THINKING
THROUGH THE
ESSAY

THINKING THROUGH THE ESSAY

JUDITH BARKER-SANDBROOK
Scarborough Board of Education
Scarborough, Ontario

NEIL GRAHAM
Scarborough Board of Education
Scarborough, Ontario

McGraw-Hill Ryerson Limited

Toronto Montreal New York Auckland Bogotá Cairo Guatemala Hamburg Lisbon London
Madrid Mexico New Delhi Panama Paris San Juan São Paulo Singapore Sydney Tokyo

THINKING THROUGH THE ESSAY

Copyright© McGraw-Hill Ryerson Limited, 1986
All rights reserved. No part of this publication may be
reproduced, stored in a retrieval system, or transmitted, in
any form, or by any means, mechanical, electronic,
photocopying, recording, or otherwise, without the prior
written permission of McGraw-Hill Ryerson Limited.

ISBN 0-07-549066-8

567890 D 54321098

Printed and bound in Canada

Canadian Cataloguing in Publication Data

Barker-Sandbrook, Judith.
  Thinking through the essay

For use in high school.
Bibliography: p.
IBSN 0-07-549066-8

1. English language – Rhetoric.   2. Exposition
(Rhetoric)   1. Graham, Neil.   II. Title.
PE1471.B37 1986   808'.0427   C86-093008-4

Care has been taken to trace ownership of copyright material
contained in this text. The publishers will gladly accept any
information that will enable them to rectify any reference or credit
in subsequent editions.

Learning without
thought
is
labour lost

Thought without
learning
is
perilous

— Confucius

Judith Barker-Sandbrook, M.A., B.Ed., is an Ontario Academic Courses teacher of English with the Scarborough Board of Education.

Neil Graham, M.A., is coordinator of English for the Scarborough Board of Education and a member of the Ontario Ministry of Education team developing the Ontario Academic Courses in English.

CONTENTS

A CKNOWLEDGMENTS

Page 4   By permission of the estate of the late Sonia Brownell Orwell and Martin Secker & Warburg Ltd.

Page 19   By permission of The Associated Press.
(top)

Page 19   By permission of The Canadian Press.
(bottom)

Page 21   Copyright © 1985 by The New York Times Company. Reprinted by permission.

Page 23   From THE MEDUSA AND THE SNAIL, by Lewis Thomas. Copyright © 1979 by Lewis Thomas. Reprinted by permission of Viking Penguin Inc.

Page 27   From WHY I AM NOT A CHRISTIAN by Bertrand Russell. Reprinted by permission of George Allen & Unwin, (Publishers) Ltd.

Page 34   By permission of Ghislaine McDayter.

Page 37   Reprinted from *Our Literary Heritage,* published by The Ryerson Press.

Page 42   "The Eichmann Trial in Retrospect," originally published in *The Reporter,* copyright 1962 by The Reporter Magazine Company. Reprinted from *Cross Currents,* Macmillan Company of Canada Limited, 1969.

Page 48   © 1985 by the Association of Canadian University Teachers of English. Reprinted from *English Studies in Canada,* Vol. XI, No. 1, March, 1985, pp. 82-90. by permission of the Association.

Page 59   From CANADIAN FORUM, December 1984, Forum 19. Reproduced with permission.

Page 70   "The Tragedy of Ugliness" appears by permission of the author.

Page 74   The School Administrator, published by the American Association of School Administrators; June 1983. Reprinted by permission.

Page 85   By permission of the author.

Page 88   Reprinted with permission — The Toronto Star Syndicate.

Page 91   Reprinted with permission of Heather Forsythe, Queen's Engineering Chemistry.

Page 96   Reprinted by permission of DODD, MEAD & COMPANY, INC., from FAMOUS AMERICAN NEGROES, by Langston Hughes. Copyright © 1954 by Langston Hughes. Copyright renewed 1982 by George Houston Bass.

PREFACE

This essay collection develops and refines critical thinking and language skills essential for post-secondary and professional success.

The approach, suggested assignments, and tips for students encourage independence, initiative, and the use of a wide range of community and school resources, especially the Resource Centre and the services of the teacher-librarian.

Part A: Essays for Language and Literature

The essays in this section have been selected to accommodate the needs and interests of students who intend to pursue different post-secondary careers. Selections have been grouped into twelve units, covering the major reading and writing formats that students will meet in post-secondary education. In each unit, a broad choice of assignments invites students to develop and refine skills. For convenient reference, these assignments are grouped under the following headings:

- Before Reading
- Exploring the Essay
- Extensive Study
- The Writing Folder
- Independent Study
- Timed Reading and Writing

Part B: Essays for the Writer's Craft and Studies in Literature

In the first seven essays, professional writers offer comments about the process of writing nonfiction, poetry, drama, and fiction. In the final five selections, scholars and critics share their ideas about approaches to literature. The reader is introduced to each selection by three preliminary questions and/or comments which provide focus and encourage students to compare ideas, approaches, and themes which recur in the essays in both Parts A and B. Finally, *An Overview: Questions for Discussion,* raises interesting issues to pursue in class.

Part C: Tips for Students

These tips encourage students to develop and refine specific skills and to learn how to work with increased independence.

Note: The Guide to Themes and Special Skills Exercises, follows Part C. It offers additional suggestions for the use of this text.

Suggested Supplementary Resources

Students in any English course would find it useful to have these key reference and language texts in the Resource Centre.

E.M. Beck, ed., *Bartlett's Familiar Quotations* (Toronto: Little, Brown and Company, 15th and 125th anniversary edition, revised and enlarged, 1980)

W.R. Benét, *The Reader's Encyclopedia* (New York: Thomas Crowell, 1965)

T.M. Bernstein, *The Careful Writer: A Modern Guide to English Usage* (New York: Atheneum, 1983)

H.W. Fowler, *A Dictionary of Modern English Usage* (New York: Oxford University Press, 1983, second edition revised by Sir Ernest Gower)

C.O.S. Mawson and K. Whiting, eds., *Roget's Pocket Thesaurus* (Toronto: Simon and Schuster, 1976)

Note: Additional references that pertain especially to Parts A, B, and C are provided in the Introduction to each section.

E SSAYS FOR LANGUAGE AND LITERATURE

INTRODUCTION

The essays in this section cover a wide range of material. Each unit begins with a KEY WORK which is followed by assignments requiring interpretation, analysis, reaction and skills application. Some of the assignments refer to the ASSOCIATED READINGS which may be used to expand ideas and provide further skills practice. The opening unit, Core Essays: The Link Between Thinking and Language, provides the focus of the text. Thereafter, units should be selected according to individual needs and the general interest of the class. The study material within each unit is organized logically under six headings. However, each area is independent of the others and could be studied separately.

The BEFORE READING suggestions focus students on the format or content of the essays. They are intended to provide warm-up exercises which facilitate class discussion and reading in context.

The EXPLORING THE ESSAY suggestions develop skills needed for close reading and analysis.

The EXTENSIVE STUDY suggestions ask students to apply and/or respond to ideas raised in the Key Work. Thus, students are encouraged to engage in high-level thinking skills — to synthesize, evaluate, assess and draw comparisons and contrasts. The Associated Readings help students learn to draw connections and discern relationships. In addition, students are encouraged to form their own connections that link the units and to articulate their perceptions. Some of the units help develop such practical skills as annotation of texts, note-taking, and library research (see the *Guide,* which appears at the end of the book). Finally, most units offer exercises that help develop and refine oral skills and peer interaction through small group and class activities.

The WRITING FOLDER suggestions are designed to help students focus on the process of writing, to engage in activities that lead to polished pieces of writing (see Tips on "Composing Essays" in Part C and the lists of additional resources listed in the Introduction to each section of the text). Again, the variety of suggestions should help students and teachers find topics that interest everyone. The length of the assignments has been left for the teacher to adjust according to various timetable constraints.

The INDEPENDENT STUDY suggestions in each unit either relate directly to the essay(s) studied or else move further afield. Some are designed to fulfill the requirements of a minor project (coded +), whereas others are coded with a double ++ to indicate a major project which would probably require five to seven weeks of work under the teacher's supervision. The many projects have been designed in a fairly open-ended and flexible manner to allow for differences in curricula and timetables in various schools. Students are encouraged to consult the Tips on Independent Study in Part C and the additional resource material listed in the Introduction to Part C for further help.

TIMED READING AND/OR WRITING suggestions are intended to help students prepare for the time constraints imposed by examinations and tests. The time requirements have been left to the teacher's discretion. Further guidance for students is offered in Tips on Preparing for the Examination in Part C.

Suggested Supplementary Resources

Students of Language and Literature courses will find it useful to have the following texts in their school's Resource Centre.

M. Abram, *A Glossary of Literary Terms* (Holt, Rinehart and Winston, 1966)

D. Brown, *Notemaking* (Toronto: Gage Educational Publishers, 1977)

R. Burchfield, *The English Language* (Oxford University Press, 1985)

D.J. Enright, ed., *Fair Speech: The Uses of Euphemism* (Oxford University Press, 1985)

Margot Northey, *Making Sense: a student's guide to writing and style* (Oxford University Press, 1983)

H. Shaw, *McGraw-Hill Handbook of English* (Toronto: McGraw-Hill Ryerson, 1985)

K. Spicer, *Winging It* (Toronto: Doubleday of Canada, 1982)

W. Strunk, Jr. and E.B. White, *The Elements of Style* (Toronto: Macmillan of Canada, 1972)

F. Watkins and W. Dillingham, *The Practical English Handbook* (Boston: Houghton Mifflin, 1982)

1. CORE ESSAYS: THE LINK BETWEEN THINKING AND LANGUAGE

Key Work:
  "Politics and the English Language" — George Orwell
Associated Readings:
  "Standards in Standard English"
  "Varieties of Canadian English"
  "There, There" — William Safire
  "Notes on Punctuation" — Lewis Thomas

The opening essay by Orwell and the Associated Readings that follow provide the major focus for *Thinking Through the Essay*. These essays explore the interconnection between thought and language and the qualities of effective language usage.

In the Key Work, "Politics and the English Language," Orwell shows that modern English is full of "bad habits" that produce slovenly thinking. He provides six rules of language that promote clear thinking and effective expression.

In the Associated Readings the essays "Standards in Standard English" and "Varieties of Canadian English" point out the dynamic nature of language and the consequences for what is known as "standard English." Finally, two humorous essays, Safire's "There, There" and Thomas's "Notes on Pronunciation," effectively show that position and punctuation are as important as clarity and word choice for effective language usage.

The ability to think clearly and to use language effectively is crucial to your success in this final year of secondary school and for your post-secondary career. As you explore these Core Essays, consider carefully how they may help improve your performance.

BEFORE READING

▪ What do you already know about Orwell? What might you expect him to say about politics and/or the English language?
▪ Consider your attitudes and biases (favourable or unfavourable) about the state of the English language and the need, if any, for improvement in usage and style.
▪ Read only the opening paragraph. Identify two generalizations Orwell makes about the English language and the nature of language. Assess the extent to which you agree with these generalizations.

POLITICS AND THE ENGLISH LANGUAGE

GEORGE ORWELL

Most people who bother with the matter at all would admit that the English language is in a bad way, but it is generally assumed that we cannot by conscious action do anything about it. Our civilization is decadent, and our language — so the arguments runs — must inevitably share in the general collapse. It follows that any struggle against the abuse of language is a sentimental archaism, like preferring candles to electric light or hansom cabs to aeroplanes. Underneath this lies the half-conscious belief that language is a natural growth and not an instrument which we shape for our own purposes.

Now, it is clear that the decline of a language must ultimately have *political and economic causes*: it is not due simply to the bad influences of this or that individual writer. But an effect can become a cause, reinforcing the original cause and producing the same effect in an intensified form, and so on indefinitely. A man may take to drink because he feels himself to be a failure, and then fail all the more completely because he drinks. It is rather the same thing that is happening to the English language. It becomes ugly and inaccurate because our thoughts are foolish, but the slovenliness of our language makes it easier for us to have foolish thoughts. The point is that the process is reversible. Modern English, especially written English, is full of bad habits which spread by imitation and which can be avoided if one is willing to take the necessary trouble. If one gets rid of these habits one can think more clearly, and to think clearly is a necessary first step towards political regeneration: so that the fight against bad English is not frivolous and is not the exclusive concern of professional writers. I will come back to this presently, and I hope that by that time the meaning of what I have said here will have become clearer. Meanwhile, here are five specimens of the English language as it is now habitually written.

These five passages have not been picked out because they are especially bad — I could have quoted far worse if I had chosen — but because they illustrate various of the mental vices from which we now suffer. They are a little below the average, but are fairly representative samples. I number them so I can refer back to them when necessary:

> 1. I am not, indeed, sure whether it is not true to say that the Milton who once seemed not unlike a seventeenth-century

Shelley had not become, out of an experience ever more bitter in each year, more alien (*sic*) to the founder of that Jesuit sect which nothing could induce him to tolerate.

> Professor Harold Laski (Essay in *Freedom of Expression*)

2. Above all, we cannot play ducks and drakes with a native battery of idioms which prescribes such egregious collocations of vocables as the Basic *put up with* for *tolerate* or *put at a loss* for *bewilder*.

> Professor Lancelot Hogben (*Interglossa*)

3. On the one side we have the free personality: by definition it is not neurotic, for it has neither conflict nor dream. Its desires, such as they are, are transparent, for they are just what institutional approval keeps in the forefront of consciousness; another institutional pattern would alter their number and intensity; there is little in them that is natural, irreducible, or culturally dangerous. But *on the other side*, the social bond itself is nothing but the mutual reflection of these self-secure integrities. Recall the definition of love. Is not this the very picture of a small academic? Where is there a place in this hall of mirrors for either personality or fraternity?

> Essay on psychology in *Politics* (New York)

4. All the 'best people' from the gentlemen's clubs, and all the frantic Fascist captains, united in common hatred of Socialism and bestial horror of the rising tide of the mass revolutionary movement, have turned to acts of provocation, to foul incendiarism, to medieval legends of poisoned wells, to legalize their own destruction to proletarian organizations, and rouse the agitated petty-bourgeoisie to chauvinistic fervour on behalf of the fight against the revolutionary way out of the crisis.

> Communist pamphlet

5. If a new spirit *is* to be infused into this old country, there is one thorny and contentious reform which must be tackled, and that is the humanization and galvanization of the B.B.C. Timidity here will bespeak canker and atrophy of the soul. The heart of Britain may be sound and of strong beat, for instance, but the British lion's roar at present is like that of Bottom in Shakespeare's *Midsummer Night's Dream* — as gentle as any sucking dove. A virile new Britain cannot continue indefinitely to be traduced in the eyes, or rather ears, of the world by the effete languors of Langham Place, brazenly masquerading as 'standard English'. When the voice of Britain is heard at nine o'clock, better far and infinitely less ludicrous to hear aitches honestly dropped than the present priggish, inflated, inhibited, school-ma'amish arch braying of blameless, bashful mewing maidens!

> Letter in *Tribune*

Each of these passages has faults of its own, but, quite apart from avoidable ugliness, two qualities are common to all of them.

The first is staleness of imagery: the other is lack of precision. The writer either has a meaning and cannot express it, or he inadvertently says something else, or he is almost indifferent as to whether his words mean anything or not. This mixture of vagueness and sheer incompetence is the most marked characteristic of modern English prose, and especially of any kind of political writing. As soon as certain topics are raised, the concrete melts into the abstract and no one seems able to think of turns of speech that are not hackneyed: prose consists less and less of *words* chosen for the sake of their meaning, and more of *phrases* tacked together like the sections of a prefabricated hen-house. I list below, with notes and examples, various of the tricks by means of which the work of prose construction is habitually dodged:

Dying metaphors. A newly invented metaphor assists thought by evoking a visual image, while on the other hand a metaphor which is technically 'dead' (e.g., *iron resolution*) has in effect reverted to being an ordinary word and can generally be used without loss of vividness. But in between these two classes there is a huge dump of worn-out metaphors which have lost all evocative power and are merely used because they save people the trouble of inventing phrases for themselves. Examples are: *Ring the changes on, take up the cudgels for, toe the line, ride roughshod over, stand shoulder to shoulder with, play into the hands of, no axe to grind, grist to the mill, fishing in troubled waters, rift within the lute, on the order of the day, Achilles' heel, swan song, hotbed.* Many of these are used without knowledge of their meaning (what is a 'rift', for instance?), and incompatible metaphors are frequently mixed, a sure sign that the writer is not interested in what he is saying. Some metaphors now current have been twisted out of their original meaning without those who use them even being aware of the fact. For example, *toe the line* is sometimes written *tow the line.* Another example is *the hammer and the anvil,* now always used with the implication that the anvil gets the worst of it. In real life it is always the anvil that breaks the hammer, never the other way about: a writer who stopped to think what he was saying would be aware of this, and would avoid perverting the original phrase.

Operators, or *verbal false limbs.* These save the trouble of picking out appropriate verbs and nouns, and at the same time pad each sentence with extra syllables which give it an appearance of symmetry. Characteristic phrases are: *render inoperative, militate against, prove unacceptable, make contact with, be subject to, give rise to, give grounds for, have the effect of, play a leading part (role) in, make itself felt, take effect, exhibit a tendency to, serve the purpose of,* etc. etc. The keynote is the elimination of simple verbs. Instead of being a single word, such as *break, stop, spoil, mend, kill*, a verb becomes a *phrase* made up of a noun or adjective tacked on to some general-purposes verb such as *prove, serve, form, play, render*. In addition, the passive voice is wherever possible used in preference to the active, and noun constructions are used instead of gerunds (*by examination of* instead of *by examining*). The range of verbs is further cut down by means of the *-ize* and *de-* formations, and banal statements are given an appearance of profundity by means of the *not un-* formation. Simple conjunctions and prepositions are replaced by such phrases as *with respect to, having regard to, the fact that, by dint of, in view of, in the interests of, on the hypothesis that*; and the ends of sentences are saved from anticlimax by such resounding commonplaces as *greatly to be desired, cannot be left out of account, a development to be expected in the near future, deserving of serious consideration, brought to a satisfactory conclusion*, and so on and so forth.

Pretentious diction. Words like *phenomenon, element, individual* (as noun), *objective, categorical, effective, virtual, basic, primary, promote, constitute, exhibit, exploit, utilize, eliminate, liquidate* are used to dress up simple statements and give an air of scientific impartiality to biassed judgements. Adjectives like *epoch-making, epic, historic, unforgettable, triumphant, age-old, inevitable, inexorable, veritable* are used to dignify the sordid processes of international politics, while writing that aims at glorifying war usually takes on an archaic colour, its characteristic words being: *realm, throne, chariot, mailed first, trident, sword, shield, buckler, banner, jackboot, clarion*. Foreign words and expressions such as *cul de sac, ancien régime, deus ex machina, mutatis mutandis, status quo, Gleichschaltung, Weltanschauung* are used to give an air of culture and elegance. Except for the useful abbreviations *i.e., e.g.*, and *etc.*, there is no real need for any of the hundreds of foreign phrases now current in English. Bad writers, and especially scientific, political and sociological writers, are nearly always haunted by the notion that Latin or Greek words are grander than Saxon ones, and unnecessary words like *expedite, ameliorate, predict, extraneous, deracinated, clandestine, sub-aqueous* and hundreds of others constantly gain ground from the Anglo-Saxon opposite numbers.[1] The jargon peculiar to Marxist writing (*hyena, hangman, cannibal, petty bourgeois, these gentry, lackey, flunkey, mad dog, White Guard*, etc.) consists largely of words and phrases translated from Russian, German or French; but the normal way of coining a new word is to use a Latin or Greek root with the appropriate affix and, where necessary, the -ize formation. It is often easier to make up words of this kind (*deregionalize, impermissible, extramarital, non-fragmentatory* and so forth) than to think up the English words that will cover one's meaning. The result, in general, is an increase in slovenliness and vagueness.

Meaningless words. In certain kinds of writing, particularly in art criticism and literary criticism, it is normal to come across long passages which are almost completely lacking in meaning.[2] Words like *romantic, plastic, values, human, dead, sentimental, natural, vitality,* as used in art criticism, are strictly meaningless, in the sense that they not only do not point to any discoverable object, but are hardly even expected to do so by the reader. When one critic writes, 'The outstanding features of Mr X's work is its living quality', while another writes, 'The immediately striking thing about Mr X's work is its peculiar deadness', the reader accepts this as a simple difference of opinion. If words like *black* and *white* were involved, instead of the jargon words *dead* and *living,* he would see at once that language was being used in an improper way. Many political words are similarly abused. The word *Fascism* has now no meaning except in so far as it signifies 'something not desirable'. The words *democracy, socialism, freedom, patriotic, realistic, justice* have each of them several different meanings which cannot be reconciled with one another. In the case of a word like *democracy,* not only is there no agreed definition, but the attempt to make one is resisted from all sides. It is almost universally felt that when we call a country democratic we are praising it: consequently the defenders of every kind of régime claim that it is a democracy, and fear that they might have to stop using the word if it were tied down to any one meaning. Words of this kind are often used in a consciously dishonest way. That is, the person who uses them has his own private definition, but allows his hearer to think he means something quite different. Statements like *Marshal Pétain was a true patriot, The Soviet press is the freest in the world, The Catholic Church is opposed to persecution* are almost always made with intent to deceive. Other words used in variable meanings, in most cases more or less dishonestly, are: *class, totalitarian, science, progressive, reactionary, bourgeois, equality.*

Now that I have made this catalogue of swindles and perversions, let me give another example of the kind of writing that they lead to. This time it must of its nature be an imaginary one. I am going to translate a passage of good English into modern English of the worst sort. Here is a well-known verse from *Ecclesiastes:*

> I returned, and saw under the sun, that the race is not to the swift, nor the battle to the strong, neither yet bread to the wise,

nor yet riches to men of understanding, nor yet favour to men of skill; but time and chance happeneth to them all.

Here it is in modern English:

> Objective consideration of contemporary phenomena compels the conclusion that success or failure in competitive activities exhibits no tendency to be commensurate with innate capacity, but that a considerable element of the unpredictable must invariably be taken into account.

This is a parody, but not a very gross one. Exhibit 3, above, for instance, contains several patches of the same kind of English. It will be seen that I have not made a full translation. The beginning and ending of the sentence follow the original meaning fairly closely, but in the middle the concrete illustrations — race, battle, bread — dissolve into the vague phrase 'success or failure in competitive activities'. This had to be so, because no modern writer of the kind I am discussing — no one capable of using phrases like 'objective consideration of contemporary phenomena' — would ever tabulate his thoughts in that precise and detailed way. The whole tendency of modern prose is away from concreteness. Now analyse these two sentences a little more closely. The first contains 49 words but only 60 syllables, and all its words are those of everyday life. The second contains 38 words of 90 syllables: 18 of its words are from Latin roots, and one from Greek. The first sentence contains six vivid images, and only one phrase ('time and chance') that could be called vague. The second contains not a single fresh, arresting phrase, and in spite of its 90 syllables it gives only a shortened version of the meaning contained in the first. Yet without a doubt it is the second kind of sentence that is gaining ground in modern English. I do not want to exaggerate. This kind of writing is not yet universal, and outcrops of simplicity will occur here and there in the worst-written page. Still if you or I were told to write a few lines on the uncertainty of human fortunes, we should probably come much nearer to my imaginary sentence than to the one from *Ecclesiastes*.

As I have tried to show, modern writing at its worst does not consist in picking out words for the sake of their meaning and inventing images in order to make the meaning clearer. It consists in gumming together long strips of words which have already been set in order by someone else, and making the results presentable by sheer humbug. The attraction of this way of writing is that it is easy. It is easier — even quicker, once you have the habit — to say *In my opinion it is a not unjustifiable assumption that* than to say *I think*. If you use ready-made phrases, you not only don't have to hunt about for words; you also don't have to bother with the rhythms of your sentences, since these phrases are generally so

arranged as to be more or less euphonious. When you are composing in a hurry — when you are dictating to a stenographer, for
instance, or making a public speech — it is natural to fall into a
pretentious, latinized style. Tags like *a consideration which we
should do well to bear in mind* or *a conclusion to which all of us
would readily assent* will save many a sentence from coming
down with a bump. By using stale metaphors, similes and idioms,
you save much mental effort, at the cost of leaving your meaning
vague, not only for your reader but for yourself. This is the significance of mixed metaphors. The sole aim of a metaphor is to call up a
visual image. When these images clash — as in *The Fascist oc-
topus has sung its swan song, the jackboot is thrown into the
melting-pot* — it can be taken as certain that the writer is not
seeing a mental image of the objects he is naming; in other words he
is not really thinking. Look again at the examples I gave at the
beginning of this essay. Professor Laski (1) uses five negatives in 53
words. One of these is superfluous, making nonsense of the whole
passage, and in addition there is the slip *alien* for akin, making
further nonsense, and several avoidable pieces of clumsiness
which increase the general vagueness. Professor Hogben (2) plays
ducks and drakes with a battery which is able to write prescriptions, and, while disapproving of the everyday phrase *put up with*,
is unwilling to look *egregious* up in the dictionary and see what it
means. (3), if one takes an uncharitable attitude towards it, is
simply meaningless: probably one could work out its intended
meaning by reading the whole of the article in which it occurs. In (4)
the writer knows more or less what he wants to say, but an ac-
cumulation of stale phrases chokes him like tea-leaves blocking a
sink. In (5) words and meaning have almost parted company. People
who write in this manner usually have a general emotional meaning — they dislike one thing and want to express solidarity with
another — but they are not interested in the detail of what they are
saying. A scrupulous writer, in every sentence that he writes, will
ask himself at least four questions, thus: What am I trying to say?
What words will express it? What image or idiom will make it
clearer? Is this image fresh enough to have an effect? And he will
probably ask himself two more: Could I put it more shortly? Have I
said anything that is avoidably ugly? But you are not obliged to go to
all this trouble. You can shirk it by simply throwing your mind open
and letting the ready-made phrases come crowding in. They will
construct your sentences for you — even think your thoughts for
you, to a certain extent — and at need they will perform the important service of partially concealing your meaning even from yourself. It is at this point that the special connexion between politics
and the debasement of language becomes clear.

In our time it is broadly true that political writing is bad writing.

Where it is not true, it will generally be found that the writer is some kind of rebel, expressing his private opinions, and not a 'party line'. Orthodoxy, of whatever colour, seems to demand a lifeless, imitative style. The political dialects to be found in pamphlets, leading articles, manifestos, White Papers and the speeches of Under-Secretaries do, of course, vary from party to party, but they are all alike in that one almost never finds in them a fresh, vivid, home-made turn of speech. When one watches some tired hack on the platform mechanically repeating the familiar phrases — *bestial atrocities, iron heel, blood-stained tyranny, free peoples of the world, stand shoulder to shoulder* — one often has a curious feeling that one is not watching a live human being but some kind of dummy: a feeling which suddenly becomes stronger at moments when the light catches the speaker's spectacles and turns them into blank discs which seem to have no eyes behind them. And this is not altogether fanciful. A speaker who uses that kind of phraseology has gone some distance towards turning himself into a machine. The appropriate noises are coming out of his larynx, but his brain is not involved as it would be if he were choosing his words for himself. If the speech he is making is one that he is accustomed to make over and over again, he may be almost unconscious of what he is saying, as one is when one utters the responses in church. And this reduced state of consciousness, if not indispensable, is at any rate favourable to political conformity.

In our time, political speech and writing are largely the defence of the indefensible. Things like the continuance of British rule in India, the Russian purges and deportations, the dropping of the atom bombs on Japan, can indeed be defended, but only by arguments which are too brutal for most people to face, and which do not square with the professed aims of political parties. Thus political language has to consist largely of euphemism, question-begging and sheer cloudy vagueness. Defenceless villages are bombarded from the air, the inhabitants driven out into the countryside, the cattle machine-gunned, the huts set on fire with incendiary bullets: this is called *pacification*. Millions of peasants are robbed of their farms and sent trudging along the roads with no more than they can carry: this is called *transfer of population* or *rectification of frontiers*. People are imprisoned for years without trial, or shot in the back of the neck or sent to die of scurvy in Arctic lumber camps: this is called *elimination of unreliable elements*. Such phraseology is needed if one wants to name things without calling up mental pictures of them. Consider for instance some comfortable English professor defending Russian totalitarianism. He cannot say outright, 'I believe in killing off your opponents when you can get good results by doing so'. Probably, therefore, he will say something like this:

> While freely conceding that the Soviet régime exhibits certain features which the humanitarian may be inclined to deplore, we must, I think, agree that a certain curtailment of the right to political opposition is an unavoidable concomitant of transitional periods, and that the rigours which the Russian people have been called upon to undergo have been amply justified in the sphere of concrete achievement.

The inflated style is itself a kind of euphemism. A mass of Latin words falls upon the facts like soft snow, blurring the outlines and covering up all the details. The great enemy of clear language is insincerity. When there is a gap between one's real and one's declared aims, one turns as it were instinctively to long words and exhausted idioms, like a cuttlefish squirting out ink. In our age there is no such thing as 'keeping out of politics'. All issues are political issues, and politics itself is a mass of lies, evasions, folly, hatred and schizophrenia. When the general atmosphere is bad, language must suffer. I should expect to find — this is a guess which I have not sufficient knowledge to verify — that the German, Russian and Italian languages have all deteriorated in the last ten or fifteen years, as a result of dictatorship.

But if thought corrupts language, language can also corrupt thought. A bad usage can spread by tradition and imitation, even among people who should and do know better. The debased language that I have been discussing is in some ways very convenient. Phrases like *a not unjustifiable assumption, leaves much to be desired, would serve no good purpose, a consideration which we should do well to bear in mind* are a continuous temptation, a packet of aspirins always at one's elbow. Look back through this essay, and for certain you will find that I have again and again committed the very faults I am protesting against. By this morning's post I have received a pamphlet dealing with conditions in Germany. The author tells me that he 'felt impelled' to write it. I open it at random, and here is almost the first sentence that I see: '(The Allies) have an opportunity not only of achieving a radical transformation of Germany's social and political structure in such a way as to avoid a nationalistic reaction in Germany itself, but at the same time of laying the foundations of a co-operative and unified Europe.' You see, he 'feels impelled' to write — feels, presumably, that he has something new to say — and yet his words, like cavalry horses answering the bugle, group themselves automatically into the familiar dreary pattern. This invasion of one's mind by ready-made phrases (*lay the foundations, achieve a radical transformation*) can only be prevented if one is constantly on guard against them, and every such phrase anaesthetizes a portion of one's brain.

I said earlier that the decadence of our language is probably curable. Those who deny this would argue, if they produced an argument at all, that language merely reflects existing social conditions, and that we cannot influence its development by any direct tinkering with words and constructions. So far as the general tone or spirit of a language goes, this may be true, but it is not true in detail. Silly words and expressions have often disappeared, not through any evolutionary process but owing to the conscious action of a minority. Two recent examples were *explore every avenue* and *leave no stone unturned,* which were killed by the jeers of a few journalists. There is a long list of fly-blown metaphors which could similarly be got rid of if enough people would interest themselves in the job; and it should also be possible to laugh the *not un-* formation out of existence,[3] to reduce the amount of Latin and Greek in the average sentence, to drive out foreign phrases and strayed scientific words, and, in general, to make pretentiousness unfashionable. But all these are minor points. The defence of the English language implies more than this, and perhaps it is best to start by saying what it does *not* imply.

To begin with, it has nothing to do with archaism, with the salvaging of obsolete words and turns of speech, or with the setting-up of a 'standard English' which must never be departed from. On the contrary, it is especially concerned with the scrapping of every word or idiom which has outworn its usefulness. It has nothing to do with correct grammar and syntax, which are of no importance so long as one makes one's meaning clear, or with the avoidance of Americanisms, or with having what is called a 'good prose style'. On the other hand it is not concerned with fake simplicity and the attempt to make written English colloquial. Nor does it even imply in every case preferring the Saxon word to the Latin one, though it does imply using the fewest and shortest words that will cover one's meaning. What is above all needed is to let the meaning choose the word, and not the other way about. In prose, the worst thing you can do with words is to surrender them. When you think of a concrete object, you think wordlessly, and then, if you want to describe the thing you have been visualizing, you probably hunt about till you find the exact words that seem to fit it. When you think of something abstract you are more inclined to use words from the start, and unless you make a conscious effort to prevent it, the existing dialect will come rushing in and do the job for you, at the expense of blurring or even changing your meaning. Probably it is better to put off using words as long as possible and get one's meanings as clear as one can through pictures or sensations. Afterwards one can choose — not simply *accept* — the phrases that will best cover the meaning, and then switch round and decide what impression one's words are likely to make on another person. This last effort of the mind cuts out all stale or mixed images, all prefabricated phrases, needless repetitions, and humbug and vagueness generally. But one can often be in doubt about the effect of a word or a phrase, and one needs rules that one can rely on when instinct fails. I think the following rules will cover most cases:

> i. Never use a metaphor, simile or other figure of speech which you are used to seeing in print.
> ii. Never use a long word where a short one will do.
> iii. If it is possible to cut a word out, always cut it out.
> iv. Never use the passive where you can use the active.
> v. Never use a foreign phrase, a scientific word or a jargon word if you can think of an everyday English equivalent.
> vi. Break any of these rules sooner than say anything outright barbarous.

These rules sound elementary, and so they are, but they demand a deep change of attitude in anyone who has grown used to writing in the style now fashionable. One could keep all of them and still write bad English, but one could not write the kind of stuff that I quoted in those five specimens at the beginning of this article.

I have not here been considering the literary use of language, but merely language as an instrument for expressing and not for concealing or preventing thought. Stuart Chase and others have come near to claiming that all abstract words are meaningless, and have used this as a pretext for advocating a kind of political quietism. Since you don't know what Fascism is, how can you struggle against Fascism? One need not swallow such absurdities as this, but one ought to recognize that the present political chaos is concerned with the decay of language, and that one can probably bring about some improvement by starting at the verbal end. If you simplify your English, you are freed from the worst follies of orthodoxy. You cannot speak any of the necessary dialects, and when you make a stupid remark its stupidity will be obvious, even to yourself. Political language — and with variations this is true of all political parties, from Conservatives to Anarchists — is designed to make lies sound truthful and murder respectable, and to give an appearance of solidity to pure wind. One cannot change this all in a moment, but one can at least change one's own habits, and from time to time one can even, if one jeers loudly enough, send some worn-out and useless phrase — some *jackboot, Achilles' heel, hotbed, melting pot, acid test, veritable inferno* or other lump of verbal refuse — into the dustbin where it belongs.

---

[1] An interesting illustration of this is the way in which the English flower names which were in use till very recently are being ousted by Greek ones, *snapdragon* becoming *antirrhinum, forget-me-not* becoming *myosotis*, etc. It is hard to see any practical reason for this change of fashion: it is probably due to an instinctive turning-away from the more homely word and a vague feeling that the Greek word is scientific. [Author's footnote.]

²Example: 'Comforts catholicity of perception and image, strangely Whitmanesque in range, almost the exact opposite in aesthetic compulsion, continues to evoke that trembling atmospheric accumulative hinting at a cruel, an inexorably serene time-lessness. . . Wrey Gardiner scores by aiming at simple bullseyes with precision. Only they are not so simple, and through this contented sadness runs more than the surface bitter-sweet of resignation.' (*Poetry Quarterly*). [Author's footnote].

³One can cure oneself of the *not un-* formation by memorizing this sentence: *A not unblack dog was chasing a not unsmall rabbit across a not ungreen field.* [Author's footnote.]

EXPLORING THE ESSAY

1. (a) In the opening two paragraphs, what general attitude does Orwell identify as an impediment to the improvement of language usage?
   (b) In the second paragraph, locate and underline Orwell's complete thesis.
   (c) After Orwell clarifies his thesis with a number of examples, show that he uses a problem-solution structure to organize the essay.
   (d) In the interaction between thought and language, which element does Orwell believe must predominate? Why?

2. Identify each of the four main "language tricks" Orwell catalogues. In a sentence for each, summarize the four points he is making.

3. What does Orwell hope to achieve through his parody of the excerpt from *Ecclesiastes*?

4. A sixth "language trick" is to write by habit, stringing together "ready-made phrases." Why does Orwell condemn this approach?

5. What are some of his concerns about political language?

6. Why does Orwell maintain that "the great enemy of language is insincerity?"

7. Orwell shows that thought and language are inexorably intermingled. He states that "if thought corrupts language, language can also corrupt thought." How does he demonstrate this interaction?

8. In *Teaching Language,* Edward DeBono says, "Language provides the handles with which we grasp the world." Explain why Orwell would agree with this statement, given his contention that "language is an instrument for expressing and not concealing thought." Make specific reference to Orwell's essay.

EXTENSIVE STUDY

1. Argue a case for calling this work "Thinking and the English Language" rather than "Politics and the English Language."

2. To what extent does Orwell take his own advice about the use of metaphor? Has he used any "dying metaphors," "verbal false limbs," "pretentious diction," or "meaningless words?"

3. Orwell makes a number of generalizations about the state of language and the links between language and thought:

    "Most people . . . would admit that the English language is in a bad way."

    "It is clear that the decline of a language must ultimately have political and economic causes."

    "In our time it is broadly true that political writing is bad writing."

    "If thought corrupts language, language can also corrupt thought."
    "The great enemy of clear language is insincerity."

    Working in pairs, demonstrate how Orwell illustrates each of these generalizations; then assess the extent to which you agree with each of his contentions.

4. Working in groups, have each person record a definition of thinking. Consider whether thinking precedes expression or is developed by it. Compare responses; try to arrive at a collective definition. Contrast your definition with those of other groups.

5. Orwell wrote that "the whole tendency of modern prose is away from concreteness." The following sample illustrates Orwell's statement: "Effective interfacing of the community with the school curriculum can manifest itself as an interesting latter-day spelling bee." Find several examples of this type of usage. Try to put your findings into straightforward English.

6. Orwell has shown the interrelatedness between thinking and language. After considering all that he has to say and reviewing your own thinking and composing, do you think you could improve your approach? Explain.

7. In January 1984, Allan Fotheringham, a political journalist, wrote about Orwell's essay and its relationship to the contemporary Canadian government: "Orwell was right. The debasement of language eventually leads to the debasement of politics" (*Maclean's* magazine, Vol. 97, #3, January 16, 1984).

    Bring to class examples of current statements by political leaders. Do you agree that Orwell's ideas about politicians' use of language apply today?

8. (a) Read the article "Standards in Standard English" and distinguish between language liberals (descriptivists) and language conservatives (prescriptivists).

    (b) Based on what Orwell said in his essay, decide whether Orwell would be classified as a descriptivist or prescriptivist.

    (c) Define what is meant by standard usage in language by consulting authorities and at least one language text.

    (d) Determine the extent to which you, your classmates, and your teacher agree with the purists or the liberals. Which side of the argument do you think university and college professors would adopt? What implications does this have for your language usage in your post-secondary career?

9. (a) Read Safire's "There, There" and Thomas's "Notes on Punctuation." Show that underneath each writer's rather whimsical approach certain rules for effective sentence structure and punctuation are set out.

(b) Demonstrate that their specific rules for sentence structure and punctuation are a refinement of Orwell's six language usage rules.

10. Working individually or in small groups, research what authorities say about style and compare their ideas with Orwell's. Use the relevant chapters in suggested texts listed below or consult your teacher-librarian:

Elements of Style by W. Strunk, Jr. and E.B. White (see the 21-point "List of Reminders" referred to in Safire's article, page 21)

Making Sense by Margot Northey

The Little English Handbook for Canadians by J. Bell and E. Corbett

11. Create a class dictionary of the "dying metaphors" or rubber-stamp expressions we often use. Use it to check your future oral and written usage.

12. After reviewing the rules, debate one of these resolutions:

That modern technology is having a detrimental effect on our language.

That the English language should become the world's international language.

13. Using one or more of the texts listed below, select several examples of quotations that have become famous because of their effective use of language. What aspects of language usage makes each especially memorable?

Canadian Quotations by John Robert Colombo

The Book of Insults by Nancy McPhee

Bartlett's Familiar Quotations or other similar texts in your library

THE WRITING FOLDER

1   How would Orwell judge your writing style? Apply Orwell's six style rules to one of the polished pieces in your folder. Your observations might be written or oral. Or you may wish to work with a partner and comment on each other's work.

2. "Effective language usage, both written and spoken, is based on certain rules of style."

   Write a reasoned response to this generalization, bearing in mind what you have learned in this introductory unit.

INDEPENDENT STUDY

Note: In this text, the independent study suggestions are coded with symbols indicating the time and effort required to complete them. The code + indicates a minor project, whereas ++ suggests a major project.

1. Orwell wrote *Politics and the English Language* in 1946. Two years later, he published *1984,* a novel that translates his concerns about the dangers of political language manipulation into fictional terms. Read *1984.* Develop a project that assesses the accuracy of Orwell's prophetic vision. Consider whether our political leaders emulate those in the novel and to what extent we live in a world of "newspeak." You may wish to include other fictional works such as Anthony Burgess's *A Clockwork Orange* or some advertising material. + or ++
2. Read Robert Burchfield's *The English Language.* Use some of its key ideas to explore language and pronunciation patterns in your school or community. In consultation with your teacher, develop a written report of your findings. + or ++
3. Read *Our Own Voice: Canadian English and How It Is Studied,* in which R. McConnell explores Canadian language heritage and patterns. Using some of his methods (research, surveys, samples) investigate your community's language heritage and patterns. Your project could stress oral or written speech, or both, if it becomes a group effort. + or ++

TIMED READING AND WRITING

Note: No time limit has been suggested for these timed reading and/or writing assignments. Your teacher will determine the time limit and length of written work when it is assigned.

1. Orwell claims that when composing hurriedly it is natural to fall into a pretentious style. Write a reasoned response to this comment, indicating whether you agree and what you might add about how time limitations influence one's writing style.
2. Compose a piece of work (perhaps a parody) that proves the point stated in the above assignment.
3. Read the article "Varieties of Canadian English" and summarize its content in a brief paragraph.

STANDARDS IN STANDARD ENGLISH

LONDON (AP) — A war of words has broken out among the keepers of the English language as it is spoken and written here.

To the horror of the purists, the compilers of Britain's leading dictionaries today accept as legitimate the sentence: "Hopefully the eggs are fresh."

In 1984, which happens to be the 100th year since the first Oxford Dictionary appeared, "hopefully" is a fine example of the clash between the conservatives (known as prescriptivists in language circles) manning the ramparts against what they regard as linguistic permissiveness, and the liberals (descriptivists) who say just about anything goes, provided it circulates widely enough.

In the latest round of battle, novelist Kingsley Amis, a purist, argues that "hopefully" is being hopelessly misused, and that the above example, which should have said "We (or I) hope the eggs are fresh," is in effect implying that the eggs are fresh and somehow infused with hope.

But Dr. Robert Burchfield, chief editor of the Oxford English dictionaries, and Betty Kirkpatrick, his counterpart at Chambers 20th Century Dictionary in Scotland, believe this usage of "hopefully" is correct because modern English has accepted it.

Last month, in a review of the new Oxford Guide to English Usage, Amis, 62, castigated modern lexicographers for "giving their followers leave to spatter their talk and prose with any old illiteracy or howler that took their fancy."

Since these experts would never use such English themselves, Amis wrote in the weekly *Observer* newspaper, they reminded him of "a parson grimly preserving his own chastity while recommending adultery to his parishioners."

Toronto Star, Mar. 8/84

VARIETIES OF CANADIAN ENGLISH

OTTAWA (CP) — John Corneil gets teased at work for the way he talks.

No wonder. The registrar of collections for the Canadian Centre for Folk Culture at the National Museum of Man uses expressions such as "gumtuckies."

In Ottawa Valley dialect, that means rubber boots — "gum" for rubber and "tuckies" because you tuck your pants into them.

Corneil, who picked up the expression while growing up in Carleton Place near Ottawa, says he hasn't heard it outside the valley.

Speech peculiarities

Gumtuckies is only one example of the peculiarities of speech that exist among the English-speaking residents of the valley. But, says Ottawa linguist Howard Woods, many expressions attributed exclusively to the valley are heard all over Canada.

Woods defines a dialect as the speech characteristics of a particular region. The characteristics include grammar, vocabulary and pronunciation. Languages are collections of dialects and everyone speaks a dialect, he says.

People pick up dialects when they are young by "subconsciously imitating people they want to identify with."

"There is no standard English that all English-speakers speak. Everybody speaks what somebody else considers a dialect."

Woods, head of the English program development division of the Public Service Commission's language program, studied spoken English in the Ottawa area while he was a doctoral student at the University of British Columbia.

In 1979, he finished his PhD thesis, The Ottawa Survey of Canadian English, and a revised version is to be published this year.

During his research and field work, Woods compiled a list of expressions people said were "Ottawa Valley talk." But many are heard in other parts of Canada, too, he said.

For example, he was told that substituting bring for take — as in "Bring it over to the neighbors" — is pure valley-speak. In fact, he says, it's a common grammatical error heard all over North America.

The remaining traces of dialects brought by 19th-century settlers are being swept away by modern communications and mass education, Woods says. From the Ottawa River westward, English has become increasingly uniform and standardized.

"Some people might find it sad, but I'm afraid there's very little local color left in terms of language. Canada west of the Ottawa River is the largest land mass in the world where a language is so similar all over."

Variety in Newfoundland

He describes standard Canadian English as the English heard on radio and television and taught in Canadian schools. It is the English spoken by broadcasters, teachers, political leaders, businessmen and other influential leaders.

What linguistic variety is left is found mainly in Newfoundland, he said.

"There are several Newfoundland accents. In fact, there are a whole bunch of them. Each bay and outport has its own accent or dialect."

Local dialects have survived longer in Newfoundland, and to a lesser extent in Nova Scotia, because these areas were settled earlier than Ottawa and the West, he said. They were also relatively isolated for a long time.

Toronto Star, Aug. 8/85

THERE, THERE

WILLIAM SAFIRE

"There's no there" was Gertrude Stein's classic slander of the city of Oakland, Calif. That was the last time a sentence was started successfully with a pronominal, impersonal *there.*

There is an inclination among weak writers to use *there* at the beginning of sentences. Look at the slow-starting agglomeration of words in the previous sentence: it's a wet noodle of a sentence, putting the reader to sleep before coming to life with the word *weak.* Compare that "pronominal there" pap to this vigorous alternative: "Weak writers are inclined to use *there* at the beginning of sentences."

Ah, you say, what about Shakespeare's "There is a tide in the affairs of men. . . ."? Face it: even the Bard had his bad days. If he had a chance, Shakespeare would pick up the phone and say: "Hello, Rewrite? I want to change Brutus's line that begins *There is a tide* to *A tide exists* . . . No, hold on — make that *Great tides appear.* . . . Yes, same iambic pentameter, and putting the noun up closer to the front gives it a little zing. *There is* is a weak way to start any speech."

Rewrite would say: "But how about the *there* in Hamlet's 'Ay, there's the rub!' That *there* sounds pretty strong to me."

Shakespeare would then patiently point out to Rewrite that *there,* when meaning a place or an intensifier for *that,* is a powerful word. (So *there!*) Moreover, when used to mean "thither" or "yon" (as in "Cassius over there has a lean and hungry look"), *there* has its place. And when meant as "at or to that point," it serves a real purpose. (What is the point of this piece? I'm getting there.) But when used in writing, as a mere "function" word for writers reluctant to bite into the subject without first fiddling around, *there* is a sign of weakness, irresolution and pusillanimity. (Brutus was, deep down, weak; maybe Shakespeare was sending a signal. O.K., on that basis, leave the *there is* bit in.)

The linking verb that follows the lazy writer's pronominal impersonal is also weak; sentences that start *There is* stagger to the starting line. Compare the wimpish *There are a couple of reasons I like to hide behind 'there is.'* . . . to the forceful *The reasons I reject 'there is' include.* . . .

Another way not to start a sentence is with a conjunction. (The reader has been euchred into a style piece about ways not to start sentences. We finally got there.) Conjunctions like *And, but* and *because* are intended to join thoughts or to subordinate one idea to another, but when used to start sentences, these conjunctions usually produce a sloppy or choppy effect. This rule can be broken with great effect: Shirley Jackson began a superb short story with "And the first thing they did was segregate me" — but her dramatic purpose in opening with a conjunction was to give the impression of not starting at the beginning. And, yes, to be totally honest, even I have started sentences with *And* — too often, frankly — when I want to give the impression of a sudden afterthought or an admission I dragged out of myself that I had not planned to set forth in my argument.

In starting sentences, you should watch out for *but*, a word that starts a withdrawal from a position. Inside a sentence, where it belongs, *but* is not as specific as *except* — "No alibis except terminal frizzies accepted" — but *but* is a stronger contradiction than *however.* If you want to contradict sharply, use *but* in the same sentence — "She's an intellectual but I like her" — and if you want to slide off a flat statement, introducing a qualification out of fairness or second thought, use *however* after a semicolon or at the start of a new sentence: "She's an intellectual. However, as I am no dummy myself, I like her."

Not every language authority agrees with me on this mild approval of *However* to start a sentence, however. "Strunk and White discourage the use of *however* as a conjunctive adverb at the beginning of a sentence," writes Leslie Brisman, a professor of English at Yale, "(allowing it when it is an adverb meaning 'no matter how'). I and many of my colleagues continue to correct this in our students' writing, but the number of grammar handbooks demonstrating the *however* in the initial position makes us wonder whether there is any ground for continuing to insist on this matter of form."

No grounds; forget it. However many purists insist that the only time *however* may be used to start a sentence is demonstrated at the start of this sentence, the fact is that such a requirement is outdated. More important (meaning "what is more important" — let us continue to resist *more importantly,* which connotes forced significance), we cannot let great old stylebooks dictate today's style.

However, don't use *however* when you mean *in spite of,* which is tougher than the broad-spectrum *but.* If you mean "I know all that, and I am not persuaded" and really want to separate yourself from all that has gone before, you can do much better than *however.* Try *despite,* or if the *spite* turns you off, use the fast-disappearing *nevertheless.* (Remember that song Eddie Fisher used to sing? Hum it on your way to English class.) You can begin a sentence, even a paragraph, with *Nevertheless;* it will have more punch than a paragraph beginning with *However.* (You are the only one reading this paragraph; everyone else skipped it because however-graphs are for timorous State Department speechwriters. Tough speechwriters at State come right out with *On the other hand.*)

We will now rewrite the next-to-last sentence to show how simpering it is to use *Because* everyone else skipped it. . . ." That use of *Because* at the start. Here's the revision: "Why are you the only one reading this paragraph? *Because* at the start creates a sentence fragment and is not as effective as "Why are you the only one reading this paragraph? *The reason is* that everyone else. . . ." (If you now ask, "Why is that more effective?" my answer is "Because I'm the Language Maven, that's why, and when I break a rule, as I do in this sentence, I break it wide open — for emphasis.")

Treat your readers to action up front. It's bad enough to dribble off, but it's worse to dribble on. With the tide running to wipe out *There is,* we will next wash away *It is.* (Bor-ing!) Such a tide, taken at the flood, leads on to fortune; omitted, all the cadence of our prose is spent in shallows and in mini-series.

NOTES ON PUNCTUATION

LEWIS THOMAS

There are no precise rules about punctuation (Fowler lays out some general advice (as best he can under the complex circumstances of English prose (he points out, for example, that we possess only four stops (the comma, the semi-colon, the colon and the period (the question mark and exclamation point are not, strictly speaking, stops; they are indicators of tone (oddly enough, the Greeks employed the semicolon for their question mark (it produces a strange sensation to read a Greek sentence which is a straightforward question: Why weepest thou; (instead of Why weepest thou? (and, of course, there are parentheses (which are surely a kind of punctuation making this whole matter much more complicated by having to count up the left-handed parentheses in order to be sure of closing with the right number (but if the parentheses were left out, with nothing to work with but the stops, we would have considerably more flexibility in the deploying of layers of meaning than if we tried to separate all the clauses by physical barriers (and in the latter case, while we might have more precision and exactitude for our meaning, we would lose the essential flavour of language, which is its wonderful ambiguity)))))))))))).

The commas are the most useful and usable of all the stops. It is highly important to put them in place as you go along. If you try to come back after doing a paragraph and stick them in the various spots that tempt you you will discover that they tend to swarm like minnows into all sorts of crevices whose existence you hadn't realized and before you know it the whole long sentence becomes immobilized and lashed up squirming in commas. Better to use them sparingly, and with affection, precisely when the need for each one arises, nicely, by itself.

I have grown fond of semicolons in recent years. The semicolon tells you that there is still some question about the preceding full sentence; something needs to be added; it reminds you sometimes of the Greek usage. It is almost always a greater pleasure to come across a semicolon than a period. The period tells you that that is that; if you didn't get all the meaning you wanted or expected, anyway you got all the writer intended to parcel out and now you have to move along. But with a semicolon there you get a pleasant little feeling of expectancy; there is more to come; to read on; it will get clearer.

Colons are a lot less attractive, for several reasons: firstly, they give you the feeling of being rather ordered around, or at least having your nose pointed in a direction you might not be inclined to take if left to yourself, and, secondly, you suspect you're in for one of those sentences that will be labelling the points to be made: firstly, secondly and so forth, with the implication that you haven't sense enough to keep track of a sequence of notions without having them numbered. Also, many writers use this system loosely and incompletely, starting out with number one and number two as though counting off on their fingers but then going on and on without the succession of labels you've been led to expect, leaving you floundering about searching for the ninethly or seventeenthly that ought to be there but isn't.

Exclamation points are the most irritating of all. Look! they say, look at what I just said! How amazing is my thought! It is like being forced to watch someone else's small child jumping up and down crazily in the center of the living room shouting to attract attention. If a sentence really has something of importance to say, something quite remarkable, it doesn't need a mark to point it out. And if it is really, after all, a banal sentence needing more zing, the exclamation point simply emphasizes its banality!

Quotation marks should be used honestly and sparingly, when there is a genuine quotation at hand, and it is necessary to be very rigorous about the words enclosed by the marks. If something is to be quoted, the *exact* words must be used. If part of it must be left out because of space limitations, it is good manners to insert three dots to indicate the omission, but it is unethical to do this if it means connecting two thoughts which the original author did not intend to have tied together. Above all, quotation marks should not be used for ideas that you'd like to disown, things in the air so to speak. Nor should they be put in place around clichés; if you want to use a cliché you must take full responsibility for it yourself and not try to fob it off on anon., or on society. The most objectionable misuse of quotation marks, but one which illustrates the dangers of misuse in ordinary prose, is seen in advertising, especially in advertisements for small restaurants, for example "just around the corner," or "a good place to eat." No single, identifiable, citable person ever really said, for the record, "just around the corner," much less "a good place to eat," least likely of all for restaurants of the type that use this type of prose.

The dash is a handy device, informal and essentially playful, telling you that you're about to take off on a different tack but still in some way connected with the present course — only you have to remember that the dash is there, and either put on a second dash at the end of the notion to let the reader know that he's back on course, or else end the sentence, as here, with a period.

The greatest danger in punctuation is for poetry. Here it is necessary to be as economical and parsimonious with commas and periods as with the words themselves, and any marks that seem to carry their own subtle meanings, like dashes and little rows of periods, even semicolons and question marks, should be left out altogether rather than inserted to clog up the thing with ambiguity. A single exclamation point in a poem, no matter what else the poem has to say, is enough to destroy the whole work.

The things I like best in T.S. Eliot's poetry, especially in the *Four Quartets*, are the semicolons. You cannot hear them, but they are there, laying out the connections between the images and the ideas. Sometime you get a glimpse of a semicolon coming, a few lines farther on, and it is like climbing a steep path through woods and seeing a wooden bench just at a bend in the road ahead, a place where you can expect to sit for a moment, catching your breath.

Commas can't do this sort of thing; they can only tell you how the different parts of a complicated thought are to be fitted together, but you can't sit, not even take a breath, just because of a comma,

2. THE GENERIC ESSAY

Key Work:
   "The Good Life" — Bertrand Russell

Associated Readings:
   "Duck Shooting on Yonge Street" — Ghislaine McDayter
                                        (student essay)

   "Excerpt from *Walden*" — Henry David Thoreau

   "The Eichmann Trial in Retrospect" — Abba Eban

Essays are categorized sometimes according to the writer's purpose (to describe, to explain, to persuade) or approach (formal or informal). The essays in this unit are labelled generic because their authors do not conform to any specialized conventions other than standard English usage. On the other hand, contained within this category are many specialized forms of the essay which adhere to criteria as seen in the essays in other units of the text: the review, the report, the scholarly essay, to name a few. These are the nonfiction formats you will likely read most often in your post-secondary career.

The Key Work, "The Good Life" by Bertrand Russell, represents the classical essay. The French essayist, Montaigne, is credited with inventing the genre; in 1580, he published a collection of short prose writings, *Essais,* which means "attempts." That is, his *essais* were his attempts to understand himself and his world. Russell's essay is "classic" in that it follows this tradition.

The Associated Readings demonstrate the scope of the generic essay. Ghislaine McDayter's wry "Duck Shooting on Yonge Street" contrasts sharply in tone with the dry definitional approach of Russell and the more lyrical philosophizing of Thoreau's "Excerpt from *Walden.*" Eban's rational approach to a highly emotional subject in "The Eichmann Trial in Retrospect" shows that a skilled writer is able to approach an intensely emotional subject and argue a point in a reasoned manner.

BEFORE READING

- Familiarize yourself with Russell's life by reading a brief biographical sketch in a reference book such as *The Reader's Encyclopedia* by Benét.
- In your view, what are the essentials of a good life?
- Who epitomizes the good life? What does your selection indicate about your values?

THE GOOD LIFE

BERTRAND RUSSELL

There have been at different times and among different people many varying conceptions of the good life. To some extent the differences were amenable to argument; this was when men differed as to the means to achieve a given end. Some think that prison is a good way of preventing crime; others hold that education would be better. A difference of this sort can be decided by sufficient evidence. But some differences cannot be tested in this way. Tolstoy condemned all war; others have held the life of a soldier doing battle for the right to be very noble. Here there was probably involved a real difference as to ends. Those who praised the soldier usually consider the punishment of sinners a good thing in itself; Tolstoy did not think so. On such a matter no argument is possible. I cannot, therefore, prove that my view of the good life is right; I can only state my view and hope that as many as possible will agree. My view is this: *The good life is one inspired by love and guided by knowledge.*

Knowledge and love are both indefinitely extensible; therefore, however good a life may be, a better life can be imagined. Neither love without knowledge nor knowledge without love can produce a good life. In the Middle Ages, when pestilence appeared in a country, holy men advised the population to assemble in churches and pray for deliverance; the result was that the infection spread with extraordinary rapidity among the crowded masses of supplicants. This was an example of love without knowledge. The late war afforded an example of knowledge without love. In each case, the result was death on a large scale.

Although both love and knowledge are necessary, love is in a sense more fundamental, since it will lead intelligent people to seek knowledge, in order to find out how to benefit those whom they love. But if people are not intelligent, they will be content to believe what they have been told and may do harm in spite of the most genuine benevolence. Medicine affords, perhaps, the best example of what I mean. An able physician is more useful to a patient than the most devoted friend, and progress in medical knowledge does more for the health of the community than ill-informed philanthropy. Nevertheless, an element of benevolence is essential even here if any but the rich are to profit by scientific discoveries.

Love is a word which covers a variety of feelings; I have used it purposely, as I wish to include them all. Love as an emotion — which is what I am speaking about, for love "on principle" does not seem to me genuine — moves between two poles: on one side, pure delight in contemplation; on the other, pure benevolence. Where inanimate objects are concerned, delight alone enters in; we cannot feel benevolence toward a landscape or a sonata. This type of enjoyment is presumably the source of art. It is stronger, as a rule, in very young children than in adults, who are apt to view objects in a utilitarian spirit. It plays a large part in our feelings toward human beings, some of whom have charm and some the reverse, when considered simply as objects of aesthetic contemplation.

The opposite pole of love is pure benevolence. Men have sacrificed their lives to helping lepers; in such a case the love they felt cannot have had any element of aesthetic delight. Parental affection, as a rule, is accompanied by pleasure in the child's appearance but remains strong when this element is wholly absent. It would seem odd to call a mother's interest in a sick child "benevolence," because we are in the habit of using this word to describe a pale emotion nine parts humbug. But it is difficult to find any other word to describe the desire for another person's welfare. It is a fact that a desire of this sort may reach any degree of strength in the case of parental feeling. In other cases it is far less intense; indeed it would seem likely that all altruistic emotion is a sort of overflow of parental feeling, or sometimes a sublimation of it. For want of a better word, I shall call this emotion "benevolence." But I want to make it clear that I am speaking of an emotion, not a principle, and that I do not include in it any feeling of superiority such as is sometimes associated with the word. The word *sympathy* expresses part of what I mean but leaves out the element of activity that I wish to include.

Love at its fullest is an indissoluble combination of the two elements, delight and well-wishing. The pleasure of a parent in a beautiful and successful child combines both elements; so does sex love at its best. But in sex love, benevolence will only exist where there is secure possession, since otherwise jealousy will destroy it, while perhaps actually increasing the delight in contemplation. Delight without well-wishing may be cruel; well-wishing without delight easily tends to become cold and a little superior. A person who wishes to be loved wishes to be the object of a love containing both elements, except in cases of extreme weakness, such as infancy and severe illness. In these cases benevolence may be all that is desired. Conversely, in cases of extreme strength, admiration is more desired than benevolence: this is the state of mind of potentates and famous beauties. We only desire other people's good wishes in proportion as we feel ourselves in need of help or in danger of harm from them. At least, that would seem to be the biological logic of the situation, but it is not quite true to life. We desire affection in order to escape from the feeling of loneliness, in order to be, as we say, "understood." This is a matter of sympathy, not merely of benevolence; the person whose affection is satisfactory to us must not merely wish us well but must know in what our happiness consists. But this belongs to the other element of the good life — namely, knowledge.

In a perfect world, every sentient being would be to every other the object of the fullest love, compounded of delight, benevolence, and understanding inextricably blended. It does not follow that, in this actual world, we ought to attempt to have such feelings toward all the sentient beings whom we encounter. There are many in whom we cannot feel delight, because they are disgusting; if we were to do violence to our nature by trying to see beauties in them, we should merely blunt our susceptibilities to what we naturally find beautiful. Not to mention human beings, there are fleas and bugs and lice. We should have to be as hard pressed as the Ancient Mariner before we could feel delight in contemplating these creatures. Some saints, it is true, have called them "pearls of God," but what these men delighted in was the opportunity of displaying their own sanctity.

Benevolence is easier to extend widely, but even benevolence has its limits. If a man wished to marry a lady, we should not think the better of him for withdrawing if he found that someone else also wished to marry her: we should regard this as a fair field for competition. Yet his feelings toward a rival cannot be *wholly* benevolent. I think that in all descriptions of the good life here on earth we must assume a certain basis of animal vitality and animal instinct; without this, life becomes tame and uninteresting. Civilization should be something added to this, not substituted for it; the ascetic saint and the detached sage fail in this respect to be complete human beings. A small number of them may enrich a community; but a world composed of them would die of boredom.

These considerations lead to a certain emphasis on the element of delight as an ingredient in the best love. Delight, in this actual world, is unavoidably selective and prevents us from having the same feelings toward all mankind. When conflicts arise between delight and benevolence, they must, as a rule, be decided by a compromise, not by a complete surrender of either. Instinct has its rights, and if we do violence to it beyond a point it takes vengeance in subtle ways. Therefore in aiming at a good life the limits of human possibility must be borne in mind. Here again, however, we are brought back to the necessity of knowledge.

When I speak of knowledge as an ingredient of the good life, I am not thinking of ethical knowledge but of scientific knowledge and knowledge of particular facts. I do not think there is, strictly speaking, such a thing as ethical knowledge. If we desire to achieve some end, knowledge may show us the means, and this knowledge may loosely pass as ethical. But I do not believe that we can decide what sort of conduct is right or wrong except by reference to its probable consequences. Given an end to be achieved, it is a question for science to discover how to achieve it. All moral rules must be tested by examining whether they tend to realize ends that we desire. I say ends that we desire, not ends that we *ought* to desire. What we "ought" to desire is merely what someone else wishes us to desire. Usually it is what the authorities wish us to desire — parents, schoolmasters, policemen, and judges. If you say to me, "You ought to do so-and-so," the motive power of your remark lies in my desire for your approval — together, possibly, with rewards or punishments attached to your approval or disapproval. Since all behaviour springs from desire, it is clear that ethical notions can have no importance except as they influence desire. They do this through the desire for approval and the fear of disapproval. These are powerful social forces, and we shall naturally endeavor to win them to our side if we wish to realize any social purpose. When I say that the morality of conduct is to be judged by its probable consequences, I mean that I desire to see approval given to behavior likely to realize social purposes which we desire, and disapproval to opposite behavior. At present this is not done; there are certain traditional rules according to which approval and disapproval are meted out quite regardless of consequences. But this is a topic with which we shall deal at some other time.

The superfluity of theoretical ethics is obvious in simple cases. Suppose, for instance, your child is ill. Love makes you wish to cure it, and science tells you how to do so. There is not an intermediate stage of ethical theory, where it is demonstrated that your child had better be cured. Your act springs directly from desire for an end, together with knowledge of means. This is equally true of all acts, whether good or bad. The ends differ, and the knowledge is more adequate is some cases than in others. But there is no conceivable way of making people do things they do not wish to do. What is possible is to alter their desires by a system of rewards and penalties, among which social approval and disapproval are not the least potent. The question for the legislative moralist is, therefore: How shall this system of rewards and punishments be arranged so as to secure the maximum of what is desired by the legislative authority? If I say that the legislative authority has bad desires, I mean merely that its desires conflict with those of some section of the community to which I belong. Outside human desires there is no moral standard.

Thus, what distinguishes ethics from science is not any special kind of knowledge but merely desire. The knowledge required in ethics is exactly like the knowledge elsewhere; what is peculiar is that certain ends are desired, and that right conduct is what conduces to them. Of course, if the definition of right conduct is to make a wide appeal, the end must be such as large sections of mankind desire. If I defined right conduct as that which increases my own income, readers would disagree. The whole effectiveness of any ethical argument lies in its scientific part, i.e., in the proof that one kind of conduct, rather than some other, is a means to an end which is widely desired. I distinguish, however, between ethical argument and ethical education. The latter consists in strengthening certain desires and weakening others. This is qute a different process.

We can now explain more exactly the purport of the definition of the good life with which this essay began. When I said that the good life consists of love guided by knowledge, the desire which prompted me was the desire to live such a life as far as possible, and to see others living it; and the logical content of the statement is that, in a community where men live in this way, more desires will be satisfied than in one where there is less love or less knowledge. I do not mean that such a life is "virtuous" or that its opposite is "sinful," for these are conceptions which seem to me to have no scientific justification.

EXPLORING THE GENERIC ESSAY

1. After the first reading of Russell's essay, make sure you are familiar with the following vocabulary in the context the author has used it: amenable, supplicant, philanthropy, sonata, utilitarian, benevolence, altruistic, sublimation, indissoluble, sentient, ascetic, sage, ethical, superfluity, potent, moralist.

2. Underline the thesis statement.

3. (a) State Russell's definition of the good life.
    (b) What does Russell say about the role of knowledge in this life, and about the two poles and the role of love? (Since this is a challenging work, you might consider rereading it before answering the remaining questions.)

4. Pick out examples of the following methods of proof:
    (i)   historical references
    (ii) illustrations that use contrast
    (iii) statements of opinion and personal belief
    (iv) literary references
    (v)   appeals to authority figures
    (vi) attempts to draw the reader into the argument
    (vii) verifiable fact, and explain why there is little of this

5. In the margin, number the major steps in Russell's argument. Then summarize the main idea of each step.

6. Examine the language. Pick out examples of phrasing and literary devices that contribute to the reader's enjoyment and/or understanding of the passage.

EXTENSIVE STUDY

1. "The Good Life" provides an excellent example of an essay that uses the technique of extended definition; that is, the whole essay functions to define Russell's subject. He claims that delight in contemplation and benevolence are "the two emotional poles" of love.
   (a) Explain the basic differences between these two aspects of love.
   (b) Give your own example which substantiates the point made in paragraph 2.

2. (a) Account for Russell's claim that he cannot prove his view of the good life. How does this affect his argument?
   (b) Compose your own example of another generalization that someone might make but could not prove.
   (c) Make a generalization that can be proved, explain the form the proof might take, and suggest how this generalization differs from the above statement.

3. What insight, if any, has Russell given you about his personality? Use your intuition and the material studied to form your observations.

4. How much human behaviour is, in your view, guided by anticipated consequences?

5. Do you agree that "all behaviour springs from desire?" Give arguments for and against this statement.

6. "We only desire other people's good wishes in proportion as we feel ourselves in need of help or in danger of harm from them." Assess the validity of Russell's discussion in paragraph 6.

7. Russell states in paragraph 10: "All moral rules must be tested by examining whether they tend to realize the ends we desire."
   (a) Do you agree with this contention? Give reasons.
   (b) How might this position affect you in later life?

8. Consider examples of how our society tries to maintain social control by altering our desires. What are the moral implications of this power?

9. Read McDayter's "Duck Shooting on Yonge Street."
   (a) Speculate about McDayter's view of the good life, judging from what she has revealed about her personality and values. Cite examples from her essay to make your points.
   (b) Would McDayter be likely to share Russell's views of what brings contentment?

10. Read the excerpt from Thoreau's *Walden*. Would Russell agree that the simplicity Thoreau sought was a key ingredient for the good life? Refer to both essays for proof.

11. Read Eban's "The Eichmann Trial in Retrospect."
    (a) Compare the types of evidence Eban and Russell use in their approach to these two significant moral issues.
    (b) Eban quotes Jean-Jacques Rousseau's famous statement:

> The fundamental principle of all morality is that man is a being
> naturally good, loving justice and order; that there is not any
> original perversity in the human heart, and that the first
> movements of nature are always right.

Working in pairs or small groups, phrase this generalization in your
own words. Do you agree with this observation? Would Thoreau or
Russell be likely to agree? Give reasons.

12. If you have read all the essays in this unit, make a list of what you
could learn about life from each writer. Beside each observation,
indicate whether you agree or not, and why. You might want to work
individually or in groups and then compare findings.

13. Read "Ethics and Engineering" and the associated letters of response
in unit 12 on Contemporary Journalism, page 213. Consider how
Russell's definition of the good life might relate to those students who
allegedly hold an "anti-arts" credo.

THE WRITING FOLDER

1. Write a polished dialogue in which conflict between two persons
arises from differing interpretations of what makes life meaningful.
Your characters should have a second major difference which
contributes to the tension — for example, they might have radically
different class or cultural backgrounds or an age gap between them.
Aim for diction appropriate for each character.

2. You are the host of a nationally syndicated talk show which
encourages controversy. Prepare a series of interview questions for a
future program; the guests will be a prominent rock star and a
professor of religious studies. The questions should encourage your
guests to convince the audience of the validity of their position on the
good life. Use language appropriate to the occasion. You may wish to
read your paper aloud.

3. Interview a teacher in your school about his or her view of the good
life. Write a polished report of the interview. Caution: avoid asking
questions that intrude upon your subject's privacy. Show the teacher
your finished report and obtain permission before submitting it for
marking.

INDEPENDENT STUDY

1. Read Graham Greene's *The Heart of the Matter*. Using Russell's
definition of the good life and the ideas raised in one other of his
essays, consider Scobie's failure to live or die well.   ++

2. Read James Joyce's *Portrait of the Artist As a Young Man*. Stephen
Daedalus's epiphanies help define his quest as an artist. Decide

whether the life Daedalus chooses for himself is in harmony with Russell's view of the good life.   ++

3.   Research the life of Gandhi. Using more than one source, analyze the ways in which Gandhi's teachings and life exemplified or differed from Russell's views of love and knowledge, and the role the two elements play in life. Your essay should provide footnotes and a bibliography. Consult your teacher about the school's or department's footnote format.   ++

4.   For other associated independent study projects, see the works listed below or consult your teacher-librarian:

> Robert Bolt, *A Man for All Seasons*
> Albert Camus, *The Myth of Sisyphus*
> Eric Fromm, *The Art of Loving*
> Charles Gore, *The Philosophy of the Good Life*
> Barrington Moore, *Reflections on the Causes of Human Misery*
> Sir Thomas More, *Utopia*
> Henry David Thoreau, *Walden*

TIMED WRITING

Using what you have learned from one or more of the essays in this unit, write an essay on one of the following topics within the time determined by your teacher. Keep the tone personal, but do not use colloquial language except in direct speech.

My View of the Good Life

My Mother's Views of the Good Life Are Very Different From Mine (or substitute friend, father, employer, etc.)

One cannot actively pursue the good life.; contentment is the byproduct of life well lived.

DUCK SEASON ON YONGE STREET

GHISLAINE MCDAYTER (student essay)

If anyone asks me where I work, I look them straight in the eye, and with a quiet deliberation that defies rebuttal, inform them that I work in an art gallery. Nothing, may I add, could be further from the truth. The 'art gallery' is on the second floor of a book shop in the biggest tourist trap in the whole of Toronto.

In an attempt to give visitors a flavour of Canadian culture, the mall's architects ingeniously latched on to a 'goose' theme. In every corner of the sprawling complex, Canada geese were strung up to the ceiling in such realistic poses that many tourists looked up at the figures with wary glances, tentatively feeling the tops of their heads for wetness. Not that one can blame the architects. In all fairness, there are few symbols identifiably Canadian, and a group of beavers swinging from the ceiling would understandably have been more disturbing than the relatively unobtrusive birds.

Not to be outdone, the manager of my gallery decided to carry on this motif. Within a month of his appointment, the store began to resemble something of a cross between Jack Miner's mating grounds and an indoor duck graveyard. Stained glass ducks swung from the ceiling, carved ducks propped up books on bird decoys, and to top off this fowl theme, prints of Canada geese stared stupidly down at American viewers.

Any chance I might have had for a good working relationship with my new employer ended abruptly when he proudly placed a package marked "fragile" on the counter before me. To my horror, it did not contain the usual shipment of "Wild Wings" cards and decoys, but a new addition for the front desk — a large wooden telephone in the shape of a duck. It had been cleverly split down the centre to form the receiver; one was expected to speak into the duck's bill. The crowning glory, said my employer, was the ring. But perhaps 'ring' was the wrong word for it quacked rather than rang and reverberated throughout the building, further intimidating the somewhat paranoid tourists who strolled under the shadows of swinging birds.

After a week of working in this environment, I understandably began to eye the merchandise with the same look of evil intent that I suspect a hunter, having spotted a particularly troublesome quarry, might acquire. The hunt was on — either the ducks went or I did. There were just too many of them; the store simply wasn't large enough for all of us, and I had the horrifying impression that the enemy was reproducing at an alarming rate. Each one I sold was a notch in my belt, a move toward sanity. The answer to my problem presented itself in the shape of American tourists.

Sorely befuddled by the apparent lack of Canadian culture — other than possibly bird watching — tourists stumbled into my trap in search of "real Canada," only to be confronted with more geese. Thoroughly persuaded that Canadians were indeed very clean, very nice, but utterly lacking in imagination, the visitors resigned themselves to souvenir birds and statues of the C.N. tower (surely just another nesting place for the beloved goose). "In this bag," they mused clutching their plastic statues and painted birds, "in this bag lies the true nature of Canada." And so began their great search for the definitive Canada goose.

Not that this solution was the perfect one. I found myself dealing with a whole new and rather awkward situation. Being a Canadian in a souvenir shop, I became the rather unwilling target of goose-trivia questions. I faced an unpleasant prospect; if the eager questioner discovered how little I knew or cared about geese, *my* birds might be sent home to roost. Suddenly I found myself relating the most intricate and certainly the most salacious details about the behavioural patterns of the Canadian goose.

I distinctly recall one especially unnerving occasion when I was confronted by a rather large American carrying a camera, a map and a small book on bird watching. Naively, I breathed a sigh of relief. Here was someone who had fallen for the propaganda, hook, line and sinker. I anticipated no problems. In this, however, I was proven wrong. He began asking rather elementary questions about the mating call of the Canada duck which even I could answer, tormented as I was each day by that very sound made by the office telephone. But his queries grew more difficult. Could he be a real duck lover who had begun to smell a rat? His next question sent me into a cold sweat. What did the Canada goose eat, as a rule? Frantically, I tried to recall every animal film I had ever seen, but I'd always been more entranced with the gourmet habits of human-kind — and my stand-by answer of "beaver" simply wouldn't suffice. In desperation, I blurted out the first thing that came to me: maple syrup.

"Maple syrup?," he puzzled.

"Yes," I lied, grimly envisioning myself buried under a mountain of refunded ducks. Lucky for me, though, my tormentor decided to cut his losses and waddled off, I assume to purchase some genuine Canadian maple syrup goose-feed.

Although certain clever tourists refused to be taken in by Canada's apparent fowl fetish and staunchly purchased soap-stone sculptures of seals and Margaret Trudeau's autobiography, others did a better job of disseminating duck propaganda than I could have ever hoped for. One steaming day, a well-dressed couple wandered into the store conversing just loudly enough in their Greenwich Village accent for me to eavesdrop as I picked my way across the duck-festooned display area.

"Excuse me," said the man, "but could you tell me the artist of this yellow-beaked decoy?"

I stared in wonderment at the man; clearly, I had much to learn about this world and my fellow human beings. This was on par with wanting to know the artist of the gold-plated C.N. tower figures that lit up when one turned them upside down. At random, I picked up a duck and read the name scratched hastily on its stomach.

"Didn't I tell you, Andrea?," he said turning to his wife. "We *met* this artist just last month at a gallery opening," he told me, conspiratorially. I wondered if he fancied that, should the word get out, the masses might descend upon him for autographs or information about this artist. Somewhat astonished, I pondered what kind of gallery opening in New York displayed ducks. After all, everyone knows New Yorkers are a strange breed, long-accustomed to decorating their subway with obscene graffiti and dancing down rickety fire-escapes boisterously singing, "I love New York!." If this represented American culture, perhaps their cultural situation was as iffy as ours. It was no wonder they so readily turned to 'our' ducks for entertainment. Regardless, it seemed a sign of social decay on both sides of the world's longest undefended border, but nothing I could remedy.

Some time later, I discovered my error. A more leisurely inspection transformed the inscription from "Madeline Kore" into "Made in Korea." But I'd learned an important lesson in the battle to rid my world of ducks. I continued to bedazzle tourists with the brilliant creations of Miss Kore and my sales grew commensurately. Indeed, I'd be very much surprised if by now some brilliant entrepreneur hasn't caught on to a very good thing, changed her name, and opened a highly lucrative duck gallery at 5th and Main — or in Hazelton Lanes, for that matter.

Don't get me wrong. Ducks and geese, as boring as I may find them, are highly profitable. So much so that I will continue to work in my gallery so long as the search for the definitive Canada goose persists. And each May, I will happily note the dwindling number of geese perched around the shop. With thanks, I settle back to watch the birds migrating *south* for a change.

*E*XCERPT FROM WALDEN

HENRY DAVID THOREAU

. . . When first I took up my abode in the woods, that is, began to spend my nights as well as days there, which, by accident, was on Independence Day, or the Fourth of July, 1845, my house was not finished for winter, but was merely a defence against the rain, without plastering or chimney, the walls being of rough, weather-stained boards, with wide chinks, which made it cool at night. The upright white hewn studs and freshly planed door and window casings gave it a clean and airy look, especially in the morning, when its timbers were saturated with dew, so that I fancied that by noon some sweet gum would exude from them. To my imagination it retained throughout the day more or less of this auroral character, reminding me of a certain house on a mountain which I had visited a year before. This was an airy and unplastered cabin, fit to entertain a travelling god, and where a goddess might trail her garments. The winds which passed over my dwelling were such as sweep over the ridges of mountains, bearing the broken strains, or celestial parts only, of terrestrial music. The morning wind forever blows, the poem of creation is uninterrupted: but few are the ears that hear it. Olympus is but the outside of the earth everywhere.

The only house I had been the owner of before, if I except a boat, was a tent, which I used occasionally when making excursions in the summer, and this is still rolled up in my garret; but the boat, after passing from hand to hand, has gone down the stream of time. With this more substantial shelter about me, I had made some progress toward settling in the world. This frame, so slightly clad, was a sort of crystallization around me, and reacted on the builder. It was suggestive somewhat as a picture in outlines. I did not need to go outdoors to take the air, for the atmosphere within had lost none of its freshness. It was not so much within-doors as behind a door where I sat, even in the rainiest weather. The Harivansa[1] says, "An abode without birds is like a meat without seasoning." Such was not my abode, for I found myself suddenly neighbour to the birds; not by having imprisoned one, but having caged myself near them. I was not only nearer to some of those which commonly frequent the garden and the orchard, but to those wilder and more thrilling songsters of the forest which never, or rarely, serenade a villager, — the wood thrush, the veery, the scarlet tanager, the field sparrow, the whip-poor-will, and many others.

I was seated by the shore of a small pond, about a mile and a half south of the village of Concord and somewhat higher than it, in the midst of an extensive wood between that town and Lincoln, and about two miles south of that our only field known to fame, Concord Battle Ground; but I was so low in the woods that the opposite shore, half a mile off, like the rest, covered with wood, was my most distant horizon. For the first week, whenever I looked out on the pond it impressed me like a tarn high upon the side of a mountain, its bottom far above the surface of other lakes, and, as the sun arose, I saw it throwing off its nightly clothing of mist, and here and there, by degrees, its soft ripples or its smooth reflecting surface was revealed, while the mists, like ghosts, were stealthily withdrawing in every direction into the woods, as at the breaking up of some nocturnal conventicle. The very dew seemed to hang upon the trees later into the day than usual, as on the sides of mountains.

This small lake was of most value as a neighbour in the intervals of a gentle rain-storm in August, when, both air and water being perfectly still, but the sky overcast, mid-afternoon had all the serenity of evening, and the wood thrush sang around, and was heard from shore to shore. A lake like this is never smoother than at such a time; and the clear portion of the air above it being shallow and darkened by clouds, the water, full of light and reflections, becomes a lower heaven itself so much the more important. From a hill-top near by, where the wood had been recently cut off, there was a pleasing vista southward across the pond, through a wide indentation in the hills which form the shore there, where their opposite sides sloping toward each other suggested a stream flowing out in that direction through a wooded valley, but stream there was none. That way I looked between and over the near green hills to some distant and higher ones on the horizon, tinged with blue. Indeed, by standing on tiptoe I could catch a glimpse of some of the peaks of the still bluer and more distant mountain ranges in the northwest, those true-blue coins from heaven's own mint, and also of some portion of the village. But in other directions, even from this point, I could not see over or beyond the woods which surrounded me. It is well to have some water in your neighbourhood, to give buoyancy to and float the earth. One value even of the smallest well is that when you look into it you see that the earth is not continent but insular. This is as important as that it keeps butter cool. When I looked across the pond from this peak toward the Sudbury meadows, which in time of flood I distinguished elevated perhaps by a mirage in their seething valley, like a coin in a basin, all the earth beyond the pond appeared like a thin crust insulated and floated even by this small sheet of intervening water, and I was reminded that this on which I dwelt was but *dry land.*

Though the view from my door was still more contracted, I did not feel crowded or confined in the least. There was pasture enough for my imagination. The low shrub oak plateau to which the opposite shore arose stretched away toward the prairies of the West and the steppes of Tartary, affording ample room for all the roving families of men. "There are none happy in the world but beings who enjoy freely a vast horizon," said Damodara[2], when his herds required new and larger pastures.

Both place and time were changed, and I dwelt nearer to those parts of the universe and to those eras in history which had most attracted me. Where I lived was as far off as many a region viewed nightly by astronomers. We are wont to imagine rare and delectable places in some remote and more celestial corner of the system, behind the constellation of Cassiopeia's Chair, far from noise and disturbance. I discovered that my house actually had its site in such a withdrawn, but forever new and unprofaned, part of the universe. If it were worth the while to settle in those parts near to the Pleiades or the Hyades[3], to Aldebaran or Altair[4], then I was really there, or at an equal remoteness from the life which I had left behind, dwindled and twinkling with as fine a ray to my nearest neighbour, and to be seen only in moonless nights by him. Such was that part of creation where I had squatted;

> There was a shepherd that did live,
>   And held his thoughts as high
> As where the mounts whereon his flocks
>   Did hourly feed him by.

What should we think of the shepherd's life if his flocks always wandered to higher pastures than his thoughts?

Every morning was a cheerful invitation to make my life of equal simplicity, and I may say innocence, with Nature herself. I have been as sincere a worshipper of Aurora[5] as the Greeks. I got up early and bathed in the pond; that was a religious exercise, and one of the best things which I did. They say that characters were engraven on the bathing tub of King Tching-thang to this effect: "Renew thyself completely each day; do it again, and again, and forever again." I can understand that. Morning brings back the heroic ages. I was as much affected by the faint hum of a mosquito making its invisible and unimaginable tour through my apartment at earliest dawn, when I was sitting with door and windows open, as I could be by any trumpet that ever sang of fame. It was Homer's requiem; itself an Iliad and Odyssey in the air, singing its own wrath and wanderings. There was something cosmical about it; a standing advertisement, till forbidden, of the everlasting vigor and fertility of the word. The morning, which is the most memorable season of the day, is the awakening hour. Then there is least somnolence in us: and for an hour, at least, some part of us awakes which slumbers all the rest of the day and night. Little is to be expected of that day, if it can be called a day, to which we are not awakened by our Genius, but by the mechanical nudgings of some servitor, are not awakened by our own newly acquired force and aspirations from within, accompanied by the undulations of celestial music, filling the air — to a higher life than we fell asleep from; and thus the darkness bear its fruit, and prove itself to be good, no less than the light. That man who does not believe that each day contains an earlier, more sacred, and auroral hour than he has yet profaned, has despaired of life, and is pursuing a descending and darkening way. After a partial cessation of his sensuous life, the soul of man, or its organs rather, are reinvigorated each day, and his Genius tries again what noble life it can make. All memorable events, I should say, transpire in morning time and in a morning atmosphere. The Vedas[6] say, "All intelligences awake with the morning." Poetry and art, and the fairest and most memorable of the actions of men, date from such an hour. All poets and heroes, like Memnon[7], are the children of Aurora, and emit their music at sunrise. To him whose elastic and vigorous thought keeps pace with the sun, the day is a perpetual morning. It matters not what the clocks say or the attitudes and labours of men. Morning is when I am awake and there is a dawn in me. Moral reform is the effort to throw off sleep. Why is it that men give so poor an account of their day if they have not been slumbering? They are not such poor calculators. If they had not been overcome with drowsiness, they would have performed something. The millions are awake enough for physical labour; but only one in a million is awake enough for effective intellectual exertion, only one in a hundred millions to a poetic or divine life. To be awake is to be alive. I have never yet met a man who was quite awake. How could I have looked him in the face?

We must learn to reawaken and keep ourselves awake, not by mechanical aids, but by an infinite expectation of the dawn, which does not forsake us in our soundest sleep. I know of no more encouraging fact than the unquestionable ability of man to elevate his life by a conscious endeavour. It is something to be able to paint a particular picture, or to carve a statue, and so to make a few objects beautiful; but it is far more glorious to carve and paint the very atmosphere and medium through which we look, which morally we can do. To affect the quality of the day, that is the highest of arts. Every man is tasked to make his life, even in its details, worthy of the contemplation of his most elevated and critical hour. If we refused, or rather used up, such paltry informations as we get, the oracles would distinctly inform us how this might be done.

I went to the woods because I wished to live deliberately, to front only the essential facts of life, and see if I could not learn what it had to teach, and not, when I came to die, discover that I had not lived. I did not wish to live what was not life, living is so dear; nor did I wish to practise resignation, unless it was quite necessary. I wanted to live deep and suck out all the marrow of life, to live so sturdily and Spartan-like as to put to rout all that was not life, to cut a broad swath and shave close, to drive life into a corner, and reduce it to its lowest terms, and, if it proved to be mean, why then to get the whole and genuine meanness of it, and publish its meanness to the world; or if it were sublime, to know it by experience, and be able to give a true account of it in my next excursion. For most men, it appears to me, are in a strange uncertainty about it, whether it is of the devil or of God, and have *somewhat hastily* concluded that it is the chief end of man here to "glorify God and enjoy him forever." . . .

---

[1]A Sanskrit epic poem of the fifth century A.D. Thoreau and Emerson were both interested in Eastern and Near Eastern religious literature.
[2]The Hindu divinity, Krishna.
[3]*Pleiades, Hyades,* constellations.
[4]*Aldebaran, Altair,* bright stars.
[5]The Greek goddess of dawn.
[6]The sacred literature of the Hindus.
[7]Son of Aurora; his statue is reputed to emit a harp-like sound at sunrise.

THE EICHMANN TRIAL IN RETROSPECT

ABBA EBAN

He who cannot remember the past is doomed to repeat it.

GEORGE SANTAYANA

On a winter day in 1944 the head of an industrial concern in Berlin calmly signed the following letter to Gestapo headquarters:

> Following our verbal discussion regarding the delivery of equipment of simple construction for the burning of bodies, we are submitting plans for our perfected cremation ovens which operate with coal and which have hitherto given full satisfaction.
>
> We suggest two crematoria furnaces for the building planned, but we advise you to make further inquiries to make sure that two ovens will be sufficient for your requirements.
>
> We guarantee the effectiveness of the cremation ovens as well as their durability, the use of the best material and our faultless workmanship.
>
> Heil Hitler!
>
> C.H. Kori

There was a good reason for the writer's complacent mood. The places in which 'full satisfaction' had been given included Dachau and Lubin, where 'the best material and faultless workmanship' had efficiently converted the bodies of men, women, and children into piles of anonymous powdered ash. Why should not the Kori Corporation now receive the Belgrade business? Competition, however, was keen. The I.A. Topf Corporation was showing great technical ingenuity, as is clear from its terse note of February 12, 1943, to the 'Central Construction Office of the S.S. and the Police at Auschwitz':

> Subject: Crematoria 2 and 3 for the camp.
>
> We acknowledge receipt of your order for five triple furnaces, including two electric elevators for raising the corpses and one emergency elevator. A practical installation for stoking coal was also ordered and one for transporting ashes.

These documents, produced at the Nuremberg trials of Nazi war criminals and at the Eichmann trial in Jerusalem, are excellently typed. There was, of course, an adequate number of carbon copies for the files. One can imagine the respectable industrialists going off to their clubs in a fine glow of patriotic duty and commercial enterprise.

But there was no point in cremation furnaces without the human fuel. Not far away in his Berlin office, Adolf Eichmann was signing a briefer document. It was a telegram to his emissaries in occupied countries. It read simply: 'Children's transports can get under way.' The reference was to children who no longer had parents with whom to embark on the journey to Auschwitz for collective gassing. Even these presented problems. The Jerusalem court sat transfixed in silent horror as Attorney-General Hausner unfolded the story: 'You will hear evidence of tender infants pressed by their mothers to their bodies in the gas chamber so that they were not immediately poisoned, until the executioners came and threw them alive into the furnaces.'

This was standard practice. But a special routine was now necessary to organize the asphyxiation of Jewish children who had no parents to accompany them. How this worked in occupied France was factually described at the Jerusalem trial.

> The children would arrive at the Drancy Camp packed in busses guarded by policemen. . . . On the arrival of the busses they would begin to remove the children and lead them in groups to the halls, the older ones holding the hands of the smaller children; or carrying them in their arms. They did not weep, the children; they walked terrified, disciplined, miserable, and complied with the orders like a flock of sheep, one helping the other. . . .
>
> On the day of deportation, they would be wakened at five o'clock in the morning. Irritable, half asleep, most of the children would refuse to get up and go down to the courtyard. The volunteer women would have to urge them, gently, patiently and so tragically, so as to convince the older children that they must obey orders and vacate the halls. On a number of occasions the entreaties did not help. The children cried and refused to leave their mattresses. The gendarmes would then enter the halls and pick up the children in their arms as they screamed with fear, struggling and grasping at each other. The halls were like a madhouse; the scene was too terrible for even the hardest men to bear.
>
> In the courtyard they would call out the names of the children one by one, mark them off in the register, and direct them to the busses. When a bus filled up it would leave the camp with its cargo. Since many of the children remained unidentified and others would not answer to their correct or assumed names, they would include them in the convoy to make up the number.
>
> Each convoy consisted of about five hundred children and five hundred adults chosen from the camp prisoners. Within a period of about three weeks, during the second half of August and the first part of September, 1943, four thousand children, thus made into orphans, were transported in this fashion to be exterminated with adult strangers.
>
> Hauptsturmführer Roethke was present at these transports and would inspect personally the parading of the children, the roll call, and the loading into the busses.

The people of Israel are the sons, the daughters, the brothers, the sisters, the fathers, the mothers of the millions whose agony was re-enacted during the twelve months of the Eichmann trial. The procedures at every stage were marked by careful decorum and high legal scholarship. But behind the reserved procedures one could see the marching ghosts.

If you were a Jew in Europe during those years, and if Adolf Eichmann knew of your existence, your fate was inexorable. You would be rounded up with your family in Amsterdam or Paris, in Belgrade or Venice, in Budapest or Brussels, in Warsaw or Kiev. You would be put on a train for Auschwitz or Treblinka, and then either lined up naked with hundreds of others behind your neat pile of clothes while German soldiers shot you in the neck on the edge of a huge ditch or else herded into a shower room for mass asphyxiation. Your hair would be shorn beforehand, your gold fillings taken afterwards, your ashes used for fertilizer. You could be useful to the German war economy. Today the capital cities and villages of Europe contain ghostlike streets with their communal buildings, synagogues, and schools in which the bustle and laughter of living men, women, and children were choked by the grim ukase issuing from the sinister office in Berlin where Adolf Eichmann pored meticulously over his files, before affixing the most macabre signatures ever inscribed by mortal hand.

All this happened in recent memory. Anybody alive today over the age of thirty-five is in some way a part of this experience. For we belong to the unique generation that committed or suffered or failed to prevent these things. In each of the three contingencies we have a direct relationship to the drama. The theme of the Jerusalem courtroom was the unending tension between the sublime attributes of man's nature and his unlimited capacity to distort the human image. And in this conflict our generation has lived the moment of man's darkest defeat.

Some would have preferred not to evoke the past. Does not the tormented human imagination deserve respite from the assault of such memories? There are people of impeccable sincerity who advocate its oblivion. Mr. Victor Gollancz, for example, has written that 'The sooner we forget the cruelties of the past, the better.'

After millions of years of evolution, a species emerges on this planet endowed with the gift of memory and articulation. Man is the only animal able to transmit experience. And the transmission of experience is the central core of education and moral progress. Memory is the father of conscience. The issue is whether we should wipe from the tablets of memory the most vivid evidence of the consequences flowing from chauvinism, racial discrimination, and inhumanity.

The question must be answered in the name of the future, not of the past. Man is the only animal that has ever shown a tendency to destroy its own species. He may now become the first and only creature to devastate its habitat. He cannot afford to ignore any experience that throws light on the social consequence of his nature. 'The fundamental principle of all morality,' wrote Jean-Jacques Rousseau, 'is that man is a being naturally good, loving justice and order; that there is not any original perversity in the human heart and that the first movements of nature are always right.'

There may have been evidence for this outlook in the eighteenth century. It is less easy to reconcile it with the memory of ordinary men — tens of thousands of them — going calmly about their work of slaughter or writing solemn minutes in impeccable commercial jargon about the 'satisfactory' attributes of machines for burning bodies. The human conscience needs an alarm bell, not a sleeping pill.

The first lesson of the trial takes us back to the moral torment of our age. The horrors of Nazism sprang from a society in which high standards of science and technology were fostered. We are reminded here of the fallacy of a technical rationalism uninhibited by moral restraint. Man has probed deeply into the spectacle of nature, but he stands baffled before the incalculabilities of his own character. He has exercised command over his external realm but seems impotent to control his inner domain. Thus the age of scientific triumph is the epoch of confusion. Man is conscious of his lack of inner and outer harmony, obsessed by a sense of helplessness before the forces generated by his own creative imagination. He looks gropingly into the past in the hope of finding a beam of light to illumine his future.

It is for this future, and for its sake alone, that the trial was held. Its lesson and counsel affect every layer of social experience. It teaches how discrimination, taking root in small beginnings, leads to vast and uncontrollable disaster. The outrages of Auschwitz and Treblinka could not have occurred had there not been tens of thousands of men who became accustomed to look at other men as though they were not human at all. A man cannot murder others in cold blood, he cannot dash a baby to the ground or fling children into a furnace, unless he is first convinced that they are not a part of his own humanity.

The trial asks urgent questions about the limits beyond which racial incitement cannot be tolerated. This is the oldest dilemma of liberalism. If a society is free and tolerant, must it even tolerate attacks on its own toleration? If a society can suppress pornography without ceasing to be free, why is it forbidden to establish some criterion whereby ideas fatal to social morality may be denied the sanction of law? The indulgence granted the Nazi doctrine in the

1930's before it reached irresistible proportions stands as an ominous warning against inertia and apathy. In the Weimar Republic this indulgence flowed from the doctrine that there is no limit to the free dissemination of opinion — not even the limit of decency and survival. On the international plane, it sheltered behind a doctrine of sovereignty applied with such rigid pedantry as to inhibit effective international intervention. In the postwar world, lesser outrages have fortunately evoked a much sharper and more insistent international reaction.

In the particular terms of Jewish history, the trial represented Israel's assertion of the dignity and equality of Jewish life. The few voices that were raised against the verdict had not questioned similar action when the allied governments inflicted condign penalties on men who had not been responsible for a small fraction of Eichmann's butchery. There has been an insidious, if unconscious, assumption across history that Jewish lives are not enclosed within the same framework of law and social morality as the lives of other peoples.

It was probably in response to this background that the Jerusalem courts took care to remain in the orbit of the Nuremberg jurisprudence and of the legal practice of other nations outraged by Nazi violence. To have done anything else would have been to convict the allied and resistance powers of excessive severity. In a world in which the capital penalty still exists and in which the precedents for penalizing racial massacre have been so clearly and recently demarcated, any other course would have been a rebellion against the established juridical standards. Israel was created in order to make Jewish history flow in harmony with the universal procession of law — and not outside its realm, as in all previous generations. It is true that the Jerusalem courts had a particular message to write. But there was no clean slate on which to write it. I can personally testify that some in the legislative and executive branches who are passionate opponents of capital punishment felt inexorably that this was not the area in which to commence the writing of new law.

The news of Eichmann's most active operation — the gassing and burning of Hungarian Jews — reached the free world in the summer of 1944. The spokesman of that world brandished an impotent fist at the distant murderer:

Prime Minister [Churchill] to Foreign Secretary,
11 July 1944.
There is no doubt that this is probably the greatest and most horrible crime ever committed in the history of the world, and it has been done by scientific machinery by nominally civilized men in the name of a great State and one of the leading races of Europe. It is quite clear that all concerned in this crime who may fall into our hands, including the people who only obeyed orders

by carrying out the butcheries, should be put to death after their association with the murders has been proved.

It is not a matter of vengeance. The children clutching each other's hands as they were herded into the slaughter chamber are beyond vengeance or expiation. The issue is whether the human society can be denied the ultimate right to banish from its midst those who massively violate its most sacred compassions. Beyond this issue is the question of whether we are safe against a renewal of the tragedy. We may become so if we save it from oblivion and deduce its lessons in the political, social, and educational domains.

The renaissance artists portrayed the human soul as being drawn upward and downward by elements in its own nature. Both the upward and the downward pull can be discerned in the life of our times. It is still not certain how the tension will be ultimately resolved. The story of this dark and evil assault enters the memory of man as one of his weapons in the struggle for the vindication of his essential humanity.

3. THE SCHOLARLY ESSAY

Key Work:
  "Spiritual Longing in Laurence's Manawaka Women" — Leslie-Ann Hales
Associated Readings:
  "Our Two Cultures" — Patricia Smart
  "The Tragedy of Ugliness" — John Hunter (student essay)

The scholarly essay is the essence of critical thinking and writing. It demonstrates insightful opinion supported by depth of research and an objective and reasoned approach.

Those who write scholarly essays may concentrate their investigation on the subject itself (primary research), as do Hales and Hunter; as well, they may consult other authorities in the field (secondary research) as does Patricia Smart. If secondary research is needed for your project, use these sources only after you have sufficiently explored your primary material.

Unlike the generic essay, the scholarly essay is a highly specialized essay form. Each subject area (English, History, Philosophy) has its own requirements for organization and format, particularly documentation of sources.

1olarly essays are written for a select audience. They are often
1ed in academic journals or periodicals such as *Atlantic Monthly,*
lay Night, or *Canadian Forum.* For example, Hales's essay was
.hed in *English Studies in Canada,* a periodical read mainly by
sh teachers. Smart's essay appeared in *The Canadian Forum,* a
magazine read mainly by informed Canadians.

BEFORE READING

■ Familiarize yourself with the titles of Margaret Laurence's work and the
controversy about her fiction that sometimes surfaces.
■ To what extent do you think the characters a writer invents are reflections of his or her self? Defend your position.
■ The publisher of *English Studies in Canada* stipulates that all submis-
sions must follow *Modern Language Association (MLA)* style and
documentation. Locate this manual and familiarize yourself with these
conventions. Some instructors use the *Chicago Manual of Style.* Determine which style your teacher expects.

SPIRITUAL LONGING IN LAURENCE'S MANAWAKA WOMEN

LESLIE-ANN HALES

Responding to Donald Cameron, who observed that there is a religious element in her fictional world, Margaret Laurence said:

> I don't know even what I mean by God, but I don't think,
> personally, that we do live in a universe which is as empty as we
> might think. A lot of my characters, like myself, inhabit a world
> in which they no longer believe in the teachings of the traditional
> church, but where these things have enormous emotional
> impact on them still, as they do on me. . . . Part of the terrific
> impact of things like the hymns derives from the fact that you
> learned these things in a much earlier era of your life, an era of
> rock-solid faith. Now you *lost* this: and part of the impact is not
> that you believe it, but you mourn your disbelief. This is Eden
> lost.[1]

Laurence's tentative wistfulness is even more apparent when
she says that she does not "really believe that God is totally dead in
our universe. . . ."[2] Both these statements suggest an almost reluctant belief in God, a belief which Laurence can only cautiously
express: God is not totally dead and the universe not as empty as we
might think. A more confident believer would affirm with as-

surance that God is alive and the universe full of God's presence. Laurence is unable to make any such assertive declaration. Yet the fact of God's existence, unfathomed, mysterious, and perhaps not completely dependable, is a fragile reality in Laurence's personal perspective.

Countering this tentative faith is Laurence's sorrowful sense that, God notwithstanding, human beings, ultimately, are sentenced to isolation, constantly thwarted in their attempts to touch each other. In the Donald Cameron interview, Laurence expressed the anguish of this human predicament:

> It's partly that I feel that human beings ought to be able, *ought*
> to be able to communicate and touch each other far more than
> they do, and this human loneliness and isolation, which
> obviously occurs everywhere, seems to me to be part of man's
> tragedy. I'm sure one of the main themes in all my writings in
> [sic] this sense of man's isolation from his fellows and how
> almost unbearably tragic this is.[3]

God may not be totally dead in our universe but, apparently however he is manifest, this in no way affects human relationships. This idea seems to represent a split in Laurence's stance since, on the whole, those who believe in God tend to think that the relationship with God provides a context, model, or way of understanding relationships with other people.

Whether Laurence's stance *really* has such a split, however, turns out to be much less certain if one examines how her personal perspective infiltrates her fictional world of Manawaka. Naturally the reader must be wary of identifying Laurence with her protagonists since, as novelist, she must be allowed the freedom to create characters who may have views radically different from her own. But in the Cameron interview, Laurence herself draws the parallel between her own beliefs and those of many of her fictional characters. It is at least evident that her Manawaka protagonists manifest a markedly similar tentative faith in God and that these protagonists are sentenced to the kind of isolation Laurence perceives to be the way of the world.

What the Manawaka protagonists do not realize is that there is an intimate connection between the way they understand the universe and God's place in it, and the way they relate, or fail to relate, with other people. Relationships do not develop in a vacuum; they are grounded in beliefs people have about themselves, other people, and the world in which they live. Whether Laurence states this systematically is not the question, for it is certainly true that her Manawaka novels demonstrate it consistently. Such frustrated communications as occur in these stories are not simply coincidental in a world where God's presence is posited with such hesitance and qualification. Rather this frustration results precisely from the protagonists' ambiguous response to God and his role in their lives.

Dostoyevsky raised the question of what happens in a world which has ceased to believe in God. How, he wondered, would people relate and how were their actions to be judged? Laurence's novels pose a different but, perhaps, related question: what happens in a world in which people believe that God is not totally dead but that his presence is only negative or indifferent? Indeed, why would one turn away from the human realm, if that is where anger and isolation begin and end, to the realm of a God who is, at best, indifferent? These questions are relevant with respect to the Manawaka novels, and the answer would seem to be that, although the protagonists would very much like to laugh God out of their universe, they are unable to do so. Their plight is that they transfer what happens in their relationships with other people to their relationship with God. But there is an important difference. Since they realize that other people, like themselves, have weaknesses, needs, and fears, the protagonists resign themselves to understanding, if not accepting, why a breakdown in relationship occurs. God, on the other hand, they believe to be all powerful. Therefore he should prevent such a breakdown. Apparently he does not, and for this reason, their relationships with him are marked by anger and fear. That they should cling to so negative a belief in God, all the while protesting that they do not believe at all, perhaps seems strange. However, it signifies that they desire more honest and loving communication not only with other people but also with God. They do not understand that they themselves make this impossible.

To spend time with the protagonists of the Manawaka novels is to have the feeling that one gets to know a family of sisters. Hagar Shipley, of course, is removed from the other protagonists by one generation, but in terms of her personality and the way she relates to other people, she is like the elder sister. Each of these women is a cauldron of conflicting emotions, conflicting responses, conflicting beliefs. With the possible exception of Rachel, who is a more timid woman in many ways, the Manawaka protagonists are strong-willed, proud, independent, tough survivors. Rachel shares these characteristics, but she is more muted, more repressed, more obedient to the expectations of society. At the same time, Hagar, Rachel, Stacy, Vanessa, and Morag are all emotional, sensitive, fragile, easily wounded, and somewhat superstitious with a superstition which is the distortion of their deep capacity for spirituality.

Laurence's novelistic technique for revealing the personalities of her protagonists allows the reader to see, simultaneously, both the apparently hard-boiled external self and the fragile inner being of the characters. One reason the Manawaka women move so realistically and credibly through Laurence's fictional world is that, not only their words, but also their thoughts, feelings, and fantasies are opened to the reader. Furthermore, the interwoven memory flash-backs to childhood, adolescence, and early womanhood eventually provide a rich context in which to understand the characters more fully. Indeed, it is only because Laurence makes the reader privy to so much of the protagonists' total selves that the consistent pattern of the intimate connection between relationships with other people and relationship with God is perceptible. In this pattern, the need to conceal what is inside, to hide vulnerability behind a mask of cavalier self-assurance or indifference, recurs. Hagar, recalling how she feared the dark because, for her, it "teemed with phan-toms, soul-parasites with feathery fingers, the voices of trolls, and pale inconstant fires like the flicker of an eye,"[4] remembers what she did with her fear in front of her husband: "But I never let him, or anyone, know that."[5] Rachel talks to her lover, Nick, and remem-bers how feelings were handled in her family: "'In my family, you didn't get emotional. It was frowned upon.'"[6] Stacy becomes wor-ried and frustrated by her increasing sense of alienation from those around her: "What goes on inside isn't ever the same as what goes on outside. It's a disease I've picked up somewhere."[7] Vanessa, whose family motto is "be then a wall of brass," recalls how she longed to reach out to her father, but resisted doing so: "I stood beside him, wanting to touch the light-brown hairs on his forearm, but thinking he might laugh at me or pull his arm away if I did."[8] And Morag, retracing her past, is haunted by the lesson she learned so well so young: "Morag doesn't let on. If you let on, ever, you're done for."[9] Even these brief quotations indicate the pattern, for they are representative of how the Manawaka protagonists respond to other people.

However, as Stacy admits, what goes on inside is not the same as what goes on outside, and what is inside is a tremendous vul-nerability, a sensitivity to rejection which each of these women finds necessary to guard jealously. As readers, we are privileged to see this side of the personality as well and, curiously, it is in this confusion, anger, pain, and isolation that the name of God keeps coming up. In other words, it is not in external dialogue but in internal monologue, reflections, and fantasies that God's ambigu-ous role in the lives of these women is revealed. As Laurence sug-gested in the Donald Cameron interview, none of the protagonists live in a world in which God is perceived as an informing presence. Yet none can wholly forget and dispense with God either. It is in this tension that Laurence's personal perspective qualifies the fictional world her protagonists inhabit. No one ever explains *why* God should be part of the picture. In fact, the presence of God seems to provoke only anger or fear. Invariably God is assumed by these women to be, if existent at all, removed, aloof, and indifferent, although there is always the possibility that God is at least interested enough in individuals to mock the hurtful things that happen to them.

Clinging to such a relationship with God seems odd and, of course, most of the protagonists would protest that they do not cling to it at all. But the fact of God as a being on whom one can vent one's frustration, or against whom one can rail, or even whose judgment one might fear, is undeniably present in the Manawaka novels. It is as true for Hagar, the woman who says she could never get the hang of praying, as it is for Morag, who suspects God does not care that little kids are being bombed in London during the war. Stacy, too, catches herself talking to God — again — and pauses to wonder why on earth she should be doing so:

> God knows why I chat to you, God — it's not that I believe in you. Or I do and I don't, like echoes in my head. It's somebody to talk to. Is that all? I don't know. How would I like to be only an echo in somebody's head? Sorry, God. But then you're not dependent upon me, or let's hope not.[10]

Perhaps this does not sound like a particularly prayerful way to talk to God. Stacy would agree since she does not even know why she talks to God in the first place. She certainly does not expect these one-sided conversations to have any effect on her life, for she believes, with the other Manawaka protagonists, that she is alone in her struggles.

In many ways, Stacy MacAindra, suburban housewife with her salesman husband, her three children, her spreading waistline, her desire for a lover, and her almost hourly gin and tonic, seems the least likely of all the Manawaka protagonists to be chatting so familiarly with God. Yet, when her son, Duncan, nearly drowns shortly after Stacy has begun a love affair with a young man, her thoughts turn spontaneously to God, to the fear that God is punishing her for her actions:

> God, if it was anything I did, take it out on me, not on him — that's too much punishment for me
> —Judgment. All the things I don't like to think I believe in. But at the severe moments, up they rise, the tomb birds, scaring the guts out of me with their vulture wings. . . . I used to think about Buckle that he was as superstitious as a caveman. I didn't know then that I was, too.[11]

Until this moment, Stacy's conversations with God have been flippant. Now, when there is a crisis, she is no longer flippant for she perceives God as judge and jury. Panic notwithstanding, Stacy fears that the world is not, after all, chaotic and abandoned. Her fear of God is spontaneous and sudden, as if it has been lurking in the depths of her mind only to surface when something as "severe" and terrifying as the near death of her son occurs.

For Stacy, as for the other protagonists, it is next to impossible to reflect on life and believe that, if God exists, he is a God of mercy. If God exists, he is a cruel jester and a righteous judge, although he may not even care enough to bother judging. Hagar, in her more cynical moments, also sees a jester-God in her mind's eye.

> I see Him clad in immaculate radiance, a short white jacket and a smile white and creamy as zinc-oxide ointment, focussing His cosmic and comic glass eye on this and that, as the fancy takes Him. Or no — He's many-headed, and all the heads argue at once, a squabbling committee.[12]

Why Hagar should bother to think about God at all if such a cynical portrait is the only one she can draw is not immediately clear. It is certainly not a portrait which can provide comfort for the dying old woman. It *does*, however, illustrate again the protagonists' tendency to transfer to God those characteristics which mark their other relationships. Yet Hagar does not rest entirely easy in this cynicism for, only moments before she describes God in this way, she wonders with far less effrontery about God's response to humanity: "What if it matters to Him, after all, what happens to us?"[13] Clearly when relationships break down, when one feels sentenced to isolation, when one's emotions are concealed behind a wall of stony silence, it is difficult to believe there is a God who actively cares about one's life. The point is that Manawaka protagonists always protest that they do *not* believe in God or that their belief is only, as Stacy says, superstition. Hence they should feel no need to repeat, in their loneliness, that God does not exist or, at least, is unconcerned with human affairs. That they *do* repeat this is a sign that, beneath their defiant stance of strength, they yearn for God to be involved in their world.

Precisely this conflict explains why the Manawaka protagonists make statements about God so riddled with contradiction. On the one hand, Hagar feels angry at God "for giving us eyes but almost never sight,"[14] but on the other, she stubbornly clings to the idea that she is irrevocably alone and so precludes opening herself to God exactly as she has prevented herself from opening up to other people:

> Pride was my wilderness, and the demon that led me there was fear. I was alone, never anything else, and never free, for I carried my chains within me, and they spread out from me and shackled all I touched. Oh, my two, my dead. Dead by your own hands or by mine?[15]

Hagar fears that she is largely responsible, if not for the deaths of her husband and son, then for the deaths of their relationships with her. She does not realize that she is similarly responsible for the death of her relationship with God, that she has shut God out just as surely as she shut out her husband and her son.

The barriers which the Manawaka protagonists inevitably raise between themselves and others do not suddenly crumble before God. The fortress walls within which they hide are fortified against God and other people. Their understanding of the world demands that pride, independence, and self-sufficiency be cultivated because these are the only shields protecting them from pain; sadly, these shields also insulate them from joy. Laurence's protagonists demonstrate powerfully that these defences effectively quash attempts to trust and to love. Hence when they do think about God, they work on the same assumptions and stand defiantly stubborn, convinced that God simply does not care.

Hagar, Rachel, Stacy, Vanessa, and Morag all understand with terrible clarity the high price of such pride. In Vanessa's family no one is able to communicate honestly and, as her Uncle Terence says, "everybody to his own shield in this family."[16] This alienation causes Vanessa frequently to fear there is no rhyme or reason to anything that happens, much as Rachel bitterly suggests that, in the face of God's indifference, she should "celebrate confusion."[17] Vanessa shares this sense of the indiscriminate, random anarchy of events, and she also blames it on God: "I could not really comprehend these things, but I sensed their strangeness, their disarray. I felt that whatever God might love in this world, it was certainly not order."[18] Loneliness, alienation, estrangement all contribute to the feeling of being unrooted in the world. Rachel experiences this unrootedness in her dreams as the feeling of being a spectral photograph, "insubstantial, unable to anchor myself, unable to stop this slow nocturnal circling."[19] The world appears to her "blurred, artificial, indefinite, an abstract painting of a world."[20] Stacy looks in the mirror to make sure she really exists. For her, as for Rachel and Vanessa, using words becomes surreal, for words provide no access to other people: "I'm surrounded by voices all the time but none of them seem to be saying anything, including mine. This gives me the feeling that we may all be one-dimensional."[21] Even Morag, who does not so readily turn to thoughts of God, decides early that God is "no good" because he makes senseless, random decisions against which no one has recourse:

> She does not love God. God is the one who decides which people have got to die, and when. Mrs. McKee in Sunday school says God is LOVE, but this is baloney. He is mean and gets mad at people for no reason at all, and Morag wouldn't trust him as far as she can spit. . . . Does He really know what everybody is thinking? If so, it sure isn't fair and is also very spooky.[22]

The feeling of being disconnected, of being unable to touch other people (as Laurence believes to be characteristic of human relations) causes the feeling of insubstantiality, the randomness and chaos these women experience. They cannot perceive order or pattern if they are unable to get outside their own minds and connect with someone else.

The Manawaka protagonists do speak *about* God. Stacy chats *with* God, and even Morag, in all her unbelief, prays *to* God: *"Help me, God; I'm frightened of myself."*[23] Yet not once do any of them feel that God is listening, that he cares, or that he may be trying to reach them. They treat God as they have treated those who have sought to love them. Morag shares the fear which haunts all Laurence's protagonists. She cannot reach out or open herself for she cannot bear the desolation and humiliation of rebuff. In her heart, Morag cannot deny her daughter's angry charge: "'You make me sick. You make me bloody sick. You're so goddam proud and so scared of being rejected. You're so stupid in that way, you really are.'"[24] But Morag's simple prayer, "Help me God," is offered more in panic than in faith, because accepting God's help would be letting on to him in a trusting way that she is frightened. And as Morag says, "if you let on, ever, you're done for."[25]

In her Manawaka protagonists, Laurence breathes life into fictional women who bear out what she said in her interview with Donald Cameron. People do not communicate with each other or touch each other as much as they should. But, and the "but" is important to Laurence, God is not totally dead in the universe. The Manawaka protagonists do not perceive in any logical way the connection between their estrangement from other people and their estrangement from God. Yet they repeatedly make this connection in less-guarded moments through their anger, their cynicism, and their "superstitious" fear of God. All unbidden, the desire to be grounded in relationship keeps cutting across the tangled knot of their unhappiness. Anger towards and cynicism about God are only the disillusioned and distorted expression of what these women actually desire in their lives. Hagar's recognition of what might have been shocks and grieves her, for it is now too late to do anything with her new understanding: "This knowing comes upon me so forcefully, so shatteringly, and with such a bitterness as I have never felt before. I must always, always, have wanted that — simply to rejoice."[26]

That none of the Manawaka protagonists ever uncover and nurture this lamented glimmer of faith, never trace it to its source, not in superstition, but in a recognition of what Hagar calls "the heart's truth,"[27] is probably a result of Laurence's own hesitation. The discovery that the universe truly *is* Godless and that honest communication between people really *is* impossible would be devastating to her protagonists. Perhaps it is also too overwhelming for Laurence to contemplate. Perhaps that is why she can only say that God is not totally dead. Yet even though the Manawaka protagonists are never able to take the tremendous risk of committing themselves to faith in a God who cares, their reluctant acknowledgment of God at all gives the lie to their cynicism. God is more real to them than they can admit, because Laurence is too honest a novelist to write him out of their lives entirely.

---

[1]Donald Cameron, *Conversations with Canadian Novelists — 1* (Toronto: Macmillan of Canada, 1973), pp. 111-12.
[2]Ibid., p. 111.
[3]Ibid., p. 105.
[4]Margaret Laurence, *The Stone Angel* (Toronto: McClelland & Stewart; New Canadian Library, 1968), p. 205.
[5]Ibid., p. 205.
[6]Margaret Laurence, *A Jest of God* (Toronto: McClelland & Stewart-Bantam Limited, 1979), p. 109.
[7]Margaret Laurence, *The Fire-Dwellers* (Toronto: McClelland & Stewart-Bantam Limited, 1969), p. 28.
[8]Margaret Laurence, *A Bird in the House* (Toronto: McClelland & Stewart Limited, 1974), p. 92.
[9]Margaret Laurence, *The Diviners* (Toronto: McClelland & Stewart Limited; New Canadian Library, 1974), p. 51.
[10]Laurence, *The Fire-Dwellers*, p. 57.
[11]Ibid., p. 266.
[12]Laurence, *The Stone Angel*, p. 93.
[13]Ibid., p. 90.
[14]Ibid., p. 173.
[15]Ibid., p. 292.
[16]Laurence, *A Bird in the House*, p. 87.
[17]Laurence, *A Jest of God*, p. 44.
[18]Laurence, *A Bird in the House*, p. 59.
[19]Laurence, *A Jest of God*, p. 21.
[20]Ibid., p. 106.
[21]Laurence, *The Fire-Dwellers*, p. 71.
[22]Laurence, *The Diviners*, p. 63.
[23]Ibid., p. 207.
[23]Ibid., p. 207.
[24]Ibid., p. 193.
[25]Ibid., p. 51.
[26]Laurence, *The Stone Angel*, p. 292.
[27]Ibid.

EXPLORING THE SCHOLARLY ESSAY

1. Sum up Laurence's religious position as revealed in the three quotations from the interview in Donald Cameron's *Conversations with Canadian Novelists*.

2. What does [sic] mean (see second quotation, paragraph 3)? Why has it been used?

3. (a) Identify the writer's thesis as she develops it in her fifth and sixth paragraphs. Make sure the key words "ambiguity" (or ambiguous) and "conflict" appear in your statement.
   (b) Explain why Hales needed to use Cameron's interview as a lead-in to her thesis.

4. Paragraphs 7 through 16 develop her thesis:
   (a) Demonstrate that these paragraphs provide a three-stage development of her thesis.
   (b) Why was the argument developed in that order?

5. Show that in the concluding two paragraphs Hales sums up her thesis and encourages the reader to continue pondering these matters.

6. (a) Find examples of Hales's effective use of diction and key images that emphasize her thesis.
   (b) Transitions are a key element for achieving clarity. Evaluate Hales's use of transitions in paragraph 7.
   (c) Identify the elements in Hales's style that create an objective and reasoned tone.

EXTENSIVE STUDY

1. Hales relies on primary research (that is, study based solely on Laurence's work), except for her references to the interview. Explain the difference between primary and secondary sources.

2. Hales refers 24 times to Laurence's works. Assess the content and length of these references. Are these references sufficient to convince you of the validity of her thesis?

3. According to Hales, Laurence's women portray the idea that our relationships with others derive from our views about ourselves and our place in the universe. Argue this idea, giving examples.

4. Laurence says in paragraph 7 that "being superstitious . . . is a distortion of . . . deep capacity for spirituality."
   (a) Explain what this generalization means.
   (b) Debate this idea.

5. (a) Read "Our Two Cultures." Judge the scholarship of the essay based on the following criteria:

   depth of research (primary and secondary)
   organization of material
   effective use of rhetorical devices

   (b) Debate the Quebec assertion that English Canada and its literature is culturally only a region of the United States.
   (c) Debate the writer's thesis that English Canadians write in the tradition of realism, morality, and openness, whereas French-Canadian writers are caught up in a passionate vision, enclosed within a patriarchal society.

6. Read the student essay "The Tragedy of Ugliness" by John Hunter. Read tips on "Evaluating an Essay" on page 316. In small groups develop criteria for evaluation based on these tips. Then assess Hunter's essay. Decide if it meets all the criteria for a scholarly essay in its thesis, organization, support, and conventions of format. As a group, see if you can agree on a mark for it. You might compare your evaluation with the findings of other groups.

7. If you have read Russell's "The Good Life" (see The Generic Essay), compare his approach to life with the observations Hales makes about Laurence's protagonists.

8.   Read "The Conscience of the Writer" by Robertson Davies (see page 173) and "Excerpt from *Walden*" by Thoreau (page 37). Do either of these essays offer us insight into the problems of Laurence's women?

THE WRITING FOLDER

1.   If you have studied fiction or drama in your course this year, write a scholarly essay on a topic arising from your reading. Or you might develop a topic based on some of the reading you have done in this text. Use primary research only. You should develop your topic by applying all the stages of critical thinking and writing outlined in the tips on "Composing Essays" in Part C.

INDEPENDENT STUDY

1.   Read two or three of Laurence's novels. Write an essay in which you study her depiction of males, determining their commonalities and drawing conclusions from your evidence.   ++

2.   Hales mentions that Dostoyevsky and Laurence "pose a different but, perhaps related question" about spirituality. Read one novel by Dostoyevsky and one by Laurence. Compare the spiritual condition of each of the protagonists.   ++

3.   Trace T.S. Eliot's spiritual quest as it is reflected in his poetry — "The Love Song of J. Alfred Prufrock," "The Waste Land," "Ash Wednesday," and "Four Quartets." You may also wish to read his later work, *Murder in the Cathedral,* and biographical information.   ++

4.   Gather a collection of poetry that depicts people's spiritual questing. Write the introduction, prologue, or preface to your collection. Your project should also include some taped readings. If you wish, submit some of your own writing.   + or ++

5.   Read a collection of Albert Camus's reflective essays such as *The Myth of Sisyphus* and one or more of Laurence's works of fiction. Compare the writers' views about the individual's place in the universe.   ++

6.   Read *Sons and Lovers* or another novel by D.H. Lawrence and one novel by Margaret Laurence. Compare the novelists' depiction of spiritual needs as reflected in the protagonists and their relationships with the opposite sex.   ++

TIMED READING AND WRITING

1.   Construct a literature-based examination question (see the tips on "Preparing for the Examination" in Part C). After deciding on a suitable time limit, answer your question. (You might exchange questions and answers with a friend and assess each other's work.)

2.   Reread Hunter's essay and make an outline in the time stipulated by your teacher.

OUR TWO CULTURES

PATRICIA SMART

One suspects our ancestors to have been possessed of a kind of divine madness to have undertaken the voyages they did to a country Jacques Cartier described as "the land God gave to Cain." But it was a madness that as another Frenchman in our own century, André Breton, commented: "took root, and has lasted" . . . and produced a culture or cultures that have begun to return full circle to their origins.

> *"Mon pays a franchi ses frontières d'exil*
> *Mon pays vient parler sur la place du monde"*

writes Gatien Lapointe, whose death last fall at the early age of 52 was mourned by all lovers of Quebec poetry.

If you are familiar with Canadian literature, you know that there is now confidence and a joy of affirmation in the writing of both our major cultures. Such confidence was fought for slowly and painfully in both Quebec and English Canada by the nationalist generation of the 1960s, a generation that had to prove in spite of all appearances to the contrary that it did have a heritage and a culture (or rather two heritages and two cultures) and a present and future reflected in the mirrors its writers were placing before it. Mirrors have a way of becoming prisons, however, unless there is sharing and growth through contact with what is outside oneself. "In order to flower," writes another Quebec poet, Gaston Miron, "poetry needs a land, a space, a light, a milieu where it can put down roots, and a great deal of friendship."

I want to reflect on the land, the space, the milieux where our two literatures have put down their roots and make some tentative suggestions about the different ways the writers of the two cultures have inhabited the territories of the real, the imaginary and of language. Linked to each other willy-nilly since the conquest in which both Wolfe and Montcalm lost their lives, we have transposed our battles and our psychological borders even onto the names we have called ourselves. From the clearly demarcated names of *les Anglais* and *les Canayens* (the English and the Canadians) used by both races until 1840, we have moved through a variety of hyphenated and non-hyphenated attempts to name ourselves, our relationship and our sense of belonging to an often contested territory.

History makes strong claims on the Canadian and *Québécois* consciousness: we have never, I think, seen ourselves as a generation of new Adams (or Eves) operating in virgin territory and in total rupture from tradition. And so, in a country where in 1984 official bilingualism — the dream of our departed Prime Minister Pierre

Elliot Trudeau — has been met with resistance strong enough to have brought the Manitoba legislature to a standstill, it is tempting to fall back in defence of bilingualism on the historically-validated description of French and English as our "two founding cultures." This term, however, is rejected by many Western Canadians, whose ancestors arrived after the geographical chess game that split that nation in two; and it is rejected with greater justification by the native peoples of the country, whose own claims rest on a more ancient historical imperative.

To speak simply of French-Canadian and English-Canadian cultures has the practical advantage of including the important members of each culture who live and write within the territory of the other — Gabrielle Roy, Antonine Maillet, Mordecai Richler and Leonard Cohen, to name only a few — but events in Quebec have coloured these terms in a decidedly federalist hue. The terms now used by many writers and intellectuals to describe the two cultures are "Quebec" and "Canada," but these too are ambiguous, for it is never quite clear whether they are meant to refer to the situation of a part within the larger whole, or to two mutually exclusive territories of the imagination which may well regard each other with affection, but do not overlap.

For compromisers like myself, who I like to think are also realists, it is perhaps most useful to speak of Quebec or *Québécois* and English-Canadian culture: for these are the two major groups which have historically battled and out of necessity have compromised, and who have passed from generation to generation the visions that have shaped our two literatures.

What are these visions or cultural traditions? How have they regarded each other? Do they contain within them any basis for the comparison of *Québécois* and English-Canadian literature? An astonishingly small amount of work has been done in the area of comparative Quebec and English-Canadian literature, for reasons that differ, I think, depending on the critic's culture of origin. For many English-Canadian critics, the border between the two cultures has traditionally not existed, and the Quebec tradition has simply been assimilated into the larger Canadian whole — an act easier to achieve on paper than it has been in historical reality. The rarity of comparative studies coming from within Quebec is on the surface simply a question of other priorities — Quebec itself, but also Europe, the United States, Latin America come first. Anywhere but English Canada, one is sometimes tempted to think. When articles on English-Canadian culture do appear in Quebec, they are likely to be headed by a title like "Does English Canada really exist?," betraying a commonly-held belief that English Canada is culturally only a region of the United States. Paradoxically then, one could say that the relationship between conqueror and conquered is reversed in the cultural sphere, and it is most often the English Canadian who expends his or her energy envying and admiring the passion, the militancy, the theoretical sophistication, the collective character of Quebec literature, while remaining unsure of his or her own discourse and guilt-ridden about the power relationships that exist in the political realm.

Critics who have reflected on the two cultures have proposed a number of geometric symbols meant to characterize their relationship — parallel lines, the "horizontality" of English Canada as opposed to the "verticality" of Quebec, a spiral staircase, an ellipse, a double helix, a lattice-work fence. But like criticism itself, especially comparative criticism, these figures remain abstract and aloof from the historical contingencies that have defined our cultures and their relationship. Looking toward the literature itself, we find a clearer sense of the images we have had of each other. Here we enter the realm of stereotypes, but with the knowledge that stereotypes grow out of a reality imposed by history, and can be played with by imaginative writers to reveal us to ourselves and create new perceptions.

In Quebec and English-Canadian literature before 1960, I think we are dealing in stereotypes rarely opened out to reveal the push-pull ambiguities that have linked our cultures in a hostile kind of togetherness. In traditional Quebec literature, from Patrice Lacombe's 1846 novel *La Terre paternelle* through the classic novels of the land *Maria Chapdelaine, Menaud, maître-draveur,* and *Trente arpents* to Gabrielle Roy's urban masterpiece *Bonheur d'occasion,* the English is the conqueror, the invader, the rich industrialist insensitive to the language and culture he is destroying through his economic expansionism. Traditional English-Canadian literature, to the extent that it deals with the *Québécois* at all, presents the other side of the same coin — the loggers in Connor's *The Man from Glengarry,* the *habitants* in the poetry of William Henry Drummond, *mutatis mutandis,* the French Canadians in MacLennan's *Two Solitudes,* are basically charming folkloric remnants of a culture doomed to be left behind in the march of Anglo-Saxon progress.

In the two literatures since 1960, however, these stereotypes begin to open up and reveal the vertiginous underside of our selves as revealed in the mirror of the other. I want to look at four of these images — taken from works by Hubert Aquin, Jacques Godbout, Margaret Atwood and Nicole Brossard — and attempt to extract from them some insights into the changes in the English-Canadian-*Québécois* relationship over the last 20 years.

In Aquin's 1965 novel *Prochain épisode,* the Quebec revolutionary seeking his own identity and union with his beloved woman-country sets out to kill the Other, the enemy, but finds in

him the benevolent and cultured conqueror, the enemy-brother
with whom fusion would equal death but also mystical ecstasy.
This Other is perceived by the *Québécois* — and this is a theme to
which I will return — as powerful and attractive in the way he
inhabits space:

> the pleasure of inhabiting a house can, then, resemble the
> overwhelming sense of awe and comfort I feel in this large and
> majestic drawingroom. H. de Heutz inhabits a second universe
> which has never been accessible to me, as I pursue my chaotic
> exile in a series of hotels that are never home to me.

Acquin's image of the relation between the two cultures is one of
fascination, struggle and finally of stasis, as in the baroque sculpture of two warriors "reaching towards each other in complemen-
tary postures, immobilized by a sort of cruel embrace, a duel to the
death that bathes the dark piece of furniture in radiant light." It is
an image which may well return to haunt us, but which at present,
in the post-referendum atmosphere of the 1980s, seems to belong to
a bygone age.

About 15 years after *Prochain épisode,* a more grotesque and
carnavalesque image is proposed almost simultaneously by writers
central to each of the two cultures. Both Margaret Atwood in her
1978 volume *Two-Headed Poems* and Jacques Godbout in his
1981 novel *Les têtes à Papineau* describe English Canada and
Quebec as Siamese twins joined by the head, on whom radical
surgery in impossible. The Siamese twin image is perhaps more
despairing than Aquin's in its sense of an inescapable biological,
geographical and historical fatality, a monstrous farce into which
we were born; but it is more liberating as well in its suggestion that
the situation can best be dealt with by laughter and acceptance of
our grotesque but real natures. Godbout's image is in fact internal
to Quebec: his Siamese twins are not precisely English Canada and
Quebec, but rather the English and French sides of the *Québécois*
psyche — a two-headed monster, named Charles-François (read
Canadien-français) Papineau. Joined at the neck, Charles and
François are basically content with each other, but are told by
ideology and modern technology that their two-headedness is unacceptable. In the course of the novel they allow themselves to be
convinced by an English-Canadian surgeon — trained of course in
the United States — to submit to an operation meant to fuse their
heads into one. The result is a triumph of technology over culture:
the two heads are in fact fused and life goes on, but the resulting
one-headed creature, Charles F. Papineau, can no longer speak
French and works in a laboratory at English Bay in Vancouver.
Better perhaps, Godbout seems to be suggesting, to accept that the
50/50 division of the French-Canadian vote in Quebec's 1980 refer-
endum on independence is a true reflection of the culture's duality,

and to learn to live with the ambiguities it involves. And yet the ending is doubly ambiguous, for Charles and François' downfall can also be seen as a result of their trust in English-Canadian power and technology.

Margaret Atwood's *Two-Headed Poems* are less science-fictionally prophetic than Godbout's novel, but equally wary of splitting the two-headed monster, which for Atwood is Canada:

> *Why fear the knife that could sever us,*
> *unless it would not cut skin but brain?*

Like Godbout, Atwood plays with the familiar stereotypes — the *Québécois* as "one big happy family" and the English Canadians as the unwanted neighbours, the uncultured merchants and technocrats of the country. What is interesting in her portrayal, I think, is the reversal of the colonizer-colonized relationship I referred to earlier — the silencing of the English Canadian as he or she finds herself trapped in the stereotype dictated by the other culture. How is dialogue possible, or even an articulation of one's own voice, when that voice is heard by the other as:

> *a language for ordering the slaughter and gutting of hogs, for*
> *counting stacks of cans. Groceries are all you are good for.*
> *Leave the soul to us.*

In spite of the cool irony of its surface, Atwood's poem is a moving plea for dialogue and an avowal of the feeling of paralysis experienced by the English Canadian in the face of *Québécois* indifference:

> *These words slow us, stumble*
> *in us, numb us, who*
> *can say even Open*
> *the door, without these diffident*
> *smiles, apologies?*

> *If I were a foreigner, as you*
> *say instead of your second head,*
> *you would be more polite. . .*

> *But we are not foreigners*
> *to each other; we are the pressure*
> *on the inside of the skull, the struggle among*
> *the rocks for more room,*
> *the shove and giveaway, the grudging love*
> *the old hatreds.*

Compared with the despairing passion of Aquin's two warriors image, the humour and self-mockery in Godbout's and Atwood's Siamese twin image can be seen as a step forward in the relation between the two cultures. But we are still trapped in the head, in the brain — in the attempt at "reasonable" dialogue between the two cultures that has never really succeeded. And so we have, as Atwood herself states:

> *not a debate*
> *but a duet*
> *with two deaf singers.*

The implication of this image, whether or not Atwood is conscious of it, is that the Siamese twins should forget their debate and concentrate on their songs — their own songs and poems and stories and not the stereotypical voice and image imposed on them by the other. The debate between *Québécois* and English Canadian has in fact never really taken place in Canada — the striking difference between the charismatic photographs of Quebec premier René Lévesque used in the Quebec media and the angry demagogical ones chosen by English-Canadian newspapers and television is only one example of the chasm between the cultures on the level of political debate. But debate functions according to the rules of logic, and there has never been anything logical about the Canadian attempt to achieve equality between the majority English and the minority French.

If there is a solution it can only be found in paradox, and in the final literary image I want to propose as an emblem of our two cultures there is a paradoxical turning away from each other that becomes an image of sharing between two autonomous partners. Nicole Brossard's image is not consciously proposed as an emblem of the two cultures, for like Jacques Godbout and other *Québécois* writers she has freed herself from the gaze of the other culture and is writing about her own primary concern: the question of the emerging voice of women. The paradox, I think, as far as Quebec and English Canada are concerned, is that in recent years there has been an unprecedented sharing between women writers and critics of the two cultures, and that this dialogue has been built not on the conscious desire to link the two cultures as such, but on the excitement of examining within the specificity of our separate cultural contexts what we have to say to each other as women. It seems appropriate then to transpose onto the larger cultural sphere Brossard's striking image of two women standing back to back but touching each other:

> *It feels like panic, confusion,*
> *this impossible romance of being*
> *face to face, this juggling of*
> *acrobatic bodies, this Berlin*
> *wall I can lean against,*
> *this shivering in the back it is marvellous: you*
> *can see everywhere at once.*
> *She can read my thoughts while*
> *I have my back turned she is*
> *amazed at my amazement. . . .*

In contrast with the geometric images proposed by the literary critics and with earlier images of aborted dialogue proposed by the writers, this image is real, incarnate and loving. And why not an image of two women as emblematic of the two cultures, given the importance of women for somewhat different cultural reasons in both English-Canadian and *Québécois* literature? Why not a bodily image, given the coming down to earth, the breaking out of the rigid garrison mentality, that has characterized both out literatures in recent years? Brossard's image is one of touching but not of fusion, of separate identities respected and shared as both partners look not at each other, but — supporting each other — out to the world. Transposed, it becomes an image of two nations and two projects, an adjacent but not a common space, a border shared in which both cultures find strength in difference.

And that, I think, is the present situation of the *Québécois* and English-Canadian cultures: involved in a process of integrating into their images of self the voices of women and of the world around them, they are beginning to find new modes of dialogue that subvert the old logic of political boundaries. No longer attached by the head, they are beginning to find ways of speaking to each other with a more bodily intelligence which does not exclude the heart or the shared history of their becomings. Special issues devoted to English-Canadian literature in two major Quebec literary periodicals this year are one sign among many of this new mood.

If there is, as I have suggested, a more detached and positive relationship developing between the two cultures, its effect is likely to be felt as well in the area of comparative literary criticism. To date, with one possible exception, the only book-length comparative studies that exist have been thematic and sociological in their methodology and undeniably if unconsciously federalist in their underlying ideology. Unrelenting in their search for similarities in the themes, literary genres and value systems of the two cultures, they have deformed both traditions by ignoring the fundamental differences in their ideological context and literary reference points. The exception, E.D. Blodgett's *Configuration: Essays on the Canadian Literatures* (1982), makes the important statement in its introduction:

> not only that all literary theory is ideological, but that any literary theory that tries to resolve the problems of nation-states that are at least bilingual in an official sense must be clear about its ideology.

Further, states Blodgett, "any literary framework that assumes equality of status between [the two major] cultural groups [in Canada] mistakes the nature of the relationship." Blodgett's own essays, however, concentrate on the plurality of Canadian immigrant literatures, European influences and uses of literary genre rather than on any real attempt to relate the *Québécois* and English-Canadian literary traditions as such.

My own suggestion as to a mode of comparison that might allow recognition of the difference between the two cultures would be an approach centered on the ways that *Québécois* and English-Canadian writers have inhabited space: the territories of reality, the imagination and language. A comment made to me by a *Québécois* friend who had tried to read the work of Margaret Laurence helped to crystallize the sense I have had of our fundamental difference: "I tried to get into her novels," he said, "but they were too real." Implicit in his comment, I think, was the question "Where is the fantasy? the dream? the excursion to the borders of madness to which my own culture has accustomed me? Where is the explosion of language that subverts the referential relationship of literature to reality and therefore subverts reality itself?"

It is not my intention to deny the importance of post-modernist writers in English Canada — Robert Kroetsch, Rudy Wiebe, Daphne Marlott, Jack Hodgins and others — and their conscious play with inversions of the relationship between reality and fiction. But I cannot escape my instinctive feeling that if there is one contemporary writer who has been regarded as typical of the English-Canadian sensibility it is Margaret Laurence and that she, as well as other major English-Canadian writers like Robertson Davies, Timothy Findley and even Margaret Atwood, are part of a tradition of realism that distinguishes them from the central tradition of *Québécois* writing. This distinction between realism and something else — utopia? despair? revolution? desire? fascination with language? — seems to me to be the essential category to be addressed if we hope to relate the two cultural traditions in any meaningful way.

By realism I mean not only an attitude with regard to narrative structures and language, which in spite of questioning and experimentation remain basically intact in English-Canadian fiction, but also a fundamentally optimistic and pragmatic relationship to society that is present in most English-Canadian writing. Teaching a novel by Margaret Atwood opposite one by Hubert Aquin or Marie-Claire Blais in a comparative Canadian-Quebec literature course, for example, leads one inescapably to the observation that for Atwood — in spite of her lucid and ironic exposure of societal and sexual injustice and her consciousness of the games of language — there is an underlying realist and essentially moralistic vision of a correctible society; while in Aquin and Blais there is a more extreme and passionate vision of the inescapable fact of death or of the necessity of total revolution.

The same structural and ideologically-based contrasts would be possible between most of the major writers of the two traditions. In the work of poets like Roberts, Lampman, F.R. Scott, Dorothy Livesay, Earl Birney and Al Purdy language is taken for granted and used as a means of entry into reality, while for Emile Nelligan, Saint-Denys Garneau and even for a political poet like Gaston Miron, a primary focus is not reality but the voyage within language itself. Is it purely accidental that landscape has been an essential category in English-Canadian poetry and literary criticism, and not in the Quebec tradition? Whether it has inspired terror or love, or has been regarded as a force to be learned from, the land has existed in English-Canadian poetry as an external reality drawing the poet out of him or herself, while in Quebec poetry it has been on the contrary a symbolic projection of self or of the quest for national identity. A comment made by Jacques Godbout on the two cultural traditions helps to clarify this relationship between landscape and realism. If you asked the average English Canadian to name a painting that represents his culture, Godbout said, he or she would choose a Group of Seven painting. If you asked a *Québécois* the same question, he or she would choose a painting by Jean-Paul Lemieux — that is, a representation of a solitary individual in the foreground against the vaguely outlined backdrop of a desolate landscape.

Despite the parallel developments of the novel genre that have been traced by critics like Ronald Sutherland — from rural to small town to urban, from alienation to liberation — the same contrasts based on attitudes to reality (and here I mean social reality) are possible between the two traditions. Seen in contrast with the Quebec *roman de la terre*, which is closed and circular in structure and unrelentingly patriarchal in its value system, the English-Canadian novel of the land appears open in structure and in its vision of accommodating technological and social change. Abe Spalding in Grove's *Fruits of the Earth* is undoubtedly a patriarch, but he is chastened and changed by his daughter's rebellion and by the necessary modernization of his agricultural way of life; while the Quebec *cultivateur* clings to patriarchal tradition and sees his world disappear, choosing (or being forced to) defeat rather than compromise. Even a novel like Sinclair Ross' *As for Me and My House*, which has often been regarded as typical of the victimization of the Canadian protagonist in the face of nature and a hostile society, seems open in its narrative structure and vision of the couple and society when compared with a Quebec analogue like *Poussière sur la ville* by André Langevin. The ambiguities of Ross' novel have been much debated, but it is surely significant that it is narrated not by the protagonist but by his wife, and that in spite of the lack of communication between husband and wife that constitutes the novel's subject, it concludes with the hope of renewed dialogue between them and the possibility of their leaving the small Western town where their misfortunes have taken place to begin again elsewhere.

In Langevin's novel, also situated in a hypocritical small town, the narrator's wife is seen only from his point of view, and her suicide constitutes a symbolic gesture suggesting the necessary explosion of a closed order. Unlike Ross' Western Canadian couple, the *Québécois* protagonist is denied the luxury of mobility: at the novel's end he remains in the town, conscious that his struggle must be played out within the limits of the enclosed space that defines his world. Such contrasts, rooted in the way the underlying ideological space of the two cultures has shaped literary structures, would also help to explain why women have had more room to exist as autonomous individuals within the English-Canadian tradition than in Quebec, where women writers from the 19th century on often seem to be writing as if they were attempting through words to break down the walls of a prison.

If we were to examine the different philosophical traditions that have shaped the cultures of English Canada and Quebec, we would discover a further dimension and explanation of these basic contrasts. Reduced to their simplest level, they seem to me to be encapsulated in a well-known motto of our federalist French-Canadian Prime Minister: "Reason over passion," or Canada over Quebec. There has in fact been in English-Canadian cultural history an overriding belief in reason, in the possibilities of compromise, in the simultaneously progressive and conservative nature of a tradition that believes reality is manageable, changeable and open to the future. On the *Québécois* side, certainly because of the colonizer-colonized relationship and also because of the absolutist character of Roman Catholic religious tradition, there has been on the contrary a traditional refusal or inability to compromise with the real. Space is basically inhabitable in English-Canadian literature, while in Quebec literature it is a prison to be exploded through the play of language and the imaginary.

Is it purely coincidental that in addition to the differences of ideology, religious tradition and historical circumstance that account for these contrasts there is a fundamental difference in the *real* space inhabited by the two literatures? The geographical space of traditional Quebec literature is enclosed, diminished, a degraded version of the huge geographical canvas occupied by New France that for many generations in Quebec was seen with nostalgia as the myth of a paradise lost through the British Conquest. The space of English-Canadian literature, on the other hand, is open, eclectic, often disorienting in its regional disparity, a space that is possessed and even taken for granted by its literary inhabitants, and that allows for exploration and expansion. Unlike the *Québécois* the English Canadian has had the luxury of being what poet Al Purdy calls a "transient," running and running without ever leaving home:

> *Riding the boxcars out of Winnipeg in a morning*
> *after rain so close to*

the violent sway of fields it's
like running and running
naked with summer in your mouth . . .
After a while there is no arrival and
no departure possibly any more
you are where you were always going
and the shape of home is under your fingernails.

To return to the image used by Hubert Aquin in *Prochain épisode*, the English Canadian has taken for granted "the pleasure of inhabiting a house," while the *Québécois*, pursuing his "chaotic exile in a series of hotels that are never home to [him]," has learned to challenge the structures of the real and to seize possession of language.

In conclusion, I am tempted by the reassuring parallelism and symmetry of movements I think are present in the most recent writings of English Canada and Quebec to say that English Canadian literature, especially on the West Coast and the Prairies and in the writing of certain feminists, is moving away from realism towards a confident inhabitation of the realms of fiction, the imaginary and language; while in Quebec literature, in the poetry and fictions of writers like France Théoret, Philippe Haeck and Nicole Brossard, the real and the present are discernible as never before. I would like, however, to add one final reflection regarding the question of realism, which I think is a central and unresolved one for writers and critics in English Canada. Realism is an unpopular word in literary circles, and there is no doubt that it can represent a too comfortable and conventional literary and ideological space. Aritha Van Herk argues convincingly in a recent article that we must "de-sire realism," and loose the hold that history has had on us, making room in Canadian writing for desire and daring to create non-mimetic fictions. In the exchanges that are presently taking place between feminist writers and critics of the two cultures, there is a growing recognition on the part of English-Canadian feminists that patriarchal society and the traditions of literary realisms have been a prison for women in search of a language and a new future, and that Quebec women writers have much to teach us about women and language.

But if realism and what Dorothy Livesay has called the "documentary tradition" have in fact been central to the English-Canadian cultural heritage, if ideological realism has provided us, even as women, with space in which to exist and evolve, realism and history must and will continue to be integrated in a particularly Canadian way into our desire and our fictions. Whatever the mutations of our writing that come about through modernist and feminist experimentation with language, English-Canadian and *Québécois* writers will undoubtedly continue to inhabit their territories in ways that are mirror images rather than replicas of one another.

THE TRAGEDY OF UGLINESS: D.H. LAWRENCE'S PORTRAYAL OF INDUSTRIALISM

JOHN HUNTER (student essay)

The collected works of any writer contain threads — themes that repeatedly appear, highlighting the writer's deepest interests. The foundation of D.H. Lawrence's work is an intense concern with the human spirit. Perhaps the vastness of this subject and Lawrence's intense desire to probe the soul explain his prolific output.[1]

One of Lawrence's chief concerns was the effect of industrialism on the individual. Lawrence's life (1885–1930) spanned the transition from traditional English cottage industry to technological, heavy industry. And just as George Eliot[2] (1819–1880) wrote about the beginnings of this change, Lawrence focussed on the end result. Lawrence believed that the ugliness and abuses of industrial society had degraded working people and obliterated much of the beauty of life. "Starting from the Village" and *Sons and Lovers* illustrate this feeling particularly well.

As every phrase seems to telegraph his perceptions to the reader, one must be highly selective in parameters to compare these two works. The key focus is industrial life as it affects people and their relationships, especially between the sexes. But the role of nature must also be considered. Other related criteria for comparison include the setting and the debilitating effects of ugliness and poverty which contribute to the decline in the quality of life portrayed in these works.

Both stories are set in the Nottinghamshire coalfield at the turn of the century. "Starting from the Village" takes place in the small village of Eastwood, Lawrence's birthplace. *Sons and Lovers* is set in a small mining town, Bestwood. The similarity of these two names is too pointed to ignore. The likeness is further enhanced by the description of each. About Bestwood, he writes, ". . . in the brook valley, they erected The Bottoms . . . blocks of miners' dwellings . . . the conditions of living were quite unsavoury . . . the kitchens opened on to the nasty alley of ash pits" (p. 8). Similarly, in Eastwood, mining families lived in "two great . . . squares of dwellings . . . looking outward onto the grim street and inward to . . . the ash pit" (p. 2). In both cases, Lawrence is appalled that the property developers have debased the beautiful countryside into an ugly 'home' for miners.

The significance of this similarity of setting lies in the contrast between the appearance of the countryside before and after the arrival of large mines. Industrialism upset the balance man had achieved with nature. Technological development took the old miners' cottages that blended with the landscape, the gin pits that made no smoke, and the rolling countryside that working people enjoyed. It gave back ash pits, slag heaps and grey-streaked sky. The incongruity between this actuality and the potential beauty depressed Lawrence: "These mining villages might have been like the lovely hill towns of Italy. And what happened?" (p. 2). The life of the common man was declining and alongside him, in a sad and inexorable parallel, the very ground on which he lived was decaying.

Lawrence's worship of nature is closely allied with these concerns. In both works, he pleads with the reader to fight against the ravaging of the countryside. Jim Morrison, a twentieth century singer, encapsulates Lawrence's sentiments very aptly:

> What have they done to the Earth?
> What have they done to Our Fair Sister?
> Ravaged and raped Her and beat Her and killed Her,
> Stuck Her with knives and . . .
> Dragged her on down . . .*

Nature is almost a physical being in Lawrence's writing, a force that profoundly affects human beings. In these two examples, three faces of nature are explored. The first presents nature as a soothing influence:

> The mountain-ash berries across the field stood fierily out from the dark leaves . . In the east, a mirrored sunset floated pink . . . With Mrs. Morel, it was one of those moments when small frets vanish and the beauty of things stands out (p. 49-50).

And in his essay, Lawrence writes:

> . . . I've seen many a collier stand looking down at a flower with that remote sort of contemplation which shows a real awareness of the presence of beauty (p. 4).

Here one sees Lawrence's almost messianic belief in the curative power of nature.

Nature is also depicted as a force that can sear a person to the very soul. Its sensuality evokes strong personal responses. About Gertrude Morel, he writes:

> The tall white lilies were reeling in the moonlight . . . the air was charged with perfume as with a presence . . she drank a deep draught of the scent. It made her almost dizzy (p. 35).

And in "Starting from the Village," Lawrence again notes how profoundly in tune women are with nature: "Most women love flowers . . . if they see a flower that arrests their attention, they must pluck it" (p. 4).

Finally, nature is portrayed as a wounded animal. Promoters of industry "are scrabbling over the face of England with miles of red-brick homes, like horrible scabs" (p. 4) which mar the landscape and drive nature ever further away from the workers. The barons of industry did not share Lawrence's belief that man needs nature and it was folly to destroy a God-given balance. Industrial society separated people from their roots.

Beauty and creativity are underminded by industrialism as we see in both works. In neither town are the miners' lives enriched with any recreational facilities. The men must vent their frustration in the pub and the consequences for family life are often negative. Lawrence blames the callous factory owners who pay no heed to the creative impulses of human beings; they are merely tools to be exploited. He portrays the miners as people who are only half alive because these needs cannot be expressed. About Walter Morel he writes, "He was a remarkably handy man — could make or mend anything . . she did not mind the mess, he was busy and happy" (p. 20). And in Eastwood, there is no encouragement for "song and dance . . . some form of beauty in dress. The human soul needs beauty more than bread" (p. 5).

This last line sums up the significance of the ugliness of the colliers' lives. People are driven to despair and drunkenness when, like Walter Morel, creativity can be expressed only through mending; indeed, when his son's painting wins a prize he can do no more than grunt, "Oh 'ave you my lad." The decline in the quality of life insidiously undermines family relationships.

In both works, life is depicted as a never-ending struggle against poverty. The free enterprise system of the time meant a life of relative ease for the middle and upper classes[3]. But in these days before trade unions, the working class toiled for long hours under poor conditions for meagre wages. Lawrence's miners work twelve hour days. Their future holds no relief from the unhealthy working environment. Their wives work scarcely less hard struggling with the children and the finances. The battle to survive with inadequate resources dominates their lives so completely there is little room for any joy. For Gertrude Morel, life seems bleak and pointless: "The world seemed a dreary place where nothing else would happen for her . . . she was sick of it, the struggle with poverty, the ugliness and meanness" (p. 12). In Eastwood, "The women . . . nagged about material things" and the males "have been beaten down with the whole human consciousness hammering on the fact of material prosperity above all else" (p. 5). Life becomes a meaningless merry-go-round for survival.

The real significance of this situation in human terms can be measured in its effect on the quality of male-female relations. The ugly circumstances forced upon men and women by industrial life mean most marriages are little more than an entrapment for both parties. The collier of Eastwood flees "from the house as soon as he could get away" (p. 4). And in *Sons and Lovers*, the situation is nasty:

> Sometimes a good husband came along with his family . . But usually the women and children were alone. . . . Mrs. Morel despised her husband . . . she turned from the father. He had begun to neglect her (p. 12-13).

Marriage is not so much a union as a form of mutual slavery. The industrial lifestyle has crippled the human soul and ruined family life. The working class were like trapped rats, closed in by the mine for which every sacrifice had to be made.

In these ways does Lawrence plead his case against the waste he saw around him. In "Starting from the Village," he concludes with a prophecy, a way out of the desert. In *Sons and Lovers*, he does this too, but more subtly. Paul, like his Biblical name-sake, is an apostle. He is the beacon pointing the way. By refusing to become a cog in the industrial wheel, by turning to art and intimate relationships with women, he escapes the trap of his society. The final image is a positive one: "Paul walked towards the faintly humming, glowing town quickly" (p. 427). Part of urban life he may be, but he will pursue his muse independent, aware, and emotionally free of the great clanging mineworks.

---

[1]In nineteen years he wrote twelve novels, nine collections of short stories, ten other books, some plays, and many poems.
[2]See *Silas Marner* for an example of her work on the same theme.
[3]See the novels *The Rainbow* and *Women in Love* for an account of how industrialism affected the middle and upper classes.

4. THE REPORT

Key Work:
   "Whole Brain Learning" — Margaret Hatcher

Associated Readings:
   "TV As a Shaper" — Christopher Reed

   "Report on Animal Research" — Tom Harpur

   "'Degree Day' Report" — Heather Forsythe (student report)

A report is a form of exposition based on investigation and experimentation; like the scholarly essay it is usually intended for a specialized audience. In essence, it summarizes the scope and findings of an endeavour, for example, see Key Essay, Hatcher's "Whole Brain Learning."

The organization of a report is generally straightforward: a statement of purpose, a review of the scope of the investigation or experiment, an elaboration of the observations, and a conclusion summarizing the findings or stating recommendations. The writer strives for an objective approach, but elements of persuasion may creep in, especially if recommendations are presented, as seen in Harpur's report.

Since the report is essentially a summary, its length is tightly circumscribed by the amount of information needed to accomplish its purpose. The range of this type of report is seen in the Associated Readings by Reed ("TV As a Shaper") and Forsythe (" 'Degree Day' Report"). Thus, reports must be carefully edited to make use of word-saving devices. Often, in the interest of clarity and brevity, the report's basic structure is outlined with headings and subheadings, and descriptions are replaced with charts, diagrams, and other visual effects.

BEFORE READING

■ What do you know about the theory of right-brain left-brain thinking?
■ Turn to Figure Two: "Specialized Functions of Left and Right Sides of the Brain" on page 77. Using your dictionary, study the material. Do you think that you have essentially a right-brain or left-brain personality?
■ Note the title of the periodical in which this report was published. Can you anticipate the writer's purpose by linking her subject and her audience?

WHOLE BRAIN LEARNING

MARGARET HATCHER

One of the more exciting and promising revolutions of our time is that of recent brain research and its mind-boggling implications for our education system. Recent brain/mind research offers undeniable evidence that we are taking the first steps toward understanding the latent, spectacular power of the mind. Yet we are tempted to ask: If our awareness is as pervasive, our brains as sensitive and infinitely complex, our memories as absorbent as research suggests, if we can indeed will changes in our physiology at the level of a single call as biofeedback and biosynergistic research indicate, why are we learning and performing at such mediocre levels?

While there are no easy, simple answers to this complex issue, it may be educators have ignored how the brain functions and have sought solutions elsewhere. In so doing, we may have neglected an organ of tremendous complexity and power. Recently, aided by new electronic tools, biomedical scientists, anthropologists, psychologists, and educators have sought to advance brain research and use this research to improve learning.

What are the educational implications of brain research?

Infinite Capacity of the Brain

The brain is essentially a circuitry of interconnecting elements called neurons or nerve cells. Each neuron consists of three major parts: dendrites, cell body (soma), and axons (*see Figure One*).

Dendrites are spongy, antenna-like receptacles which conduct information from the neural field surrounding the neurons into the *cell body* (soma) where the information is coded and stored as a sensory image. When we need the information stored in the cell body, it is sent from the cell body along the *axon* and forms a *synapse*, an electrical quasi-juncture with a neighboring dendrite, thus transmitting information along the entire neural circuit.

The process we call "thinking" is actually the neural process of synaptic action. The simple act of blinking the eye takes about one million neural connections (Galyean, 1981). Researchers have concluded that "it is within the synapse itself that knowledge takes place" (Sagan, 1977; Teyler, 1978; Thompson, Berger, and Berry, 1980).

What is outstanding about the research on the neural structure

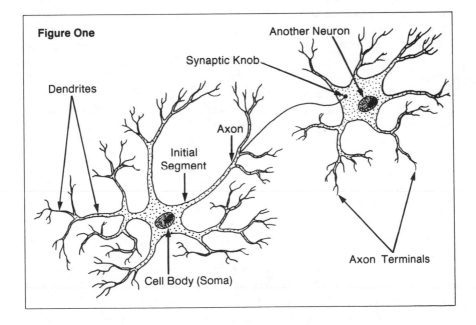

Figure One

Another Neuron

Synaptic Knob

Dendrites

Axon

Initial Segment

Cell Body (Soma)

Axon Terminals

of the brain is the undeniable evidence of the apparently infinite capacity of the brain. Although estimates vary, Galyean summarizes research that indicates the brain is composed of ten to 100 billion neurons constantly firing and exchanging information among themselves (Hart, 1975; Sagan, 1977; Teyler, 1978). Add to this the fact that every neuron is capable of storing up to five billion bits of information (Galyean, 1981), whereas our most advanced computer chips can store only one billion. In addition, it is estimated that *each* neuron has ten to 100 thousand dendrites reaching to collect information, and each neuron, because of expansive dendritic branching, can connect with as many as 1,000 other neurons at any given moment (Galyean, 1981). According to Sagan, "Ten to 100 billion neurons interacting with a thousand each at one time implies that the brain is capable of processing from ten to 100 trillion bits of information in a lifetime." Since these are infinite numbers, from a mathematical point of view, it seems that the brain's capacity for learning is infinite. Leonard observes: "A brain composed of such numbers of neurons obviously can never be 'filled up'." Perhaps the more it knows, the more it can know and create. Perhaps, in fact, we can now propose an incredible hypothesis: "*The ultimate creative capacity of the brain may be, for all practical purposes, infinite.*" (Leonard in Ferguson, 1973).

Right Brain/Left Brain Functions

One of the most exciting and dramatic findings of brain/mind research is that the right and left cortical hemispheres of the brain have certain specialized, predictable functions and process information differently. One of the first to report this "split brain" phenomenon was Robert Ornstein in the *Scientific American* in 1967. Other research followed (Bogen, 1969; Kinsbourne, 1980; Ornstein, 1972; Wittrock, 1978) and verified the thesis of *hemisphere differentiation.* By using brain scans of both cortices while subjects perform specific tasks such as daydreaming, counting, reading, writing, or drawing, researchers have been able to determine specialized functions for the right and left brains (*see Figure Two*).

Although each hemisphere has specialized functions, there is also a *bilaterality* of the brain, meaning that each hemisphere also shares some functions — both participate in most activities, but each hemisphere simply *processes* information differently. The corpus callosum, a bundle of nerves and fibers connecting the right and left cortices of the brain, functions to allow information perceived by one side of the brain to be received by the other. Without this, our right hand literally would not know what our left hand was doing.

In addition to specialized functions of the right and left hemi-

Figure Two. Specialized Functions of Left and Right Sides of the Brain.

Left Brain	Right Brain
1. Controls the right side of the body	1. Controls the left side of the body
2. Verbal/numerical	2. Visual/spatial
3. Logical/vertical	3. Perceptual/sensual/lateral thinking
4. Rational	4. Intuitive
5. Linear time	5. Space, infinity
6. Focus	6. Diffusion
7. Sequential/orderly	7. Spontaneous/creative
8. Analytic, the arrangement of parts	8. Gestalt, viewing the whole
9. Explicit	9. Tacit
11. Literal	11. Metaphorical/symbolic
12. Convergent	12. Divergent
13. Fact/Reality	13. Dream/fantasy/mystical

spheres, other findings emerging from brain/mind research hold dramatic implications for personal growth and increasing our intellectual capacities. For example, we now know that the right brain cannot verbalize what it knows; its language is practically wordless, speechless. Information in the right brain is stored in images, senses, symbols, and metaphors. The left brain, on the other hand, must recognize and reformulate the images of the right brain into words before information in the right brain can be communicated. In short, the left brain is the "alphabet of the mind" (Galyean, 1981). The implications of that one fact alone are far-reaching. Like the dream we vividly experienced during the night, only to have it evaporate in the morning, the right brain world of intuitive, symbolic, holistic knowing is lost unless we capture it in words through the left brain.

Another significant finding relating to hemispheric differentiation is that, like a computer, the function of the left brain is to recognize, organize, and assimilate new information into *already existing frameworks;* its function is to recognize the relationship of stimulus to what it already knows. The left brain, in other words, is unable to create meaning or generate new ideas. It is from the right brain that new ideas, total contexts, creativity of meaning emerges. Hence, "without the right brain, there would be no idea; without the left brain, the idea would not be encoded, understood or communicated," observes Galyean.

Unfortunately, research indicates that our traditional educational system often emphasizes left hemispheric functioning to the neglect and even denial of right hemispheric activity (Bogen, 1969; Frostig and Maslow, 1979; Wittrock, 1978). Also, tests are designed to measure predominantly left brain analytical skills as the major determinant of IQ, and often the creative individual who perceives holistically rather than analytically is left little opportunity to achieve well on most IQ tests. Only recently has research begun to attach equal importance to right and left brain learning styles (Brown, 1971; Galyean, 1981; Valett, 1977; Weinstein and Fantini, 1970).

The point of research on hemispheric specialization is *balance;* let us not neglect either hemisphere in favor of the other. The goal is to become equally familiar, equally proficient in both modes. Ornstein notes:

> Our highest creative achievements are the product of the complementary functioning of the two modes. Our intuitive knowledge is never explicit, never precise in the scientific sense. It is only when the intellect can begin to *process* the intuitive leaps, to explain and "translate" the intuition into operational and functional knowledge that the scientific becomes complete. (Ornstein, 1972).

Educational implications of "whole brain learning" are just now being explored. Some of the major techniques currently being used to tap the power of the right hemisphere and to form a bridge between right and left hemispheres include:

■ **Synectics** is a new field of educational psychology that focuses on techniques teaching metaphorical thinking (Ferguson, 1973). The metaphor is a natural bridge between the right and left hemispheres because metaphors symbolically carry knowledge and make connections from the mute right brain so that it may be recognized by the left as being *like* something. Often the depth and significance of our experiences are related to the quality and intensity of our metaphorical insights, and indeed the more intense our experiences, the less words are useful. Also, metaphorical thinking is a key to *pattern* seeing, the ability to see relationships. Thus, to detect meaning from parts, to see wholes, the interrelatedness of things.

■ **Multi-Sensory/Discovery/Experiential Learning Techniques.** Because the sense of space, the five physical senses, and body movement are all predominantly right brain processes, more and more educational strategies are involving total body experiences in learning. Discovery and experiential programs provide opportunities for learning by *doing,* for real-life situations within which students can find and solve problems that are relevant to their lives, and opportunities for observing and accomplishing skills/ concepts not possible in the classroom. Such activities provide the right hemisphere with the stimulus to activate and bridge whole brain functioning. Techniques involving body movement, improvisation, role-playing, multi-sensory expression, and synesthesia are all being used to facilitate learning.

Some interesting research suggests that extra-sensory perception (telepathy, clairvoyance, precognition and psychokinesis) could also be viewed as a total combination of senses throughout the body so that the body as a whole acts as a perceptual organ. Research is in its infancy in relating this concept to intuitive and creative thinking processes, but the implications for education in the future are staggering.

■ **Divergent and Creative Thinking Techniques.** Research tells us that the brain apparently does not require our conscious (left brain) effort to form bridges to creative (right brain) functions; it requires only our *attention*, our openness to let the information through and to recognize its significance. Because the left brain is logical and verbal, we often tend to listen and to give attention only to it. Divergent and creative thinking techniques rest on the premise of the significance of *open-focus.* These techniques emphasize the use of contradiction and paradox; problem-solving techniques; organizing skills; Gestalt techniques to focus on patterns and wholes rather than isolated parts; information processes that emphasize asking the right questions rather than having the right answers; open-ended problems/situations; use of discovery, exploratory and imagination games, "mind-benders," and other mind expansion devices; and futuristics. A recent study showed that creativity scores invariably drop about 90 percent between ages five and seven; by age 40 an individual is only about 2 percent as creative as at age five (Ferguson, 1973). This suggests that the almost total emphasis on logical, linear thought in our educational system may effectively suppress creativity.

Use of Emotions in Learning

A fascinating area of brain research deals with the role of emotions in the process by which information is transmitted smoothly and rapidly throughout the brain's neural circuitry. The axons of each neuron are coated with a fatty substance called myelin. Several research teams have verified that heavily myelinated axons conduct information more rapidly from the cell body than do less myelinated axons (Galyean, 1981; Thompson, Berger and Berry, 1980). In addition, and even more significantly, independent studies conclude that myelin production is heavily affected by the presence or absence of two factors: *emotional closeness and enriched experiential learning environments* (Sagan, 1977). The educational implications of this finding are clear: if it is true that highly intelligent people have an abundance of healthy myelinated axons to assure smooth and rapid transmission of vast amounts of information, then *increased learning capacity might possibly be nurtured through physical affection and enriched learning environments* (Clark, 1979).

Related to this finding is the relationship between emotions and thinking. We now know that the brain operates on an emotional bias system and on a programmatic basis. The information stored within the cell soma of each neuron represents not only isolated bits of information, but chains of information, or programs, as well (Hart, 1975). What merits careful consideration for educators is *how the brain selects its programs.* Research tells us that *the brain processes only that information that is perceived by the learner as helpful, interesting, rewarding* (Hart, 1975; MacLean, 1978, 1980; Sagan, 1977) *and/or "gamey"* (Wittrock, 1978). In short, our brain's chemistry seems to be controlled by inner images of pleasure or displeasure, and if the learning environment or the information is negative, it is not allowed passage, the stimuli are never encoded, never stored, never remembered, and consequently, never learned.

Thus, the way we perceive ourselves, the inner images we hold about ourselves, others, and our environment determine how we think, behave, and ultimately determine what we learn. Research and experience have long verified that intellectual output can be enhanced through increasing the quality and quantity of affective motivators such as desire, excitement, and social/cultural approbation. More and more these are tied to the degree of the learner's positive self-image, to exercising focused concentration on performing tasks well on a daily basis, and to seeing oneself as thoroughly successful, capable, and confident throughout the day. It seems evident that one of the major thrusts of education of the future will be to find ways of providing students with means of discovering their own intentions and sources of their own learning motivation.

Alpha Consciousness

Research into how the brain prepares to receive new ideas and new material shows us that there must be sufficient flexibility for change to take place, for old behavioral patterns to mollify, eventually break down, and to create new forms and new patterns. The brain performs dissipative action (breakdown and creation) through the creation of electric waves. Brain wave patterns are based on four basic frequency ranges: *Beta* waves are most often recorded in the ordinary waking state of conscious or in analytical thinking and are most often recorded when left hemisphere tasks occur such as externally focused attention, goal orientation, and problem solving. Beta waves are short and rapid, and they allow little or no room for disturbance of already existing patterns.

Alpha waves, however, are emitted when we are deeply relaxed, engaged in daydreaming, reverie, creative endeavors, intuitive thinking, or symbolic expression. These waves shake up already existing patterns, allowing new ones to emerge. Galyean notes that "The alpha state is the *sine qua non* exponent of creativity, insight, and illumination" (Galyean, 1981). Also the alpha state is usually characterized by feelings of psychological integration and unity, and that, although the alpha state involves both hemispheres, the right hemispheric processes appear to be predominant. Studies have shown that highly intelligent people produce more alpha waves and work in an alpha state for longer periods of time than do persons of average intelligence (Galyean, 1981).

Delta waves are recorded most frequently during deep dream states. *Theta* waves are usually recorded during semi-sleep, characterized by creative insights, and are often associated with creativity and right brain functioning.

Researchers such as Galyean, Clark, and Ornstein have documented dramatic results in the use of inducing alpha consciousness through relaxation techniques, such as deep breathing and yoga, meditation techniques, such as inner focusing, centering, visualization and guided imagery. These alpha states influence both the rapidity and quantity of information being retained over long periods of time. More and more, it is becoming evident that it might be necessary to structure periods for creative incubation as a part of the standard curriculum, including such elements as time for reverie, guided imagery, mind/body integrative activities nurturing intuitive development, and meditation approaches, all of which quiet brain activity and increase synchronous brain activity.

If we accept overwhelming evidence offered us by brain research that we *are* smarter than we think, that we *are* capable of functioning far beyond the limits of ordinary three-dimensional existence, it follows that we, as educational leaders, have much rethinking to do about the educational premises on which our schools are founded. Educational methodologies derived from brain research are still in the neophyte stages of development and should be treated as such — much research into individual learning styles still needs to be accomplished.

However, one thing remains certain: the promises and expectations of actualizing the full spectrum of human potential loom enticingly before us. The great challenge for educators is to discover ways to expand the greatest of all human gifts — a clear, sharp, constantly expanding, centered mind — to teach others how to acquire and nurture this gift for themselves.

SELECTED READINGS

Battung, Diane. "An Educator's Guide to the Brain/Mind Revolution: Implications for Learning and Expanded Human Potential." Long Beach, California: KenZel, 1980.

Bogen, Joseph. "The Other Side of the Brain, I, II, III." *Bulletin of the Los Angeles Neurological Societies* 34, 3 (July 1969).

Brown, George, ed. *Human Teaching for Human Learning.* New York: Viking Press, 1971.

Clark, Barbara. *Growing Up Gifted.* Columbus, Ohio: Merrill Publishing Co., 1979.

Ferguson, Marilyn. *The Brain Revolution.* New York: Taplinger, 1973.

Frostig, Marianne, and Maslow, Phyllis. "Neuropsychological Contributions to Education." *Journal of Learning Disabilities* 8 (October 1979): 40-54.

Galyean, Beverly. "The Brain, Intelligence and Education." *Roper Review* (Fall 1981).

Galyean, Beverly, "Guided Imagery in Education." *Journal of Humanistic Psychology* (Spring 1981).

Hart, Leslie. *How the Brain Works.* New York: Basic Books, 1975.

Kinsbourne, Marcel. "Cognition and the Brain." In M.C. Wittrock, ed., *The Brain and Psychology.* New York: Academic Press, 1980, 325-342.

MacLean, Paul D. "A Mind of Three Minds: Educating the Triune Brain." In Jeanne Chall and Allan Mirsky, eds., *Education and the Brain.* The Seventy-Seventh Yearbook of the National Society for the Study of Education. Part 2. Chicago, Ill.: University of Chicago Press, 1978, pp. 308-342.

MacLean, Paul D. "A Meeting of Minds," *Dromenon. A Journal of New Ways of Being.* 3, 1 (1980): 12-19.

Maslow, Abraham. *Toward a Psychology of Being.* 2nd edition. New York: Van Nostrand Reinhold, 1968.

Ornstein, Robert E. *The Psychology of Consciousness.* New York: Viking Press, 1972.

Sagan, Carl. *The Dragons of Eden.* New York: Ballantine, 1977.

Teyler, Timothy J. "The Brain Sciences: An Introduction." In Jeanne Chall and Allan Mirsky, eds., *Education and the Brain.* The Seventy-Seventh Yearbook of the National Society for the Study of Education. Part 2. Chicago, Ill.: University of Chicago Press, 1978, pp. 1-32.

Thompson, Richard E.; Berger, Theodore W.; and Berry, Stephen D. "Brain Anatomy and Function." In M.C. Wittrock, ed., *The Brain and Psychology:* New York: Academic Press, 1980, 3-32.

Valett, Robert E. *Humanistic Education.* Saint Louis, Mo.: C.V. Mosby Company, 1977.

Weinstein, Gerald, and Fantini, Mario. *Toward Humanistic Education: A Curriculum of Affect.* New York: Praeger, 1970.

Wittrock, M.C. "Education and the Cognitive Processes of the Brain." In Jeanne Chall and Allan Mirsky, eds., *Education and the Brain.* The Seventy-Seventh Yearbook of the National Society for the Study of Education. Part 2. Chicago, Ill.: University of Chicago Press, 1978, pp. 61-102.

THE SCHOOL ADMINISTRATOR

Exploring the Report

1. (a) Make an outline of this report showing that it follows the four-stage format referred to earlier. Incorporate the headings and subheadings used.

   (b) What heading should have appeared before the paragraph on page 77 beginning, "Unfortunately, research indicates . . .?" Why?

2. Explain the following:

   (a) the most recent theory of how we actually think;

   (b) why current research argues that "the ultimate creative capacity of the brain may be infinite";

   (c) the concept of "hemisphere differentiation," related findings, and the implications for "personal growth and intellectual capacities";

   (d) the interrelationship between the brain's two parts.

3. What elements of the current educational system run counter to the implications of this research?

4. In a sentence or two for each, explain these terms and phrases: synetics, multi-sensory/discovery/Experiential Learning Techniques, and Divergent and Creative Thinking Techniques.

5. Explain the connection between emotion, thinking, and learning.

6. Why is a positive self-image vital for learning?

7. Identify the four basic frequency ranges of brain waves and their functions.

8. What challenge does the writer direct to her audience?

9. Because of the strongly persuasive language used (e.g., "exciting and dramatic," "mind-boggling," and "undeniable"), this report is not as objective as some. Find other examples of the writer's persuasive language and describe the tone it achieves.

10. How does the documentation format of a report differ from that of a scholarly essay?

11. What do the "figures" add to the report's impact?

12. Is the persuasive tone of this report necessary to achieve its purpose? Give reasons.

EXTENSIVE STUDY

1. "An almost total emphasis on logical, linear thought in our educational system may effectively suppress creativity."
   In small groups, explore your educational background and decide to what extent your particular educational experiences have enhanced and/or repressed your creativity. (You might begin by making a list of subjects that are essentially right-brain or left-brain oriented.)

2. "The brain operates on an emotional bias system . . . inner images of pleasure or displeasure enhance or prevent learning."
   Cite evidence for your views on this generalization.

4. Research current findings about the differences between female and male right- and left-brain capacities and their interrelatedness. Report your findings to the class, considering also the personal and social implications.

5. Determine the number of left-handed people in the class. First, consider whether logic indicates that left-handed people have their brain functions reversed. Next, attempt to find evidence about this issue. (You could begin by exploring the bibliography or consult your teacher-librarian.)

6. If you were an architect commissioned to design a school or learning environment, what have you learned from this report that could improve your building?

7. If you were a new teacher, how might Hatcher's findings help you to become more skilled at your profession? Attempt to provide specific examples of ways of teaching material to appeal to a variety of learning styles.

8. Working in pairs or small groups, consider ways parents might help their children to develop a more balanced hemispheric ability. Judging from what you have learned from Hatcher's report and perhaps further

library research, try to make a list of activities, including games, that seem to call on both spheres.

9. Read " 'Degree Day' Report" by Heather Forsythe, an engineering student, and explain why she received a high grade.

10. Research into brain functioning and learning is still in its infancy. Locate additional information that supports, qualifies, or refutes the theory of left-brain/right-brain thinking.

11. Read the summary of Dr. George Gerbner's report in "TV As a Shaper" (a summary of a summary) on the impact and implications of television on American audiences. Do the television viewing habits of Americans develop right- or left-brain capacities? Give reasons. If you have not done so already, you might find it interesting to read "An Interview with David Suzuki" (see Contemporary Journalism, page 224) and note his comments about the impact of television on children.

12. What would Orwell likely have thought about the findings mentioned in question 11 concerning the relationship between language and learning, judging from the views he expressed in "Politics and the English Language," page 4? Refer especially to the section on synetics research.

13. (a) What are the moral implications of regarding the brain as a "circuitry of interconnecting elements," in other words, a sophisticated computer?

    (b) Read the review of *The Second Self: Computers and the Human Spirit* (see The Review, page 138). Assess the apparent effects of computer technology on people's self-image.

THE WRITING FOLDER

1. Research the television viewing habits of some of your peers, a selected group of elementary school children, or a group representing your community. Record your findings in report form.

2. Write a report on any subject that particularly interests you. Follow report format.

3. Locate a report in a well-known magazine or journal and evaluate it.

INDEPENDENT STUDY

1. The more we know about the human mind, the more possible it becomes to control it. The novels *Brave New World, A Clockwork Orange,* and *1984* explore the world of mind control. After reading these works, write a report in which you outline the commonalities and differences in the writers' attitudes and approaches to this prospect.

++

2. Research the circulation files in your Resources Centre. Ask several

teachers or teacher-librarians what they might like to know about students' reading habits. Write a report on your findings.   +

3.   Examine the literature on how television viewing affects children. In co-operation with an elementary school's P.T.A., deliver your report to concerned parents.   + or ++

4.   With the co-operation of your school's administration, investigate the vandalism of school property. Deliver a report on your findings to the administration and Student Council. Ask Student Council members to offer solutions.   +

5.   Prepare a set of lesson plans for the teaching of one or two novels or plays your class might enjoy studying. Provide such teaching aids as dittos, overheads, films or filmstrip titles. Take into account the needs of students with different learning styles.   + or ++

6.   Ideas for other related independent study projects may be found by consulting some of the titles Hatcher lists in her bibliography, Selected Readings, at the end of her report.

TIMED READING AND WRITING

1.   Write an outline for Reed's report on American television viewing habits.

2.   Read Tom Harpur's report about his visit to the University of Toronto's Research Laboratory. Write a reasoned response assessing the extent to which he managed to write a rational, objective report on this highly emotional subject.

3.   "If I had a child, I'd be vigilant about her or his viewing habits until the age of . . . ." Argue this statement, giving specific reasons relating to what you have read and talked about in this unit.

TV AS A SHAPER

CHRISTOPHER REED

Professor George Gerbner, an authority on contemporary television, likes to quote the seventeenth-century Scottish thinker, Andrew Fletcher of Saltoun, who wrote: "If a man were permitted to make all the ballads, he need not care who should make the laws."

Dr. Gerbner's point is that the TV screen is now our balladeer, today's source of the stories, legends and characters that shaped earlier cultures. Yet because of the pervasiveness of TV, its influence on our attitudes may go beyond ephemeral politics and laws and into fundamental social dispositions.

Now Dean of the Annenberg School of Communications at the

University of Pennsylvania, Dr. Gerbner has been studying TV for 17 years. His conclusions have been published mainly in academic journals, but his findings on North American TV society are provocative enough to interest a wider audience.

Even a casual student of the United States, puzzled by the paradoxes of Reaganism and the New Populism, the social beatification of the U.S. medical profession, or even why Americans have such slovenly eating habits, may turn to Dr. Gerbner for enlightenment. His may not be the last word, but he offers startling examples of life imitating artifice.

The popularity of so many exported U.S. TV shows and what some critics call U.S. cultural imperialism may also mean that many of his findings apply to the rest of the industrialized English-speaking world.

Dr. Gerbner's studies cover light viewers (those who watch up to two hours a day) and heavy viewers (four hours and above). Commercial TV's need for a vast audience pulls its content and its viewers toward mainstream blandness. Thus, heavy viewers tended to regard themselves as "average," "middle class" and politically "moderate" despite their actual status or opinions, Dr. Gerbner found.

In fact, these "moderates" were usually well to the right of what would normally be regarded as centrist on such social matters as race, minorities, personal rights, freedom of expression and law and order. This reflects TV's portrayal of the world as dangerous and nasty through its dramatization of crime and violence and obsession with disasters and mayhem.

Heavy viewers were not conservative on economics and social services, however. Here they demonstrated distrust of big government and resentment of taxes, yet they demand beneficial government services and the quick economic "fix".

Dr. Gerbner believe this stems from commercial TV's "mass mobilization of consumption". As a temple devoted to the glorification of instant gratification via its advertising, TV is bound to encourage fast and simple solutions to material desires.

The world on the small screen and those who people it are far from reality. Average viewers see 300 screen characters a week in prime time. They are portrayed in apparent realism, but bear little relation to their real-life counterparts or to the viewers' actual world.

Watchers see 30 police officers, seven lawyers, three judges, 12 nurses and 10 doctors a week, but only one engineer or scientist. Service or manual workers comprise 10 per cent of the screen cast but are 65 per cent of the real world. Men outnumber women on TV three to one.

The popular male age range is from 25 to 55, but for women 25 to 35. People under 18 are a third, and those over 65 a fifth of their actual presence in the U.S. population.

Violence is seen six times an hour in peak time, of which two incidents per evening are fatalities (so that in 10 years a heavy viewer will have seen about 7,000 screen deaths). Women and the elderly, although actually under-represented in comparison with reality, are disproportionately the victims. Young white males occur most often in violent scenes, but are least likely to be victims — the opposite of the real world where they are the most likely — after young black males — to be injured or killed.

Since this is TV's version of mainstream reality, no wonder heavy viewers believe they are moderates and no wonder their opinions are conservative. TV violence contributes to apprehension and increased support of right-wing "law and order" campaigns.

Aggravating the anxiety is the medium's preoccupation with crime — among the week's 300 characters are 23 criminals and crime is at least 10 times more frequent on the screen than in life. Nor are children spared: during their weekend daytime programs, the "kid-vid ghetto," as advertisers call it, there are 18 violent acts an hour.

A curious side-effect of the violence is the role of medicine. Screen violence rarely causes pain or suffering and never seems to need medical attention. On the average, only 6 to 7 per cent of major characters require treatment.

Nevertheless, the doctors are beyond reproach: fewer than 4 per cent are shown as evil — half the percentage shown in other professions. Doctors are also characterized as fairer, more sociable and warmer than other characters and are rated as more intelligent, more rational and more stable and fair than the (female) nurses. The MD "symbolizes power, authority and knowledge and possesses an almost uncanny ability to dominate and control the lives of others".

If this helps to explain the demi-god status of physicians, the daytime soap operas must contribute to what strikes many foreigners as rampant U.S. hypochondria.

Nearly half of all soap opera characters are involved in health-related occurrences. Half the pregnancies end in miscarriage and 16 per cent in the mother's death. Health is the most frequently discussed topic. The second most common location in the soaps is a doctor's surgery.

This preoccupation with health could have something to do with the TV characters' reckless attitude toward it. On most shows, seatbelts are rarely used and few safety precautions are taken at work. Eating, drinking or talking about food occur nine times an hour in peak time, yet characters almost always remain sober — and slim.

TV may explain why Americans eat and drink in public so much — gobbling and gulping junk food and sticky drinks while going up in elevators, driving cars, or shopping. TV people eat on the run all the time (one commercial shows two men eating pizzas while practicing basketball) and scenes of families sitting down to a balanced dinner hardly ever appear in the shows. Dr. Gerbner links this constant snacking with an attempt to resolve frustration, a point echoed by U.S. dieticians, who constantly warn the overweight millions against compulsive eating.

Junk food is much advertised on TV, of course, but Dr. Gerbner believes the programs are "worse" than the commercials.

As the advertising criterion for TV's content is cost per 1,000 viewers, rather than pure income from commercials, TV shows may be put together with little concern for quality or accuracy in the infinite quest for the impossible: a show costing nothing but seen by everyone.

"We are only now discovering our environment of symbols and messages," says Dr. Gerbner, "rather than in the conventional sense of our surroundings — and only now realizing that, as with other things, these are also mass-produced. We should alert our citizens to this . . . Perhaps what we need most now is a prime-time program alerting viewers to the hidden political messages behind the messages they know about."

Simpler might be a warning like the one now carried on cigaret packets, to precede a soap-opera or prime-time drama: "This show may turn you into a neurotic right-winger."

The Globe and Mail, May 30, 1985

REPORT ON ANIMAL RESEARCH

TOM HARPUR

The shedding of blood in animal sacrifice is something we associate with crude attempts to placate angry gods by primitive peoples. But, in reality, we ourselves are part of a culture which daily sacrifices millions of animals.

Most of these are killed for food — something we seldom think about in the supermarket. Many become grist for the mills of fashion or other facets of our consumerism. Millions are used for research.

Each of these categories raises significant ethical questions about our relationships with other living things, particularly the use and sacrifice of animals in laboratory experiments.

Greater importance?

The fundamental moral issue raised is: By what right do we treat animals as legitimate means to our human ends? Who or what says our lives and well-being are of greater importance than theirs?

"Obviously people matter more than dogs, cats, or monkeys," you may say.

But, morally, it's not that simple. It is nowhere engraved in stone or self-evident in logic that humans are of more value. When you state that they are, you are asserting a tenet of faith or belief.

Such a faith may be based on the philosophy of humanism, i.e. that humanity is the highest value and the good of humanity the norm by which all else is decided. Or, it may be based upon the Judeo-Christian faith that we are created in the image of God and have been given dominion over the earth and all its life forms.

I must say I was somewhat surprised during a media tour of the animal research facility at the University of Toronto this week to hear an eminent surgeon justifying the use of animals in experimentation by citing the Judeo-Christian tradition.

Since he is a practising Christian, his appeal to religion made sense for him. But to put this kind of faith forward as a defence of the scientific community's animal research seemed far-fetched. This community is not necessarily more devout than the rest of Canadians. Some would say it is profoundly less so.

A note of clarification: Some, indeed too many, down through history, have taken the Judeo-Christian tradition — especially some verses in Genesis — to mean humans have the right to exploit nature in any way we want. Ecological rape has been the result.

I agree with contemporary theologians who argue that the chief model in the Bible for our relationship to the planet and its creatures is one of stewardship.

Responsible stewards

Adam, we are told in the great myth, was put in the garden "to dress it and to keep it." Our dominion is to be one of caring, loving concern. A good steward hands over to others what has been entrusted to him — hands it over in better shape than when he received it.

It is out of this two-fold context — belief in the ultimate value of human persons and belief that we are called to be responsible stewards of all the earth — that I formulate my own response to the unpleasant reality of animal experiments.

On these grounds, I can see no justification for the use of animals in experiments having to do with war, weapons or defence.

Nor can I justify the exploitation of animals in the production of ever-proliferating cosmetics and other needless, so-called consumer items. This is not stewardship but collective irresponsibility.

Medical research, however, is different. This week I watched as a surgical team removed the liver of a pig in preparation for a transplant into another pig. It is precisely because of this operation and others like it — conducted with all the sedation, hygiene, and consummate care of any human surgery — that persons dying of liver disease in this country will soon be offered a new hope.

Medical school

In another room at the university's medical school, I saw a doctor preparing a dog for surgery in an attempt to discover ways of making heart pacemakers more energy-efficient in order to avoid frequent operations for replacements. The dog, an unclaimed stray, felt no more pain than anyone who has ever been sedated for a similar procedure.

In fact, after spending several hours there, I have no trouble in accepting the comment of Dr. George Connell, the university president: "These animals are extremely well cared for. They're well housed and fed and most of them suffer no traumatic experience . . . in the course of experimentation.

It is because of such experimentation that millions now live longer, healthier lives than ever before. (Our average lifespan has lengthened by 25 years since 1900, and animals have benefited by the increased knowledge as well.) Nearly every advance in medicine — from Banting and Best's discovery of insulin for diabetes, to organ transplants, medications to control epileptic seizures, artificial joints, cataract removal and artificial lens implants, and radiation therapy for cancer — has been due to animal research.

Wherever possible today's medical researchers avoid the use of live animals. Work with dead tissues, cultures, or computer models is infinitely easier and less costly. These people are dedicated scientists bent on the relief of human misery, not mad sadists.

But for those diseases still unsolved — cancer, multiple sclerosis, heart disease, Alzheimer's disease, cystic fibrosis and the rest — research involving animals offers the best and, in some cases, the only hope of a cure.

If you are thinking about the rightness or wrongness of this kind of research yourself, here are a few figures for the University of Toronto's animal research — and they are fairly typical of research across Canada — that may be of help:

- rats and mice — 92 per cent of the total of animals used;
- rabbits, sheep, and pigs — 3.5 per cent;
- cats and dogs — 1.3 per cent;

- primates (monkeys, etc.) — .03 per cent;
- frogs — 1.4 per cent;
- others, including fish and birds — 1.7 per cent.

Toronto Star, June 2, 1985

'DEGREE DAY' REPORT

HEATHER A. FORSYTHE (student report)

The student was asked to write a report proposing a suitable change to the "degree day" definition currently used by the Department of the Environment. The audience was specified as "a general interest publication read by engineers and scientists of all disciplines (e.g., *Canadian Consulting Engineer*)."

Current Definition

A "degree day" is the measure of the degree of heating needed for a particular day. The Department of Environment calculates this index by subtracting from 18°C an average of the high and low temperature readings taken between midnight of consecutive days. The degree days may be summed to arrive at a measure of the amount of heating needed in the homes, offices, etc., during a given period (e.g., a month, or the whole winter season).

Some Problems with the Current Method

The current definition, although quick and easy to calculate, is oversimplified so that large errors can occur. If the average temperature for the day is greater than 18°C, a degree day of zero is reported (since there can be no negative degree days), even though heating may have been required during some part of the day. Because the hours of daylight are fewer than the hours of darkness during the winter, and temperature highs and lows are related to day-time and night-time, single readings of high and low are a poor basis for an "average" temperature. This method of single readings also does not account for any fast swings of temperature which may occur. In addition, no allowance is made for the effects of wind and sun on heating requirements, nor for the different heating needs of homes, office buildings, and factories.

Proposed Changes — New "Degree Day" Definition

By modifying the measurement and calculation method, the above problems can be largely eliminated.

■ Two degree days should be used, one for residential buildings and one for industrial buildings (including large offices and schools). Several of the proposed corrections will be common to both, but some will be specific for one type of building.

■ Both averages should be corrected from the ratio of the hours of darkness to the hours of daylight. The temperature highs and lows should be obtained and averaged for three periods: midnight to dawn, dawn to sunset, and sunset to midnight. An average of the three should give a good basis for an average temperature weighted for the darkness to daylight ratio.

■ Since wind velocities greatly affect the heating required (both for homes and larger buildings), a rating system for the wind velocity is required. The wind velocities will be taken in the same time periods as the temperatures and averaged in the same manner. A basis of 5 km/h wind speed should be used, and for every 5 km/h above this, a correction factor of 1°C should be subtracted from the average temperature for that time period.

■ Sunlight also affects the heating requirements, especially in large buildings with many windows (e.g., high-rise office buildings). Therefore, for every hour of moderate sunlight, 1°C should be added to the daytime average which is used in calculating the industrial degree day.

■ It is also necessary to correct the industrial average for the lower temperature required on the weekends when most factories, schools and offices are unoccupied. On Saturday and Sunday, the outdoor average temperature should be subtracted from 16°C rather than 18°C. This correction should also be for each midnight to dawn temperature average when calculating the residential degree day since many people turn down the thermostat during the sleeping hours.

■ Although the new "degree day" definition requires several extra measurements, and much calculation, any cost and time increase will be balanced by a large gain in accuracy.

5. THE BIOGRAPHY, AUTOBIOGRAPHY, AND PROFILE

Key Work:
   "Harriet Tubman: The Moses of Her People" —
      Langston Hughes
Associated Readings:
   "Excerpt from An Unfinished Woman: A Memoir" —
      Lillian Hellman
   "Linda Thom: An Olympic Champion"
   "Profile" — Greg Hollyer (student)

When the essay takes the form of biography or autobiography, its purpose is to render a fascinating, true account of a person's life. A clever blend of fact, anecdote, and dialogue often produces a work that reads like fiction. The writer may, indeed, use devices employed in a successful novel — suspense, building to a climax, irony, and reconstruction of events which reinforce character details, as you may notice in the accompanying essays by Hughes and Hellman. Whether the portrait is sympathetic, neutral, or critical in tone, the work should address this question: what makes this person's life worth exploring? Thus, it should transcend the particular to illustrate some general truth(s) about the human condition.

Although the narration may cover the same material as an autobiography, a biography distances the reader from the subject as it offers an interpretation filtered through another's point of view; in this sense, one might say biography offers less opportunity for bias. But even the details presented, and the manner in which they are recounted by the biographer, inevitably reflect personal preferences. You may notice these differences in tone as you read the works about Harriet Tubman and Linda Thom.

The profile, a specific form of autobiography, is usually written for a specific audience. You will probably be asked to write a profile of yourself at some point in your post-secondary career — when applying for university or employment. Sometimes you will also need to submit a resumé or curriculum vitae, which provides specific details about your education and employment record. When composing a profile, your purpose is to introduce yourself to a specific audience and encourage a positive response through your self-portrait.

write a biography, who would be your subject? Why?
you know about Tubman, just from reading the essay's

personal qualities might help human beings survive successfully
extremely difficult situations?

HARRIET TUBMAN: THE MOSES OF HER PEOPLE

LANGSTON HUGHES

Biography
She could have been content with her own freedom, but she wasn't. Time and time again, she risked her life to free hundreds of slaves in the South.

"Then we saw the lightning, and that was the guns; and then we heard the thunder, and that was the big guns; and then we heard the rain falling, and that was the drops of blood falling; and when we came to get in the crops, it was dead men that we reaped." So the escaped slave, Harriet Tubman, described one of the battles of the Civil War in which she took part, for she was in the thick of the fighting. Before the War Harriet Tubman devoted her life to the cause of freedom, and after the War to the advancement of her people.

She was born in Maryland a slave, one of eleven sons and daughters. No one kept a record of her birth, so the exact year is not known. But she lived so long and so much was written about her that most of the other facts of her life are accurately recorded. She was a homely child, morose, willful, wild, and constantly in rebellion against slavery. Unlike Phillis Wheatley[1] or Frederick Douglass,[2] Harriet had no teaching of any sort, except the whip. As a little girl, on the very first day that she was sent to work in the Big House, her mistress whipped her four times. Once she ran away and hid in a pig sty for five days, eating the scraps thrown to the pigs. "There were good masters and mistresses, so I've heard tell," she once said, "but I didn't happen to come across any of them."

Harriet never liked to work as a servant in the house, so perhaps because of her rebellious nature, she was soon ordered to the fields. One day when she was in her early teens, something happened that affected her whole life. It was evening, and a young slave had, without permission, gone to a country store. The overseer followed him to whip him. He ordered Harriet to help tie him up. As Harriet refused, the slave ran. The overseer picked up a heavy iron weight from the scales and threw it. But he did not hit the fellow. He struck Harriet's head, almost crushing her skull, and leaving a deep scar forever. Unconscious, the girl lingered between life and death for days. When at last she was able to work again, Harriet still suffered fits of unconsciousness. These lasted all her life. They would come upon her at any time, any place, and it would seem as if she had suddenly fallen asleep. Sometimes in the fields, sometimes leaning against a fence, sometimes in church, she would "go to sleep," and no one could wake her until the seizure had passed. When she was awake, this did not affect her thinking. But her master thought the blow had made her half-witted. Harriet continued to let him believe this. Meanwhile, she prayed God to deliver her from bondage.

When she was about twenty-four years old, she married a jolly, carefree fellow named Tubman, who did not share her concern for leaving the slave country. A few years later, when her old master died, Harriet heard that she and two of her brothers were to be sold, so they decided to run away together. It was dangerous to tell anyone. Harriet had no chance to let even her mother know directly. But on the evening that she was leaving, she went about the fields and the slaves' quarters singing:

> "When that old chariot comes
> I'm gwine to leave you.
> I'm bound for the Promised Land. . . ."

And the way she sang that song let her friends and kinfolks know that to Harriet the Promised Land right then meant the North, not heaven. That night she left the Brodas Plantation on the Big Buckwater River, never to return. Before dawn her brothers became frightened and went back to the slave huts before their absence was discovered. But Harriet went on alone through the woods by night, hiding by day, having no map, unable to read or write, but trusting God, instinct, and the North star to guide her. By some miracle she eventually got to Philadelphia, found work there, and was never again a slave.

But Harriet could not be happy while all her family were slaves. She kept thinking about them. So some months later, she went back to Maryland, hoping to persuade her husband to come North with her. He said he did not wish to go. She led others Northward, however, and, within two years of her own escape, she had secretly returned to the South three times to rescue two brothers, a sister and her children, and a dozen more slaves. The Fugitive Slave Law of 1850 now made it dangerous for runaways to stop anywhere in the United States, so Harriet led her followers to Canada, where she spent a winter begging, cooking, and praying for them. Then she returned to Maryland to rescue nine more Negroes.

During the first years of her own freedom, Harriet spent most of her time showing others how to follow in her footsteps. Her fame as a fearless leader of "freedom bands" spread rapidly. Shortly, large rewards were offered by the slaveholders for her capture. But she was never captured, and she never lost any of her followers to the slave catchers. One reason for this was that once a slave made up his mind to go with her and started out, Harriet did not permit any turning back. Perhaps her experience with her two brothers when she first ran away accounted for this insistence. Her method of preventing frightened or weak travelers on the freedom road from returning to slavery, and perhaps being whipped into betraying the others, was simple. Harriet Tubman carried a pistol. When anyone said he could not, or would not, go on, Harriet pulled her gun from the folds of her dress and said, "You *will* go on — or you'll die." The strength or the courage to continue was always forthcoming when her faltering companions looked into the muzzle of Harriet's gun. Through swamp and thicket, rain and cold, they went on toward the North. Thus everyone who started out with Harriet Tubman lived to thank her for freedom.

Long before the Civil War came, so many slaves were escaping and so many white people in the North were helping them, that the routes to freedom became known as the Underground Railroad. Secret "stations" where escaping slaves might be hidden, warmed, and fed were established in houses, barns, and sometimes even churches along the way. The Quakers were especially helpful and active in this regard. And a strong Anti-Slavery Society supported such activities. Slave owners were losing thousands of dollars worth of slaves by escape every year. Harriet Tubman became known as a "conductor" on the Underground Railroad. She was not the only "conductor," but she was the most famous, and one of the most daring. Once she brought as many as twenty-five slaves in a single band to freedom.

Another time she had in her party of runaways a big strong slave worth $1500. His name was Josiah Bailey, and the Maryland countryside was plastered with posters offering a reward for his capture. There were ads in the papers for his return. On the way through New York City, a friend of freedom recognized Bailey from the description in the papers and said, "I'm glad to meet a man whose head is worth fifteen hundred dollars!" Josiah was so shocked at being recognized and so afraid that he would be captured that a mood of deep despair descended upon him, and he would not speak the rest of the trip. When the train was carrying the runaways across the bridge at Buffalo into Canada, Bailey would not even look at the wonder of Niagara Falls. But when they got on free soil and he was finally safe, he burst into song, and nobody could stop him from singing. He cried that at last, thanks to God, he was in Heaven! Harriet Tubman said, "Well, you old fool, you! You might at least have looked at Niagara Falls on the way to Heaven."

Harriet had a great sense of humor. She enjoyed telling the story on herself of how, not being able to read, she once sat down and went to sleep on a park bench right under a sign offering a big reward for her capture. When she began to make speeches to raise money for the cause of freedom, she often told jokes, sang, and sometimes even danced. She might have been a great actress, people said, because without makeup she could hollow out her cheeks and wrinkle her brow to seem like a very old woman. She would make her body shrink and cause her legs to totter when she chose to so disguise herself. Once, making a trip to Maryland to rescue some relatives, she had to pass through a village where she was known. She bought two hens, tied them by their feet and hung them heads down around her neck, then went tottering along. Sure enough, a slave catcher came up the street who might, she thought, recognize her, tottering or not. So she unloosed the squalling chickens in the middle of the street and dived after them, purposely not catching them so she could run down the road in pursuit and out of the slave catcher's sight, while all the passers-by laughed.

Sometimes, knowing that her band of fugitives was pursued by angry masters, she would get on a train headed South — because nobody would suspect that runaway slaves would be going South. Sometimes she would disguise the women in her party and herself as men. Babies would be given a sleeping medicine to keep them quiet and then wrapped up like bundles. Sometimes she would wade for hours up a stream to throw the hounds off scent. . . . Often when all seemed hopeless — although she never told her followers she had such feelings — Harriet would pray. One of her favorite prayers was, "Lord, you've been with me through six troubles. Be with me in the seventh." Some people thought that Harriet Tubman led a charmed life because, within twelve years, she made nineteen dangerous trips into the South, rescuing slaves. She herself said, "I never run my train off the track, and I never lost a passenger."

Her father and mother were both over seventy years of age when she rescued them and brought them North to a home she had begun to buy in Auburn, New York. At first they stayed in St. Catharines, Canada, where escaped slaves were safe, since in 1833 Great Britain had declared all slavery illegal. But it was too cold for the old folks there. And Harriet's work was not on foreign soil. She herself seemed to have no fear of being captured. She came and went about the United States as she chose, and became so famous that, although she never sought the spotlight, it was hard for her not to be recognized wherever she was. Once at a great woman's suffrage meeting where her old head wound had caused her to go sound asleep in the audience, she was recognized, and awoke to find herself on the platform. Her speech for women's rights was roundly applauded. In those days neither Negroes nor women could vote. Harriet believed both should, so she followed the woman's suffrage movement closely.

In appearance "a more ordinary specimen of humanity could hardly be found," but there was no one with a greater capacity for leadership than she had. Among the slaves, where she walked in secret, Harriet began to be known as Moses. And at the great public meetings of the North, as the Negro historian William Wells Brown wrote in 1854, "all who frequented anti-slavery conventions, lectures, picnics, and fairs, could not fail to have seen a black woman of medium size, upper front teeth gone, smiling countenance, attired in coarse but neat apparel, with an old-fashioned reticule or bag suspended by her side, who, on taking her seat, would at once drop off into a sound sleep. . . . No fugitive was ever captured who had Moses for a leader." She was very independent. Between rescue trips or speeches, she would work as a cook or a scrubwoman. She might borrow, but she never begged money for herself. All contributions went toward the cause of freedom in one way or another, as did most of what she earned.

But when the Civil War began and she became a nurse for the Union Armies, and then a military scout and an invaluable intelligence agent behind the Rebel lines, she was promised some compensation. Technically she was not a registered nurse, and being a woman, she could not be a soldier. Yet she carried a Union pass, traveled on government transports, did dangerous missions in Confederate territory, and gave advice to chiefs of staffs. But she never got paid for this, although she had been promised $1800 for certain assignments. To Harriet this made no difference, until after the War she badly needed money to care for her aged parents. Petitions were sent to the War Department and to Congress to try to get the $1800 due her. But it was never granted.

Harriet Tubman's war activities were amazing. She served under General Stevens at Beaufort, South Carolina. She was sent to Florida to nurse those ill of dysentery, small pox, and yellow fever. She was with Colonel Robert Gould Shaw[3] at Fort Wagner. She organized a group of nine Negro scouts and river pilots and, with Colonel Montgomery, led a Union raiding contingent of three gunboats and about one hundred fifty Negro troops up the Combahee River.[4] As reported by the *Boston Commonwealth*, for July 10, 1863, they "under the guidance of a black woman, dashed into the enemy's country, struck a bold and effective blow, destroying millions of dollars worth of commissary stores, cotton and lordly dwellings, and striking terror into the heart of rebeldom, brought off near eight hundred slaves and thousands of dollars worth of property.'' Concerning Harriet Tubman, it continued, ''Many and many times she has penetrated the enemy's lines and discovered their situation and condition, and escaped without injury, but not without extreme hazard.''

One of the songs Harriet sang during the War was:

''Of all the whole creation in the East or in the West,
The glorious Yankee nation is the greatest and the best.
Come along! Come along! Don't be alarmed,
Uncle Sam is rich enough to give you all a farm.''

But Harriet Tubman never had a farm of her own. Her generous nature caused her to give away almost all the money she ever got her hands on. There were always fugitives, or relatives, or causes, or friends in need. She was over forty years old when Abraham Lincoln signed the Emancipation Proclamation, making legal the freedom she had struggled to secure. She lived for almost fifty years after the War was over. Some people thought she was a hundred years old when she died in 1913. Certainly she was over ninety.

A number of books have been written about her. The first one, *Scenes in the Life of Harriet Tubman,* by Sarah H. Bradford, appeared in 1869, and the proceeds from its sale helped Harriet pay for her cottage. She wrote her friend, Frederick Douglass, who had hidden her and her runaway slaves more than once in his home in Rochester, for a letter about her book. In his reply he compared their two careers:

''The difference between us is very marked. Most that I have done and suffered in the service of our cause has been in public, and I have received much encouragement at every step of the way. You, on the other hand, have labored in a private way. I have wrought in the day — you in the night. I have had the applause of the crowd and the satisfaction that comes of being approved by the multitude, while the most that you have done has been witnessed by a few trembling, scared, and footsore bondsmen and women, whom you have led out of the house of bondage, and whose heartfelt *God bless you* has been your only reward. The midnight sky and the silent stars have been the witnesses of your devotion to freedom and of your heroism.''

When years later, in her old age, a reporter for the *New York Herald Tribune* came to interview her one afternoon at her home in Auburn, he wrote that, as he was leaving, Harriet looked toward an orchard nearby and said, ''Do you like apples?''

On being assured that the young man liked them, she asked, ''Did you ever plant any apples?''

The writer confessed that he had not.

''No,'' said the old woman, ''but somebody else planted them. I liked apples when I was young. And I said, 'Someday I'll plant apples myself for other young folks to eat.' And I guess I did."

Her apples were the apples of freedom. Harriet Tubman lived to see the harvest. Her home in Auburn, New York, is preserved as a memorial to her planting.

---

[1]Phillis Wheatley: Born in Africa, she came as a slave to Boston. She later gained recognition as a poet.
[2]Frederick Douglass: Born into slavery, he escaped to freedom in the North.
[3]Robert Gould Shaw: the commander of a free Negro regiment from Massachusetts.
[4]Combahee River: in South Carolina.

EXPLORING THE BIOGRAPHY

1. Quote the sentence that expresses Hughes's thesis and explain how this sentence relates to the title.

2. Tubman's courage and humility dominate this biographical sketch. Demonstrate how Hughes achieves this impression through judicious selection and interpretation of his material.

3. Show that Hughes uses figures of speech and informal diction to create a tone that he feels is appropriate to achieve his goal.

4. What relative weight did Tubman apparently assign to each of the following: God, circumstance, and personal control? How did these attitudes affect the nature of her life?

5. What does the structure of this biographical sketch have in common with a short story?

EXTENSIVE STUDY

1. This library exercise will acquaint you with reference sources for use in this course and future university and college arts and science courses. Your teacher may ask the teacher-librarian to introduce the class to appropriate sources before you begin. In some cases, your teacher-librarian may assess the results of this orientation. Major references include:

    - special encyclopedias (e.g., Benét's *The Reader's Encyclopedia*)
    - handbooks and special reference tools (e.g., *A Reader's Guide to Literary Terms*)
    - biographical references (e.g., *Who's Who in Canada*)
    - bibliographies and historical references (e.g., *The Literary History of the United States*)
    - abstracts and indexes (e.g., *Reader's Guide to Periodical Literature*
    - specialized dictionaries which provide rules and examples for language usage (e.g., Fowler's *A Dictionary of Modern English Usage* and Bernstein's *The Careful Writer*)

Working in pairs, look for answers to questions (a) through (j) listed below. If suitable reference texts aren't available, ask your teacher-librarian for guidance or visit the local public reference library, or university library, if possible. Take point form research notes.

(a) Find biographical data about Langston Hughes that may provide clues about his interests, credibility, and biases.
(b) Locate two biographical sketches of Harriet Tubman. What details are presented differently or omitted? Can you account for these differences?
(c) Find the titles of two other books about Tubman or the escape of southern slaves.
(d) Identify the Quakers.
(e) Record the title of a source containing the Fugitive Slave Law of 1850.
(f) Note five facts about Fredrick Douglass's life.
(g) Identify Moses and his role in the Promised Land.
(h) Write definitions of biography and autobiography as literary forms.
(i) Record the names of two famous slave catchers.
(j) Quote the rule about the usage of the word "but," which suggests that Hughes has employed it correctly in his sentence beginning "But Harriet could not be happy while all of her family were slaves." (You may wish to refer to "There, There" by William Safire in The Core Essays, page 21.)

Compare your findings with another pair of students. Consult your teacher or teacher-librarian about any problems you encountered.

2. Working in a small group, explore these questions. You might take notes on your conversation and share your observations with another group when you are finished:
(a) How did you feel about Tubman, the woman, after reading the essay? Why?
(b) Which of Tubman's traits could have contributed to her success in contemporary society?
(c) Read the accompany profile, "Linda Thom: An Olympic Champion." What personal qualities have contributed to Linda Thom's success? Compare these traits with Tubman's.
(d) Define the characteristics of a hero. Which of these criteria do Tubman and Thom meet? Which of the standards in your definition apply to the classical hero and which are peculiar to our time and culture?
(e) What lessons in living can we learn from the experiences of Tubman and Thom?

3. Read the excerpt from Hellman's autobiography, An Unfinished Woman: A Memoir. Show how Hellman has used diction and personal

details to create a more personal tone than Hughes has used in his biography of Tubman.

4. If you have read John F. Kennedy's "Inaugural Address" and/or Martin Luther King's "I Have a Dream" (see The Speech, page 152), consider how Tubman's life relates to Kennedy's and/or King's aspirations.

THE WRITING FOLDER

1. Reread the letter from Fredrick Douglass which appears at the end of Hughes's essay. Following the same style, contrast the character and achievements of any two people. (They might be famous individuals, personal friends, or fictitious characters.) Assume you are writing for a specific friendly audience of your choice.

2. Assume the role of a reporter interviewing Tubman near the end of her career. Compose the interview, filling in answers based on what you have learned about Tubman from this essay. (See a model interview with David Suzuki in Contemporary Journalism, page 224.) Your audience is a magazine read by high school students.

3. If you are familiar with the life and work of Martin Luther King, assume his point of view and compose a speech that he might have delivered during the days of the Civil Rights Movement in which he pays tribute to Tubman's contribution to society. Your audience is a public rally and the date is 1964.

4. Analyze Hellman's writing style as it appears in the Associated Readings, page 104. In your analysis, describe the tone she creates and give specific examples of how she uses language and presents details to achieve this tone.

5. Write a brief biographical sketch of someone you admire and know well. Then write an autobiographical sketch of the same person as you think that individual perceives him or herself.

6. Write a profile to accompany your application for university or for a job.

INDEPENDENT STUDY

1. Investigate the life and work of Martin Luther King. After reading one or two biographies and a number of his speeches such as "I Have a Dream," develop a specific topic with your teacher's guidance. Tape or deliver in person a dramatic reading of one of King's famous speeches. + or ++

2. After reading one full-length biography about Tubman, develop a specific essay project with your teacher. (You might compare tone, biases, sources, and devices used by Hughes and the other biographers to enhance reader interest.) +

3. After reading one or more sources about Tubman or an issue raised by Hughes's essay, write a short story in which the characters confront a challenging situation that reveals their inner qualities (e.g., the Underground Railway, slave catchers, unusual bravery in the face of physical danger). Accompany your fiction with a brief oral analysis that ties your story to your reading.   + or ++

4. Read two biographies of a famous person. Contrast the depiction of the individual in question. (Consider point of view, bias, focus, omissions, interests, and interpretation). See your teacher-librarian for titles. You might provide your class or teacher with a presentation of your findings, if your work relates to an author or theme studied by the class.   ++

5. Read a biography and an autobiography about one famous person. Compare the two works with regard to approach, objectivity, interpretation of the same events, tone, and point of view. See your teacher-librarian for titles. Include a brief oral report in which you discuss which book you preferred and why.   ++

6. Read material about how to write biography. Write an original work of biography about a living person you know (perhaps one of your grandparents) whom you believe to be worthy of such attention. Base your work on in-depth interviews with the individual. Be sure you clearly establish the universal dimension of your project. Also submit one of your interview tapes and a bibliography of works consulted.   +

7. These biographies and autobiographies may suggest other independent study topics or lead you to read further for pleasure:

    Barbara Amiel, *Confessions*
    Simone de Beauvoir, *Memoirs of a Dutiful Daughter*
    Hugh Garner, *One Damn Thing After Another!*
    Margaret Lane, *The Brontë Sisters*
    Ralph G. Martin, *Jennie: The Life of Lady Randolph Churchill*
    Nancy Mitford, *Zelda*
    Heather Robertson, *Willie: A Romance*
    Michèle Sarde, *Colette*
    Theodore Sorenson, *Kennedy*
    William Styron, *The Confessions of Nat Turner*

TIMED READING AND WRITING

1. Write an essay which begins with either of:

    If I had met Harriet Tubman, the first thing I would want to ask her is . . .

    OR

    The best way to meet a challenge is to . . .

2. Compose a dialogue between Tubman and King or Thom in which

they compare the challenges they faced one hundred years apart and how they handled them.

3. Read the profile by Greg Hollyer, page 110. In memo form, write a first impression reaction of acceptance or rejection, using only this information. What else would you like to know about this person before employing him?

EXCERPT FROM AN UNFINISHED WOMAN: A MEMOIR

LILLIAN HELLMAN

I was born in New Orleans to Julia Newhouse from Demopolis, Alabama, who had fallen in love and stayed in love with Max Hellman, whose parents had come to New Orleans in the German 1845–1848 immigration to give birth to him and his two sisters. My mother's family, long before I was born, had moved from Demopolis to Cincinnati and then to New Orleans, both desirable cities, I guess, for three marriageable girls.

But I first remember them in a large New York apartment: my two young and very pretty aunts; their taciturn, tight-faced brother; and the silent, powerful, severe woman, Sophie Newhouse, who was their mother, my grandmother. Her children, her servants, all of her relatives except her brother Jake were frightened of her, and so was I. Even as a small child I disliked myself for the fear and showed off against it.

The Newhouse apartment held the upper-middle-class trappings, in touch of things and in spirit of people, that never manage to be truly stylish. Heavy weather hung over the lovely oval rooms. True, there were parties for my aunts, but the parties, to a peeping child in the servants' hall, seemed so muted that I was long convinced that on fancy occasions grown people moved their lips without making sounds. In the days after the party one would hear exciting stories about the new suitors, but the suitors were never quite good enough and the parties were, obviously, not good enough for those who might have been. Then there were the Sunday dinners with great-uncles and aunts sometimes in attendance, full of open ill will about who had the most money, or who spent it too lavishly, who would inherit what, which had bought what rug that would last forever, who what jewel she would best have been without. It was a corporation meeting, with my grandmother unexpectedly in the position of vice-chairman. The chairman was her brother Jake, the only human being to whom I ever saw her defer. Early, I told myself that was because he was richer than she was, and did something called managing her money. But that was too simple: he was a man of great force, given, as she was given, to breaking the spirit of people for the pleasure of the exercise. But he was also witty and rather worldly, seeing his own financial machinations as natural not only to his but to the country's benefit, and seeing that as comic. (I had only one real contact with my Uncle Jake: when I graduated from school at fifteen, he gave me a ring that I took to a 59th Street hock shop, got twenty-five dollars, and bought books. I went immediately to tell him what I'd done, deciding, I think, that day that the break had to come. He stared at me for a long time, and then he laughed and said the words I later used in *The Little Foxes:* "So you've got spirit after all. Most of the rest of them are made of sugar water.")

But that New York apartment where we visited several times a week, the summer cottage where we went for a visit each year as the poor daughter and granddaughter, made me into an angry child and forever caused in me a wild extravagance mixed with respect for money and those who have it. The respectful periods were full of self-hatred and during them I always made my worst mistakes. But after *The Little Foxes* was written and put away, this conflict was to grow less important, as indeed, the picture of my mother's family was to grow dim and almost fade away.

It was not unnatural that my first love went to my father's family. He and his two sisters were free, generous, funny. But as I made my mother's family all one color, I made my father's family too remarkable, and then turned both extreme judgments against my mother.

In fact, she was a sweet eccentric, the only middle-class woman I have ever known who had not rejected the middle class — that would have been an act of will — but had skipped it altogether. She liked a simple life and simple people, and would have been happier, I think, if she had stayed in the backlands of Alabama riding wild on the horses she so often talked about, not so lifelong lonely for the black men and women who had taught her the only religion she ever knew. I didn't know what she was saying, when she moved her lips in a Baptist church or a Catholic cathedral or, less often, in a synagogue, but it was obvious that God could be found anywhere, because several times a week we would stop in a church, any church, and she seemed to be at home in all of them.

But simple natures can also be complex, and that is difficult for a child, who wants all grown people to be sharply one thing or another. I was puzzled and irritated by the passivity of my mother as it mixed with an unmovable stubbornness. (My father had not been considered a proper husband for a rich and pretty girl, but my mother's deep fear of her mother did not override her deep love for my father, although the same fear kept my two aunts from ever marrying and my uncle from marrying until after his mother's death.)

Mama seemed to do only what my father wanted, and yet we lived the way my mother wanted us to live. She deeply wanted to keep my father and to please him, but no amount of protest from him could alter the strange quirks that Freud already knew about. Windows, doors and stoves haunted her and she would often stand before them for as long as half an hour, or leaving the house, would insist upon returning to it while we waited for her in any weather. And sad, middle-aged ladies would be brought home from a casual meeting on a park bench to fill the living room with woe: plain tales of sickness, or poverty, or loneliness in the afternoon often led to their staying on for dinner with my bored father.

I remember a time when our apartment was being painted and the week it was supposed to take stretched into three because one of the two painters, a small, sickly man with an Italian accent, soon found that my mother was a sympathetic listener. He would, in duty, climb the ladder at nine in the morning but by eleven he was sitting on the sofa with the tale of the bride who died in childbirth, the child still in Italy, his mother who ailed and half starved in Tuscany, the nights in New York where he knew nobody to eat with or talk to. After lunch, cooked by our bad-tempered Irish lady, and served to him by my mother to hide the bad temper, he would climb the ladder again and paint for a few hours while my mother urged him to stop work and go for a nice day in the sunshine. Once, toward the end of the long job — the other painter never returned after the first few days — I came home carrying books from the library, annoyed to find the painter in my favorite chair. As I stood in the doorway, frowning at my mother, the painter said, "Your girl. How old?"

"Fifteen," said my mother.

"In Italy, not young, fifteen. She is healthy?"

"Very healthy," said my mother. "Her generation has larger feet than we did."

"I think about it," said the painter. "I let you know."

I knew my mother didn't understand what he meant because she smiled and nodded in the way she always did when her mind had wandered, but I was angry and told my father about it at dinner. He laughed and I left the table, but later he told my mother that the painter was not to come to the house again. A few years later when I brought home for dinner an aimless, handsome young man who got roaring drunk and insisted upon climbing down the building from our eighth-floor apartment, my father, watching him from the window, said, ''Perhaps we should try to find that Italian house painter.'' My mother was dead for five years before I knew that I had loved her very much.

My mother's childbearing had been dangerously botched by a fashionable doctor in New Orleans, and forever after she stood in fear of going through it again, and so I was an only child. (Twenty-one years later, when I was married and pregnant, she was as frightened for me, and unashamedly happy when I lost the child.) I was thirty-four years old, after two successful plays, and fourteen or fifteen years of heavy drinking in a nature that wasn't comfortable with anarchy, when a doctor told me about the lifelong troubles of an only child. Most certainly I needed a doctor to reveal for me the violence and disorder of my life, but I had always known about the powers of an only child. I was not meaner or more ungenerous or more unkind than other children, but I was off balance in a world where I knew my grand importance to two other people who certainly loved me for myself, but who also liked to use me against each other. I don't think they knew they did that, because most of it was affectionate teasing between them, but somehow I knew early that my father's jokes about how much my mother's family liked money, how her mother had crippled her own children, my grandmother's desire to think of him — and me — as strange vagabonds of no property value, was more than teasing. He wished to win me to his side, and he did. He was a handsome man, witty, high-tempered, proud, and — although I guessed very young I was not to be certain until much later — with a number of other women in his life. Thus his attacks on Mama's family were not always for the reasons claimed.

When I was about six years old my father lost my mother's large dowry. We moved to New York and were shabby poor until my father finally settled for a life as a successful traveling salesman. It was in those years that we went back to New Orleans to stay with my father's sisters for six months each year. I was thus moved from school in New York to school in New Orleans without care for the season or the quality of the school. This constant need for adjustment in two very different worlds made formal education into a kind of frantic tennis game, sometimes played with children whose strokes had force and brilliance, sometimes with those who could barely hold the racket. Possibly it is the reason I never did well in school or in college, and why I wanted to be left alone to read by myself. I had found, very early, that any other test found me bounding with ease and grace over one fence to fall on my face as I ran towards the next.

LINDA THOM: AN OLYMPIC CHAMPION

The 1984 summer Olympics in Los Angeles were tailor-made for Carleton alumna, Linda Thom, BJ/67.

The Olympics featured for the first time ever, a women's pistol competition, the event that propelled Linda's name onto the headlines of Canada.

With her gold-medal-winning shot, Linda became legend.

She was the first woman in history to win an Olympic shooting competition; the first Canadian to win a gold medal in a pistol event (shooting events have always been held for men in the modern Olympics); the first Canadian to win a gold medal at the 1984 Games; the first gold-medallist for Canada since 1968 (when the Equestrian team won in Mexico); the first Canadian individual to win a gold medal since shooter Gerry Ouellet won the prone rifle event in 1956; and the first Canadian woman to win a gold medal in the summer games since 1928.

"I call them 'My Olympics' because so many things came true for me," she says. "It was like a Hollywood script."

The road to Olympic fame began for Linda back in the 1960s. Her father had been a competitive rifle shooter in his youth in Great Britain before immigrating to Canada, and she herself took up pistol shooting in 1969.

She quickly became a member of the Canadian national team, and competed internationally. Between 1972 and 1975, while living in Paris where her husband Donald was posted, she shot with the Paris police team, travelling with them to competitions in France and other European countries.

In Paris, she also earned a Grand Diplôme from the Cordon Bleu Cooking School, and the "Certificate d'Aptitude Professionelle en cuisine" granted by the French government.

Upon returning to Ottawa, she turned her attention to a highly successful catering business and to raising two children, born in 1976 and 1978. Then in 1980, while visiting Calgary, she learned that the women's pistol competition would be included in the 1984 Olympics.

It took a lot of lobbying to get the women's pistol competition in the 1984 games, she says. "The Olympic Committee has more than 200 events and 10,000 athletes to put through their paces in two weeks and is loathe to increase the number of events."

Although women used to be eligible to compete alongside men in Olympic shooting, not having separate events was a big barrier, she says, and only 10 women had ever managed to participate in the history of the games.

"I had wanted to compete in the Olympics since I was a child," she said, "so you can imagine how delighted I was by the news."

Linda came back to Ottawa to talk to her husband about getting involved in the Olympics ("He backed me all the way, right from the start") before committing herself to the training program.

It took her two years to get organized and save enough money before she could train seriously. "We were self-funded then," she says. "I had to get to the competitions . . . we didn't have a car at the time . . . I had to save to buy one. There were expenses for travel, meals, ammunition, equipment, all that sort of thing."

The financial burden became easier once she became a 'carded' athlete, partly funded by Sport Canada.

In addition to practice on the range, she says, training involved strengthening her shoulders through weight training and an exercise holding the pistol, aerobics, stretching, and mental exercises to develop positive thinking.

"I had not been in international competition for quite some time," she recalls. "It took a lot of training."

The Olympics themselves were "pretty fantastic" she says.

"It was the realization of a lifetime dream for me, and I certainly wasn't disappointed. There was a psychological boost at every turn. The atmosphere was tremendous because the entire Olympic team had a lot of confidence and self-assurance. Canadian athletes were there to do their personal best and were determined to achieve their goals. The feeling was so strong, it was practically tangible."

She says she knew she would win the Gold medal before she won it.

"I had a really good feeling," she recalls. "When my coach announced there would be a shoot-off for the medal, I knew I would win it. I had made up my mind. That's all there was to it.

"Pressure is something you put on yourself. Having said that, I have to admit that my heart was going like a trip hammer during the shoot-off. But I had a very positive attitude, a great deal of control, and was very determined . . . It carried me through."

The things most memorable to her about the games, she says, are "First, winning the gold medal; second, being told, and coming to realize, I was an inspiration for the Canadian team; and third, carrying the Canadian flag in the closing ceremonies."

She also notes with pride that the shooting team as a whole did very well, with solid placing in several events.

Since the games, she says public attitude to the sport has changed.

"A lot more people realize it is a recreational sport, not just for policemen and army types," she says. "It's a sophisticated, technical, stylized form of shooting, that has as much to do with combat as archery, javelin throwing, shotput, or any one of a number of similar events."

Her life now is very hectic, she says.

"I haven't been able to take up my catering business again. I've been in demand for appearances all over the place. I'm also trying to promote shooting as much as I can, to get sponsors for the team and for myself.

"The problem is, if you get too busy, sometimes your health fails."

In fact, she says she was ill for five weeks over the winter. ("I find it difficult to say no, but I'm learning there are some things that have to go on the back burner for a while.")

In addition to her public appearances, Linda is writing a cookbook and continuing to train and compete in shooting matches.

"Shooting is one of the sports you can pursue over a career," she says. And it comes as no surprise when she confirms that she has her sights set on the 1988 summer Olympics in Seoul, South Korea.

ALUMNI NEWS

PROFILE

GREG HOLLYER (student)

This profile accompanies an application for a part-time job.

I am a 23 year old male currently attending Queen's University in Kingston, Ontario. This school year marks the last of a four-year program in engineering geophysics. Last summer I was employed as a research assistant doing lab and field work aimed at the prediction and prevention of mine cave-ins. This on-the-job experience helped me get a feel for the career I have chosen to pursue.

At present, my interests are largely centred around campus life, in which I play an active part. Academically, I am involved in the branch of geology known as geophysics which endeavours to characterize the physical properties of the earth for exploration (petroleum and mineral) and civil engineering purposes.

Extracurricular activities include writing columns for a campus newspaper, being Queen's editor of *Project Magazine* (a national student engineering magazine) and writing and editing a geology departmental newsletter. I also enjoy participating in hockey, baseball, and football at the intramural level.

My interests outside the university include reading (especially 20th century fiction), following current events and politics, and camping in isolated areas. I enjoy a well-rounded life, part of which I hope will someday include writing an obscure novel and raising a family.

6. THE DIARY OR JOURNAL

Key Work:
   "The Vintage Time" — Lawrence Durrell
Associated Reading:
   "Excerpt from *Willie: A Romance*" — Heather Robertson

A diary or journal, unlike the letter, allows the writer to express private emotions and reactions that might otherwise never be expressed, let alone shared. For this reason, some people feel journal-keeping is a healthy form of self-expression. Some individuals make regular notations in their diaries and record intimate details of their lives and relationships with others; therefore, they may stipulate that their reflections cannot be published for a number of years after their death. But even people who do not normally keep a journal may do so to record special experiences such as travel to a foreign land.

The diary's style and tone may be more personal and informal than other forms of the essay; unless the writer plans to publish the work, expression usually remains spontaneous and unpolished. The thesis may appear more as a point of view or orientation than as a clear statement of intent. Unless the diaries are published, the only audience is the writer. In these ways, they differ from their close relative, the autobiography.

For the student researching the past, certain published diaries may be an invaluable tool. Whether the writer is a famous scientist like Marie Curie, an important historical figure like Mackenzie King, or an artist or literary personality like Lawrence Durrell, readers may catch a glimpse of another side of their personalities. These revelations may shed new light on their work.

BEFORE READING

■ Do you keep a journal or diary? How might this habit benefit your expression?
■ Make a mental list of your images of an exotic country.
■ If you could travel anywhere in the world, where would you go? Why?

THE VINTAGE TIME

LAWRENCE DURRELL

> *'No tongue: all eyes: be silent.'*
> The Tempest

Somewhere between Calabria and Corfu the blue really begins. All the way across Italy you find yourself moving through a landscape severely domesticated — each valley laid out after the architect's pattern, brilliantly lighted, human. But once you strike out from the flat and desolate Calabrian mainland towards the sea, you are aware of a change in the heart of things: aware of the horizon beginning to stain at the rim of the world: aware of *islands* coming out of the darkness to meet you.

In the morning you wake to the taste of snow on the air, and climbing the companion-ladder, suddenly enter the penumbra of shadow cast by the Albanian mountains — each wearing its cracked crown of snow — desolate and repudiating stone.

A peninsula nipped off while red hot and allowed to cool into an antarctica of lava. You are aware not so much of a landscape coming to meet you invisibly over those blue miles of water as of a climate. You enter Greece as one might enter a dark crystal; the form of things becomes irregular, refracted. Mirages suddenly swallow islands, and wherever you look the trembling curtain of the atmosphere deceives.

Other countries may offer you discoveries in manners or lore or landscape; Greece offers you something harder — the discovery of yourself.

20.9.38

Riding southward in the spluttering bus from Kouloura to Ypso at the end of a bright September you can feel the altered accent in things — for the vintage is beginning. Everywhere the turtle-doves are calling in the arbours and orchards; and washed by the brilliant sunlight the whole coast glitters and expands under the swinging blows of the waves. The bay is alive with sails glowing in their many colours, and the atmosphere is so clear that one can see, miles away, the distinct figures of friends holding sails and tillers; my brother's boat *Dugong* lies just off Agni, heading for the house. I can see his characteristic pose, legs stretched out, head on one side and eyes closed against the smoke of his cigarette. He has stowed his guns in their leather cases under the half-decking where the faithful Spiro sits scanning the horizon for something to shoot at. *Dugong* slaps and yaws as she meets the small race of water thrown back, yellow and curdled, from the Butrinto Estuary. He will be sorry to miss us on his way up to the northern lake Antiniotissa ('Enemy of youth') where he is after quail and woodcock.

As we move slowly down from the dead lands the road becomes more and more precipitous, and the green valley comes up at us in a trembling wave of fronds and branches. We roar through several small hamlets, scattering smoke and stones. A woman stands frowsily at her door and empties coffee grounds upon the stones. Two children sit under a bench playing with a tortoise. A policeman shouts something unintelligible. The bus is crammed with peasants going to market, and the air in it smells almost inflammable with garlic and exhaust fumes. Father Nicholas and his son sit just behind us. He has finally conquered his prejudice against southern women, and they are on their way to try and arrange a match with the Gastouri girl whom we had seen at the Kastellani dance. Father Nicholas is in great voice and keeps the whole bus in a roar of laughter. Our feet rest upon a fluttering floor of chickens, all tied by the legs in bunches, like vegetables. His son looks rather ashamed of himself. It is not altogether restful, this journey. At each of Father Nicholas's jests the driver lets off a peal of laughter in a high piping voice and, letting go his hold upon the wheel, hugs himself with extravagant joy. At these moments the bus shows signs of wanting to mount the stone parapet of the road and fly down into the valley. This tendency is corrected at the last moment, when all except the hardiest travellers have commended themselves to St. Spiridion and flung one arm across their eyes. With prodigious roaring and scraping of brakes we rattle down the mountain like some iron cockroach, and draw up at last in clouds of dust, before the little tavern at the crossroads where Spiro had already parked his great Dodge under the olives, and is busy arguing about the price of wine with the innkeeper.

We sit for a while over a glass of wine with him. He gives us the gossip of the town in his wonderful Brooklyn argot — strange fragments of words with whole syllables discarded from them when they are beyond his pronunciation. Spiro's noble stomach reposes comfortably on his knees. His forearms are covered in a black pelt of hair. He is sweating easily and comfortably from every pore. In the dark shadow thrown by the trees, with the red reflections of the tablecloth playing about his dark, good-natured face, he reminds me of nothing so much as a great drop of olive oil. He informs us, with self-importance mixed with a certain shame, that a fire broke out the previous afternoon at a garage. As one of the firemen he had had his first practical experience of fire-fighting. On the whole the affair had been rather a scandal. The brigade had arrived in good time, clinging importantly to the new fire-engine which the Government had provided, each in his gleaming helmet. Spiro himself had arrived, but riding majestically in his own car, with his helmet on. The garage was well alight. The balconies of the surrounding houses were thronged with sightseers, waiting to see the recently formed Fire Brigade prove itself in its first baptism of fire. All went well. While the hose was being uncoiled, the Chief of Police made a short but incisive speech exhorting everyone to stay calm and not to give way to panic. The fire hydrant was unlocked and everything placed in position to extinguish the blaze. At this point, however, a disgraceful argument broke out as to who was going to hold the nozzle of the hose. Words became gestures. Gestures became acts. A push here, a scuffle there, and riot had broken out. A struggling mass of firemen began to fight for possession of the nozzle. At this point the hose bulged and began to emit a creditable jet of water, and what was to be a baptism of fire became a baptism of water for the onlookers. A slowly rotating fountain of water moved across the square. The Minister for the Interior, who had been standing innocently on his balcony in heliotrope pyjamas, was all but swept into the street by the force of the jet. Women screamed. The long-averted panic against which the Chief of Police had warned them broke out. The affair ended with a baton charge and a number of arrests. The garage was left to burn itself out. The engine was driven home in disgrace by a civilian. And Spiro tendered his resignation.

Driving easily across the low hills where the vineyards have already taken on their ochre tones, he seems a little hurt that we find the story funny. 'It's not a good thing', he tells N. repeatedly, 'for the nation when the bastards do that.'

We sweep up the long drive and round to the side of the house. The Count is sitting at the edge of the orchard, under a tree, reading with his dogs beside him. He is clad in pyjamas and a straw hat. He waves his hand and signals us to cross the sunlight-dappled walks.

'Ah! you will forgive my pyjamas,' he says. 'The others have not arrived yet. I am half drunk just reading through Mazziari's description of the grapes. Come, let us take our pick.'

The vineyards are already beginning to look gutted and burnt out with shrivelling leaves. The Count walks ahead with us stopping here and there in all the profusion to clip a bunch of grapes with his scissors, which he carries tied round his waist on a piece of string. 'Ah, my dear, where have you ever seen such plenty?' he says. Indeed the variety is astonishing. 'We will ignore these plump ones with the thick skins. But try these violet coloured ones. You may find them too sweet. We have had three days' torture preparing for the gathering. So many extra mouths to feed. Plasterers, treaders, and whatnot hanging about the house.' The great doors of the magazine are ajar. The huge vats and butts have been dragged out into the meadow for caulking and patching. Under a tree a small army of men is at work upon them. Some have been turned upon logs, and are being filled with gravel and water, before being rolled. Others are being mended and scoured. 'The big one in the corner,' says the Count, 'she is the one you have to thank for the crimson robola wine which you think so good — and which even Zarian likes.'

The shadow of the cottage-pergolas seems rich with the scent of grapes — of blunt sweet muscatel and lisabetta. Ourania cuts down heavy clumps of them for the table, holding them in her brown arms and smiling. They are covered in a rich misty bloom still.

Meanwhile across the orchard the Count is in full voice: 'The little amber ones and those which look ice-green and closely packed — they have done very well this year. Farther on we shall see the *rhoditi*. They run blood-red when the sun shines through them; coral rather, like the lobe of an ear. Dear me, we shall all have indigestion. Ah! Here comes the Doctor and Zarian — beyond the olive-trees there. And his wife. Zarian looks extremely puffed as usual. And Nimiec.'

By lunch-time the rest of the guests have arrived, and are seated at tables laid under the arbour which bounds the last terrace. A tremendous meal has been prepared, and three of the prettiest village girls are there to serve it. Zarian openly bemoans having brought his pleasant American wife with him. 'Where do you keep these beauties?' he asks. They are never here when we come alone.'

'They would distract us perhaps,' says the Count seriously. The crimson *robola* is passed round. Each pours a drop upon the ground before drinking — the peasant libation. The grounds are swarming with workmen to prepare for to-morrow's picking.

'This year we are going to begin on the hill there. It should be specially good, this year's *robola*. I feel it in my bones. We shall call it, I think, Prospero's Wine. What do you say?'

The valley curves away below the arbour with its delicately curved panels of landscape. From the orchard a guitar strikes up, and after a few moments' hesitation the sound of voices — the men's deep and rough, the women's high and shrill as herring-gulls'. The gatherers have arrived in the hope of an extra day's work. The faint crack of guns sounds in the valley. A puff of smoke here and there marks a sportsman with a muzzle-loader shooting doves. The conversation wells up in waves — overstepping the boundaries of language. The vintage holiday has begun.

Lunch prolonged unconscionably becomes tea. Some of us wander away to bathe or sleep out the long hot afternoon. By nightfall the gang of workmen have done their job, and the vine-vats are ready. They sit upon doorsteps or on the grass among the olive-trees, eating their frugal meal of bread and fruit. But wine there is in plenty for them.

At the end of the terrace Zarian lies majestically sleeping in a hammock, while his wife pauses from her reading at intervals to brush a fly off his face. Theodore and Nimiec have disappeared on a journey of exploration with N.

The Count is pottering round the magazine in his pyjamas giving orders in a peremptory voice to his overseers. 'To-morrow we shall start on the *robola* vat,' he says, and gives orders for it to be moved out of the shadow into the angle of the wall where the sunlight strikes. 'Niko is going to come and do the treading. I can always trust him.' Niko is a slim young man, dressed in a dark suit, who holds his hat modestly in his hand as he hears the Count speak. 'If we put all the women on to the vineyard at once we should have the first vat gathered by sundown to-morrow. Niko can begin at dusk.' His face is radiant and empty of preoccupation. Meanwhile the cellars must be tidied, the magazines dusted and all vanishable goods removed beyond the reach of the pickers' temptation. Ourania is filling the bowls with flowers — autumn crocus and cyclamen from the walls of the vineyards. Donkeys unload mounds of red tomatoes at the outhouse and everywhere the brisk sound of bargaining goes on. Caroline is playing patience upon the balcony, stopping from time to time to pop a grape into her mouth. 'We cannot complain,' says the Count. 'It will be a lovely vintage. We can start Niko off to-morrow. We might bathe to-night. We can use the car. I see that Spiro has stayed on with us. It's bad for trade but he can't bear to miss a party.'

The sound of singing is beaten out thin upon the late afternoon air. I can hear Spiro's bass notes sounding like the eructations of a giant. The Count sits for a while on the garden wall with one slipper off and lights a cigarette. 'And perhaps we shall have an engage-ment or something to remind us that we are getting old men.' Caroline pretends she does not hear.

Bocklin has brought his flute. Its quaint twirls and flourishes sound unearthly on the empty lawns where the nymph stands. The Count walks slowly down the garden path. 'There is going to be a war, of course. But on days like this one feels that it will go on for ever — I mean this lovely lambent weather: no sense of time, except that the fruit upon our tables changes. By the way, figs are in. Let us hope they will outlive your foreign policy, my dear boy. I see you have been reading Mackenzie. It will be just the same. The Royalists will let us down all the way along. Don't you see that Nimiec and Caroline are falling in love with each other? There is that subtle unspoken polarity of feeling you can see when they are together. They both know it will happen. They both know that the other knows. They both avoid each other's company. And yet the invisi-ble cobweb is drawing tighter. That is happiness — the certainty and inevitability of an attraction like that. It remains for the lock to turn on the event and already it is spoiled. They have had a hundred opportunities to confess themselves — and there he is walking round with the Doctor, holding his test-tubes, while she sits and plays patience and imagines that she does not want him to come and find her there. You know, there is no philosophic compensation for growing beyond the reach of love — that is the one wall one never breaks through. To think that *that* will never happen again. That *that* moment, the germinating half-second during which you recognize your completement in someone else, will never happen again. . . . Any of the peasant girls would supply the physical simulacrum of the event. Ah, but the thing itself is gone. Let us have a glass of wine, shall we? It's thirsty work talking like a Norman Douglas character. Caroline, have a glass of wine with us and let me tell your fortune.'

Just after dawn the cries of the pickers wake us. The grass is still heavy with dew and the sun not yet above the trees. A long line of coloured women are setting forth for the vineyard with their baskets. Mark and Peter are the overseers, and they follow with lordly strides behind them smoking and talking, proud in their blue smocks and straw hats. Spiro follows with the brindled puppy. As we watch the procession the window below us opens and the Count puts his head out to cheer them with some parting pleasantry. The early breakfast daunts everyone but Zarian, who has eaten himself into a state of feverish indigestion and cannot sleep. Spiro sits on the terrace, cap in hand, and prophesies a sunny day in the voice of such heartiness that Zarian becomes all at once quite peevish. The Count, having reassured himself that the pickers have set out to gather the favourite *robola* vineyard, sleeps on for a couple of hours.

By mid-morning we are all up on the hillock overlooking the vineyard, surrounding our pyjama'd host like staff officers watching a battle. On the brilliant dappled sunlight of the slopes below the women have put on their wimples and are moving with swift grace from shrub to shrub, cutting the long branches with their sickle knives — branches of crimson *robola* which drop in their baskets with the weight of human limbs.

In the shade of an olive cloths have been spread, and here the women converge, each with her blooming basket load. Two donkeys with panniers stand by apathetically, flicking flies with their tails. Everything goes with a terrific pace for this the first day of picking and the Count himself is looking on.

Presently, when the Count has been reassured as to the picking, we retire to the arbours by the house to drink coffee and pass the long morning in idle talk. Bocklin plays his flute. And gradually, by journeys, the donkeys bring in the fruit which is emptied into the great wooden vat under the careful eyes of Niko himself. The Count cannot sit still until he has supervised everything himself, and seen everything with his own eyes. 'Niko is a wonderful boy,' he says. 'Don't think that any oaf can tread wine. No, he is pure as island water. Don't imagine that the wine-treader doesn't transform the wine with his feet — that there isn't a communication I mean between his style and technique and state of soul and the response of the fruit. It's an aesthetic performance. No, Doctor. It is no use you smiling in that ironical scientific manner. We could easily use a machine-treader and you would soon see what sort of wine my *robola* had become. Niko treads a part of himself into the vat. He is an angel on earth. Ah! dear me. How over-exotic one sounds when one translates from Greek to English.'

By four o'clock the vat is heaped full and from the sheer black weight of the fruit the must has begun to force the crude spigot. The Count is extremely excited, for it is the moment to begin the treading. Niko has been standing in the trough by the well, washing himself in the icy water. Now he advances to the vat, clad only in a white shirt which is knotted at the thighs. His pale face looks remote and far-away as he hoists himself up. His white feet dangle for a second in the sunlight and vanish. The Count is hoarse with emotion. 'You remember everything now,' he says nervously. 'The old way — as you have done it always.' Niko does not answer. He smiles, as if at some remembered joke, and nods. Gently moving his feet he begins by treading a small hole to stand in and begins to work into it the grapes piled above the rim.

The spigot is now uncorked and the must begins to come out in an opaque crimson spurt. This beautiful colour stains the trough, lacquers the tin measure, and stabs the shadows of the magazine with splashes of red. Keeping the same tireless pace Niko labours deeper and ever deeper into the great vat until by the latest dusk his white face has quite vanished into the depths and only his two crimson grape-splashed hands can be seen holding the edges of the vat. He perches himself up every now and again and rests, hanging his head like a bird. He has become almost intoxicated himself by the fumes of the must, and by the long six-hour routine of his treading — which ends at ten o'clock. His face looks pale and sleepy in the red light of the lanterns. Mark encourages him with gruff pleasantries as he measures the must back into the vat. Since the wine is red the skins and stalks are left in. Now the huge wooden lid, weighted with stones, is floated upon the top, and by to-morrow morning all the leavings will have risen up under it into a scarlet froth of crust, from under which the liquid will be crackling with fermentation. For ten days now the fermentation will go on, sending its acid smell on the gusts of wind from the meadow, into the bedrooms of the great house.

Now that the *robola* is safely on the way, the Count can turn his attention to the kitchens with their gleaming copper ware and dungeon-like ovens. Here he busies himself with Caroline and Mrs. Zarian in the manufacture of *mustalevria* — that delicious Ionian sweet or jelly which is made by boiling fresh must to half its bulk with semolina and a little spice. The paste is left to cool on plates and stuck with almonds; and the whole either eaten fresh or cut up in slices and put away in the great store cupboard.

Sykopita, Zarian's favourite fig cake, will come later when the autumn figs are literally bursting open with their own ripeness. But for the time being there are conserves of all kinds to be made — orange-flower preserve and morella syrup. While the Count produces for the table a very highly spiced quince cheese, black and sticky, but very good.

The ravished vineyards are a sad sight on the brown earth of the property. The Count pauses from time to time in his passage between the kitchen and the dining-room terrace to contemplate them. He is happy with the full weight of his resignation: because October is coming with its first sweep of rain and mist. The remaining vine-leaves and fig-leaves — strange butterfly-like shapes against the massive platinum-grey trunks — will be gathered for fodder. The earth will die shabbily and dully in russet patches, tessellating the landscape with its red squares and octagons. In November the cleaning of guns, the first wood fires, and the putting away of summer clothes. Then the earth will spin inexorably into winter with its gales and storms — the wild duck screaming from Albania, the seas shrieking and whistling off the barren northern point beyond Turtle-Dove Island.

These few days pass in a calm so absolute, that to regret their passing would be unworthy of them. Zarian is bound for Geneva next week. Nimiec for Poland until next spring.

We picnic for supper on these warm nights by the Myrtiotissa monastery. Spiro lights a fire of pine-branches and twigs, and the three wicker hampers of the Count are brimmed with food and drink. In the immense volume of the sea's breathing our voices are restored to their true proportion — insignificant, small and shrill with a happiness this landscape allows us but does not notice. The firelight etches the faces so clearly. The Count with his bright eyes looking over N.'s shoulder as she draws. Theodore's golden beard lowered over a pool in complete abstraction. Nimiec and Caroline walking with linked fingers into the sea. Zarian's lips shiny with wine, his silver scruff of hair flying like a halo round his head. Spiro's great charred features. Everyone. The night around us edges slowly on towards the morning, silent except for the noise of the sea, and the sleepy chirp of cicadas in the plane-tree who have mistaken our fire for sunlight. 'You have noticed how we talk less and less together as the days go on,' says the Count. 'It is not because we have less to say to each other, it is because language becomes inadequate to our parting. I do not know when we shall meet again. Will you all be back by next spring I wonder?'

It is already very late, and the donkeys have stumbled off home with the hampers. Theodore lies asleep in the firelight. His lips move slowly. Zarian has taken the guitar from Bocklin and has started to play it inexpertly. He is trying to find the key for the little island song which Theodore has taught us.

> 'Sea, you youth-swallower,
> O poison-bearing element, Sea,
> Who make our island folk
> Always be wearing their black clothes.

> Have you not had enough of it,
> Sea, in all this long time,
> With the bodies you have swallowed
> Down in your insatiable waves?'

Presently Theodore will wake and ask Caroline to sing 'Greensleeves' and 'Early One Morning' — airs sounding in all that emptiness so Lydian and remote coming from those American lips with their limping southern drawl.

To-morrow we are separating.

1.1.41

A postcard from the Count: 'Christmas Day. I spent it alone in happy memory of the year before when we walked across the northern marshes and you were attacked by a wounded hare — remember? To remind myself (and hence you also) of our perpetual spring I gathered a bunch of flowers from the valley — flowers from every season. Cyclamen and snowdrop. February's irises and a jonquil, cinquefoil, bugloss, corn marigold, orange blossom, clover, and wild roses. Spiro has asked one of his pilots to fly them to you so you will have them by now. They are my invitation for next year. Don't forget us.'

EXPLORING THE DIARY

1. As you read this diary extract, practise annotating your book. This process can sometimes replace note-taking, because you create explanatory notes, critical comments and an "instant" summary of the content. During class or seminar discussions, it becomes simpler to find discussion points and make relevant additions. The act of annotation forces attentive reading and thinking. Individuals develop their own annotating styles; however, here are some ideas to help you begin.

   ■ Using a highlighter pen, mark the thesis statement and the key phrases in each paragraph's topic sentence. Or underline these points in a coloured pen or pencil.

- In the margin beside each paragraph, write one word or a brief phrase which summarizes the content or remarks in point form.
    - See the tips about note-taking in Part C for suggested short forms.
2. Durrell begins the book from which this diary passage is extracted with the verse:

> "A Greekish isle, and the most pleasant place that ever our eyes beheld for the exercise of a solitary and contemplative life. . . . In our travels many times, falling into dangers and unpleasant places, this only island would be the place where we would wish ourselves to end our lives."
>
> Anthony Sherley, *His Persian Adventures*, 1601

   (a) How does this verse help set the tone of the book, judging from the excerpt you have read?
   (b) Does Durrell appear to have selected an apt verse? Give reasons.
3. What changing visual impressions strike Durrell as he travels through Italy to Greece?
4. Why does Durrell go to Ypso?
5. Show how Durrell conveys a sense of movement and change in paragraphs 3 and 4 in the entry dated 20.9.38.
6. (a) Select examples of literary devices and interesting phrases Durrell uses to create a sense of local colour.
   (b) Evaluate the success with which each is used.
7. Durrell describes a number of people he encounters. How do these characterizations help to convey Durrell's enjoyment of these experiences?
8. What does the dialogue in the entry contribute to the portrait Durrell is drawing?
9. Diaries are often edited and adapted before publication. If you had to shorten the excerpt from Durrell's journal by one-third, what revisions could you make and still retain the integrity of the piece?

EXTENSIVE STUDY

1. Durrell's writing style is highly impressionistic and sensual.
   (a) For what formats and audiences would this language be inappropriate? Why?
   (b) Of the works you have studied in this text, whose style does Durrell's most resemble? Justify your decision.
2. In your class discussions of this or other essays, have you observed any examples of culturally biased or stereotyped thinking? If so, give examples.
3. Account for the fact that some people become very attached to a

particular place. What, if anything, do these personal attachments reflect about our personalities?

4. Read the accompanying "Excerpt from *Willie: A Romance*" by Heather Robertson. Compare King's and Durrell's diary excerpts, using the following headings: preoccupations, revelations about the writers' personalities, use of language and the tone achieved, and intended audience.

5. If you have read Dilworth's "Foreword to *Klee Wyck*" (see The Foreword, Prologue and Preface, page 197), compare the poetic quality of the passages quoted from Emily Carr's work with the language used in Durrell's diary excerpt. (Durrell has published a number of poetry collections.) Which style do you prefer? Why?

6. If you have read Conrad's letter to his Aunt (see The Letter, page 129), compare Durrell's and Conrad's reactions to foreign environments. What do their different reactions suggest about their characters?

THE WRITING FOLDER

1. In an impressionistic passage about a place you have visited or know well, attempt to capture the poetic quality of Durrell's style. Use diary or letter format. Specify your audience (e.g., private diary not to be published or a letter to a friend or the newspaper).

2. Assume the role of a contributing editor to the travel section of a newspaper with which you are familiar. Write a column about the city (or area) you were sent to review. Your purpose is to acquaint your readers with the flavour of your experience. Use the journalistic style found in this newspaper. Specify your audience (e.g., a mass circulation tabloid or a newspaper read by influential people).

3. Assume the role of someone travelling in a foreign country very unlike Canada. Write a series of "postcards" for a variety of people about an unusual experience.

4. Write a dialogue between a couple honeymooning in a foreign country. One of them is enjoying the cultural differences, but the other wants to go home.

5. Write a poem that captures the spirit of Durrell's experience in Greece.

INDEPENDENT STUDY

1. Research the type of review articles that appear in *The New York Review of Books*. Read two travel books by a famous author. Write a review article similar in audience and purpose. Link the works in terms of themes, approaches, and revelations about the writer's personality, attitudes, and interests. The oral component of the project might take

the form of a taped reading of your review prepared for radio
broadcast.   ++

2. Read D.H. Lawrence's *Twilight in Italy.* Compare the themes and
   preoccupations with those in one of his fictional works such as *Sons
   and Lovers* or *Women in Love.*   ++

3. Read two works, one by Ernest Hemingway and one by Graham
   Greene, that are set in exotic countries. Examine the influence of
   setting on the theme and plot. If you are studying either of these
   writers in class, you might prepare a brief seminar on one aspect of
   your research.   ++

4. Read one of *The Diaries of Anaïs Nin* and a journal by another famous
   person. Develop a specific comparative topic with your teacher.   ++

5. After reading one or two of the travel books, write a short story in
   which the setting reflects your reading. The conflict should arise from
   a situation derived from the setting. Accompany your short story with
   a written or taped analysis of the links between the book(s) you read
   and your short story.   + or ++

6. Read Heather Robertson's fictionalized interpretation of William Lyon
   Mackenzie's life, *Willie: A Romance. Volume One of the King Years.*
   Then read an historical account that deals with the same time period
   in King's life. Develop a specific comparative project with your
   teacher. (You might, for example, write a major review article in which
   you consider the merits and weaknesses of each work.)   ++

7. For further ideas you might read travel studies such as:
   D.H. Lawrence, *Mornings in Mexico* and *Etruscan Places*
   Lawrence Durrell, *Bitter Lemons*
   M.F.K. Fisher, *Two Towns in Provence*
   Karen Blixen, *Out of Africa*
   Margaret Laurence, *The Prophet's Camel Bell*
   Gerald Durrell, *My Family and Other Animals*
   Alan Moorehead, *The Blue Nile*

TIMED READING AND WRITING

1. Write an essay in the time specified by your teacher, using one of
   these opening sentences.

   If I could spend a year travelling in any country, I think it would
   be . . .

   I'd rather spend my summer at the cottage than travel around
   foreign cities.

   Yes, there's some place I'd rather be!

2. Write a descriptive sketch of a place you've visited and found
   enjoyable or unpleasant.

3. Use twelve of these randomly selected words in an essay related to travel or another idea raised by Durrell's essay. You may change the verb tenses and parts of speech.

   journey, experience, stranger, ancient, reflection, sadness, supreme, evaporate, infinite, reaction, encounter, recapture, baffle, dream, symbol, elusive, liberty, exotic, exult, reflect, memory, language, water.

   Title the essay.

4. Summarize the content of King's diary excerpt in 150 words.

*E*XCERPT *FROM* WILLIE: A ROMANCE

HEATHER ROBERTSON

Prime Minister's Papers: Public Archives of Canada

King; William Lyon Mackenzie (1874–1950), prime minister of Canada, 1921–1930, 1935–1948. Private Diary (handwritten) 1916. p. 362.

Wednesday, December 27, 1916

Mother and I arrived safely at the Union Station about 8:30 this morning having had a remarkably good night on the train. The porter brought Mother an orange at 6 and she was up and dressed when the train reached the station. Not a sign of illness, or even train sickness the whole way.

We drove to the Roxborough in a covered sleigh, and had breakfast in my rooms, before the flowers, with the bright window opening out before.

McGregor had some carnations on the table to greet Mother and myself, red and white and prettily arranged. Col. Foster sent a lovely cyclamen, to me, a box of sweetmeats to mother. The servants were all pleasant in expressing their thanks for 'Xmas gifts.

I went through a pile of letters and cards awaiting our arrival — such a lot of beautiful cards from friends in the United States and Canada and England. Among the letters were three from Mr. Rockefeller, one acknowledging my letter proposing two months salary off, which he said must be placed before the Committee, one enclosing his cheque for $365.00 in payment for the expenses of my illness, & one informing me tentatively of renewal of my engagement with the Foundation for another year. All were beautifully expressed, & in most considerate and kindly terms. The last rests my mind for the coming year. It gives me that time to complete the work in hand for the Foundation & lets the year's events intervene, with a chance to be governed by them as to what may be best at the close. Truly I have reason for profound gratitude at this great good fortune, and at possessing so loyal and true a friend. How grateful I am that everything has worked out. Instead of being poor and stranded as we once feared & might have been but for the care and foresight of recent years under the Providence of God, the independence I had hoped for as a basis of public life is gradually being accumulated. I am trying to put my affairs on a solid basis, providing for Mother and myself in the event of politics and marriage come what may.

I wrote thanking Mr. R. and answered other letters.

This morning and afternoon I got busy with McGregor and two servants, and pulled my office out of the room in which I have had it & which I changed into a room for Mother & converted my bedroom into an office & bedroom combined. It was a heavy and dirty job but we made splendid progress and by evening I was able to show Mother into the little room I have tastefully arranged for her, and to give her a welcome to it, which as I expected, would be appreciated so feelingly that words could not be expressed. She has been wonderful all day, went downstairs to both lunch and dinner.

After dinner, when I spoke of going out for a little walk, she asked if she could come along. A perfectly wonderful spirit. If the body were only strong, it could achieve anything. It gives me a great deal of happiness to have her near me, and now I shall provide for her happiness always. God grant she may be long spared. God has answered my prayers in letting me see father's affairs well straightened out, during his lifetime, and provision made for his age, free of debt and obligation of any kind, and He has answered it, in preserving Mother for me, and restoring my nature to its noblest self, where I find the highest joy in unselfish service for her. For all this my heart is filled with a gratitude beyond words.

To bed at 11.

Thursday, December 28, 1916

The maid in the rooms has a cough and I gather has tuberculosis. She said "Wherever you go you have to work." What a lot the poor have! I feel I should like to give my life in service to help improve theirs, that is my real ambition. I wish I had the right person with whom to share it.

Most of today has been spent continuing yesterday's arranging of furniture and belongings. Also some little time spent shopping. Bought a brass bed (single size) mattress and springs for Mother's room for $35.00. Then I attended a meeting of the Patriotic Fund. Met the new Governor-General, the Duke of Devonshire. I thought he was a man of force of character and ability, essentially practical and with a good business head. He spoke very well. One million Frenchmen have been killed in the war so far! What a sacrifice! How can men love war, how can nations tolerate it!

At the Rideau Club I had lunch with Mr. Fraser and Sir Henry Egan, two of Ottawa's millionaire lumbermen. Both very modest and agreeable men. After lunch I wrote letters of condolence to Frank Oliver, Col. J.W. Woods and J. Turiff, MP, on the loss of their sons in the war.

Took Mother with me for a little walk between 4 and 5. It was not too cold and she enjoyed the air, but she is very frail. She came down to dinner but did not eat much. Tonight she went early to bed after we finished reading the balance of *A Sunny Subaltern,* a splendidly written series of letters & wonderfully descriptive of the boy's experiences in all phases of war.

The Tory papers are beginning mean attacks on me because of the Rockefeller association. Trying to raise enmity with Labour because of this association. How sinister and cruel the world is to those who would befriend it!

Friday, December 29, 1916

Today has been spent putting things away. McGregor and I have worked like Trojans cleaning cupboards and drawers from the bottom up and putting in the storeroom below everything we can manage to get along without. We have had shelves put in below and are removing all our transfer cases there, the entire correspondence of past years is now in the basement. Also we packed away many of the pictures which I have had since coming to Ottawa.

I am trying to 'put behind those things that are behind' that I may the better 'press on to the mark of the calling in Christ.' Mother has developed a heavy cold which threatens bronchitis. Mother took both meals in bed and ate very little at either of them. I have sought to get her the things required, fruit, medicines, etc. but I find it difficult to remember, and with the cramped quarters doubly hard. I try not to be impatient, but somehow illness in others is very hard for me to bear. Still, I shall seek to be brave in this, and overcome myself, realizing how great is the privilege. No joy can equal making her remaining time peaceful and happy. I fear greatly at times that it may not be long, yet if I do keep her bright and of good cheer it may be for years. God help me to do this with all the love of which my nature is capable, love worthy of her dear life and love. Mother will I think throw this cold off soon.

Hon. Mr. Casgrain, Postmaster General, died today from pneumonia. I liked him & he was one of the best of the present government.

Very cold tonight — to bed 11:45.

Saturday, December 30, 1916

Today McGregor and I continued our task of cleaning up. We spent

part of the morning completing the correspondence and this afternoon we worked in the storeroom downstairs, hauling boxes, sorting papers etc. By 8 o'clock we had every cupboard & drawer in the
place cleaned out, its contents duly sorted and packed, and the
rooms transformed in appearance. I purchased a few articles for
Mother's room, a little wagonette to cook on & serve meals on, an
umberella (sic) stand for the Hall, and gave McGregor a small gift in
recognition of his faithful services through the year. Mother is
better but still has a heavy cold. I veritably believe she could not
have lived long and might not have been alive now had she remained where she was. I got in a few groceries.

It was about 1 a.m. when I got to bed this morning having cont'd
to work getting off cards and letters and straightening out things. It
is a duty job well out of the way. So far as I know not a single
business matter is outstanding or a single business communication
unanswered or a single account unpaid (the club and Roxborough
excepted). We end the year with a perfectly clean slate.

Sunday, December 31, 1916

All day I have worked very hard to clean the slate of all obligations. I
owe no man or woman living a letter or a cent, nor even an acknowledgment of a kindness done or a courtesy shown. *Everything*
has been acknowledged though it has taken a herculean effort and
has prevented me enjoying Mother's society through the day.

Have had breakfast & tea in my rooms & greatly enjoyed sharing
them with Mother and having them cooked on our little electric
heater. C. came for tea. She brought Mother a perfectly lovely violet
in a pot, a mass of blooms & just right for the sunny window. She is a
sweet, modest girl, quite transformed now she is out of the 'royal'
set. I can't help but feel she may be the one to share my life's work. I
have in the past perhaps been a little too critical and missed opportunities that way.

Tonight I found a five cent piece in the snow in the middle of
Sparks St. Picked it up, was surprised to see the King's head. If it be
an omen it may mean a King's commission with sufficient to carry it
out in the New Year.

My last thought in the year was of dear old father and little Bell,
and the loved ones still on earth. We are all one family although two
have gone before. I thank God for sparing me Mother, and for
restoring me to a nobler manhood than any I have hitherto known.
Withal God has been kind and good. I see life more clearly. My faith
is stronger, my life purer, my character nobler than a year ago.
Passing through the furnace of physical and mental suffering has
taken some of the dross away. I look out on life with a wider vision
and spiritual insight and have greater self-control & a greater faith
in God. Goody-bye old year, and God forgive all that has been amiss
in it and bless the good that He has sent. All we owe to Him.

7. THE LETTER

> **Key Work:**
>   "Conrad's Letter to His Aunt" — Joseph Conrad
> **Associated Reading:**
>   "Dear Fellow Canadian" — Farley Mowat
>   "Meditating" — Joyce Howe

A letter is a special form of essay in which the writer conveys a written message to a specific person or group. Although most letters are written for a private audience (e.g., friend, business correspondent), some are specifically designed for public consumption; the latter includes letters to the editor of a newspaper or magazine, or an open letter appearing in the form of a petition or appeal about a controversial issue such as the acid rain problem, which is raised by Mowat in the Associated Reading, page 134.

Letters vary in a number of other ways. Whether a letter is intended for private or public consumption, the level of formality and tone depends on the writer's purpose. A business letter may be formal and curt if the writer wishes to express dissatisfaction, for example. Similarly, a personal letter to a friend may express negative feelings in a like manner. The thesis in personal letters, as with diaries, may appear in a rambling form that calls upon the reader to intuit, or read between the lines. However, in public letters such as Mowat's appeal and letters to the editor such as Howe's "Meditating," the thesis is generally clearly stated near the beginning.

BEFORE READING

■ Approximately how many letters of any sort have you read or written in the last year? Try to account for the contention that the private letter is a dying form of expression which has been replaced by "junk mail, circulars, and the telephone."

■ If you were to write a letter to the editor today, what would your subject be? Peruse two local newspapers and draw a tentative generalization about why people write these letters.

■ Letters are often an important research source. Consult your Resource Centre's card catalogue to locate collections of letters that might be helpful for scholarly research.

CONRAD'S LETTER TO HIS AUNT

JOSEPH CONRAD

Kinshasa, 26 September 1890

Dearest and best of Aunts!

I received your three letters all at once on my return from Stanley Falls, where I went as supernumerary in the vessel *Roi des Belges* to learn the river. . . . My days here are dreary. Make no mistake about that! I am truly sorry to have come here. Indeed, I regret it bitterly. . . .

Everything is repellent to me here. Men and things, but especially men. And I am repellent to them, too. From the manager in Africa — who has taken the trouble of telling a good many people that I displease him intensely — down to the lowest mechanic, all have a gift for getting on my nerves; and consequently I am perhaps not as pleasant to them as I might be. The manager is a common ivory-dealer with sordid instincts who considers himself a merchant though he is only a kind of African shopkeeper. His name is Delcommune. He hates the English, and I am of course regarded as an Englishman here. I can hope for neither promotion nor increase of salary while he remains here. Moreover, he has said that he is but little bound here by promises made in Europe, so long as they are not in the contract. Those made me by M. Wauters are not. Likewise I can look forward to nothing, as I have no vessel to command. The new boat will be finished in June of next year, perhaps. In the meanwhile my status here is vague, and I have been having troubles because of this. So there you are!

As a crowning joy, my health is far from good. *Keep the secret for me*, but the truth is that in going up the river I had the fever four times in two months, and then at the Falls (its native country) I had an attack of dysentery lasting five days. I feel rather weak physically and a little bit demoralized, and upon my word I think I am homesick for the sea and long to look again on the plains of that salt-water which has so often cradled me, which has so many times smiled at me under the glittering sunshine of a beautiful day, which many times too has flung the threat of death in my face with a whirl of white foam whipped by the wind under a dark December sky. I regret having to miss all that. But what I regret most of all is having bound myself for three years. True, it is hardly likely I shall serve

From LETTERS OF JOSEPH CONRAD TO MARGUERITE PORADOWSKA, translated from French and edited by John A. Gee and Paul J. Sturm. Reprinted by permission of Yale University Press.

them out. Either those in authority will pick a German quarrel with me to ship me home (and on my soul I sometimes wish they would), or another attack of dysentery will send me back to Europe, if not into the other world, which last would be a final solution to all my troubles!

For four whole pages I have been talking about myself! I have said nothing of the delight with which I read your descriptions of men and things at home. Truly, while reading your dear letters I forgot Africa, the Congo, the black savages and white slaves (of whom I am one) who inhabit it. I was happy for an hour. Know that it is not a small thing (or an easy thing) to make a human being happy for a *whole* hour. You may well be proud of having done it. And so my heart goes out to you in a burst of gratitude and sincerest, deepest affection. When shall we meet again? Alas, meeting leads to parting; and the more often one meets, the more painful become the separations. Fatality.

While seeking a practical remedy for the disagreeable situation into which I have got myself, I have thought of a little plan — still pretty much up in the air — with which you might perhaps help me. It seems that this Company or another affiliated with it is going to have some ocean-going vessels, and even has one already. Probably that big (or fat?) banker who rules the roost at home will have a sizeable interest in the other Company. If my name could be submitted for the command of one of their ships (whose home-port will be Antwerp), I might on each voyage run off to Brussels for a day or two when you are there. That would be ideal! If they decided to call me home to take a command, I should of course bear the expense of my return passage. This is perhaps not a very practical idea, but if you return to Brussels during the winter you might find out through M. Wauters what is going on, mightn't you, dear little aunt.

I must close. I leave in an hour by canoe for Bamou, to select wood and have it cut to build the station here. I shall remain encamped in the forest two or three weeks, unless ill. I rather like that. Doubtless I can have a shot or two at buffalo or elephant. . . .

EXPLORING THE LETTER

1. Why is Conrad in the Congo?
2. What does the letter reveal about his state of mind?
3. (a) What does the language Conrad uses reveal about his personality and character?
    (b) Based on the tone of the letter and his choice of anecdotes, suggest the nature of Conrad's relationship with his aunt and the response he anticipates.
    (c) Examine the metaphor in Conrad's description:

I . . . long to look again on the plains of that salt-water which has
so often cradled me, which has so many times smiled at me
under the glittering sunshine of a beautiful day, which many times
too has flung the threat of death in my face with a whirl of white
foam whipped by the wind under a dark December sky.

What is Conrad expressing? Assess the success of his
comparison.

(d) Pick out and examine the writer's culturally biased
generalizations.

(e) Find examples of emotionally loaded diction that illustrate his
subjective reactions to his experiences.

4. Conrad writes that "everything is repellent to me here. Men and
things, but especially men."

Judging from the limited evidence offered in his letter, assess the
extent to which he was personally to blame for the situation in which
he finds himself. What role has apparently been played by factors
such as other people, uncontrollable events, and Conrad's manner of
responding to alien circumstances?

Note: A pertinent piece of biography concerns Conrad's upbringing by
his uncle. You might consult your teacher-librarian about standard
references for biographical information such as W.R. Benét's *The
Reader's Encyclopedia.*

EXTENSIVE STUDY

1. Working in pairs or small groups, compose a specific example of each
of the following. Then discuss how one might cope with these
situations in emotionally healthy ways:
    (a) a childhood fantasy is fulfilled but the reality falls far short of the
    dream;
    (b) having to stay alone in a totally alien country;
    (c) enforced idleness for six months in a remote area which does not
    offer the usual distractions of modern civilization (e.g., radio and
    television).

2. Read Mowat's "Dear Fellow Canadian." What difference in style, tone,
and purpose can you discern between this public letter and Conrad's
private letter?

3. If you have read the essay by Durrell about his European experiences
(in The Diary and Journal, page 112), suggest why Durrell enjoyed
cultural differences, whereas Conrad was apparently repelled.

4. If you have read Hughes's essay about Harriet Tubman (see The
Biography, Autobiography, and Profile, page 96), suggest how
Tubman's reactions to Conrad's Congo experience might have
differed from Conrad's. Working as a group, you might compose a
brief letter from Tubman in the Congo to a friend back home.

5.   If you have read the essays by Shadbolt and Dilworth about Emily Carr (in The Foreword, Prologue and Preface, page 196), consider whether the type of isolation and loneliness Carr endured were in any way similar to Conrad's.

THE WRITING FOLDER

1.   Write a selection of public and/or private letters for three different audiences in which you recount the experiences of one day in your life. Adapt the language, subject matter, and tone to suit your audience.

2.   Prepare an exchange of letters between two fictional characters you have created or encountered in your reading. Provide brief background information about each character to identify them for your audience. Develop a conflict or theme.

3.   Assume the role of the injured party in a three-sided romance. Write appropriate letters to the new couple. Your diction should reflect your feelings about each party, but should allow you to retain your dignity.

4.   Find a letter to the editor. Write a response in language appropriate to that particular newspaper.

INDEPENDENT STUDY

1.   Read Conrad's The Heart of Darkness. Complete one of the following assignments:
     (a) Assuming the point of view of Kurtz, write an excerpt from Kurtz's journal in which Kurtz explains his feelings and the changes that took place in his values and behaviour during his sojourn in the Congo. Attempt to capture the flavour of the character and the era through the use of appropriate diction. Note: your piece should reflect a working knowledge of the text. You might tape a reading from your work.   +
     (b) The Congo experience is a test for both Kurtz and Marlow. Marlow survives; Kurtz fails. In a comparative study of these two characters, account for their different "fates."   +
     (c) Read Conrad's letters in the Norton Critical Edition or other collections. Give a reasoned response to this question: to what extent do the letters deepen one's emotional and intellectual appreciation of the novel?   +

2.   Read two of Conrad's novels. Develop an essay topic after reading a number of critical commentaries that discuss the psychological aspects of these novels. In the Norton Critical Edition, see, for example, A.J. Guerard's "The Journey Within," A.M. Hollingsworth's, "Freud, Conrad and the Future of Illusion," J. Thale's "Marlow's Quest," and L. Feder's "Marlow's Descent into Hell."   + or ++

3. Read Coleridge's "The Rime of the Ancient Mariner" and one of Conrad's novels that explores the quest for self-knowledge. Write an epic or narrative poem that dramatizes this theme. Accompany your work with a taped dramatic reading and a brief analysis that links your poetry with the themes in your reading.   ++

4. One critic wrote that Conrad saw the world as "a place of unending confrontation and contention between the forces of dissolution and ideal brotherhood." Assess this statement of Conrad's world vision in an essay that deals with two of Conrad's novels.   ++

5. Read *Lord Jim* by Conrad and *The Great Gatsby* by F. Scott Fitzgerald. Assess the validity of this statement: "Fitzgerald and Conrad shared the same concern — the plight of the romantic egoist, the extravagant dreamer imprisoned by personal illusions."   ++

6. Read one or two modern works by Africans about Africa. Develop a specific essay topic with your teacher. (Some suggestions include the portrayal of the African's struggle for personal and/or political freedom, racism or tribalism in the modern state, corruption within the society or government of independent states, the conflict between the individual's needs and the demands of society, or the political novel.) Interesting selections: Ayi Kwei Armah, *The Beautyful Ones Are Not Yet Born* (a novel about Ghana); Ali A. Mazrui, *The Trial of Christopher Okigbo* (a novel about a poet who was killed fighting for Biafra in the Nigerian war); Chinua Achebe, *A Man of the People* (a novel about Nigeria); Ngugi wa Thi 'ongo, *Petals of Blood* (a novel set in independent Kenya); Okot p'Bitek, *Two Songs* (poetry about the problems facing independent Africa). You might prepare a brief talk for the class about the aspect of African literature you found most surprising.   + or ++

7. Read the collected letters and one major work of a famous writer such as Lawrence, Conrad, Eliot, Beckett, Joyce, or Colette. Consider how the preoccupations, attitudes, and themes in these letters reflect the concerns in the author's fiction, drama, or poetry. Consult your teacher-librarian for titles. Develop a specific topic with your teacher. If your class is studying the work of the writer you select, you might prepare a brief reading of excerpts from the letters.   ++

TIMED READING AND WRITING

Read the accompanying letter by Mowat (or skim it again if you have already read it), and answer these questions in the time specified by your teacher:

1. What are the purposes of this letter?

2. To what extent does the presentation of this letter affect the reader's response?

3. Does Mowat present sufficient evidence for his argument?

4. Does the letter accomplish its apparent purpose? Why or why not?

5. After reading Mowat's letter, write a reply — intended either for Mowat's consumption or as a letter to the editor.

OR

Read Howe's "Meditating" and summarize it in 50 words or less.

DEAR FELLOW CANADIAN

FARLEY MOWAT

Spring, 1985

Canada's lakes and forests, our fish and wildlife belong to all of us. But in your lifetime <u>the wilderness will die bit by bit unless you act now.</u>

Throughout North America pollution creates rain that is 40 to 50 times more acid than normal. Some rain is literally as acidic as vinegar! This acid rain has killed 1,400 of our lakes and streams in eastern Canada and placed another 90,000 lakes on the danger list.

Also on the <u>danger list</u>:

▪ <u>our fish</u>: dozens of species of fish, including the beleaguered Atlantic salmon, in lakes and rivers that are hundreds of miles from the nearest city;

▪ <u>our forests</u>: the Canadian lumber industry, as forests suffer damage from acid rain and associated air pollutants. The West German government estimates 50 per cent of its forests are affected by this mix of pollutants;

▪ <u>our health</u>: asthmatics and others whose breathing problems are worsened by the pollutants that cause acid rain — urban areas like Greater Vancouver, Toronto, and Montreal are particularly hard hit;

▪ <u>our economy</u>: tourism and sport fishing businesses are threatened with substantial financial losses;

▪ <u>our heritage</u>: historic buildings, cars, homes — <u>anything that stands out in the rain is being eaten away.</u>

In other words, we all suffer. Canada is facing the slow death of industries that are major earners of foreign exchange dollars. The economic losses will be enormous and every tax payer will feel the blow. But we can halt this destruction.

We have known for many years that sulphur and nitrogen oxides from smelters, coal-fired generators and auto exhaust pipes are the culprits. But, until recently, governments in Canada refused to take unilateral action to stop acid rain, and in the United States the Reagan Administration still refuses to admit that action is needed.

The Canadian Coalition on Acid Rain exists to fight acid rain. You have probably seen Michael Perley or Adele Hurley, the executive co-ordinators, on television. I am proud to be associated with them.

The Canadian Coalition now numbers 50 groups whose memberships total nearly 2 million Canadians. They are listed elsewhere in this package. The Coalition monitors polluters, researches waste control acid emissions, and pushes governments in both countries . . . hard.

The Coalition's efforts have shown results. Fourteen months ago, in a major breakthrough, the federal and provincial governments signed an agreement to cut acid pollutants by 50 per cent within 10 years. In February, the eastern provinces decided how much pollution should be reduced in each province to meet this target. Following this meeting, Quebec passed final regulations to control acid pollutants. And the giant Inco smelter at Sudbury, Ontario will cut its sulphur dioxide emissions in half by 1994. Finally, the federal government has agreed to contribute $150 million towards a cleanup of Canadian smelters, and has tightened auto emission regulations to conform with those already in place in the U.S.

Nevertheless, even with the above reductions, the job is not yet finished. Ways must still be found to cut eastern Canadian sulphur dioxide emissions by another 1.5 million tonnes, so that acid rain cleanup in Canada becomes a reality. Responsibility for these reductions must still be assigned, regulations passed, and financing arranged.

Furthermore, at least half the acid rain that falls on Canada originates in the United States. And the Reagan Administration — despite strong protest from Canada and from state Governors and from Congress — refuses to act on acid rain.

So the fight isn't over. The process of passing regulations and approving funds for cleanup has really just begun. Please join us. A contribution in the postage paid envelope enclosed will ensure the Canadian Coalition on Acid Rain can continue to produce results.

The Coalition has already started working on a timetable for Canada's cleanup and proposals for funding and legislation to make the federal and provincial governments honour their acid rain commitments.

In the United States, the Coalition will step up governmental efforts in Washington with concerned Americans all across the country.

Your help is needed.

I am asking you to donate to the Canadian Coalition on Acid Rain to help make Canada's good intentions a reality and to make the U.S. government see they have to stop raining acid on us.

You may be able to afford $100 or $500 or $25 . . . your donation will go a long way to stop acid rain.

Send in your contribution right now. You will be glad you did.

Help the Canadian Coalition on Acid Rain win more victories. You can stop the rain . . . please send your donation today.

Sincerely,

Farley Mowat
for the Canadian Coalition on Acid Rain

P.S. Canada needs a cleanup not an acid bath. Help solve the problem with a donation today.

MEDITATING

JOYCE HOWE

I am writing with regard to the recent articles on total allergy syndrome or what has been termed the Twentieth Century Disease.

Twenty-eight months ago, I too was confined to one decontaminated room, unable to eat and depressed to the point of suicide. Today I am leading a normal life, teaching as I did before I became ill and happier than I ever was before. I would like to share some of the strategies which led to my recovery.

In the beginning I went to a clinical ecologist, but the expense was great and the results not so satisfactory. I took what I had learned from him and the group which supports the movement and struck off on my own. (It is, indeed, a very isolating disease and the first effort seemed beyond me.)

I used exercise, walking in fresh air everyday and a series of stretching exercises such as one gets in yoga. I used massage, particularly shiatsu massage.

I abandoned the four-day rotation diet when it became obvious I was not getting good nourishment and I adopted a macrobiotic way of eating. (There are a number of books by George Ohsawa and Michio Kuchi about this ancient grain-based diet.)

I eat primarily organic brown rice and organic vegetables plus my own unyeasted bread.

I meditated and through reading explored the role of the spirit in relation to the body. Finally, I had several homeopathic remedies prescribed which produced profound results.

Exactly what made me better, I do not know. Perhaps it was the recognition that, in fact, I was not alone, no matter how things seemed, but rather that I was in the constant care and attention of something much greater.

It is a difficult task to live in the 20th century when voices are raised in the agony of global misery and our mother, the earth, is suffering such rape. Living requires devotion and a recognition that there is a purpose to it as well as stedfast love. Fortunately, there is a lot at our disposal.

Joyce Howe
Scarborough

Toronto Star, July 29/84

8. *THE REVIEW*

Key Work:
   "Review of *The Second Self*" — Howard Gardner
Associated Readings:
   "Byting Back" — J.D. Reed
   "Computers: Pro and Con" — Mark Derr
   "Reviews of Tremblay's *Albertine, in Five Times*" —
   Ray Conologue and Robert Crew

The review is an essay that offers an informed opinion on some type of artistic endeavour: a film, concert, book, or play, for example. Reviews range from informal to scholarly, depending on the readers, listeners, or viewers for whom they are intended. A good review informs the audience about the nature of the work or person and suggests whether it is worthy of attention and why. A reviewer/critic may, therefore, have a profound impact on the success or failure of an artistic endeavour. Certain reviewers such as the film critic Pauline Kael and the modernist critic Hugh Kenner have made the review an art form in its own right. In some cases, artists such as Margaret Laurence, Alice Munro, D.H. Lawrence, T.S. Eliot, and Samuel Beckett have even reviewed each other's work.

As with prologues and forewords, reviews are useful time-savers. Reading one or more reviews is often a handy way to begin exploring a topic. However, as with any piece of criticism, the reader should realize that these reviews represent the informed opinion of only one person.

The Key Work by Howard Gardner and two of the Associated Readings present three different critical responses to a recent publication on the impact of computers, *The Second Self: Computers and the Human Spirit* by Sherry Turkle. The other Associated Reading, comprising two reviews by Conologue and Crew, demonstrates that two critics may have different responses to the same work, in this case a play, *Albertine, in Five Times.* The essays in this unit illustrate that reviews strongly reflect the personal tastes of individual critics.

BEFORE READING

■ In what specific ways has the computer affected the individual and society?

■ Survey the class to determine how many of your peers are ''computer literate.'' Assess the extent to which computer literacy will be necessary for your post-secondary career.

■ List some possible reasons reviewers might differ in their response to the same material.

REVIEW OF THE SECOND SELF: COMPUTERS AND THE HUMAN SPIRIT

HOWARD GARDNER

By Sherry Turkle
362 pp. New York:
Simon and Schuster

Millions of words have been written — or processed — about the impact of computers on individuals and society. Like earlier writings about the automobile or television, these views are primarily the commentator's personal projections. In authors' comments about computers, one may readily discern their deep-seated beliefs about technology and culture, as well as about other persons, the self, rationality and emotion.

Sherry Turkle, a sociologist and a clinical psychologist who teaches at Massachusetts Institute of Technology, has immersed herself in several milieus where people interact with computers. In what may well be the first ethnographic study of the ''computer world,'' she has interviewed young children, some experienced with computers and some not; adolescents, both the casual and the serious users of computers, and several groups of adults, including experts in artificial intelligence, ''hackers'' who spend most of their waking hours at terminals and lay purchasers of personal computers. Though armed with a set of concerns, she has given her subjects considerable leeway to express their own opinions. Along the way, she has assembled a wealth of fascinating observations about the impact of computers on these groups.

Beyond question, her rich survey has brought together information which was previously available only in scattered writings. She has conducted a far more thorough investigation than had been carried out before and has written about her conclusions in a clear and lively way. Anyone who wishes to know about the effects of computers on American society today would do well to read "The Second Self." Moreover, because of her abundant data, Miss Turkle is in a favorable position to go beyond the idiosyncratic projections of earlier commentators.

She views each group through a particular social scientific lens. In dealing with young children, she follows the lead of the pioneering Swiss developmental psychologist Jean Piaget. In broad outline, she discerns in children who use computers a mirroring of the stages of intellectual development proposed by Piaget in other realms of experience.

But there are illuminating divergences. As a sign of what it means to be alive, children typically speak about movement, but when asked about computers, they invoke psychological expressions — "It thinks" or "It doesn't really think." Children engaged in games also talk a lot about whether the computer can cheat, another characterization missing from the descriptions of "ordinary" machines. Children as young as 8 offer shrewd characterizations. An 8-year-old Bostonian said computers "don't have a family. They have a maker."

In describing the adolescent computer user, Miss Turkle adopts the perspective of the American psychoanalyst Erik Erikson. The central issue is the individual's own sense of identity. Adolescents caught up in computers begin to wonder whether they are free agents or whether their selves (and those of others around them) are simply programmed.

We also visit the groups of children who are heavily involved with computers. There are the enthusiasts of video games who find challenges, but also opportunities for power and control, as they match their wits against the programmers from Silicon Valley. And there are the school children who learn how to program with LOGO, or other "user-friendly" languages. Echoing observations of her close associate, Seymour Papert of M.I.T., Miss Turkle shows how the most successful youngsters make the computer an integral part of their thought processes while others, particularly young girls, may be intimidated by the computer. She contrasts these "middle-aged" children, who seek "mastery," with the younger users who are "metaphysicians" and the adolescents, who are enmeshed in issues of identity.

Miss Turkle becomes more of a sociologist, and more original as well, as she describes the adult world of computer users. She brings alive the organizations formed by the first home computer owners, the magazines over which they pored. She also nostalgically recalls the somewhat unrealistic political expectations with which these people — successors of the organization men of the 50's and young radicals of the 60's — came to surround their cherished possession. For example, she recalls the early expectation that home computers would usher in a fully democratic era, with votes instantly being tabulated on every matter of concern. The pioneering generation of the mid-70's, whose members possessed a very intimate knowledge of the machine, contrasts with the current crop, whose members ignore technical aspects of the hardware, use higher level languages and often lack a pressing reason for purchasing a computer.

In discussing two other groups of users, Miss Turkle returns to relatively familiar ground. She describes the hackers, individuals who live for their time at the terminals. We learn about their elaborate rites of passage, their often empty personal lives and their need for escape. Trying to explain why hackers are nearly all male, Miss Turkle quotes an informant who feels that a computer can occupy for a male the same all-consuming role that a baby does for a female. While she attempts to be sympathetic, I found her portrait of hackers nearly as devastating as that presented in Joseph Weizenbaum's "Computer Power and Human Reason."

Finally, Miss Turkle visits the scientists of artificial intelligence, experts who build programs which ostensibly exhibit intelligent behavior. Such researchers often see their activities as providing a privileged position for addressing fundamental philosophical questions — what is thought, what is mind, what does it mean to understand or to learn? Miss Turkle reviews the bitter fights stimulated by two philosophical critiques issued by faculty members of the University of California at Berkeley — Hubert Dreyfus's defiant book, "What Computers Can't Do," and John Searle's recent claim that computers are simply formal symbol manipulators, inherently unable to "understand" anything. In keeping with her hands-off policy Miss Turkle avoids taking a stand on these heavily charged debates.

In a suggestive allusion to her discussion of children, Miss Turkle discerns the trio of computational stances in her adult subjects as well. The members of the artificial intelligentsia are engaged in metaphysical inquiry, the hackers are preoccupied with mastery and the lay computer owners are concerned with personal identity.

While my overall impression of this book is favorable, I have to register disappointment in two areas. The first, more readily discussed reservation has to do with the excessively nontechnical nature of this book. Except for two brief appendices, Miss Turkle does not share her data with her readers. She has not indicated how representative any of her case studies are. For instance, we do not know whether the computer programmers she interviewed are typical of the whole population of programmers, or whether they represent an extreme. Too often anecdotes are substituted for analysis of data. Moreover, some of the writing borders on the simple-minded: "But there is something new. There is a new focus for a forbidden experiment. A new mind that is not yet a mind. . . . This is the computer."

My second area of disappointment stems from Miss Turkle's failure to tell her readers what she makes of all she has observed. Having been intensively involved in the "computer culture" at M.I.T. since 1977 and having interviewed 400 individuals, including many major scientists, she should have formed some views on the substantive debates in the study of computers and on the likely effects of computers on individuals or on the larger society. Instead, she tends to borrow the perspective of other researchers, to quote interview subjects without comment and to state all sides of a dispute without taking a stand. Very fair, to be sure, but ultimately unsatisfactory.

I think that Miss Turkle does have a perspective but one has to tease it out of the book. Clearly she believes that an encounter with a computer is an inherently pregnant experience. It stimulates people to confront issues they had not grappled with before, or to think about them in a new way. But she says little about whether such effects are unique to computers. Perhaps many experiences in other times had the same evocative effect. Perhaps the current craze about computers is a peculiarly American phenomenon.

A clue to Miss Turkle's own stand comes from her involvement in psychoanalysis. An analytically oriented psychotherapist and author of a book on Lacanian psychoanalysis in France, she is evidently fascinated by confrontations between reason and emotion. The obscure analyst Jacques Lacan in the archetypical land of reason, the rationalist Freud probing the unconscious, the ultimate logic machine as it affects the human personality — these themes lurk in the title, the subtitle, and the fertile first chapter, "The Evocative Object."

Miss Turkle abuts but never really confronts these antinomies. As I read her, she is inclined to accept the computer scientists' belief that a computer can think, but disinclined to accept the claim of some enthusiasts that a computer can experience emotions or otherwise fully simulate human experience. At one point, in an apparent effort to discourage simple dichotomies or formulas, she warns: "Thought and feeling are inseparable. When they are torn from their complex relationship with each other and improperly defined as mutually exclusive, the cognitive can become mere logical process, the cold, dry, and lifeless, and the affective is reduced to the visceral, the primitive, and the unanalyzable." And yet in her concluding passage, she is reduced to simple slogans: "Where we once were rational animals, now we are feeling computers, emotional machines. The hard-to-live with, self-contradictory notion of the emotional machine captures the fact that what we live now is a new and deeply felt tension."

Perhaps to expect a more comprehensive formulation on such vexed issues is unreasonable. All the same, if the computer is as evocative an object as she has portrayed, and if she is as involved in issues of reason and emotion as she appears to be, it would have been helpful for Miss Turkle to share with us her own perspective on the computational worlds. Unless, of course, the experience itself has produced an intense ambivalence, which she has "projected" in this highly suggestive, but ultimately incomplete account.

EXPLORING THE REVIEW

1. Why does Gardner feel Turkle is qualified to write about the impact of computers on the individual and society?
2. Account for Gardner's belief that Turkle's book is important.
3. Identify the groups Turkle has surveyed in her research. What she has discovered about each group?
4. Specify the two faults Gardner found in Turkle's treatment of the subject. Why does he see them as faults?
5. In the margins of the text or in your notebook, outline the review, indicating its major sections.

EXTENSIVE STUDY

1. Consult appropriate reference sources to research Piaget's impact on our thinking about children and how they learn.
2. "Adolescents caught up in computers begin to wonder whether they are free agents or whether their selves are simply programmed." Examine this generalization by Turkle. Determine whether it applies to you or to anyone you know.
3. (a) Make a list of social factors that may account for the findings that so-called hackers are "nearly all male" and "young girls are intimidated by the computer."
    (b) How might Virginia Woolf (see "Professions for Women," page 153) have accounted for these findings?
4. Is it valid for Gardner to criticize Turkle for not clearly taking a stand in the computer debate?

5. Are "thought and feeling inseparable?" In your response, you should refer to Hatcher's "Whole Brain Learning," page 74 and the comments about thinking in the tips on composing essays (see Part C).

6. (a) Read the other two reviews of Turkle's book; draw out apparent differences in opinion. (*Note*: Before you begin, check out the authorship of the other two reviews.)

    (b) Decide the extent to which the intended audience determined the content and language of each review. (You may need to check the nature of *Discover* magazine.)

7. If you can locate Peter Gzowski's CBC interview tapes with Turkle (1984), listen to them. The TV Ontario program "Realities," where Turkle was interviewed on Sept. 13, 1985, provides transcripts for a small fee. In what ways do these interviews supplement your understanding and appreciation of Turkle and her work?

8. Make a list of the computer-related expressions and images we use to describe human behaviour. Decide if this habit is changing the way we think of ourselves. If so, what are the implications of this habit?

9. Debate one of these topics. Resolved that:

    Machines add stress to human life.
    The machine plays too big a role in everyday life.
    Our society has gained more from technological advances than it has sacrificed in terms of the human spirit.

THE WRITING FOLDER

1. Write a review of a play or film you have seen, a book you have read, or an interview you have heard or seen. Locate a published review and compare it with your own judgment. Give possible reasons for differences of opinion.

2. Find two reviews of the same work (film, play, book); write a comparative evaluation.

3. Analyze your feelings about the impact of the computer on your life in essay or letter format.

4. Write a dialogue in which the reviewer, Howard Gardner, interviews Turkle about her books. (See the model interview with David Suzuki in the Contemporary Journalism section, page 224.)

5. Compose a short story that dramatizes the issues raised by the impact of the computer on the human spirit.

INDEPENDENT STUDY

1. Read Turkle's book, *The Second Self: Computers and the Human Spirit.* Conduct your own survey to determine if her findings are valid

for your environment. Present your findings in the form of a report with an oral and written component. +

2. Read E.M. Forster's *The Machine Stops* and a major science fiction classic such as A.C. Clarke's *2001: A Space Odyssey.* Compare the writers' themes about the effects of technology on the human spirit. ++

3. Read Alvin Tofler's *The Third Wave* and Turkle's *The Second Self.* Compare the writers' views about the impact of technology on the individual and society. Consider the implications for future generations. ++

TIMED READING AND WRITING

In the time specified by your teacher, read the two reviews of *Albertine, in Five Times,* Tremblay's play. Write a summary of each. In a separate response, decide which reviewer is more persuasive and why.

BYTING BACK

J.D. REED

THE SECOND SELF: COMPUTERS AND THE HUMAN SPIRIT
by Sherry Turkle
Simon & Schuster; 362 pages

When a talking electronic game chides a child of six for a wrong answer, she talks back to it. "My God," says her mother, "she treats that thing like a person. Do you suppose she thinks that people are machines?" She may indeed, according to author Sherry Turkle, an M.I.T. sociologist and psychologist. And as this study makes clear, that little girl is part of a cultural upheaval.

Bookstore shelves sag under the weight of volumes quantifying what computers will do for our math, medicine and management, but *The Second Self* explores a broader futurescape. Like the telescope, which forced man to accept a less exalted position in creation, says Turkle, the computer is challenging the manner in which we think about ourselves. "The question," she writes, "is not what will the computer be like in the future, but instead, what will *we* be like?"

To find out, Turkle became the Margaret Mead of silicon. During six years of study, she interviewed more than 400 computer users (about half of them children), lived in the subculture of virtuoso programmers, called hackers, asked electronic questions on home-user telephone networks and explored the wizardry of M.I.T.'s Artificial Intelligence Laboratory. In a series of vivid vignettes, she reports the various ways the computer "brings philosophy into everyday life."

Because hand-held electronic games are "smart" and talk back, children grant them a new existence, somewhere between the living and the inanimate. Alice, 5, thinks batteries are "like their food." Robert, 8, believes they are intelligent because they cheat. What then, Turkle asked, is special about people if it is not thinking? Feelings, children concluded.

Although Turkle suggests that computers have positive qualities — they teach math to the unscientific, for instance — addiction to them is a way to avoid human emotion. Jarish, 12, is a loner who relentlessly plays video games because, unlike people, they obey strict rules. "You walk out of the arcade," he says, "and it's . . . nothing that you can control." Arthur, 34, bought a computer to speed up his architectural business, but spends hours at the console, "poking" and "peeking" into programs, an experience he likens to a sexual kick. Says he: "Sometimes I feel guilty when I do it for too long."

Many home-computer owners believed they had bought a tool to simplify their lives. Others discovered that programming could become an end in itself. Hackers, says Turkle, are social misfits who construct digital utopias, hang out in pancake houses and admire the recursive art of M.C. Escher. At M.I.T. their nerdy abdication from society is "sport death" — programming for up to 30 hours without sleep before "crashing." Alex, a dedicated hacker, describes it as feeling "totally telepathic with the computer."

Artificial-intelligence theorists play more potent games. Teaching machines to play chess or ask questions like a psychotherapist's is only the beginning. M.I.T.'s Edward Fredkin, for instance, believes not only that machines will eventually think better than the best human minds but that "we'll be enormously happier once our niche has limits to it." What of people? David, 12: "They will be the ones who will love each other, have families and . . . go to church."

Like a proper social scientist, Turkle seems to pass no judgment on the mind-machine debate she so cogently portrays. But she is, after all, human, and hence can feel awe at the computer's potential. It is becoming, she says, "what sex was to the Victorians — threat and obsession, taboo and fascination." No printout could convey a clearer or more readable forecast.

Time, August 27, 1984

COMPUTERS, PRO AND CON

MARK DERR

The Second Self
BY SHERRY TURKLE
Simon and Schuster

Technostress
BY CRAIG BROD
Addison-Wesley

The computer is unlike any new machine in history. Because it seems to think, it challenges basic notions about the mind — a faculty that man has always thought distinctively his own. For that reason, Sherry Turkle argues in *The Second Self*, the computer is not only a useful analytical machine but an evocative presence in our lives — one that fascinates us, appalls us, and makes us reconsider what it means to be human, to think and to feel. To Turkle, the power of computers can be liberating. To Craig Brod, who presents a pessimistic case in *Technostress*, that power is menacing. It is the source, he claims, of a serious new disease induced by technology.

For her lucid, scholarly study, Turkle, a sociologist and psychologist at MIT, immersed herself in the computer culture for six years. The exercise left her intrigued but not alarmed. A 35-year-old advertising executive who plays video games for several hours each day told her, for example, that playing the shoot-'em-up arcade game Asteroids is "like playing with a mind." In Turkle's view, he is one of many players for whom video games provide a sense of control and completeness that they do not find elsewhere. The games, moreover, are only a small part of a culture in which young and old become "players in their own game, makers of their own mysteries," who find "a new intensity of relationship with the intimate machine."

At a private school she calls Austen, Turkle watched children from pre-school to fourth grade deal with their computers in different ways. Fourth graders Jeff and Kevin designed interesting programs showing space-age scenes of rockets and shuttles. But while Jeff approached the machine like a scientist or an engineer, "with determination and a need to be in control," Kevin proceeded like an artist, in an "impressionist and dreamy" way. For Turkle, Jeff and Kevin represent opposite poles in dealing with the machines: "hard mastery," the technological approach, and "soft mastery," the artistic approach. She observes that girls tend to be soft masters and boys hard masters, but takes care to emphasize the virtues of each approach.

When Turkle finds anyone involved with computers to the exclusion of nearly all else, she looks to underlying personality traits for the explanation. Henry, an Austen student, was awkward in dealing with people and relaxed only at the computer. But the computer was Henry's solution, not his problem, which turned out to be both a terror of human intimacy and a fear of being alone. Turkle concedes that the computer cannot resolve Henry's emotional difficulties, and indeed may only keep him "lost in the world of things."

Turkle is at her best explaining how the computer invites both young and old to explore their minds. Many begin asking questions: How am I different from the machine? Are we all programmed? Do computers really think? And if only things that are alive can think, are computers alive? Although computers may encourage people to view their minds as machines, Turkle concludes, they are also leading them to ponder their own souls and spirits.

This conclusion stands in sharp contrast to the downbeat report of Craig Brod, who has seen considerable service as a psychotherapist in California's Silicon Valley. Though he claims to be no technophobe, he speaks darkly of the computer's capacity to "alter the human brain," and argues rather sweepingly that it can do more harm to people's personalities, behavior, jobs, and relationships with their families than any other machine in history.

Brod's description of technostress, as he calls this disease, derives largely from his practice, but his argument proceeds more by anecdote than by detailed analysis. Some of his tales are real horror stories, some of them just amusing if painful encounters. Bonnie, a secretary in a Silicon Valley research center, resisted learning how to use the computers in her office. Finally, she apparently poured coffee into her terminal, causing its breakdown — and her dismissal. Bob, a research biochemist, identified so completely with his computer that he spent weekends creating models of new chemical compounds on it rather than talking to his wife.

Brod grants that new office technology has always upset some workers, but argues that the changes the computer has wrought are of a different order. It creates new tasks, a new environment in which workers focus on a screen in isolation from each other, and an assembly-line atmosphere in which productivity can be rigorously measured by the machine itself.

Far from being intimidated by the machines, Bob is "techno-centered," as Brod puts it — a creature of computer technology to whom productivity is all-important. Brod deems this the most virulent form of technostress because it can lead to complete identification with the computer at the expense of essential human contacts. He fails to prove, however, that computers are different from other familiar addictions like golf, hobbies, televised sports, or compulsive careerism.

Brod finds more distressing symptoms among children who fall victim to the computer's lure. Video games, for example, shorten children's attention spans, provide them with a false sense of omnipotence when they master a game, make the fantasy world more compelling than the real world, and in general draw children away from friendship and group play. Brod's surprisingly mild prescriptions for controlling the dread new disease include greater parental control and sensitivity to early symptoms in children, and more attention by management and labour to computer-related problems in the workplace.

Both books can usefully serve a society that appears eager to embrace the brave new computer world. Anybody who thinks that computers are unfailingly benign should read Brod. Anybody who thinks they will rot our minds will learn from Turkle that they need not.

Discover Magazine

REVIEWS OF TREMBLAY'S 'ALBERTINE, IN FIVE TIMES'

REVIEW
BY RAY CONLOGUE

Albertine, in Five Times.

It's a lovely title. Now, if only they'd done it five times faster.

The latest Michel Tremblay play, which opened Tuesday night at the Tarragon Theatre, is symptomatic of the Quebec writer's increasing introspection. The theatrical rough-and-tumble of his early plays is gone. Even plays such as L'impromptu of Outremont, with its static and musing quality, at least had separate characters.

But Albertine, as much a poem as a play, has one character. We see her at five different times of her life, one Albertine for each decade from 30 to 70, played by five actresses. The ingenious idea is that they can talk to each other across the years, giving dramatic form to the wistful re-running of one's life that everyone indulges in from time to time. There is the fantasy of talking to one's younger self: impressing him or her with the accomplishments of a decade, or apologizing for the failures, noting with chagrin the diminution of one's idealism and trust. And there is, of course, the horror of

Reprinted from the *Globe and Mail*, April 11, 1985

talking to one's older self, the reminder of death, the fate of golden boys and girls.

Tremblay, realizing the possible claustrophobia of the situation, has even introduced a second character, the best friend Madeleine.

There is nothing wrong with the idea, or the structure, but the execution is soporific. For Albertine is an unconvincing character.

The doubts started, for me, not with Albertine's older (or, we must say in the present case, oldest) self, played by Doris Petrie. Here we have Tremblay's sympathetic and clear-eyed view of the elderly — the resigned exterior person settling into a nursing home, the vital and angry interior person quite unresigned to age and to being patronized. And we have Doris Petrie's accomplished performance, the wandering eyes, the wistfulness, the focusing on the middle distance.

The problem started with the youngest self, Susan Coyne's 30-year-old Albertine. She has been abandoned by her husband, her 11-year-old daughter is playing sex games with a park attendant, and she confesses to being filled with a rage that could overflow the sky. It is rage against everything. No, it is against men. No, it is because (here, a bare political bone juts out) women must be either drones or whores and why isn't there a third choice?

Coyne is affecting but far too sweet to be convincing as a bearer of rage. And the script leaves her adrift. Without seeing what has happened to this woman, or meeting the daughter, the viewer can only accept her rage as a given, as the poet's *diktat*, which is unsatisfying.

Then the rage is carried through the rest of her life; it becomes the dramatic character. But it follows no clear development. At 40, she is terminally bitter; at 50, she has achieved a happiness of self-deception; at 60, she has relapsed into anger; at 70 she is pretending to have escaped it again.

The only sunlight that falls on this vacillating and futile life is Madeleine. She knows her happiness is "trite," but she senses that it has truth, and she feels sorry for Albertine. Susan Wright plays Madeleine with straightforward goodness, no hint that she is really parading her happiness to torment her choleric friend (as Albertine charges). The character is at first a relief to the viewer, but as the script muddles along she simply becomes part of the confusion.

The three in-between Albertines were troubling. There is no physical resemblance, which is fair enough, but there is also no stylistic resemblance. Each plays her character exactly as it suits her: Clare Coulter plays 40 with the stolid, dog-in-the-manger malevolence of which she is so capable; Patricia Hamilton plays 50 with the sunny vulnerability that comes easily to her; Joy Coghill is a snarky 60, lowering out from behind a mesh curtain; and Petrie as 70 is the image of a wistful and helpless elderly lady.

Can these really be the same person?

The script explores recollections and significant events in the random style of Quebecois poetic drama, and it becomes most difficult finally to see where it is going. Events do not really build, and I suspect it was this, rather than opening-night jitters, which made it so difficult for several of the actors to remember lines.

Every so often Albertine strikes a spark of wit and of Tremblay's mercilessly accurate observation of human nature. When sunny 50 tells angry 40, "this too will pass," and surly 60 mutters, "yeah, and it'll come back again, too," there is deserved laughter.

But the laughter and the tears are few and far between. This strange, eventful history is neither as strange nor as eventful as it should have been.

REVIEW
BY ROBERT CREW

It's the moment that every theatregoer lives for, that oh so rare occasion when everything works.

A great play, full of resonance and depth; a superb cast, working in perfect harmony to bring it to life; unobtrusive direction and fine staging. The result is pure theatrical magic. The barrier between actors and audience is gone; you hang on every word and there are shivers playing up and down your spine.

Such is the impact of *Albertine, In Five Times,* the new play by Quebec's Michel Tremblay that received its English-language premiere last night at Tarragon Theatre, which has done so much to introduce Tremblay to audiences outside Quebec.

Albertine is, in a word, awesome. There are two actual characters in the play, Albertine and her sister/confidante Madeleine. But we meet Albertine in five stages of her life, each played by a different actor.

Logical progression

Susan Coyne is Albertine at age 30, a widow with two problem children. She is still young enough to dream but old enough to feel the potential for anger welling up within her. She is with Madeleine on the verandah of her mother's home, having just experienced a family crisis involving her and her 11-year-old daughter. Coyne, a relative newcomer, gives a shining performance of rare promise.

Clare Coulter is Albertine at 40. The anger has now taken over and she is bitter, depressed and prickly. The progression is a logical one, with Albertine consumed by rage and love for her wayward daughter and retarded son. Of Coulter's fine performance, suffice it to say that it is hard to imagine anyone else bringing so much to the role.

Patricia Hamilton is Albertine at 50. Now working in a restaurant, she has become sunny and good-natured, enjoying her new life without her family and without men. The change of direction here appears to be a violent one, but Tremblay and Hamilton do more than just make it work.

Joy Coghill is Albertine at 60, an almost bed-ridden, pill-popping wreck. Again there has been a major transformation but again all is explained. An expert, edgy performance by Coghill, with suppressed anger finally bubbling to the surface.

Doris Petrie is Albertine at 70. An empty shell of a woman "cured of everything except memories," she's just arrived at an old people's home. Petrie gives a sensitive performance, hitting all the right notes of despair, fear and utter loneliness.

The foil for the instinctive, passionate Albertine is Susan Wright's Madeleine. She is seemingly everything that Albertine is not; smarter, happily married with thoughtful husband and nice children. Wright's portrayal has a clever, delicate touch of smugness and self-satisfaction about it.

Lovingly directed

Tremblay's technique is daring and subtle. All the characters interact with each other, casting new light on events in the past, and Madeleine moves freely between all five ages of Albertine.

It's like watching a wriggling earthworm chopped into five pieces, each with a life of its own, but gradually knitting together into a unified whole. At the end of this spare, poetic 90-minute play, there's nothing much left to know about the unhappy Albertine.

Not all is gloom and doom, however. Lovingly directed by Bill Glassco (recently appointed CentreStage's director of theatre), with an oppressive, wedge-shaped tunnel of a set by Astrid Janson, the play is leavened with much wry humor. As usual with Tremblay, deep anger is mixed with deep compassion.

This is as fine a new play as I have seen in many a long age comparable to the very best being written today. Quite simply, it is not to be missed.

Albertine, in Five Times

By Michel Tremblay. Translated by John Van Burek and Bill Glassco.

9. THE SPEECH

> *Key Work:*
> "Professions for Women" — Virginia Woolf
> *Associated Readings:*
> "Inaugural Address" — John F. Kennedy
> "I Have a Dream" — Martin Luther King
> "United Nations' Declaration of Women's Rights"

A speech is an oral essay. Although it may appear in print form, the writer's primary concern is the immediate physical presence of the audience. To avoid yawns and a parade to the door, the writer-speaker must capture a rapport with the audience through familiarity with the subject, appropriate tone, and effective delivery. The audience should be engaged at the auditory and visual levels; the sound of the words and what they mean should blend harmoniously. Good speakers often make clever use of rhetorical devices; especially effective techniques of oral rhetoric include repetition of key phrases and images, evocative language, and parallelism.

Some of the best speeches are carefully polished before delivery such as Woolf's "Professions for Women." John F. Kennedy's "Inaugural Address" was composed by his professional speech writers and delivered on January 20th, 1961, when he took the oath of office. On the other hand, speakers occasionally find it more effective to abandon their prepared texts and follow the mood and responses of their audience, as some say Martin Luther King did. As you read King's "I Have a Dream," which was delivered at a 1963 peace rally at Lincoln Memorial in Washington, look for evidence that King adopted this extemporaneous strategy; when he made this speech to thousands of people of all races, they repeatedly shouted back their approval.

Woolf delivered "Professions for Women" to The Women's Service League in Britain in the early twentieth century. As you read this Key Work, you might look for evidence that she prepared her speech for an all-female audience.

BEFORE READING

■ Recall speeches you have given in previous years. List your strongest emotional associations with the concept of a speech.
■ Make a mental list of any three people you would like most to hear speak, and specify their topics.

■ Woolf's speech considers problems often encountered by women in dealing with personal and social expectations. Explore the nature of these expectations in your community, citing examples.

PROFESSIONS FOR WOMEN

VIRGINIA WOOLF

When your secretary invited me to come here, she told me that your Society is concerned with the employment of women and she suggested that I might tell you something about my own professional experiences. It is true I am a woman; it is true I am employed; but what professional experiences have I had? It is difficult to say. My profession is literature; and in that profession there are fewer experiences for women than in any other, with the exception of the stage — fewer, I mean, that are peculiar to women. For the road was cut many years ago — by Fanny Burney, by Aphra Behn, by Harriet Martineau, by Jane Austen, by George Eliot — many famous women, and many more unknown and forgotten, have been before me, making the path smooth, and regulating my steps. Thus, when I came to write, there were very few material obstacles in my way. Writing was a reputable and harmless occupation. The family peace was not broken by the scratching of a pen. No demand was made upon the family purse. For ten and sixpence one can buy paper enough to write all the plays of Shakespeare — if one has a mind that way. Pianos and models, Paris, Vienna and Berlin, masters and mistresses, are not needed by a writer. The cheapness of writing paper is, of course, the reason why women have succeeded as writers before they have succeeded in the other professions.

But to tell you my story — it is a simple one. You have only got to figure to yourselves a girl in a bedroom with a pen in her hand. She had only to move that pen from left to right — from ten o'clock to one. Then it occurred to her to do what is simple and cheap enough after all — to slip a few of those pages into an envelope, fix a penny stamp in the corner, and drop the envelope into the red box at the corner. It was thus that I became a journalist; and my effort was rewarded on the first day of the following month — a very glorious day for me — by a letter from an editor containing a cheque for one pound ten shillings and sixpence. But to show you how little I deserve to be called a professional woman, how little I know of the struggles and difficulties of such lives, I have to admit that instead of spending that sum upon bread and butter, rent, shoes and stockings, or butcher's bills, I went out and bought a cat — a beautiful cat, a Persian cat, which very soon involved me in bitter disputes with my neighbours.

What could be easier than to write articles and to buy Persian cats with the profits? But wait a moment. Articles have to be about something. Mine, I seem to remember, was about a novel by a famous man. And while I was writing this review, I discovered that if I were going to review books I should need to do battle with a certain phantom. And the phantom was a woman, and when I came to know her better I called her after the heroine of a famous poem, The Angel in the House. It was she who used to come between me and my paper when I was writing reviews. It was she who bothered me and wasted my time and so tormented me that at last I killed her. You who come of a younger and happier generation may not have heard of her — you may not know what I mean by the Angel in the House. I will describe her as shortly as I can. She was intensely sympathetic. She was immensely charming. She was utterly un-selfish. She excelled in the difficult arts of family life. She sacrificed herself daily. If there was chicken, she took the leg; if there was a draught she sat in it — in short she was so constituted that she never had a mind or a wish of her own, but preferred to sympathize always with the minds and wishes of others. Above all — I need not say it — she was pure. Her purity was supposed to be her chief beauty — her blushes, her great grace. In those days — the last of Queen Victoria — every house had its Angel. And when I came to write I encountered her with the very first words. The shadow of her wings fell on my page; I heard the rustling of her skirts in the room. Directly, that is to say, I took my pen in my hand to review that novel by a famous man, she slipped behind me and whispered: 'My dear, you are a young woman. You are writing about a book that has been written by a man. Be sympathetic; be tender; flatter; deceive; use all the arts and wiles of our sex. Never let anybody guess that you have a mind of your own. Above all, be pure.' And she made as if to guide my pen. I now record the one act for which I take some credit to myself, though the credit rightly belongs to some excellent an-cestors of mine who left me a certain sum of money — shall we say five hundred pounds a year? — so that it was not necessary for me to depend solely on charm for my living. I turned upon her and caught her by the throat. I did my best to kill her. My excuse, if I were to be had up in a court of law, would be that I acted in self-defence. Had I not killed her she would have killed me. She would have plucked the heart out of my writing. For, as I found, directly I put pen to paper, you cannot review even a novel without having a mind of your own, without expressing what you think to be the truth about human relations, morality, sex. And all these questions, according to the Angel of the House, cannot be dealt with freely and openly by women; they must charm, they must conciliate, they must — to put it bluntly — tell lies if they are to succeed. Thus, whenever I felt the shadow of her wing or the radiance of her halo upon my page, I took up the inkpot and flung it at her. She died hard. Her fictitious nature was of great assistance to her. It is far harder to kill a phantom than a reality. She was always creeping back when I thought I had despatched her. Though I flatter myself that I killed her in the end, the struggle was severe; it took much time that had better have been spent upon learning Greek grammar; or in roaming the world in search of adventures. But it was a real experience; it was an experience that was bound to befall all women writers at that time. Killing the Angel in the House was part of the occupation of a woman writer.

But to continue my story. The Angel was dead; what then remained? You may say that what remained was a simple and common object — a young woman in a bedroom with an inkpot. In other words, now that she had rid herself of falsehood, that young woman had only to be herself. Ah, but what is 'herself'? I mean, what is a woman? I assure you, I do not know. I do not believe that you know. I do not believe that anybody can know until she has expressed herself in all the arts and professions open to human skill. That indeed is one of the reasons why I have come here — out of respect for you, who are in process of showing us by your experiments what a woman is, who are in process of providing us, by your failures and successes, with that extremely important piece of information.

But to continue the story of my professional experiences. I made one pound ten and six by my first review; and I bought a Persian cat with the proceeds. Then I grew ambitious. A Persian cat is all very well, I said; but a Persian cat is not enough. I must have a motor-car. And it was thus that I became a novelist — for it is a very strange thing that people will give you a motor-car if you will tell them a story. It is a still stranger thing that there is nothing so delightful in the world as telling stories. It is far pleasanter than writing reviews of famous novels. And yet, if I am to obey your secretary and tell you my professional experiences as a novelist, I must tell you about a very strange experience that befell me as a novelist. And to understand it you must try first to imagine a novelist's state of mind. I hope I am not giving away professional secrets if I say that a novelist's chief desire is to be as unconscious as possible. He has to induce in himself a state of perpetual lethargy. He wants life to proceed with the utmost quiet and regularity. He wants to see the same faces, to read the same books, to do the same things day after day, month after month, while he is writing, so that nothing may break the illusion in which he is living — so that nothing may disturb or disquiet the mysterious nosings about, feelings round, darts, dashes and sudden discoveries of that very shy and illusive spirit, the imagination. I suspect that this state is the same both for men and women. Be that as it may, I want you to imagine me writing a novel in a state of trance. I want you to figure to yourselves a girl sitting with a pen in her hand, which for minutes, and indeed for hours, she never dips into the inkpot. The image that comes to my mind when I think of this girl is the image of a fisherman lying sunk in dreams on the verge of a deep lake with a rod held out over the water. She was letting her imagination sweep unchecked round every rock and cranny of the world that lies submerged in the depths of our unconscious being. Now came the experience, the experience that I believe to be far commoner with women writers than with men. The line raced through the girl's fingers. Her imagination had rushed away. It had sought the pools, the depths, the dark places where the largest fish slumber. And then there was a smash. There was an explosion. There was foam and confusion. The imagination had dashed itself against something hard. The girl was roused from her dream. She was indeed in a state of the most acute and difficult distress. To speak without figure she had thought of something, something about the body, about the passions which it was unfitting for her as a woman to say. Men, her reason told her, would be shocked. The consciousness of what men will say of a woman who speaks the truth about her passions had roused her from her artist's state of unconsciousness. She could write no more. The trance was over. Her imagination could work no longer. This I believe to be a very common experience with women writers — they are impeded by the extreme conventionality of the other sex. For though men sensibly allow themselves great freedom in these respects, I doubt that they realize or can control the extreme severity with which they condemn such freedom in women.

These then were two very genuine experiences of my own. These were two of the adventures of my professional life. The first — killing the Angel in the House — I think I solved. She died. But the second, telling the truth about my own experiences as a body, I do not think I solved. I doubt that any woman has solved it yet. The obstacles against her are still immensely powerful — and yet they are very difficult to define. Outwardly, what is simpler than to write books? Outwardly, what obstacles are there for a woman rather than for a man? Inwardly, I think, the case is very different; she has still many ghosts to fight, many prejudices to overcome. Indeed it will be a long time still, I think, before a woman can sit down to write a book without finding a phantom to be slain, a rock to be dashed against. And if this is so in literature, the freest of all professions for women, how is it in the new professions which you are now for the first time entering?

Those are the questions that I should like, had I time, to ask you. And indeed, if I have laid stress upon these professional experiences of mine, it is because I believe that they are, though in different forms, yours also. Even when the path is nominally open — when there is nothing to prevent a woman from being a doctor, a lawyer, a civil servant — there are many phantoms and obstacles, as I believe, looming in her way. To discuss and define them is I think of great value and importance; for thus only can the labour be shared, the difficulties be solved. But besides this, it is necessary also to discuss the ends and the aims for which we are fighting, for which we are doing battle with these formidable obstacles. Those aims cannot be taken for granted; they must be perpetually questioned and examined. The whole position, as I see it — here in this hall surrounded by women practising for the first time in history I know not how many different professions — is one of extraordinary interest and importance. You have won rooms of your own in the house hitherto exclusively owned by men. You are able, though not without great labour and effort, to pay the rent. You are earning your five hundred pounds a year. But this freedom is only a beginning; the room is your own, but it is still bare. It has to be furnished; it has to be decorated; it has to be shared. How are you going to furnish it, how are you going to decorate it? With whom are you going to share it, and upon what terms? These, I think are questions of the utmost importance and interest. For the first time in history you are able to ask them; for the first time you are able to decide for yourselves what the answers should be. Willingly would I stay and discuss those questions and answers — but not tonight. My time is up; and I must cease.

EXPLORING THE SPEECH

1. (a) Who is the Angel in the House?
   (b) State her main characteristics.
   (c) Why did the Angel become symbolic of the emotional turmoil Woolf experienced when trying to work?
   (d) Why must Woolf kill her?

2. According to Woolf, why have women succeeded as writers before they have succeeded in other professions?

3. What point does the writer make through the sardonic mention of her Persian cat?

4. Woolf claims that many men have attitudes toward women that hamper women's imaginations. Identify the attitudes to which she refers.

5. (a) Identify elements of the speech that create its successful oral quality.
   (b) The vividness of the language used in this speech often provokes strong emotional reactions. Cite examples which accomplish this.

EXTENSIVE STUDY

1. Woolf's essay raises the issue of sex role stereotypes which influence the behaviour of both men and women. Use these famous quotations to help articulate some of these stereotypes. For each statement consider:

   (a) whether it is based on a sexist assumption and, if so, what that assumption is;

   (b) whether it is based on valid evidence;

   (c) possible ways the attitude conveyed by the statement could affect both men and women.

   ■ "The fickleness of women I love is only equalled by the infernal constancy of the women who love me."
   George Bernard Shaw, *The Philanderer*

   ■ "In revenge and in love, woman is more barbarous than man."
   Frederick Nietzsche, *Beyond Good and Evil*

   ■ "As long as you know that most men are like children, you know everything."
   Coco Chanel — remark

   ■ "Women have served all these centuries as looking-glasses possessing the magic and delicious power of reflecting the figure of a man at twice its natural size."
   Virginia Woolf, *A Room of One's Own*

   Use sources such as *Bartlett's Familiar Quotations* to find half a dozen more generalizations that reveal biased or stereotypical thinking on any subject.

2. Woolf states that "It is far harder to kill a phantom than a reality." Is this a valid statement? Explain your response. Divide into small groups, composed of an equal balance of males and females, if possible. Tape your discussion of the following questions which arise from the above statement.

   (a) "Both men and women are sometimes held back from achieving their full potential — in personal and professional spheres — by their fears and other irrational reactions."
   Judging from your personal experiences and observations, assess the extent to which you feel this statement is a valid generalization. If you think the generalization is invalid, amend it to represent the feelings of your group. Be prepared to defend your position with evidence.

   (b) Are there social factors in your community that make it more likely for women to experience fears and other irrational reactions than men? If so, what are these factors?

(c) What authorities are most likely to have valid data on this subject?

(d) Are men less likely to give in to their fears than women? Give evidence other than your own opinion. Identify a number of social factors that account for this situation.

(e) Create a hypothetical situation in which a man and a woman are not achieving their goals because of their inability to resolve certain fears. For each person, articulate the concern or fear, state the goal, and explain how the fear stands between the individual and success, and suggest at least one realistic strategy the individual can use to resolve the problem.

(f) Psychiatrists tell us that we are permanently influenced by our parents' child-rearing practices, values, and attitudes — even though many of these feelings are largely unconscious. List at least half a dozen ways parents might help their daughters and sons develop a strong sense of personal security and self-esteem.

Self-assessment: Consider the group dynamics of this situation. Listen carefully to your completed tape to see if your group engaged in stereotypical thinking and sex role bias. Were the males or females more assertive? What are the implications for your post-secondary career, judging from the role you played in this discussion?
Peer assessment: If you wish, trade tapes with another group. In what ways did this group's dynamics differ from yours?

3. Debate this statement. Resolved that:
   Men as well as women need to be liberated.

4. Read the "U.N. Declaration on Women's Rights." Do you disagree with any of its points? Why? Are there important omissions? Can values and attitudes be legislated?

5. Read the accompanying speeches by John F. Kennedy and Martin Luther King.
   (a) Compare the rhetorical devices employed and evaluate their effectiveness insofar as the intended purpose and audience.
   (b) Which speech do you prefer? Account for your reaction.
   (c) Make a list of any other essays that you have read in this text that raise social and/or political issues similar to those that Woolf, King, and Kennedy address.

6. If you have read the essays about Emily Carr (see The Foreword, Prologue and Preface, page 196), consider whether Woolf's speech gives any insight into the way Carr lived, and why.

7. Read Robertson Davies's "The Conscience of the Writer" (see The University Lecture, page 173). What category of writer would he be likely to place Carr in? Why?

8. George Orwell (1903–1950) and Virginia Woolf (1882–1941) were contemporaries who spent at least some of their lives in Britain working as professional writers. What similarities, if any, do you see in

their writing styles? Did Woolf follow Orwell's six language usage rules? (See The Core Essays, page 3.)

THE WRITING FOLDER

1. Write a dialogue between Woolf and the Angel. Develop the conflict that leads up to the murder of the Angel and reveals what Woolf learns during the struggle.

2. Write a journal entry from a woman's viewpoint that expresses her conflicts about her personal and/or professional priorities.

3. Write a journal entry or dialogue that depicts one of these conflicts:
   (i) a husband whose wife tells him she intends to return to work two months after the birth of their first child;
   (ii) a man whose wife writes a bestseller that earns half a million dollars — substantially more than he makes as a mathematics teacher;
   (iii) a father who encourages his daughter to take over the presidency of his multinational corporation when he retires.

4. Write a speech that you might deliver if you were running for a student council position. Before you polish the speech, practise delivering it to a friend.

INDEPENDENT STUDY

1. Read *The Awakening* by Kate Chopin (1851–1904), an American contemporary of Woolf.

   In her essay, "Professions for Women," Woolf claims that women artists are "impeded by the extreme conventionality of the other [male] sex." Weigh the extent to which this factor helps to explain Edna Pontellier's suicide.   ++

3. Read *The Scarlet Letter* by Nathaniel Hawthorne. Is Hester's silent acceptance of her punishment a tribute to her character or an indictment of the society in which she lives?   +

4. Read *Hedda Gabler* and *A Doll's House* by Henrik Ibsen. Explore Ibsen's depiction of women. Develop a specific topic with your teacher.   ++

5. Read Woolf's famous nonfiction work, *A Room of One's Own* and Margaret Atwood's *The Edible Woman*. Compare their analyses of the position and needs of women, or develop a more specific topic with your teacher.   ++

6. Read a book by one or more of the writers listed in question 7. Then

preview a film depicting images of women. Plan to show it to the class. Question your classmates about the issues raised in the film concerning male-female relations. Present your analysis to the class.

A word of caution: the availability of these films will vary from community to community. Be sure that your teacher has seen the film, as some suggestions may not be suitable for your particular class or community. Submit a report or essay that compares the position of women in the book(s) you read and the film you showed.   + or ++

Films depicting images of women:*
Cries and Whispers, My Brilliant Career, Taming of the Shrew, Norma Rae, Julia, Swept Away, The Turning Point, The Marriage of Maria Braun, The French Lieutenant's Woman, Autumn Sonata, Tess, Kramer vs. Kramer, The Unmarried Woman, Annie Hall, Coal Miner's Daughter, An Officer and a Gentleman

You may prefer to use an old film. (Consider such classics as: *Casablanca, Wuthering Heights, Blood and Sand,* and *The African Queen.*)

7. Related ideas for independent study may be found by reading Margaret Atwood, F. Scott Fitzgerald, Jane Austen, Margaret Laurence, Henry James, D.H. Lawrence, Sylvia Plath, Jean Rhys, Shakespeare, Simone de Beauvoir, Michelle Landsberg, Mary McCarthy, Gloria Steinem, Betty Friedan, Kate Chopin, Colette, Anaïs Nin, Doris Lessing, Katherine Mansfield, and Katherine Anne Porter.

8. Read at least one collection of famous speeches. Develop a specific topic with your teacher. (You might analyze or compare effective political speeches and then write and deliver one of your own.) + or ++

TIMED WRITING

1. Write a personal essay on one of the following topics in the time specified by your teacher:
    (a) Sexual Equality Is for the Birds
    (b) Why Can't a Woman (Man) Be More Like a Man (Woman)

2. Write an outline for an impromptu speech; deliver the speech in the time specified by your teacher:
    (a) Parenting: An Equal Opportunities Job?
    (b) Sexual Stereotyping: Society Is the Loser.

---

*This list appears in *The Critical Concept* (p. 56) available from the Ontario Secondary School Teachers' Federation.

INAUGURAL ADDRESS *INTO OFFICE*

JOHN F. KENNEDY   [Jan 20, 1961]

both inspiring and directional

We observe today not a victory of party but a celebration of freedom — symbolizing an end as well as a beginning — signifying renewal as well as change. For I have sworn before you and Almighty God the same solemn oath our forbears prescribed nearly a century and three quarters ago.

The world is very different now. For man holds in his mortal hands the power to abolish all forms of human poverty and all forms of human life. And yet the same revolutionary beliefs for which our forebears fought are still at issue around the globe — the belief that the rights of man come not from the generosity of the state but from the hand of God.

We dare not forget today that we are the heirs of that first revolution. Let the word go forth from this time and place, to friend and foe alike, that the torch has been passed to a new generation of Americans — born in this century, tempered by war, disciplined by a hard and bitter peace, proud of our ancient heritage — and unwilling to witness or permit the slow undoing of those human rights to which this nation has always been committed, and to which we are committed today at home and around the world.

 Let every nation know, whether it wishes us well or ill, that we shall pay any price, bear any burden, meet any hardship, support any friend, oppose any foe to assure the survival and the success of liberty.

This much we pledge — and more.

To those old allies whose cultural and spiritual origins we share, we pledge the loyalty of faithful friends. United, there is little we cannot do in a host of cooperative ventures. Divided, there is little we can do — for we dare not meet a powerful challenge at odds and split asunder.

To those new states whom we welcome to the ranks of the free, we pledge our word that one form of colonial control shall not have passed away merely to be replaced by a far more iron tyranny. We shall not always expect to find them supporting our view. But we shall always hope to find them strongly supporting their own freedom — and to remember that, in the past, those who foolishly sought power by riding the back of the tiger ended up inside.

To those peoples in the huts and villages of half the globe struggling to break the bonds of mass misery, we pledge our best efforts to help them help themselves, for whatever period is required — not because the Communists may be doing it, not because we seek their votes, but because it is right. If a free society cannot help the many who are poor, it cannot save the few who are rich.

To our sister republics south of our border, we offer a special pledge — to convert our good words into good deeds — in a new alliance for progress — to assist free men and free governments in casting off the chains of poverty. But this peaceful revolution of hope cannot become the prey of hostile powers. Let all our neighbors know that we shall join with them to oppose aggression or subversion anywhere in the Americas. And let every other power know that this hemisphere intends to remain the master of its own house.

To that world assembly of sovereign states, the United Nations, our last best hope in an age where the instruments of war have far outpaced the instruments of peace, we renew our pledge of support — to prevent it from becoming merely a forum for invective — to strengthen its shield of the new and the weak — and to enlarge the area in which its writ may run.

Finally, to those nations who would make themselves our adversary, we offer not a pledge but a request: that both sides begin anew the quest for peace, before the dark powers of destruction unleashed by science engulf all humanity in planned or accidental self-destruction.

We dare not tempt them with weakness. For only when our arms are sufficient beyond doubt can we be certain beyond doubt that they will never be employed.

But neither can two great and powerful groups of nations take comfort from our present course — both sides overburdened by the cost of modern weapons, both rightly alarmed by the steady spread of the deadly atom, yet both racing to alter that uncertain balance of terror that stays the hand of mankind's final war.

So let us begin anew — remembering on both sides that civility is not a sign of weakness, and sincerity is always subject to proof. Let us never negotiate out of fear. But let us never fear to negotiate.

—Let both sides explore what problems unite us instead of belaboring those problems which divide us.

—Let both sides, for the first time, formulate serious and precise proposals for the inspection and control of arms — and bring the absolute power to destroy other nations under the absolute control of all nations.

— Let both sides seek to invoke the wonders of science instead of its terrors. Together let us explore the stars, conquer the deserts, eradicate disease, tap the ocean depths and encourage the arts and commerce.

Let both sides unite to heed in all corners of the earth the command of Isaiah — to "undo the heavy burdens . . . [and] let the oppressed go free."

And if a beachhead of cooperation may push back the jungles of suspicion, let both sides join in creating a new endeavor — not a new balance of power, but a new world of law, where the strong are just and the weak secure and the peace preserved.

All this will not be finished in the first hundred days. Nor will it be finished in the first thousand days, nor in the life of this Administration, nor even perhaps in our lifetime on this planet. But let us begin.

In your hands, my fellow citizens, more than mine, will rest the final success or failure of our course. Since this country was founded, each generation of Americans has been summoned to give testimony to its national loyalty. The graves of young Americans who answered the call to service surround the globe.

Now the trumpet summons us again — not as a call to bear arms, though arms we need — not as a call to battle, though embattled we are — but a call to bear the burden of a long twilight struggle, year in and year out, "rejoicing in hope, patient in tribulation" — a struggle against the common enemies of man: tyranny, poverty, disease and war itself.

Can we forge against these enemies a grand and global alliance, north and south, east and west, that can assure a more fruitful life for all mankind? Will you join in that historic effort?

In the long history of the world, only a few generations have been granted the role of defending freedom in its hour of maximum danger. I do not shrink from this responsibility — I welcome it. I do not believe that any of us would exchange places with any other people or any other generation. The energy, the faith, the devotion which we bring to this endeavor will light our country, and all who serve it — and the glow from that fire can truly light the world.

And so, my fellow Americans: ask not what your country can do for you — ask what you can do for your country.

My fellow citizens of the world; ask not what America will do for you, but what together we can do for the freedom of man.

Finally, whether you are citizens of America or citizens of the world, ask of us here the same high standards of strength and sacrifice which we ask of you. With a good conscience our only sure reward, with history the final judge of our deeds, let us go forth to lead the land we love, asking His blessing and His help, but knowing that here on earth God's work must truly be our own.

I HAVE A DREAM

MARTIN LUTHER KING

I am happy to join with you today in what will go down in history as the greatest demonstration for freedom in the history of our nation.

Five score years ago, a great American, in whose symbolic shadow we stand today, signed the Emancipation Proclamation. This momentous decree came as the great beacon light of hope for millions of Negro slaves who had been seared in the flames of withering injustice. It came as the joyous daybreak to end the long night of their captivity.

But 100 years later the Negro still is not free. One hundred years later, the life of the Negro is still badly crippled by the manacles of segregation and the chains of discrimination. One hundred years later, the Negro lives on a lonely island of poverty in the midst of a vast ocean of material prosperity. One hundred years later, the Negro is still languished in the corners of American society and finds himself an exile in his own land. So we have come here today to dramatize the shameful condition.

In a sense we've come to our Nation's Capital to cash a check. When the architects of our republic wrote the magnificent words of the Constitution and the Declaration of Independence, they were signing a promissory note to which every American was to fall heir. This note was a promise that all men, yes, black men as well as white men, should be guaranteed the unalienable rights of life, liberty, and the pursuit of happiness.

It is obvious today that America has defaulted on this promissory note insofar as her citizens of color are concerned. Instead of honoring this sacred obligation, America has given the Negro people a bad check, a check which has come back marked "Insufficient Funds." But we refuse to believe the bank of justice is bankrupt. We refuse to believe that there are insufficient funds in the great vaults of opportunity of this nation. So we have come to cash this check, a check that will give us open demand, the riches of freedom and the security of justice. We have also come to this hallowed spot to remind America of the fierce urgency of now.

This is no time to engage in the luxury of cooling off or to take the tranquilizing drug of gradualism. Now is the time to make real the promises of democracy. Now is the time to rise from the dark and desolate valley of segregation to the sunlit path of racial justice. Now is the time to lift our nation from the quicksand of racial injustice to the solid rock of brotherhood. Now is the time to make justice a reality for all of God's children.

It would be fatal for the nation to overlook the urgency of the moment. This sweltering summer of the Negro's legitimate discontent will not pass until there is an invigorating autumn of freedom and equality. Nineteen sixty-three is not an end but a beginning. Those who hoped that the Negro needed to blow off steam and will now be content will have a rude awakening if the nation returns to business as usual. There will be neither rest nor tranquility in America until the Negro is guaranteed his citizenship rights. The whirlwinds of revolt will continue to shake the foundations of our nation until the bright day of justice emerges.

But there is something I must say to my people who stand on the warm threshold which leads them to the palace of justice. In the process of gaining our rightful place we must not be guilty of wrongful deeds. Let us not seek to satisfy our thirst for freedom by drinking from the cup of bitterness and hatred. We must forever conduct our struggle on the high plane of dignity and discipline. We must not allow our creative protest to degenerate into physical violence. Again and again we must rise to the majestic heights of meeting physical force with soul force.

The marvelous new militancy which has engulfed the Negro community must not lead us to a distrust of all white people, for many of our white brothers, as evidenced by their presence here today, have come to realize that their destiny is tied up with our destiny. They have come to realize that their freedom is inextricably bound to our freedom. We cannot walk alone.

And as we walk we must make the pledge that we shall always march ahead. We cannot turn back. There are those who are asking the devotees of civil rights: "When will you be satisfied?" We can never be satisfied as long as the Negro is the victim of the unspeakable horrors of police brutality. We can never be satisfied as long as our bodies, heavy with the fatigue of travel, cannot gain lodging in the motels of the highways and the hotels of the cities. We cannot be satisfied as long as the Negro's basic mobility is from a smaller ghetto to a larger one. We can never be satisfied as long as our children are stripped of their selfhood and robbed of their dignity by signs stating: "For Whites Only." We cannot be satisfied as long as the Negro in Mississippi cannot vote and the Negro in New York believes he has nothing for which to vote. No, no, we are not satisfied and we will not be satisfied until justice rolls down like waters and righteousness like a mighty stream.

I am not unmindful that some of you have come here out of great trials and tribulations, some of you have come fresh from narrow jail cells, some of you have come from areas where your quest for freedom left you battered by the storms of persecution and staggered by the winds of police brutality. You have been the veterans of creative suffering. Continue to work with the faith that unearned suffering is redemptive.

Go back to Mississippi, go back to Alabama, go back to South Carolina, go back to Georgia, go back to Louisiana, go back to the slums and ghettos of our northern cities, knowing that somehow this situation can and will be changed. Let us not wallow in the valley of despair.

I say to you today, my friends, even though we face the difficulties of today and tomorrow, I still have a dream. It is dream deeply rooted in the American dream. I have a dream that one day this nation will rise up and live out the true meaning of its creed: "We hold these truths to be self-evident: that all men are created equal."

I have a dream that one day on the red hills of Georgia the sons of former slaves and the sons of former slaveowners will be able to sit down together at the table of brotherhood.

I have a dream that one day even the State of Mississippi, a state sweltering with the heat of injustice, sweltering with the heat of oppression, will be transformed into an oasis of freedom and justice. I have a dream that my four little children will one day live in a nation where they will not be judged by the color of their skin but by the content of their character. I have a dream today.

I have a dream that one day down in Alabama with its vicious racists, with its Governor having his lips dripping with the words of interposition and nullification — one day right there in Alabama, little black boys and black girls will be able to join hands with little white boys and white girls as sisters and brothers.

I have a dream today.

I have a dream that one day every valley shall be exalted, every hill and mountain shall be made low, the rough places will be made plain and the crooked places will be made straight, and the glory of the Lord shall be revealed, and all flesh shall see it together.

This is our hope. This is the faith that I go back to the South with. With this faith we will be able to hew out of the mountain of despair a stone of hope. With this faith we will be able to transform the jangling discords of our nation into a beautiful symphony of brotherhood. With this faith we will be able to work together, to pray together, to struggle together, to go to jail together, to stand up for freedom together, knowing that we will be free one day.

This will be the day when all of God's children will be able to sing with new meaning:

put aside injustice,

My country 'tis of thee,
Sweet land of liberty,
Of thee I sing:
Land where my fathers died,
Land of the pilgrims' pride,
From every mountain-side
Let Freedom ring.

And if America is to be a great nation, this must become true. So, let freedom ring from the prodigious hill tops of New Hampshire. Let freedom ring from the mighty mountains of New York. Let freedom ring from heightening Alleghenies of Pennsylvania. Let freedom ring from the snowcapped Rockies of Colorado. Let freedom ring from the curvaceous slopes of California. But not only that, let freedom ring from Stone Mountain of Georgia.

Let freedom ring from Lookout Mountain of Tennessee.

Let freedom ring from every hill and molehill of Mississippi. From every mountainside, let freedom ring. And when we allow freedom to ring, when we let it ring from every village, from every hamlet, from every state and every city, we will be able to speed up that day when all of God's children, black men and white men, Jews and Gentiles, Protestants and Catholics, will be able to join hands and sing in the words of the old Negro spiritual: "Free at last! free at last! thank God almighty, we are free at last!"

U.N. DECLARATION ON WOMEN'S RIGHTS

Following is the text of a declaration on discrimination against women, as adopted 7 November 1967 in the General Assembly:

The General Assembly,

Considering that the peoples of the United Nations have, in the Charter, reaffirmed their faith in fundamental human rights, in the dignity and worth of the human person and in the equal rights of men and women,

Considering that the Universal Declaration of Human Rights asserts the principle of nondiscrimination and proclaims that all human beings are born free and equal in dignity and rights and that everyone is entitled to all the rights and freedoms set forth therein, without distinction of any kind, including any distinction as to sex,

Taking into account the resolutions, declarations, conventions and recommendations of the United Nations and the specialized agencies designed to eliminate all forms of discrimination and to promote equal rights for men and women,

Concerned that, despite the Charter, the Universal Declaration of Human Rights, International Covenants on Human Rights and other instruments of the United Nations and the specialized agencies and despite the progress made in the matter of equality of rights, there continues to exist considerable discrimination against women,

Considering that discrimination against women is incompatible with human dignity, and with the welfare of the family and of society, prevents their participation on equal terms with men, in the political, social, economic and cultural life of their countries, and is an obstacle to the full development of the potentialities of women in the service of their countries and of humanity,

Bearing in mind the great contribution made by women to social, political, economic and cultural life and the part they play in the family and particularly in the rearing of children,

Convinced that the full and complete development of a country, the welfare of the world and the cause of peace require the maximum participation of women as well as men in all fields,

Considering that it is necessary to insure the universal recognition in law and in fact of the principle of equality of men and women,

Solemnly proclaims this Declaration:

ARTICLE 1

Discrimination against women, denying or limiting as it does their equality of rights with men, is fundamentally unjust and constitutes an offense against human dignity.

ARTICLE 2

All appropriate measures shall be taken to abolish existing laws, customs, regulations and practices which are discriminatory against women, and to establish adequate legal protection for equal rights of men and women, in particular:

(a) The principle of equality of rights shall be embodied in the constitution or otherwise guaranteed by law;

(b) The international instruments of the United Nations and the specialized agencies relating to the elimination of discrimination against women shall be ratified or acceded to and fully implemented as soon as practicable.

ARTICLE 3

All appropriate measures shall be taken to educate public opinion and direct national aspirations toward the eradication of prejudice and the abolition of customary and all other practices which are based on the idea of the inferiority of women.

ARTICLE 4

All appropriate measures shall be taken to ensure to women on equal terms with men without any discrimination:

(a) The right to vote in all elections and be eligible for election to all publicly elected bodies;

(b) The right to vote in all public referenda;

(c) The right to hold public office and to exercise all public functions.

Such rights shall be guaranteed by legislation.

ARTICLE 5

Women shall have the same rights as men to acquire, change or retain their nationality. Marriage to an alien shall not automatically affect the nationality of the wife either by rendering her stateless or by forcing on her the nationality of her husband.

ARTICLE 6

1. Without prejudice to the safeguarding of the unity and the harmony of the family which remains the basic unit of any society, all appropriate measures, particularly legislative measures, shall be taken to insure to women, married or unmarried, equal rights with men in the field of civil law, and in particular:

(a) The right to acquire, administer and enjoy, dispose of and inherit property, including property acquired during the marriage;

(b) The right to equality in legal capacity and the exercise thereof;

(c) The same rights as men with regard to the law on the movement of persons.

2. All appropriate measures shall be taken to insure the principle of equality of status of the husband and wife, and in particular:

(a) Women shall have the same right as men to free choice of a spouse and to enter into marriage only with their free and full consent;

(b) Women shall have equal rights with men during marriage and at its dissolution. In all cases the interest of the child shall be paramount;

(c) Parents shall have equal rights and duties in matters relating to their children. In all cases the interest of the children shall be paramount.

3. Child marriage and the bethrothal of young girls before puberty shall be prohibited, and effective action, including legislation, shall be taken to specify a minimum age for marriage and to make the registration of marriages in an official registry compulsory.

ARTICLE 7

All provisions of penal codes which constitute discrimination against women shall be repealed.

ARTICLE 8

All appropriate measures, including legislation, shall be taken to combat all forms of traffic in women and exploitation of prostitution of women.

ARTICLE 9

All appropriate measures shall be taken to insure to girls and women, married or unmarried, equal rights with men in education at all levels, and in particular:

(a) Equal conditions of access to, and study in, educational institutions of all types, including universities, vocational, technical and professional schools;

(b) The same choice of curricula, the same examinations, teaching staff with qualifications of the same standard, and school premises and equipment of the same quality, whether the institutions are coeducational or not;

(c) Equal opportunities to benefit from scholarships and other study grants;

(d) Equal opportunities for access to programs of continuing education, including adult literacy programs;

(e) Access to educational information to help in insuring the health and well-being of families.

ARTICLE 10

1. All appropriate measures shall be taken to insure to women, married or unmarried, equal rights with men in the field or economic and social life, and in particular:

(a) The right without discrimination on grounds of marital status or any other grounds, to receive vocational training, to work, to free choice of profession and employment, and to professional and vocational advancement;

(b) The right to equal remuneration with men and to equality of treatment in respect of work of equal value;

(c) The right to leave with pay, retirement privileges and provision for security in respect of unemployment, sickness, old age or other incapacity to work;

(d) The right to receive family allowances on equal terms with men.

2. In order to prevent discrimination against women on account of marriage or maternity and to insure their effective right to work, measures shall be taken to prevent their dismissal in the event of marriage or maternity and to provide paid maternity leave, and the guarantee of returning to former employment, and to provide the necessary social services, including childcare facilities.

3. Measures taken to protect women in certain types of work, for reasons inherent in their physical nature, shall not be regarded as discriminatory.

ARTICLE 11

The principle of equality of rights of men and women demands implementation in all states in accordance with the principles of the United Nations Charter and of the Universal Declaration of Human Rights.

Governments, nongovernmental organizations and individuals are urged, therefore, to do all in their power to promote the implementation of the principles contained in this Declaration.

10. THE UNIVERSITY LECTURE

Key Work:
   "The Conscience of the Writer" — Robertson Davies
Associated Reading:
   "Civil Disobedience: Nature and Origin" —
   George Woodcock

The university lecture is a formal speech delivered to a specific audience. Predating the printing press, the lecture originated in the Middle Ages as an easy way of dispensing information; it was used in the early days of Oxford University. The lecturer assumes the listeners have certain background knowledge — through assigned readings, the nature of their interests, or their general level of education — and then explores the topic. Audiovisual aids are rarely employed and the audience may number several hundred or more. Although certain lecturers permit the audience to pose questions as they arise, more often queries are held until the end. In exploring the thesis, the speaker synthesizes information and steers the audience toward the conclusion. If you listen carefully, you should be able to pick out the steps of the argument as you take notes under headings and subheadings. Students who regularly attend their lectures and take well-organized notes usually find they are invaluable tools for exam study.

Robertson Davies, a writer and professor at University of Toronto, delivered this guest lecture at Glendon Campus, York University. The sophisticated level of diction and syntax and the challenging content are representative of the lectures you will encounter in your post-secondary career.

The Associated Reading, George Woodcock's "Civil Disobedience: Nature and Origin," is the text of one of his half-hour radio lectures on the nature of civil disobedience. The seven lectures, later published under the title *Civil Disobedience,* also assume a sophisticated background among his audience; like Davies, Woodcock often alludes to famous literary and historical figures and assumes some knowledge of mythology by the listener.

BEFORE READING

■ Have someone deliver the lecture and practise taking notes (see the tips on effective note-taking in Part C).
■ What problems did you encounter? Consider suggestions for overcoming these difficulties.

■ Have you ever attended a university lecture? What do you think of this method as a teaching technique? How might you prepare yourself now to get the most out of future lectures?

THE CONSCIENCE OF THE WRITER

ROBERTSON DAVIES

My subject is 'The Conscience of the Writer', and I have accepted your invitation to speak not because I think I have anything new to say about it, but because I think that the familiar and basic things demand constant repetition, in an age when familiar and basic things are so often cast aside, as if we had outlived them. The writer's calling has been greatly romanticized — more so, I believe, than that of any other artistic creator. Painters, sculptors, and composers are regarded with a degree of awe by the public in general, but writers possess a special sort of magic, and I believe that in part it is the magic of what seems to be a familiar and attainable, yet somehow unrealized, element in the lives of many people who are not artists of any kind. Anybody can see that he is not going to paint like Picasso, or write music like Benjamin Britten; he is not so sure that he is not going to write like somebody whose writing he admires. He has learned the humblest techniques of the writer at school; he can put down words on a page; he has some idea of grammar, or he may have decided that grammar is an unworthy shackle on his inspiration; he is constantly meeting with experiences, or observing people, that seem to him to be the stuff of writing. But somehow he never writes.

He could do so, of course. Every writer is familiar with the person who buttonholes him and tells him about the book he could write — if he had the time. Or else they have fathers or uncles who are screamingly funny characters whose lives ought to be written at once. These people sometimes offer to collaborate with the author, providing the raw material if he will do the actual work of writing.

Such people are usually middle-aged. Younger people with the urge to write do not want to collaborate; they are, on the contrary, often suspicious that older writers will snatch their splendid inspirations and capitalize on them. These young people are often daring experimenters in technique, because their ideas can only be given adequate form in some wholly new way of writing — leaving out all the verbs, or perhaps writing nothing but verbs, but most often in the present day by describing, with gloating particularity, various sexual acts which they have just discovered, and of which they wish to make the innocent old world aware. But after a few months during which they burn with a hard, gem-like flame, these people cease to write.

The world is full of people who think they could write, or who have, at some time, written. But they do not stay with it. Why?

Is it because the real writer, the serious writer, who is a writer all his life, is a special kind of person? Yes, it is. And what kind of person is he? I do not pretend to be able to answer that question fully, for there are many kinds of writers, some of whom I do not understand at all, and some whom I understand but do not admire, although I am well aware of their talents. But they all have a characteristic — indeed a distinguishing trait in their psychological make-up — which makes them recognizable, and it is this that I have called the writer's conscience, although that is not a very satisfactory name for it. I use that phrase to describe the continuing struggle that goes on in the psyche of every writer of any importance. And by that expression 'of any importance' I exclude the journalistic word-spinners, the ghost-writers, the concocters of literary confectionery, although some of these are remarkable technicians. I am talking about the writers who try — perhaps not all the time but certainly during the greater part of their careers — to write the best they can about the themes that concern them most.

This is not a moral judgement, and has nothing to do with the themes that writers choose. Perhaps I can make myself clear by instancing two books — Dostoevsky's *Crime and Punishment* and Max Beerbohm's *Zuleika Dobson*. One is an agonized exploration of the psychology of a criminal intellectual; the other is a charming joke about youth and love. One is clumsily written, with long passages of over-heated and perversely sensitive emotion; the other is elegantly and exquisitely written, in a fashion so subtle that it yields up its secrets only after several careful readings. Both are great books, and I think it is foolish to say that one is greater than the other, as if one were marking an examination, and giving Dostoevsky higher marks because he tries harder. He didn't try harder. He just wrote the best book he could in the circumstances in which he found himself. So did Max Beerbohm. Both books appeal strongly to large numbers of readers, who encounter them at particularly fortunate moments in their lives. And I believe that it is because both writers wrote under the domination of conscience, and it is the subsequent revelation that gives the books their particular weight and value.

There are no absolutes in literature that can be applied without reference to personal taste and judgement. The great book for you is the book that has most to say to you at the moment when you are reading. I do not mean the book that is most instructive, but the book that feeds your spirit. And that depends on your age, your experience, your psychological and spiritual need. These days I find myself reading poetry rather a lot. But when I was ten what I liked to read best were bound volumes of a boys' paper called *Chums*. It had just what I needed, and it extended my world remarkably; however, when I looked at some of that stuff recently I could not endure it. But I am sure I should not be reading what I read now if I had not read *Chums* then, and I am grateful. We do not read to make ourselves cultured, but to nourish our souls. Real culture is the evidence, not the reality, of the fully realized spirit.

This is one of my great quarrels with university courses in English; they require students to read lists of fine books, and to profess a knowledge of them that is usually superficial, though even this sort of knowledge is better than none at all. But for every masterpiece that is on the reading-list, there are five that are not, and many students fall into the trap of thinking that anything that is not on the list is not Blue Brand Literature, and may be disregarded. This is not the intention of English courses, but it is what happens. The great difficulty is that the emphasis in universities is likely to be on criticism of literature, rather than on delighted discovery and surrender to it. Every student — BA. MA. or PH D — knows what is wrong with Charles Dickens, though they have probably read nothing but *Great Expectations*, and read it once, when they were too young to understand it. The reason for this is perfectly clear: criticism is comparatively easy in its showy but superficial aspect. Anybody can pick up its techniques and use them with a display of skill, just as anybody can make a spectacular cut with a surgeon's scalpel, simply because it is so sharp. But the vastly more difficult business of discovering literature, and giving oneself wholly into its embrace, and making some of it part of oneself, cannot be done in large classes, and not everybody can do it even in small classes. A surprising number of people can get PH D'S in criticism; to be a worthy reader of what writers of conscience have written is a very different matter.

Which brings us back to our theme — the writer and his conscience. Moral judgements based on the themes a writer chooses, I have said, are irrelevant. Evelyn Waugh was a writer of extraordinary conscience, and his novels, even when most serious, have a comic guise, and are spare and elegant in form. Tolstoy was similarly a writer of extraordinary conscience, but *Anna Karenina* and *War and Peace* are solemn and almost portentous in tone, and their greatest admirers will admit that they might have been the better for the cutting of large passages. It is of little use to say that *War and Peace* is a masterpiece because it tells us all there is to say about war; it tells us wonderful things, but Waugh's little novel *Scoop* tells us something that Tolstoy did not. This is not to say that the two books are equally 'great' or 'good' but only that every good book is good in its own way, and that comparisons are of extremely limited value. Unless, of course, you are a superficial critic, in which case you had better banish all humility in the face of genius and get on with your self-appointed task of awarding marks and establishing hierarchies. But if you want to know and feel what genius knows and feels, you must be a reader first, and a critic a very long way afterward.

Now — what is this conscience I have been talking about? It is the writer's inner struggle toward self-knowledge and self-recognition, which he makes manifest through his art. Writers, and artists generally, are notoriously resistant to psycho-analysis, and to put hundreds of thousands of words by both Freud and Jung into a nutshell it is because they are continuously psycho-analysing themselves in their own way, which is through their work, and it is the only way to peace of mind, to integration, open to them. It is a life process, and in the work of a writer of great abilities who has been so fortunate as to live long it presents an awesome achievement. Consider the case of Thomas Mann; from *Little Herr Friedemann,* which he published when he was twenty-three, and *Buddenbrooks,* which appeared when he was twenty-five, the succession of his books reveals to us, beneath the themes, the fables, and the philosophical explorations, the development of an extraordinary spirit: *The Magic Mountain* (1924), the great *Joseph* tetralogy, which was sixteen years in the writing, *Lotte in Weimar* (1939), *Doctor Faustus* (1948), and that extraordinary book which appeared when the writer was eighty, *The Confessions of Felix Krull* — these are a few mountain peaks in a career of an artist's self-exploration. And what is revealed? A deep preoccupation with themes of death and disease, of sin and remorse and redemption, of myth and the irrationalities of life, of the wellsprings of the creative spirit, and at the last, in *Felix Krull,* a triumphant return and exploration of one of Mann's lifelong preoccupations, which was the link between the artistic and the criminal instinct, embodied in what I regard as quite the subtlest and most hair-raisingly erotic novel I have ever read. A concern, as you see, with some of the deep and continuing problems of human life.

Here we have what the great literary artist does; he explores his own spirit to the uttermost, and bodies forth what he finds in a form of art that is plain to anyone who can read it — though not necessarily to anyone who picks up his books.

The struggle is not easy and its results are sometimes disastrous, for reasons that we shall explore a little later. Psycho-analysis is notoriously demanding and disagreeable, when undertaken by a sympathetic and skilled physician: consider what it means when it is a solitary venture, undertaken as a life sentence and carried out under the circumstances in which most authors live. Is it any wonder that the domestic lives of some of them are rumpled and unseemly? Or that many of them take to drink? Or that others escape into that attractive world of action where they can get so much easy acclaim by protesting or sitting-in or freaking-out or setting themselves up as great friends and patrons of youth, or whooping it up for the Pill or LSD — doing anything, in fact, except getting on with the laborious task to which their gift and their temperament calls them?

Henrik Ibsen knew all about it, and he was one of the heroes who remained chained to his task until finally it broke him; for the last years of his life he toiled painstakingly every day over a copybook, trying to force his hand to learn, for the second time, the skill of making readable writing. Did you know that Ibsen was a poet? Here is a translation of one of his verses, full of meaning and warning for writers:

To live — is a battle with troll-folk
In the crypts of heart and head;
To write — is a man's self-judgement
As Doom shall judge the dead.

'A man's self-judgement' — that is the conscience of the writer. Whatever he writes, and whatever the summing-up of that mysterious inner court may be, if it is carried through truthfully and manfully, we shall sense in it that quality that makes literature one of the greatest of the arts, and well worth the sacrifice and the frequent misery of a writer's life.

Sometimes I laugh when aspiring writers assure me that if they could get enough money — usually in the form of a grant from some handout agency subsidized by the government — they would go to Mexico, or the Mediterranean, or to Capri, and there they would be able to write — so readily, so fluently, so happily. Fools! 'A man's self-judgement' will go with him anywhere, if he is really a writer, and he will not be able to command either inspiration or happiness or serenity. Of course if he is a mere scribbling tourist, or a work-shy flop, or both, it does not really matter much where he goes. But if he is a writer he will be wise to write wherever he finds himself. The history of literature is full of writers who have thought that the judgement of the inner court would be easier in some country outside his own.

This is not to say, of course, that a writer should not travel or gain experience. But if he is really a writer his task may be, not to seek experience, but to survive the experience that crowds upon him for every quarter. As Aldous Huxley has written, 'experience is not a matter of having actually swum the Hellespont, or danced with the dervishes, or slept in a doss-house. It is a matter of sensibility and intuition, of seeing and hearing the significant things, of paying attention at the right moments, of understanding and co-ordinating. Experience is not what happens to a man: it is what a man does with what happens to him.' Many years ago I read a book by the travelling journalist Richard Halliburton; he had climbed a very high mountain somewhere — I forget where because the book was not of the sort that sticks in the mind — and he recorded the reflection of his companion at the top. It was 'Now I can spit a mile!' We are familiar with the reflections of Wordsworth, who climbed a few quite unremarkable hills in the Lake District. There is the contrast in what experience meant to a man of trivial mind, and to a poet.

Let us continue the theme of the writer's artistic experience considered in terms of psycho-analysis. To do so, I want to talk from the standpoint of C.G. Jung, rather than that of Sigmund Freud. Great as Freud was, and unassailable as his position is among the great liberators of the human mind, his actual technique seems more suited to the consulting-room than to the university lecture-room; his mind dealt more strikingly with problems of neurosis than with matters of aesthetics, and his cast of mind was power-fully reductive. After the Freudian treatment most things look a little shabby — needlessly so. Jung's depth psychology, on the other hand, is much more aesthetic and humanistic in its general tendency, and is not so Procrustean in its effect on artistic experi-ence. The light it throws on matters of literature and on the tem-perament of the writer is extremely useful and revealing.

Jung is insistent on a particular type of development in the mind of anyone who meets the problems of life successfully; it is the change, the alteration of viewpoint, that transformation of aims and ambitions, that overtakes everybody somewhere in the middle of life. In women this change is physiological as well as mental, and consequently it has always been a matter of common observation. But in men the change is an intellectual and spiritual one of pro-found consequence, and this is something observable in the careers of virtually all writers of the kind we are talking about here — the committed writers, the servants of the writer's conscience.

Example is probably better than explanation at this point. The career of the late Aldous Huxley will be familiar to many of you. During the early part of his career his work was remarkable for its strongly satirical edge, for the brilliance of its wit, for its concern with matters of morality and especially morality as it relates to sex, which seemed to many people revolutionary and perhaps dan-gerous and destructive. He is rather out of fashion at present, but when the usual slump in reputation that follows a writer's death is over — it takes about ten or fifteen years — I think these novels will be prized for their stringent charm. But I well remember the sur-prise and excitement that was caused by the appearance of *Eyeless in Gaza* in 1936; it seemed to be a work by a new man, for its tone was inquiring, mystical, and tormented beyond anything we had found in him before. Of course the fashionable people chattered about his probable conversion to Roman Catholicism, and those who had chiefly valued the bitterness of the early books thought that he had 'gone off' terribly, and lamented him as one lost. But the change in direction had been heralded for anybody with eyes to see it in his earlier book *Point Counter Point*, which was a tortured and questing book; the bitterness in it was born of revulsion rather than glee at the follies of mankind. And what was significant about *Eyeless in Gaza* was that it was written when Huxley was forty-two, and ripe for a change. If there had been no change, we should soon have tired of the old Huxley wearing the young Huxley's intellectual clothes. And from that time until the end of his life his exploration of mystical religion and his discussions of morality were at the root of everything he wrote.

Much the same sort of foolish hubbub broke out when Evelyn Waugh wrote *Brideshead Revisited* in 1945. Has our favourite jester gone serious on us, cried the people who admired his earlier books only because they were funny, and not because they were wise. But Waugh was forty-two, and his point of view had changed.

What is the nature of this change? It is part of intellectual and particularly spiritual growth. As Jung explains it, in the early part of life — roughly for the first half of it — man's chief aims are personal and social. He must grow up, he must find his work, he must find out what kind of sex life he is going to lead, he must achieve some place in the world and attempt to get security within it, or else decide that security is not important to him. But when he has achieved these ends, or come to some sort of understanding with this part of existence, his attention is turned to matters that are broader in scope, and sometimes disturbing to contemplate. His physical strength is waning rather than growing; he has found out what sex is, and though it may be very important to him it can do little to surprise him; he realizes that some day he is really going to die and that the way he approaches death is of importance to him; he finds that without God (using that name to comprehend all the great and inexplicable things and the redemptive or destructive powers that lie outside human command and understanding) his life lacks a factor that it greatly needs; he finds that, in Jung's phrase, he is not the master of his fate except in a very modest degree and that he is in fact the object of a supraordinate subject. And he seeks wisdom rather than power — though the circumstances of his early life may continue to thrust power into his hands.

Now, the paradox of this change is that it does not make him an old man. What will make him an old man is a frightened clinging to the values of the first half of life. We have all seen these juvenile dotards whose boast is that they are just as young as their sons or their grandsons; they do not realize what a pitiful boast that is. They prate about their sympathy with youth, but they mean only the superficialities and ephemera of youth. Many of the sad smashups in marriages that we all see among middle-aged people have their origin in this attempt to dodge an inescapable fact. The values that are proper and all-absorbing during the first half of life will not sustain a man during the second half. If he has the courage and wisdom to advance courageously into the new realm of values and emotions he will age physically, of course, but his intellectual and spiritual growth will continue, and will give satisfaction to himself and to all those associated with him. And such courage and wisdom are by no means rare; they may show themselves among many people who have never thought along these lines at all but who have a knack for living life wisely; and they also are to be found among those who regard self-awareness as one of the primary duties of a good life. Paradoxically, such people are on better terms with youth than the shrivelled Peter Pans who dare not be their age.

How does this affect the writer, who is our chief concern here? It is important to him to manage this change in outlook with skill and humility, for a failure to do so can be his ruin. He may be one of those whose special gifts fit him for the kind of writing a man does before middle life. This has been the case with many poets, who appear to have lost everything but technical skill after the appearance of a number of fine — perhaps great — early works. One wonders what Byron would have been like after forty-five. One regrets that Keats did not live to give us the mature works of one of the greatest geniuses of youth. On the other hand, we recall that Cervantes, whose works written during his early life were capable, but not the sort of thing that it would occur to anybody to translate, astonished the world with *Don Quixote* when he was fifty-eight, and wrote the second part of it ten years later. We think of Goethe, who wrote the first part of *Faust* when he was fifty-six, and completed the mighty second part of that play between his seventy-fifth and his eighty-second year. I have already spoken of Thomas Mann, whose genius survived triumphantly until his death at the age of eighty, and I do not suppose it is necessary to point out that all the finest work of Bernard Shaw belongs to the second half of his life.

There are those who do not choose to make this necessary advance, or who repress evidence of it in their writing. It would be impertinent to speculate superficially on such a subject, but one may wonder if that is not what happened to Ernest Hemingway. And certainly if we examine the works of our own best-known writer, the late Stephen Leacock, with care, we wonder whether he was not trapped in the manner of his earliest writing. He did not set out on his career until he was in his early forties, but it was in the manner of his youth; his success was so great that he may have hesitated to introduce a new and deeper note into what was so gratefully accepted by his readers. The result is writing that is often thin and perfunctory. But in one of his last books — the short autobiographical sketch called *The Boy I Left Behind Me* — we are given a tantalizing sample of what he might have done if he had chosen.

There are exceptions to all rules, and you may be surprised to hear me name a writer who is one of the greatest technicians of the last fifty years, P.G. Wodehouse, who continues to produce novels — they have been discerningly called 'musical comedies without music' — that are much like his earlier successes in tone, and are so brilliantly adapted to his aims that they continue to astonish us. He is in his eighty-seventh year and still writing. But he invented a highly artificial mode which no one has successfully imitated. Wodehouse, however, is no case of arrested development; if you think him immature, read his autobiographical volume called *Performing Flea*, which he wrote in 1951. Sean O'Casey, with characteristic spleen, had referred to Wodehouse as a performing flea, and in this book Wodehouse makes it plain that he is certainly no trivial entertainer, but a man of maturity, irony, and keen perception — qualities not overwhelmingly demonstrated by O'Casey, whose best work was done by the time he was forty-four.

How does the real writer — the man with the writer's conscience, or temperament, or whatever label you choose — set about his work? There are as many ways as there are writers, but there are a few well-worn paths, and of these I can only speak with certainly about the path I have chosen for myself. It would be more correct to say, the path my temperament has chosen for me. I combine writing with other sorts of work. For twenty-eight years I have been a journalist — not just a writer, but an editor, an employer, a man who had to make sure that his newspaper did not lose money, who had to worry about new machinery, new buildings, new contracts with unions, and continually to be concerned with an obligation to a community. When I had spent the day doing this I went home and wrote, altogether, works that fill eighteen volumes; I am at work on the nineteenth, and the twentieth exists in the form of extended notes. I am not counting four full-length plays that were produced but are not yet in print. I am not saying this to dazzle you with my industry, but to tell you how I do my work. I have always been grateful for my journalistic experience, which amounts to millions of words of writing, because it kept my technique in good muscular shape. I can write now without that humming and hawing and staring at the ceiling which plagues so many writers who have trouble getting started.

I have of late become a university professor and head of a college, and these tasks can hardly be regarded as a rest-cure. My most difficult work in this realm is the correcting of student essays and marking examinations. Reading inexpert writing is deeply exhausting. It is like listening to bad music.

I have also had the ordinary family experiences. I am married and have three children, now all grown up, and I have spent countless happy hours in domestic pursuits — gardening, family music-making, getting together some modest but pleasant collections of things, amateur theatricals as well as some professional theatre-work, and a kind of family life that seems perhaps to be more characteristic of the nineteenth century than of our streamlined era. I have sat on committees, and boards; I have made a great many speeches, and I have listened to what seem, in recollection, to be millions of speeches.

All of this I consider necessary to my life as a writer. It has kept me from too great a degree of that fruitless self-preoccupation which is one of the worst diseases of the literary life. It has provided me with the raw material for what I write. The raw material, you observe; before it becomes the finished product it must undergo a process of distillation and elimination. An author is a very different thing from a reporter, or an autobiographer. This way of living has confirmed a theory I formed many years ago, when I was at the age you have reached now, that myth and fairy-tales are nothing less than the distilled truth about what we call 'real life', and that we move through a throng of Sleeping Princesses, Belles Dames sans Merci, Cinderellas, Wicked Witches, Powerful Wizards, Frog Princes, Lucky Third Sons, Ogres, Dwarves, Sagacious Animal Helpers and Servers, yes and Heroes and Heroines, in a world that is nothing less than an enchanted landscape, and that life only seems dull and spiritless to those who live under a spell — too often a spell they have brought upon their own heads.

Do not misunderstand me. I am not being whimsical, and my world is not the cosy nursery retreat of Winnie-the-Pooh. It is a tough world, and it only seems irrational or unreal to those who have not grasped some hints of its remorseless, irreversible, and often cruel logic. It is a world in which God is not mocked, and in which a man reaps — only too obviously — what he has sown. I do not think I understand it all, but I think I am acquainted with a few corners of it. And I may as well tell you that I regard the writing I have done as little more than a preparation for the work I mean to do.

Although I have been telling you about what I have done that is not the primary work of a writer, I would not have you believe that I have merely fitted my writing into odd corners of my life. Writing has always been central to my life, and my real work. But I said that I was glad to have the ordinary occupations of a busy man to protect me against that self-preoccupation that is one of the worst diseases of the literary life. Let me explain: I do not write in my spare time, I write all the time; whatever I may be doing, the literary aspect of my mind is fully at work: it is not only the hours at the desk or the typewriter, but the hours spent in other kinds of work and in many kinds of diversion when I am busily observing, shaping, rejecting, and undergoing a wide variety of feelings that are the essential material of writing. Notice that I said feelings — not thoughts, but feelings. One of the burdensome parts of the writer's temperament, as I understand it, is that one feels quite strongly about all sorts of things that other people seem to be able to gloss over, and this can be wearisome and depleting. This is the famous 'artistic sensitivity' that one sometimes hears people boasting about — very often people who show no other awareness of it. It is not a form of weakness. A writer is very rarely a wincing, delicate kind of man; in my experience he is often rather a tough creature, though given to hypochondria and sudden collapses of the spirit. I rely on a routine of daily work, and the necessities of a busy life, to keep me from succumbing too completely to the demands of a particular kind of temperament. My kind of writer — I can speak for no other — needs other work and a routine to keep him sane.

Let me return once again to the emphasis I laid on feeling, rather than thinking, in the writer's temperament. All sorts of people expect writers to be intellectuals. Sometimes they are, but it is not necessary to their work. Aldous Huxley was an intellectual, but he was not so good a novelist as E.M. Forster, who is not and does not like to be considered one. The writer is necessarily a man of feeling and intuition; he need not be a powerful original thinker. Shakespeare, Dickens, Dostoevsky — we do not think of them as intellectuals; Tolstoy's thinking was vastly inferior to his fiction; Keats was a finer poet than Arnold, though no one would deny Arnold the title of intellectual. I do not say that writers are child-like creatures of untutored genius; often they are very intelligent men: but the best part of their intelligence is of the feeling and intuitive order. Sometimes they are impatient and even rude with people who insist on treating them as intellectuals. It is not pleasant to be treated like a clock by some clever but essentially unsympathetic person who wants to take you apart to see what makes you tick. But the modern passion for this sort of thing has led to the establishment on many campuses of a man called the Writer in Residence, who is there, in part at any rate, for intellectuals to pester, take apart, and reassemble, under the impression that they are learning something about writing.

As I draw to a conclusion, I want to return to something I said at the beginning of this address, which is that the life of a writer may be likened to a long self-analysis. I suggested that the process was painful, and indeed it frequently is so. But it is something else — something that Freud never mentioned, because of his preoccupation with neurosis, but which Jung suggests: it is sometimes joyous, victorious, and beautiful. It is not fashionable nowadays to say that one's life has moments of piercing beauty, or that it brings hours which are not merely recompense, but ample and bounteous reward for all the anxieties and dark moments. But I am not a fashionable person, and I am saying that now.

The degree of self-examination that is involved in being a writer, and the stringency of the writer's conscience, which holds you to a path that is often distasteful, necessarily takes you on some strange journeys, not only into the realm of the personal Unconscious, but into the level below that. It is assumed, by many people who have read Freud and Jung, that these descents must always be alarming experiences, because Freud and Jung were so much occupied with people who were very seriously disordered. But the writer is not necessarily disordered, and great rewards await him in this realm, if he approaches it with decent reverence. He will have serious struggles, but sometimes his struggles are like those of Jacob when he wrestled with the angel at Peniel, and cried in his extremity, 'I will not let thee go, unless thou bless me.' And he received the blessing, and bore it all his life. That realm of the Unconscious, which is the dwelling-place of so many demons and monsters, is also the home of the Muses, the abode of the angels. The writer, in his traffic with that realm in which dream, and myth, and fairy-tale become mingled with the most ordinary circumstances of life, does not lack for rewards and very great rewards. Self-examination is stern and often painful, as Ibsen tells us in the verse I quoted to you, but it is not all bitterness.

I have spoken to you seriously, because I presume that you are serious people. Certainly I am one, though such reputation as I have as a writer rests — rests perhaps a little too heavily — on my qualities as a humorist. Never be deceived by a humorist, for if he is any good he is a deeply serious man, moved by a quirk of temperament to speak a certain kind of truth in the form of jokes. Everybody can laugh at the jokes; the real trick is to understand them.

I have spoken of the conscience of the writer, trying to give you some insight into what it is that distinguishes the writer by temperament, the writer who cannot help being a writer, from someone who may write very well, but who writes for a different purpose — to instruct, to explain, to criticize — and for whom therefore writing is a necessary technique rather than an all-absorbing art. If I have discouraged anyone, I am sorry, but honesty comes before even courtesy in such matters as this. And if I have made anybody look searchingly into himself, to determine whether or not he has the kind of artistic conscience I have described, I shall think myself greatly rewarded.

EXPLORING THE LECTURE

1. A lecturer will assume you know this vocabulary: collaborate, psyche, hierarchy, psychoanalysis, redemption, sensibility, aesthetic, paradox, impertinent, and temperament. A *Thesaurus* is a handy learning tool, well worth the investment.

2. What initial disclaimers does Davies offer his audience?

3. What effect does he create by starting with two negatives?

4. Davies uses contrasting anecdotes to build up to his central question.
   (a) State this question.
   (b) Quote Davies's answer to the question — his thesis.

5. Davies alludes to famous people, books, and characters whom he expects his audience to know. Use the Resource Centre to acquaint yourself with these unfamiliar names and allusions. You might consult the list of specialized reference texts suggested in the exercises following Hughes's essay (see The Biography, page 100) or ask your teacher-librarian.

6. Examine the language in this lecture:
   (a) What clues suggest this work was originally prepared for oral delivery?
   (b) Davies refers to many famous male artists in his lecture. What well-known female artists might he have used to illustrate his points? You may wish to research this topic in the Resource Centre.
   (c) Give a number of specific examples that demonstrate how the diction might be altered to include the contribution women have made to the arts. You may want to rewrite one or more paragraphs that express this change in emphasis and/or tone.

7. (a) According to Jung, what healthy changes in focus occur at mid-life?
   (b) How does Davies apply these observations to the task of the writer?
   (c) Why is he personally grateful for all the other aspects of his life that have kept him from being a full-time writer, even though he writes "all the time" despite his other activities?

8. Examine the lecture's structure. Why should you pay particular attention to the introduction and conclusion of a lecture?

9. Compare your lecture notes with a partner's. Now that you have explored the lecture's content in questions 1 through 5, which set of notes do you feel would be more helpful for studying? Why?

EXTENSIVE STUDY

1. (a) Do you accept the distinction Davies draws between two different types of writers? Give reasons.

   (b) Davies claims he is not making any moral judgment when he excludes "journalistic word-spinners, the ghost writers, the concocters of literary confection" from the realm of "the real writer, the serious writer." Do you agree that his statement is a neutral one? Explain.

2. Would Davies be likely to agree that the study of English could be improved by the suggestions and recognitions in "Whole Brain Learning" on page 74?

3. Davies alludes to Aldous Huxley's definition of experience as not "what happens to a man; it is what a man does with what happens to him."

   Show that Joseph Conrad and Harriet Tubman exemplify this distinction. (See "Conrad's Letter to His Aunt" on page 129 and Hughes's essay on page 94.)

4. (a) Davies talks about thinking, feeling, and intuition and ranks the importance of each for a writer. Demonstrate that you understand these differences by outlining a situation that shows a person reacting to a potentially real problem according to the three different types of responses mentioned above.

   (b) Abraham Maslow, a famous psychiatrist, has observed that people tend to relate to the world in characteristic ways; his personality types include, among others, the thinker, the feeler, and the intuiter. Review this material in the Resource Centre. Determine which type you are and consider how this may affect your post-secondary career.

5. Davies speaks of "the path my temperament has chosen for me."
   (a) What does he mean?
   (b) Does this imply people lack free will?
   (c) What evidence have you personally observed or read about that supports or refutes the notion of an "artistic temperament?"

6. Read the accompanying radio lecture by George Woodcock. Compare his lecture with Davies's:
   (a) Examine the rhetorical devices and level of language and account for any significant differences.
   (b) Show how Davies's and Woodcock's lectures differ from King's, Kennedy's, and Woolf's speeches (see The Speech, on page 152) in tone, purpose, and level of language.

7. If you have read:
   (a) Hughes's essay, consider what personality characteristics Harriet Tubman and a successful "real" writer might share;

(b) Russell's essay, consider how Russell's definition of the good life pertains to Davies's perceptions about being a writer.

8. Debate the statement. Resolved that:
   Creativity can be taught.
   Canadian classics are first-rate literature.

THE WRITING FOLDER

1. You are a would-be writer rationalizing your lack of productivity. Present the rationalizations in one of the following forms:
   (i)   interior monologue, stream of consciousness;
   (ii) a conversation at a cocktail party;
   (iii) a dialogue in which the writer plays both the roles: the excuse-maker and the truth-teller. The final product should demonstrate that you have understood the relevant points in Davies's argument.

2. Write two letters using suitable diction for each audience: letter one is to your publisher "explaining" why you have not mailed in the third chapter of your novel; letter two is to your best friend back home explaining that your new home in the Greek Islands hasn't removed your "writer's block."

3. Write a short story that depicts two people with "artistic temperaments" having difficulty living together. Develop a specific conflict.

4. Write an essay in which you support or refute this statement: The author who writes "to instruct, to explain, to criticize" is somehow different from "the writer by temperament." (Consider whether you identify with either of these types and whether you see possible implications for your post-secondary career.)

5. "Serious artists in all fields should be financed by the government; that way Canada would have a better chance of developing a first-rate cultural life."

   Argue for or against this proposition in a letter to the editor of our national newspaper, the *Globe and Mail*. *Note*: Canada Council, a tax-supported federal body, does make grants to the Arts.

INDEPENDENT STUDY

1. Investigate Jung's views about the relationship between art and the psychic life of the writer. Develop a specific topic with your teacher. Recommended reading includes Jung's autobiography, *Memories, Dreams, Reflections*; excerpts from his *Man and His Symbols*; and *The Portable Jung* and *Psychological Reflections* (brief selections edited according to topic by Jolande Jacobi).   ++

2. "The best Canadian writing not only reflects the uniqueness of our national experience, but also speaks to the universal aspects of life."

    Read Margaret Atwood's *Survival.* With your teacher's help, select a Canadian novel, play, or collection of short stories and analyze the work in relation to Atwood's criticism and the above generalization. If the class is studying a Canadian literature unit, you might contribute an oral analysis of Atwood's thesis. (Consider, for example, works by Margaret Laurence, Alice Munro, Robertson Davies, Marian Engel, Sheila Watson, Gabriel Roy, David French, Anne Hébert, Mordecai Richler, Timothy Findlay, and Sinclair Ross).   ++

3. Read one or more collections of Canadian poetry. Good beginnings are *The Oxford Anthology of Canadian Literature* and *Mirrors.* Write an essay that analyzes the depiction of nature or man's relationship with nature in Canadian poetry. You might present an overview of poetry from the nineteenth and twentieth centuries. Or you might identify another theme such as "Changing Urban Images," "Childhood in Canada," "The Alienated Individual," "The Many Faces of Canada," "The Immigrant Experience," "Growing Up Female in Canada," "Portraits of the Canadian Identity," and "Native Peoples." Prepare a dramatic reading of several of your favourite poems.   + or ++

4. Read a Canadian novel, play, or collection of short stories. Write a short story or a play based on some aspect of the Canadian experience depicted in that book. Tape a brief analysis of the links (theme, setting, conflict) between your creative writing and the book you read.   + or ++

5. Write a research essay about the special problems facing the writer in Canada. Refer to specific examples of contemporary Canadian writers. If possible, include material from an interview you conducted with a writer (would-be or published). Append a bibliography.   + or ++

6. Suggestions for further independent study projects may arise from reading these authors who write in the field of psychology: Alfred Adler, Eric Berne, Sigmund Freud, Eric Fromm, Carl Jung, and R.D. Laing.

*T*IMED READING AND WRITING

1. Write an essay using one of these titles or topic sentences:

    Self-Absorption: A Necessary Evil for the Artist?

    The myth of the "artistic temperament" is no more than an excuse for egocentric behaviour.

2. Read or reread "Civil Disobedience: Nature and Origin," and make an outline.

CIVIL DISOBEDIENCE: NATURE AND ORIGIN

GEORGE WOODCOCK

On a day in July, 1846, a young man named Henry David Thoreau was walking along the street of a small Massachusetts town. He was going to the cobbler to pick up a pair of shoes, but on that particular day he did not reach his destination. Instead he was arrested and taken to the local jail on a charge of failing to pay his taxes. It was one of those small incidents that fall like stones into the collective memory of mankind, and set going ripples which, instead of subsiding, mount into waves of influence as the generations go by. By now, that day in the life of a long-dead American writer has assumed such a symbolic importance that when we look back on it we are surprised to be reminded how trivial the incident actually was. Did the unpaid tax really amount only to one dollar and fifty cents? Did Thoreau really spend only one night in jail before a friend slipped in to pay up on his behalf and release him to continue his walk to the cobbler? We feel vaguely defrauded. For Thoreau was not, in fact, one of the great martyrs for human liberty, and never claimed to be, though if the need had arisen he would probably have died for his beliefs. The reason why his very small defiance of the state assumed such importance was that the experience set going the line of thought which led him to write the celebrated essay published in 1849 under the title of *Resistance to Civil Government.* Later it was given its more familiar name, *On the Duty of Civil Disobedience.*

When Thoreau spent his night in the cell he shared with a barn-burning farmhand, he was protesting in the only way then possible to him against what he regarded as an immoral war — the unprovoked American invasion of Mexico in 1846. But there were other things rankling in his mind. In particular, he was anxious to draw attention to the fact that, although the state of Massachusetts had abolished slavery, its laws provided for the return of fugitive slaves to the southern states where slavery still prevailed: this seemed to him both unjust and hypocritical. In his essay, *Resistance to Civil Government,* he elaborated the point of view that prompted his act of disobedience. His argument was that we do not develop principles merely for the luxury of enjoying their possession. To give them meaning we must act in accordance with them, no matter how we may offend the law or public opinion. "Unjust laws exist", he states, and he goes on to put the question: "Shall we be content to obey them, or shall we endeavour to amend them and obey them until we have succeeded, or shall we transgress them at once?" His answer is that if the laws only cause us personal inconvenience, it is better to put up with them, but if they force us to perform or condone acts of injustice against other people, such as invading their territory or keeping them in slavery, then, he says, "Break the law!" It is all very clear and unequivocal — when a man's conscience and the laws clash, it is his conscience that he must follow.

Thoreau was a great friend of the subject peoples of the world, of the victims of imperialism and slavery, which from his particular viewpoint meant Mexicans and Negroes; it is therefore appropriate that his ideas should have come into their own in the present century when the underdeveloped and underprivileged races are struggling for freedom and equality. Mohandas Gandhi, the man who led India into freedom by means of mass Civil Disobedience, regarded the day he read Thoreau's essay as one of the turning points of his life; ironically, he first read it in a prison library in South Africa. And in the recent struggles to gain equal rights for American Negroes, Thoreau's words have been quoted repeatedly by the thousands of people who have taken part in acts of Civil Disobedience throughout the southern United States. Perhaps the most quoted passage of all has been this: "As for adopting the ways which the state has provided for remedying the evil, I know of no such ways. They take too much time, and a man's life will be gone." Urgency, the sense that justice belongs here and now, and not in some promised future, is one of the essential elements in Civil Disobedience.

I have approached the idea of Civil Disobedience through the example of Thoreau because he seems to stand at a pivotal point in the history of the movement. In one way or another the concept of Civil Disobedience has been voiced and acted upon for at least 2,400 years, but never has it received such mass support, never has it been the object of so much public attention as during the century since Thoreau laid down in such clear intellectual terms the reasons why men should seek to govern their own actions by justice rather than by legality.

But it is the experience of the past that conditions the action of the present, and in these talks, I shall discuss the development of the idea of Civil Disobedience since its beginnings in the Athens of antiquity, where so much else in our civilization began. I shall examine its claims to have been a salutary and even a revolutionary influence in correcting those sicknesses of human institutions which Shakespeare recognized so long ago, "the oppressor's wrong . . . the law's delay . . . the insolence of office". I shall also discuss the historic failures and the inherent limitations of Civil Disobedience. But before starting on the long narrative journey that runs from Aeschylus in Athens to Dr. Martin Luther King in Alabama, I would like to get a little nearer to what we mean by the phrase Civil Disobedience.

The essence of its meaning, which distinguishes this type of disobedience from mere lawlessness, is contained in the word *civil* — a word of many and varied connotations. First of all, *civil* is an adjective relating to the responsibilities of the citizen, and the whole justification for Civil Disobedience lies in the idea that the man who practices it fulfils his responsibilities by demonstrating in action his disapproval of an evil law or social situation which ordinary democratic procedures will not eliminate. Secondly, we think of *civil* as being opposed to *military*, in other words as opposed to physical force, and it is basic to the whole philosophy of Civil Disobedience that it be carried out without any recourse to violent methods. The man who disobeys is willing to suffer for his own defiance of the law; he is not willing to make others suffer. Finally, the word civil also suggests all the nuances of meaning clustering around the ideas of courtesy and civilized behaviour; and the advocates of Civil Disobedience enjoin their followers to behave with impeccable courtesy, and to follow in all ways the advice of St. Paul: "Recompense to no man evil for evil. Provide things honest in the sight of all men." So we arrive at a final composite picture of Civil Disobedience as the breaking, on principle, of evil laws, rules or taboos, with a full acceptance of the possible consequences to oneself and a resolution to cause as little harm to others as possible. Implied in this definition is the requirement that an act of Civil Disobedience be neither furtive nor selfish. A man who falsifies his tax returns for personal profit is not committing Civil Disobedience, he is merely breaking the law. A man who publicly refuses to pay his taxes on grounds of principle and risks going to prison for it is both breaking the law and committing Civil Disobedience.

Civil Disobedience, in other words, places a man's inner sense of justice above the laws imposed by society. It erects principles above political expedients, and it has been rather well described as "an application of absolute moral truths in the realm of historical action". It invokes the idea of responsibility as against the idea of obedience, and for this reason it appeals strongly to a doubt about conventional ideas of duty which has become very widespread since the rise and fall of Nazism. It was this doubt that made the trial of Adolf Eichmann such a morally significant event. What was being tried in that Israeli courtroom was not merely a man who had sent millions of innocents to their death; it was not even merely the general record of the Nazis. It was the cult of unquestioning obedience to law and authority. If we accept duty as meaning that kind of obedience, then Eichmann was innocent; he merely acted under orders. If Eichmann was guilty, then we have to accept the idea of a point at which a man is morally bound to disobey rather than to perform acts that go beyond his conceptions of morality or justice, even if these acts were ordered by the state. Here, in its most dramatic form, is the negative justification of Civil Disobedience. The Nazis have made it impossible to condone any longer that blind sense of duty which Tennyson characterized more devastatingly than he intended in his famous phrase, "Their's not to reason why". And in ceasing to condone blind duty, we have to accept the right to Civil Disobedience.

Civil Disobedience presupposes the use of reason and independent judgment in those who practice it. It also presupposes a rather awesome austerity of outlook, since the man who disobeys must be prepared to endure physical suffering and the enmity of the obedient, while at the same time he cannot allow himself to retaliate; otherwise his whole stance would be destroyed.

Here we come to the relationship between Civil Disobedience and a whole cluster of concepts which are often associated with it when the subject comes up for discussion — in particular non-violence, passive resistance and pacifism. I think that only one among these three concepts is consistently linked with Civil Disobedience, and that is non-violence. Passive resistance, as Gandhi suggested, is a weapon of the weak; it implies the obstinate endurance of suffering without giving in, but it implies very little else, whereas Civil Disobedience seeks to take the initiative in exposing and bringing an end to unjust conditions. When we go on to pacifism, we find that it involves the total rejection of violence as a matter of principle, the idea that under no circumstances should a human life be taken. But this is not necessarily the view of those who practice Civil Disobedience. Many of the tens of thousands of volunteers engaged in the great Civil Disobedience campaigns which Gandhi organized to shake British rule in India were not pacifists — the late Prime Minister Nehru was one example — and the same applies to the civil rights demonstrators in the United States. Such people support the use of non-violent means to attain a particular end, but they do not believe it is necessarily right in all circumstances — for example, they might be willing to kill a potential murderer in self-defence or in defence of other people. And nowadays more and more people of this kind, who are not pacifists in principle, are accepting the practicality of non-violence, at least on the level at which civil rights battles are fought. It is a curious and significant paradox that the atomic age, when war, violence and power should theoretically be total, is actually the age in which the peaceful tactics of Civil Disobedience appear to be coming into their own.

These tactics have varied from century to century, and so have the objectives of Civil Disobedience. Sometimes it has been practiced to make a personal statement of principle, as in the case of Socrates. Sometimes it has been used to safeguard existing liberties, as in the successful non-violent resistance to the Nazis by Norwegian schoolteachers in 1941, an incident which I shall later describe more fully. On other occasions it has been used by people trying to win rights that have been denied them, like the Negroes in Montgomery and Selma. And occasionally it has provided the grand strategy to liberate a whole nation from foreign rule, as in the case of India. But however the tactics and the goal may change, the principle is always the same, and as a principle it emerges at the very point in history when men begin to think deeply on the relationship between the judgment of the individual and the laws of society. That point is the Athens of the fifth century B.C., the Athens of Pericles and Phidias, at the time when the great tragedies were performed in honour of the wine-god Dionysus, and Socrates walked barefoot in the narrow streets, putting his embarrassing questions to the people. Greece had emerged from tribal into city life. The days of the Homeric heroes were long past, the tyrants had been cast out, and the sophists who swarmed in the shadows of the Athenian groves were beginning to argue about the relationship of the individual to the state and of the state to the world. Were there perhaps higher loyalties than the laws of Athens? And if so, what were they, and how should a man obey them?

That thoughts of this kind widely troubled the Athenians is shown by the fact that the first man to develop them effectively were the dramatists whose plays were written for the eyes and ears of ordinary citizens. Aeschylus in the first part of the fifth century and Sophocles towards its end took as a theme the idea of an established power defied in the name of a conflicting conception of justice. In each case the dramatist develops his idea within the relatively safe framework of an ancient myth. In *Prometheus Bound* Aeschylus presents the story of the Titan who defied the decision of Zeus, the King of the Olympian Gods, to wipe out the human race. Prometheus not only rescues men from this unjust fate. He also takes them the gift of fire, and raises them out of the condition of brutes by teaching the arts of civilization. At the beginning of the play Prometheus is being shackled to the rocks of the Caucasus in punishment for his disobedience. He discusses his plight with the chorus and with various visitors, and at the climax of the play Hermes, the messenger of Zeus, comes to offer terms for submission, which Prometheus proudly rejects. Throughout the play Zeus appears as established and tyrannical authority, and Prometheus appears as the just being who follows his own conscience. "You did not tremble at the name of Zeus," says the chorus. "Your mind was yours, not his." And later Prometheus says to Hermes, "When I compare my sorrow to your slavery, I would have it no different." The play ends with the hero calling on the heavens to witness how he suffers and how unjustly.

If *Prometheus Bound* shows the rebel on the celestial plane, it puts a lesson that can be transferred to the terrestrial realm. Prometheus stands as the prototype of the civil disobeyer who, with his own mind, his own sense of justice and his own will, suffers for breaking established but unjust laws. Sophocles brought the moral a great deal nearer home in his play *Antigone,* which deals with Civil Disobedience in an earthly setting. Antigone, daughter of the tragic Oedipus, defies the ruling of Creon, King of Thebes, that the body of her brother Polyneices, who has fought against the city, shall go unburied. Creon speaks in the name of the state. Antigone answers in the name of mercy. "I cannot share in hatred but in love," she says, when she has performed the sacred rites over her brother's body and is brought into Creon's presence. Creon sentences her to death, and for his act incurs not only the wrath of the gods, so that he loses both son and wife, but also suffers the displeasure of the citizens of Thebes, who are moved by the loyalty of Antigone and by her sense of the merciful. There is no doubt Sophocles meant the citizens of Athens to be moved in the same way.

What veiled references to actual Athenian incidents are concealed in these dramatizations of ancient myths we no longer know. But we do know the case of Socrates, who in 399 B.C. was accused of not believing in the gods of the city and of corrupting the young by sceptical discources. There seems little doubt that Socrates' enemies merely wished to scare him into leaving the city, which he could easily have done like so many other unpopular philosophers before him. He chose to stay, and in his speech to the 501 citizens who sat in judgment he answered some of the charges against him; but on the charge of holding heterodox views he turned instead to defend what he called "the philosopher's mission" of searching into his own mind and those of other men, and he declared that if he were offered his life on condition that he ceased to speculate, his reply would be that, much as he loved his fellow Athenians, he would still obey the voice of God and would never abandon philosophy and free inquiry. The judges found him guilty, and now it was for Socrates to suggest a penalty lighter than the death sentence which the accusers demanded. All he offered was a small fine, and this deliberately derisory gesture infuriated the Court into sentencing him to death by a larger majority than that which had condemned him originally.

The accounts of the trial and death of Socrates are not entirely satisfactory, since they have come down to us through his followers, one of whom, Plato, was a rather imaginative literary artist, but it is certain that Socrates was standing for the right of a man not to be restricted by any law in his search for truth, and this was how his attitude was interpreted by the schools of philosophers who came afterwards. The Stoics, who greatly admired Socrates for his way of dying, taught that a man's conscience must be the final arbiter of his conduct and that his ultimate loyalty was not to the state but to all mankind. The Cynics went further. They proclaimed brotherhood with animals as well, denounced slavery, and taught that true philosophers should opt out of the state and live regardless of the law. The most famous of these beatniks of antiquity was Diogenes, who sought to break all the taboos, including those of decency; he is said to have lived in a tub, but in fact he lived in a very large oil jar, and when Alexander the Great, who was something of a culture snob, visited him and asked if there were anything he could do for him, Diogenes looked coldly at the world conqueror and said, "Just get out of my light!" By now the atmosphere of Athens had changed so much that the most heterodox of philosophers went his way in peace. The witness Socrates had made for freedom of thought and inquiry, and the shame which the Athenians felt for having forced so unusual a man to drink the poisoned cup, were largely responsible for the change.

While the intellectuals of Athens were talking and acting out the drama of individual judgment versus established law, other people in the ancient world were making the first recorded experiments in collective Civil Disobedience. Twice at least under Roman rule the monotheistic Jews gathered unarmed in the streets of Jerusalem to prevent pagan images being installed in the Temple. They stood their ground, maintaining that they would die unresisting rather than let their holy places be defiled. Their action was successful. In Rome itself, during the early days of the Republic, there were even more striking examples of Civil Disobedience. In the third century B.C. there was great discontent among the plebeians, who had no rights as Roman citizens but were still expected to fight for the city. For two years running they refused to enroll in the legions when the call went out, and on each occasion agreed to join up after promises of reforms. On returning from the second campaign, they found that the reforms had still not been carried out. Thereupon, deserting their commanders, the legions marched away peacefully and in perfect order to found a city of their own away from Rome. The result was immediate capitulation on the part of the patricians, and the appointment of the first official delegate to look after popular interests — the Tribune of the People. "There was," as Mommsen the historian has said, "something mighty and elevating in such a revolution, undertaken by the multitude itself without definite guidance under generals whom accident supplied, and accomplished without bloodshed; and with pleasure and pride the citizens recalled its memory."

Finally, there was the resistance of the early Christians to the

Roman attempts to make them accept pagan worship. The stories of martyrdoms in the arena are well known. Less familiar are the instances of Christians who refused military service. This kind of resistance, which was supported by Fathers of the Church, such as Origen and Lactantius, went on until the end of the third century A.D. A few of the trial records of these early war resisters have survived. A certain Maximilianus, called up in A.D. 295 because he was the son of a soldier, refused to serve partly from a religious objection to bloodshed and partly from an objection to wearing a lead badge bearing the image of the deified Emperor. The last of the Christian martyrs to pagan Rome was a centurion who became converted in A.D. 298, and his statement brings to a dignified close the record of Civil Disobedience in the ancient world. "If . . . those who render military service must be compelled to sacrifice to gods and emperors," he said, "then I cast down my vine-staff and belt, I renounce the standards, and I refuse to serve as a solder." Fifteen years later, in 313, the Emperor Constantine made Christianity the official religion of the Empire.

11. THE FOREWORD, PREFACE, AND INTRODUCTION

> *Key Work:*
> "Foreword to *Klee Wyck*" — Ira Dilworth
>
> *Associated Reading:*
> "Prologue to *The Art of Emily Carr*" — Doris Shadbolt

A foreword, preface, or introduction is a type of essay with a specific purpose — to introduce the reader to the book. It not only familiarizes the reader with the subject matter, but also may, like a review, inform about approaches, biases, and tone. In some cases, these preliminary remarks put the author and the work into historical and/or social context. When considered in conjunction with the table of contents and index, this section should help the reader decide whether the text is relevant to his or her needs and interests.

Sometimes a book's author also writes the foreword, preface, or introduction, as Shadbolt did for *The Art of Emily Carr*. On other occasions, this introductory material is written by the editor — an authority in the field — or a famous person who makes a collection of short stories or essays by others, for example. In the case of the "Foreword to *Klee*

Wyck," a friend of the author of *Klee Wyck* has introduced the book by sharing some of his personal memories of Emily Carr.

BEFORE READING

■ Consult the Contents pages of this text and the Preface. Consider how these two pieces of information help you to orient yourself to the structure of this textbook.

■ How would you benefit from skimming the preliminary notes in texts you read?

■ What do you know about Emily Carr? Find out if more recent material than this foreword about Carr has been published.

*F*OREWORD TO KLEE WYCK

IRA DILWORTH

MY EARLIEST vivid memories of Emily Carr go back to a period considerably more than a quarter of a century ago, to a time when she was living in Victoria, British Columbia, still largely unnoticed as an artist and, by most of those who did know her in that capacity, unappreciated or treated with ridicule and even hostility. In those days she was a familiar figure passing down Simcoe Street in front of our house which was little more than a stone's throw away from her home. With methodical punctuality by which you could almost have set your clock, she passed by each morning on her way to the grocer's or butcher's. She trundled in front of her an old-fashioned baby carriage in which sat her favourite pet, Woo, a small Javanese monkey dressed in a bright costume of black, red and brown which Emily had made for her. Bounding around her as she went would be six or eight of the great shaggy sheep dogs which she raised for sale. Half an hour later you could see her returning, the baby carriage piled high with parcels, Woo skipping along at the end of a leash, darting under the hedge to catch succulent earwigs which she loved to crunch or sometimes creeping right through the hedge into the garden to have her tail pulled by the children hiding there. The great sheep dogs still bounced around the quaint figure whom they recognized as their devoted mistress. I thought of her then, as did the children behind the hedge and as did most of her fellow-citizens who thought of her at all, as an eccentric, middle-aged woman who kept an apartment house on Simcoe Street near Beacon Hill Park, who surrounded herself with numbers of pets — birds, chipmunks, white rats and the favourite Woo — and raised English sheep dogs in kennels in her large garden.

Emily Carr was a great painter, certainly one of the greatest women painters of any time. It has been said that for originality, versatility, driving creative power and strong, individual achievement she has few equals among modern artists. Her talent in drawing revealed itself when she was still a small child and was encouraged by her father. Emily set herself, early, and with singleness of devotion, to master the technique of painting and, despite discouragement and many difficulties, worked with great courage and experimental enthusiasm until the time of her death.

After the turn of the century, with study in San Francisco and England behind her, she became particularly concerned with the problem of devising a style in painting which would make it possible for her to express adequately not only what she saw but also what she felt in her subject matter — the great totem poles, tribal houses and villages of the West Coast Indians and, later, the tangled, solemn, majestic beauty of the Pacific Coast forest. Nothing ever meant so much to her as the struggle to gain that power; she was never satisfied that she had achieved her aim. In this connection, therefore, it is interesting to have the opinion of Lawren Harris, himself a great original Canadian painter and for years one of Emily Carr's closest and most valued friends. He says in an article, "The Paintings and Drawings of Emily Carr",

> It (British Columbia) is another world from all the land east of the Great Divide. Emily Carr was the first artist to discover this. It involved her in a conscious struggle to achieve a technique that would match the great, new motifs of British Columbia. It was primarily this long and deepening discovery which made her work modern and vital, as it was her love of its moods, mystery and majesty that gave it the quality of indwelling spirit which the Indians knew so well. It was also her life with the Indians and their native culture which led her to share and understand their outlook on nature and life, and gave her paintings of totems, Indian villages and the forest a quality and power which no white person had achieved before.

Emily Carr is now also recognized as a remarkable writer. Her diaries, which first came to light after her death and remain still unpublished, make it clear that her desire to express herself in words began in the late 1920's. As in the case of her painting, she worked very hard to master this medium. She was fascinated by the great range of new possibilities which it opened up but mastery of it did not come easily.

Why did she turn to writing? Sometimes, undoubtedly, merely for comfort in her loneliness, sometimes quite consciously to relive experiences of the past. She once told me that when she was working on the first stages of a painting, trying to put down in pictorial form a subject for which she had made field sketches, she found it of great value to "word" her experience. In this way, she said, the circumstances and all the details of the incident or place would come back to her more vividly and she could reconstruct them more faithfully than was possible with paint and canvas alone. From this developed, I suspect, one of the controlling principles of her method and style in literary composition.

I have seen her "peeling" a sentence, as she called it, — a process which involved stripping away all ambiguous or unnecessary words, replacing a vague word by a sharper, clearer one until the sentence emerged clean and precise in its meaning and strong in its impact on the reader. As a result, there is in her writing the quality of immediacy, the ability, by means of descriptive words chosen with the greatest accuracy, to carry the reader into the very heart of the experience she is describing, whether it be an incident from her own childhood or a sketch of an Indian and his village — and that so swiftly as to give an impression almost of magic, of incantation.

She has spoken many times in her diaries of the difficulties she had to overcome in writing. Late in October, 1936, she made a characteristic, vivid entry:

> There's words enough, paint and brushes enough and thoughts enough. The whole difficulty seems to be getting the thoughts clear enough, making them stand still long enough to be fitted with words and paint. They are so elusive — like wild birds singing above your head, twittering close beside you, chortling in front of you, but gone the moment you put out a hand. If ever you do catch hold of a piece of a thought it breaks away leaving the piece in your hand just to aggravate you. If one only could encompass the whole, corral it, enclose it safe — but then maybe it would die, dwindle away because it could not go on growing. I don't think thoughts *could* stand still — the fringes of them would always be tangling into something just a little further on and that would draw it out and out. I guess that is just *why* it is so difficult to catch a complete idea — it's because everything is always on the move, always expanding.

A very closely related characteristic of her writing is its sincerity. I shall let her speak again for herself in her own forceful, inimitable style.

> Be careful that you do not write or paint anything that is not your own, that you don't know in your own soul. You will have to experiment and try things out for yourself and you will not be sure of what you are doing. That's all right, you are feeling your way into the thing. But don't take what someone else has made sure of and pretend that it's you yourself that have made sure of it, till it's yours absolutely by conviction. It's stealing to take it and hypocrisy and you'll fall in a hole. . . . If you're going to lick the icing off somebody else's cake you won't be nourished and it won't do you any good, — or you might find the cake had caraway seeds and you hate them. But if you make your own

cake and *know the recipe and stir the thing with your own
hand* it's *your* own cake. You can ice it or not as you like. Such
lots of folks are licking the icing off the other fellow's cake!

Consequently, Emily Carr's style is characterized by a great
simplicity and directness — a simplicity, it's true, that is a little
deceptive in view of the sustained discipline from which it resulted
— but perhaps it is just in that way that the only true simplicity is
achieved. Words are used by her with great courage, sometimes
taking on new and vivid meanings. They are in her writing the
equivalent of the quick, sure brush strokes and dramatic, strong
colours which are so characteristic of her canvases.

It has been remarked by many readers — and with justification
— that Emily Carr's prose style has much in common with poetry.
This is to be seen in her rigid selectivity in the use of diction
described above, in her daring use of metaphorical language, in the
rhythm, the cadence of her writing and in her consciousness of
form. Look, for instance, at this passage from "Century Time":

> In the late afternoon a great shadow mountain stepped across
> the lake and brooded over the cemetery. It had done this at the
> end of every sunny day for centuries, long, long before that piece
> of land was a cemetery. Dark came and held the shadow
> mountain there all night, but when morning broke, it was back
> again inside its mountain, which pushed its grand purple dome
> up into the sky and dared the pines swarming around its base to
> creep higher than half way up its bare rocky sides.
>
> Indians do not hinder the progress of their dead by embalm-
> ing or tight coffining. When the spirit has gone they give the
> body back to the earth. Cased only in a box it is laid in a shallow
> grave. The earth welcomes the body — coaxes new life and
> beauty from it, hurries over what men shudder at. Lovely tender
> herbage bursts from the graves — swiftly — exulting over
> corruption.

and again at this passage from "Bobtails":

> The top of Beacon Hill was bare. You could see north, south, east
> and west. The dogs rested, tongues lolling, while I looked at the
> new day, at the pine trees, at the sky, at the sea where it lay flat,
> and at the near broom bushes drooped with early morning
> wetness. The song of the meadow-lark crumbled away the last
> remnants of night, three sad lingering notes followed by an
> exultant double note that gobbled up the still vibrating three.
>
> For one moment the morning took you far out into vague
> chill; your body snatched you back into its cosiness, back to the
> waiting dogs on the hill top. They could not follow out there;
> their world was walled, their noses trailed the earth.

or at this from "Canoe":

> The canoe passed shores crammed with trees, trees overhanging
> stony beaches, trees held back by rocky cliffs, pointed fir trees

> climbing its dark masses up the mountain sides, moonlight
> silvering their blackness.
>
> Our going was imperceptible, the woman's steering paddle
> the only thing that moved, its silent cuts stirring phosphorus like
> white fire.
>
> Time and texture faded, ceased to exist — day was gone, yet
> it was not night. Water was not wet or deep, just smoothness
> spread with light.

Such writing transcends the usual limits of prose and becomes (but without aesthetic offence) lyrical.

The quality of form, not a surprising attribute in view of her distinction as a painter, can be seen over and over again but notably in the exquisite lyric, "White Currants", in the simply shaped but touchingly effective "Sophie" and in "D'Sonoqua" which has the quality of a musical symphony with its dominant themes, its sectional development and its use of suspense and tense emotional crescendo.

As a final point in this discussion of Emily Carr's literary style it should be noted that she was not a great reader. Her style is, therefore, not the result of imitation of literary models. Undoubtedly it is better so, for the originality and simplicity which marked all her work, whether in painting, rug-making, pottery or writing, remained uninhibited by academic literary standards. Of these Miss Carr knew little or nothing. But there is some literary influence. She was a devoted reader of the poems of Walt Whitman, attracted to them by Whitman's deep feeling for nature and by his vigorous style. There is too, I think, a discernible influence at times of the Bible, notably of the Psalms, and of the English Prayerbook.

But above everything else, Emily Carr was a truly great Canadian. Her devotion to her own land marked everything she did. She approached no subject in writing or painting with any condescension or purely artistic self-consciousness. She was driven always by a passion to make her own experience in the place in which life had set her vivid and real for the onlooker or the reader and to do this with dignity and distinction. She found life in her part of Canada often hard and baffling but always rich and full. It was her single purpose to share through the medium of her art and in as memorable a fashion as possible the experiences of her life. She was never happy outside Canada. Indeed, during her sojourns in England and France she was the victim of such overwhelming homesickness that she became physically ill and was ordered by her physician to return to her Canadian home.

She was an amazing woman. May I take the liberty of quoting a note which I set down in 1941? I hold the views as firmly today as then:

I have heard her talking and watched her devour the conversation of others, of Lawren Harris, of Arthur Benjamin, of Garnet Sedgewick; I have watched her anger tower over some meanness in the work or conduct of an artist and I have seen her become incandescent with generous enthusiasm for another's fine work; I have seen her gentleness to an old woman and to an animal; I have beheld the vision of forest and sky enter and light her eyes as she sat far from them — and I am convinced that Emily Carr is a great genius and that we will do well to add her to that small list of originals who have been produced in this place and have lived and commented in one way or another on this Canada of ours.

Emily Carr was herself more modest. Asked a few years before her death to state what had been the outstanding events of her life, she wrote,

Outstanding events! — work and more work! The most outstanding seems to me the buying of an old caravan trailer which I had towed to out-of-the-way corners and where I sat self-contained with dogs, monk and work — Walt Whitman and others on the shelf — writing in the long, dark evenings after painting — loving everything terrifically. In later years my work had some praise and some successes, but the outstanding event to me was the *doing* which I am still at. Don't pickle me away as a "done".

It is impossible to think of that vivid person as a "done". No, she goes on in her work. As surely as Wordsworth marked the English Lake District with his peculiar kind of seeing and feeling, leaving us his experience patterned in poetry, so surely this extraordinary, sensitive, gifted Canadian touched a part of our landscape and life and left her imprint there so clearly that now we, who have seen her canvases or read her books must feel, as we enter the vastness of the western forest or stand before a totem pole or in the lonely ruin of an Indian village, less bewildered and alone because we recognize that another was here before us and humanized all this by setting down in paint or words her reaction to it.

EXPLORING THE FOREWORD

1. State the function of each of the major divisions of Dilworth's foreword as indicated by the spacing.

2. Working in pairs, phrase half a dozen questions on the content of the foreword. Use clear command words to indicate each task. If you aren't sure of the differences, consult your teacher and the tips on

"Preparing for Examinations" in Part C about such words as analyze, explain, illustrate, relate, compare, show, and assess. Pose your questions to another pair of students. If they have difficulty, review the phrasing or re-evaluate your expectations.

3. (a) How does Dilworth's diction influence your impression of Carr's greatness as an artist and painter? Give specific examples.
    (b) Select specific examples of Carr's phrasing that reinforce Dilworth's portrait of Carr's greatness.

EXTENSIVE STUDY

1. Working independently or in pairs, make a list of two famous people and two general topics (nineteenth century architecture or the art of cartooning, for example) which interest you. Go to the Resource Centre with your class. Complete this exercise using the card catalogues and other library resources.
    (a) If your school's Resource Centre has a microfilm file of public library titles, your teacher-librarian can familiarize the class with its operation. (If not, move directly to exercise (b).) Using the list you drew up in class, note two titles in the form they appear on the screen for each person and subject. If the texts have forewords or prologues, record this. (*Note:* Occasionally, the section entitled Introduction performs the same function, but this is not always the case.)
    (b) Using the author and subject card catalogues, note the titles of two works for each item on your list. Look for titles different from those on the microfilm. Find four of the texts with a prologue or foreword; two should deal with one of the famous persons and two with one of the subjects. Skim the forewords or prologues. Compare the works:
    (i)   Which one most effectively conveys a sense of what the book is about? Why?
    (ii) What differences in emphasis are evident in the works that deal with the famous person and the works that pertain to a particular subject?
    (iii) Do you think that the tables of contents and forewords or prefaces give you a good sense of what the book is about? If not, cite reasons.
2. Artists sometimes feel alienated from society.
    (a) Read Woolf's "Professions for Women" (see The Speech, page 152). Compare the reasons for this alienation as portrayed by Woolf with the isolation and loneliness of Carr's experiences. What are the common elements, if any?
    (b) Read Davies's "The Conscience of the Writer" (see The University

Lecture, page 174). What does Davies's lecture help us better understand about Carr's life?

3. Read the accompanying "Prologue" by Shadbolt. Compare the impressions each work gives of Emily Carr. Which piece of writing do you prefer? Why? Argue your point in class or in a small group discussion.

4. Dilworth quotes a number of passages that Carr wrote. Examine the style of these passages. On what points of style, if any, do Carr and Orwell apparently agree?

5. Debate one or more of these statements. Resolved that:

    Artists are generally more eccentric than other people.

    A classic work of art is one that transcends personal experience to make a universal statement.

    The school system should more diligently nurture creativity. (You might read Hatcher's "Whole Brain Learning" in the unit on The Report, page 74 if you have not done so already.)

THE WRITING FOLDER

1. Observers claim Carr's prose style has a poetic quality. Prepare one of the following:
    (a) Rewrite the passage from "Canoe" in a verse form of your own choosing. You may alter the punctuation, but do not change the wording. Accompany this piece with a composition that explains the effects you achieved by arranging the lines and punctuation as you did.
    (b) Write a poem in which you attempt to capture the essence of Carr's uniqueness as she is depicted in paragraph 1. Aim for a sympathetic tone. Title the work.

2. Compare Dilworth's foreword to *Klee Wyck* with Shadbolt's prologue to *The Art of Emily Carr*. Consider such aspects as the aim, tone, language, audience, and effectiveness of each. Account for the differences in the final products. Which do you prefer? Why?

3. Write a prologue or introduction to a work you have recently read.

INDEPENDENT STUDY

1. Interested students may wish to prepare a seminar or a panel discussion with slides of Carr's paintings and sculpture and consider how her visual and written artistry are related.   +

2. Read two of Carr's books such as *The Book of Small*, *The House of All Sorts*, *Klee Wyck*, or *Growing Pains*. Write an essay on one of the topics listed below or define your own idea with your teacher.

The Loneliness of Emily Carr
The Depiction of Childhood in the Writings of Emily Carr
The Life of the Female Artist in Canada
Emily Carr's Relationship with Nature

Tape an oral report for your teacher. You might follow Emily Carr's example and discuss the questions she asked herself before painting a picture to answer in the fewest possible words: (i) "What attracted me to this subject?" (ii) "What is the thing I am trying to express?" ++

3. Read one of Carr's works listed above. Imitate her style in an anecdotal essay on a topic of your choice. Show, through specific examples from your essay, that you have followed two of Carr's principles: "Get to the point as directly as you can; never use a big word if a little one will do." ++

4. If you are especially interested in art history, examine the relationship between Carr's verbal and visual depictions of such subjects as the West Coast native people, nature, or certain individuals in her life. Narrow the focus of this project through discussions with both your Art and English teachers. + or ++

5. "The outstanding event [of my life] was the *doing* which I am still at. Don't pickle me away as a 'done,' " Carr said several years before her death.
Compare this view of life and aging with the attitude of Hagar in Margaret Laurence's *The Stone Angel* and two protagonists from the short stories in M.F.K. Fisher's *Sister Age.* ++

6. Carr was attracted to the poetry of Walt Whitman because of his "deep feeling for nature and his vigorous style." Using at least six of Whitman's poems and one collection of Carr's writings about nature, compare the writers' styles and interests. + or ++

7. Other independent study projects may arise from these suggested readings:
Margaret Atwood, "The Paralyzed Artist" and "First Peoples: Indians and Eskimos as Symbols" in *Survival*
William and Christine Mowat, eds., *Native Peoples in Canadian Literature*
Virginia Woolf, *A Room of One's Own*
(See also the Themes in Canadian Literature series published by Macmillan.)

TIMED READING AND WRITING

1. Write an essay using one of these ideas for an opening sentence:
If I could meet Emily Carr, I would like to talk to her about . . .
To be an artist, one must always be distanced from the society one depicts.
Loneliness is no more than a state of mind.

> Hard work can bring joy regardless of what one achieves.
> To live life well one must love it passionately.

2.   Reread "The Painting As Autobiography," the last section of Shadbolt's prologue. Write a one-sentence summary.

PROLOGUE TO
THE ART OF EMILY CARR

DORIS SHADBOLT

ARTIST OF THE CANADIAN WEST COAST   Emily Carr was born in Victoria on Vancouver Island 13 December 1871, died there 2 March 1945, and lived most of her life within a few blocks of the house where she was born in the James Bay district of that city. Her genius throve in the island's isolation from mainland British Columbia and in the province's isolation from the rest of Canada and the world. The two great themes of her work derived from the most characteristic features of that region — a unique and vanishing Indian culture, and a powerful coastal nature. It is logical to think of Carr and the Canadian West Coast at the same time, for her painting and her writing bear the indelible imprint of her long attachment to the place where she was born and where she chose to remain.

Despite persistent regional ties, she was not an artist who lacked broader contact, for as a girl in her late teens and early twenties she studied in San Francisco and spent altogether a little over three years there. Another five were spent in England and a little over one year in France at a time when some of the ideas crucial in the development of twentieth-century art were just emerging. Her work was admitted to a major Paris exhibition in 1911, where she was in the company of some of the progressive European artists of the day. There were trips to eastern Canada and to New York and Chicago. Through these travels she gained access to the general tradition of western European art within whose broad outlines she was to produce her work.

During one phase of her career, Carr painted in a French postimpressionist manner and at times revealed a distinctively Fauvist influence; during another period, her work showed stylistic links with Cubism. Late in her life, her passionate search for identification with universal primal energies produced occasional paintings that evoke van Gogh or suggest spiritual affinities with German Expressionism. Closer to home, her relationship to Canadian art and to the work of Lawren Harris and other members of the Group of Seven can be more readily observed. Yet she remained a highly individualistic artist, never truly part of larger world movements or their Canadian expressions, even though from time to time she borrowed their mannerisms.

Her long and productive career was marked by interruptions in style and continuity. She made a conventional early start and then, in her early middle age, a courageous and promising break into a larger international art stream, but at that point she lost her momentum in a sudden lapse of spirit. This lapse, though prolonged, was only a prelude to an explosive burst into sudden authority and a brilliant late flowering. Despite a substantial body of early work of interest and quality, that for which she is best known — and justly so — was done between her fifty-sixth and seventy-first years — paintings of dark and silent forests, monumental Indian carvings, towering trees, wild storm-tossed beaches and infinite skies, which spring from her lifelong Pacific coast experience.

THE WOMAN BEHIND CARR'S WRITING   Happily, Carr's urge for expression also took the form of writing. She produced five books of stories and reminiscences, as well as her published Journals, and fortunately some of her letters have now been deposited in public collections where they are available for study. The material is largely autobiographical, and in addition to its intrinsic interest and merit as writing, it reveals much of the person behind the artist.

The books were written some time after the events they recounted, however, and the uncertain process of memory, heightened — even distorted — by her literary skill and sense of drama, has made them unreliable sources for biographical detail. She frequently understates her age and is given to self-dramatization and idealization. The pieces in *Klee Wyck* are based on her experiences with Indians and on visits to Indian communities, but they are also stories in which time collapses and events are reshaped and interpreted to make a point in a story rather than to provide documentation.

Growing Pains is subtitled "The autobiography of Emily Carr," but it is really a collection of episodes recalled in later life when self-mythologizing had become habit, and there is no attempt to bridge the large gaps in time that separate the episodes. Even though information culled from her books of sketches and stories must be sifted and examined cautiously, it is invaluable for glimpsing her life and for seeing the face she wanted to show the world.

Hundreds and Thousands, the title she chose for her published Journals, refers to tiny English candies, so small they must be consumed by the mouthful to be appreciated. The Journals offer especially reliable information, and one wishes they had been begun before 1927 when she was already fifty-six. Still, they illumine the mature and important years of her painting life. They were intended for publication, and at times there is a self-consciousness about the writing as if she were aware of the reader looking over her shoulder, but on the whole the Journals are a spontaneous reflection of her mood and spirit and are, to a lesser degree, a record of her activities. Their form and style vary with her state of mind: rich descriptive passages followed by outbursts of frustration; thoughts on painting; soul searchings; reminiscences — broken by long silences. They represent an important personal and passionate manifesto, full of contradiction and at times irritating in their diffidence but nonetheless a powerful confession of artistic faith.

Carr was also a compulsive letter-writer and she knew that "there is a side of friendship that develops better and stronger by correspondence than contact, especially with some people who can get their thoughts clearer when they see them written. Another thing — that beastliness, self-consciousness, is left out, shyness, shamedness in exposing one's inner self face to face before another, getting rattled and mislaying words. The absence of the flesh in writing perhaps brings souls nearer."[1]

As a correspondent who greatly needed to feel in close communication with absent friends, she had the knack of writing on a moment's impulse with a directness of speech and from the edge of her thought. The letters cover a wide range, depending on the recipient. With some correspondents she reported on day-to-day events and exchanged gossip about acquaintances; naturally she was particularly interested in the activities of fellow artists.

Unfortunately Carr's many letters to Lawren Harris, written between the late 1920s and early thirties, have not turned up to date; it is believed that he did not keep them. Harris, this leading Canadian artist, whom she met in Toronto in 1927, became the most important single influence in her artistic life. Her letters to him were obviously earnest communications about religion and work, and they revealed her insecurity in both these areas at that time.

This is made clear by his letters to her which were, as she was to comment when going through old correspondence many years later, "almost all work, one artist to another."[2] Many of Carr's letters are still in existence, however, and there are snappy letters to art gallery officials concerning their alleged mismanagement of matters relating to the shipping, exhibiting or purchasing of her paintings, which can be found in the files of several art institutions.

There are also letters containing emotional outpourings which reveal her misery and loneliness in her old age. This was particularly the case in the letters to her friend and mentor Ira Dilworth. They became friends, and it was he who brought her first book to the attention of Oxford University Press and edited all her later manuscripts. Carr met Dilworth when he was regional director of the western division of the Canadian Broadcasting Corporation. After her death he became her literary executor and, like Lawren Harris, one of the trustees of her estate. In her correspondence with him she touchingly splits herself into two personae: Small (which figures in the title of one of her books and was a name Dilworth used when writing to her), the imaginative, free child spirit in her; and

Emily, the pragmatic, aging and sometimes, by her own admission, mean and nasty self. With this dual personality she could claim the privileges of a close relationship and yet, when necessary, be an ordinary, practical person, and give vent to frustration and anger.

The letters are written with whatever was handy and at any time: in pencil, on scraps of paper torn from notebooks, on board ship, in bed. And, demonstrating a characteristic lack of concern for providing peripheral information, the letters are often dated only "Sunday" or "midnight," or "3 a.m." Together they constitute a vivid and often moving portrait of a woman who, her provincialism and streak of sentimentality notwithstanding, possessed an individuality and strength of character that marked all she said and did.

Carr tells of her birth during a December snowstorm: "Contrary from the start, I kept the family in suspense all day. . . . I dallied. At three o'clock in the morning I sent Father" out in the snow for help.[3] She is evidently satisfied with this early display of will against her father, who ordinarily got his way in everything. Her account appeals as delightful story-telling and it also points to an essential attribute in her make-up: her unshakeable sense of self. Her confidence in her abilities was shaken at times but never her confidence in herself. The autobiographical component of her writing implies this sureness, a characteristic that is frequently brought out as she observes her difference from others. Her impatience, her rebelliousness, her contrariness run through *The Book of Small* and *Growing Pains* almost like a leitmotif. She was naughty as a child and lacked restraint as a young girl. As an adult she resisted the nice Victorian social conventions, scorned religious piety and dutiful good works, expressed her real feelings in angry outbursts. She smoked, rode astride a horse rather than sidesaddle, kept a monkey. She claimed that when she returned from a five-year stay in England as a woman in her early thirties, Victorians found her disappointingly unchanged. Instead of "an English Miss with nice ways," she wrote, "I was more *me* than ever, just pure me."[4] Clearly she felt her difference as strength, a needful attribute for defence against a society in which narrow-mindedness prevailed.

A reflection of the difference she felt was the large number of they's who loomed in her life: those who in one way or another formed the opposition. They included do-gooders, society ladies, clergymen with empty rhetoric, fussers, analysts, statistic-minded curators, critics and the affected. They were the snobs (though it might be said that she had her own inverted form of snobbery). They were the convention-bound (though from her upbringing she had retained her own set of conventions), who naturally belonged to the vague mass of those who were uninterested in or hostile to her work.

Whatever the dramatic licence in her writing and however much she enjoyed her eccentricity, she was different. In small and large ways she forced her will on the patterns of her life. Some of the small ways made her conspicuous in Victoria's everyday world, and those with a small-town attitude regarded her as someone outside the pale of ordinary society, something of the village oddity. The supreme statement of her difference was, of course, her stance as artist, and her Journals repeatedly confirm how completely she committed all her resources and personality into being that artist: her enormous will, her obstinacy, her sensory vitality, her sublimated erotic energy, her observation of nature and her identification with its forces, her yearning for spiritual fulfillment, her immense need for self-expression.

And, not unexpectedly, it was the greater difference entailed in being a dedicated artist that had more serious consequences for her. In periods of low self-confidence or dejection, the exhilaration of aloneness as a working condition turns into the pain of loneliness as a living condition. "I haven't one friend of my own age and generation. I wish I had. I don't know if it's my own fault. I haven't a *single thing* in common with them. . . . None of them like painting and they particularly dislike my kind of painting. . . . Oh Lord, I thank Thee for the dogs and the monkey and the rat."[5]

At a crucial time in her career her dialogue with Lawren Harris gave her immeasurable sustenance. His letters continued their patient, generous support and encouragement, though after a while he began writing advance disclaimers and reassurances into them against the hints of criticism she might find there, for he understood her great sensitivity and her insecurity within the artistic isolation she chose. The years of correspondence and the occasional visit with him were the only times while her art was still forming that she had a friend with whom she could communicate deeply and sympathetically about the things that mattered most to her. Later, when they had ceased to correspond regularly, a chance visit from a European artist drew the comment: "It is wonderfully heartening to speak with another artist. I have missed the contact with Lawren bitterly. To both of us religion and art are one."[6]

At the end of 1939 when she had just turned sixty-nine she felt that there was not one solitary soul she could open up to. There were others in her life besides Harris — towards the latter part, many others — who bolstered her spirits; but throughout the Journals and in many of her letters, especially those to Ira Dilworth, with whom she had a close bond in the last years, along with the moments of elation or contentment runs the theme of the artist's loneliness. Once when she had been reading *The Autobiography of Alice B. Toklas*, she wrote: "Oh, if there was only a really kindred spirit to *share* it with [the lagoon at sunset], that we might keep each other warm in spirit, keep step and tramp uphill together. . . . all the artists there in Paris, like all the artists in the East, jogging along, discussing, condemning, adoring, fighting, struggling, enthusing, *seeking* together, jostling each other, instead of solitude, no shelter, exposed to all the 'winds' like a lone old tree with no others round to strengthen it against the buffets. . . . It must be my fault somewhere, this repelling of mankind and at the same time rebelling at having no one to shake hands with but myself. . . . Stop this yowl."[7]

Still, her difference and aloneness were strengths to draw from, and one concludes that she acquired toughness in a climate of adversity, even if she had to help create it. She needed response to her work and longed for success, but when compliments came her way she often thought them cloying or insincere, or plain rubbish when they emanated from art critics who were inclined to be analytical or "aesthetical." Easiest to accept were compliments from ordinary people of no importance in the art world (and therefore incapable of conferring success on her), who were exercising no judgement on her work but simply responding intuitively. After a party in her studio at which her guests appeared to like her paintings, she confided: "All that 'goo' trickles over me and runs down the other side and makes not one indentation. I do not think it is empty flattery. I think most of them *felt* something but it kind of nauseates me. I liked the little Chinaboy's remarks much better, badly expressed but from his heart."[8]

Failure was painful, but she knew how to deal with it and so sometimes interpreted events negatively when they could have been read otherwise. She speaks of the response she had had to her solo exhibition in Seattle late in 1930, some of it warmly congratulatory; yet when she had not heard from the gallery's director six weeks later she concluded that the show was not a success and read herself a moral lesson: "It did me good to have to rattle around and work and get ready for it. The fact that it fell flat was good for my conceit. If the work had been big enough — hit the bull's-eye — people would *have* to acknowledge it." She goes on to berate the "lazy minds and shrinking hearts of us who shirk the digging grind,"[9] exhorting herself to continue the struggle.

Like most artists, she wanted success but feared what it might do to her and to her work, and so for much of her life she created a protective shell to guard against flattery, minimizing success when it came her way. Her concept of the creative process — and of life itself, as she was fond of reiterating — is that of a never-ending struggle; she feared that success might make her smug and would interfere with her self-criticism. Also, she found the equation that relates paintings and "filthy money" repellent; she knew that art and money belong to different aspects of life and cannot be meaningfully equated, and that if she began to see the "dollar sign"[10] as she worked, she would lose her bearings as an artist.

More frequently in later years, when her confidence was stronger and the risks involved were less, she was able to resolve the conflict and could gauge and accept her successes. In February 1936, as she was packing to leave the memory-filled House of All Sorts, and in a mood of reminiscence and self-analysis, she faced the ambivalence in herself. "When I look over things I see that I have been careless over my receipts. I have had lots of recognition. Way over West it has come to me and I have not properly appreciated it. Why? It did not seem to mean much to me. I was wasteful of it, did not follow it up. I might have, and perhaps would have, become well off and financially successful. Things were suggested but I let them slip, was saucy over them. Now bad times have come; I cannot reach the public and the public soon forget. Some tire and look for a new person of interest. I would not kowtow. I did not push. Praise embarrassed me so that I wanted to hide. You've got to meet success halfway. I wanted it to come all the way, so we never shook hands."[11]

THE PAINTING AS AUTOBIOGRAPHY   Carr's writing, which achieved popularity before her painting, reveals the intense individuality of this woman who lived the life of an artist — as much as her upbringing and her abilities would allow — fully, romantically, passionately. And so, in addition to the rich legacy she left behind as painter and author, she emerges as a fascinating human being. Although it is not the perspective of this book to portray the woman Emily Carr, an understanding of her work is inseparable from some knowledge of her life. Not to recognize the autobiographical nature of her evolving art, the sense in which her painting is the most powerful expression of her existence and a necessity of her life, is to miss one of the dimensions of her work.

Her art is autobiographical not in the superficial sense that it follows her movements and relates to periods of her life, nor as a reflection of her changing moods. It is in the nature of some art to find its sources in the deepest wellspring of the self, and so it was with Carr in her mature work, once she had learned to make that mysterious connection with her intense psychic energy. She was one of those artists who, in the words of the psychoanalyst Otto Rank, live themselves out completely in their work.

NOTES

1. Emily Carr, *Hundreds and Thousands: The Journals of Emily Carr* (Toronto: Clarke, Irwin & Co., 1966) p. 206.
2. Carr to Dilworth, c. 1941–42, Emily Carr Papers (MG 30, D 215), Public Archives of Canada, Ottawa.
(All subsequent references to the Public Archives of Canada are from these papers.)
3. Emily Carr, *Growing Pains: The Autobiography of Emily Carr* (Toronto: Clarke, Irwin & Co., 1966) p. 5.
4. *Growing Pains*, p. 203.
5. *Hundreds and Thousands*, p. 141-42.
6. *Hundreds and Thousands*, p. 238.
7. *Hundreds and Thousands*, p. 108.
8. *Hundreds and Thousands*, p. 145.
9. *Hundreds and Thousands*, p. 24.
10. *Hundreds and Thousands*, p. 289.
11. *Hundreds and Thousands*, p. 224.

12. CONTEMPORARY JOURNALISM

Key Work:
   "Ethics and Engineering" — John Aitken
Associated Readings:
   "Letters of Response"
   "An Interview with David Suzuki" — Ron Wideman

Magazines, newspapers, and periodicals are prepared for specific audiences. As these publications compete for readership, articles are often selected for their ability to sell the publication. (Sometimes, this consideration — especially in mass circulation publications — overrides the merit of the content.) You should, therefore, consider not only the piece itself, but also the possible biases, interests, and image of the publication. "Ethics and Engineering," the Key Work, and "Letters of Response" appeared in *The Graduate,* a free periodical mailed to all University of Toronto alumnae. The Associated Reading, "An Interview with David Suzuki," was also published originally in a periodical, *The Forum,* with a specialized audience; it is read mainly by teachers in Ontario.

However, not all of today's journalism is published for a narrow audience. The breadth of contemporary journalism is demonstrated by the scope of material in this text. In "The Core Essays: The Link Between Thinking and Language," you will find examples such as Safire's "There, There" from *The New York Times* and "Varieties of Canadian English" from a popular newspaper.

BEFORE READING

■ Make a class list of favourite magazines and newspapers. In each case, identify the publisher, the intended audience, and the possible biases or leanings you might expect to find in these publications.
■ What plans do you have for a post-secondary career? Make a mental list of the factors you might weigh in formulating your choices.
■ Do such professionals as ministers, nurses, and police officers have special responsibilities to society?

ETHICS AND ENGINEERING

JOHN AITKEN

ZEV FRIEDMAN, TENSE, SHOULDERS SCRUNCHED, listens to the questions coming from students who have surrounded him. They are asking about determinism and freedom and want to bounce their ideas off him. He is drawn back to the blackboard where he scribbles some points and repeats a portion of what he has been trying to get across for the past hour: that while science depends upon determinism — events and actions are caused by preceding events and actions — determinism is inadequate for an understanding of humanity. There is freedom in humanity: the freedom to make moral judgements and choices. Where determinism absolves us, freedom holds us responsible for our actions.

Friedman, an associate professor of philosophy, has been lecturing on philosophical concepts of right and wrong, of *rights*, to 300 first year engineering students. It is the first time he has taught engineering students, although he has been teaching at U of T ever since he received his doctorate here 15 years ago.

"It's murder in there," he says later. "There is hostility to you and what you're trying to say." But what of the students, questioning, demanding more, interested? Surely that's encouraging? He shrugs. "There's no contact. You're not a person at all."

Derek Allen, associate professor of philosophy, teaches the first part of the course and Friedman the second. Allen has been at it for four years. "I'm more relaxed now, "he says, "less formal. But it's hard work. These students have a different cast of mind. They're technically oriented toward quantitative issues and they're used to the idea that a problem can be solved according to a definite procedure. They're not used to dealing with questions that don't lend themselves to that sort of treatment. The anti-arts credo runs very deep, or at least voluble lip service is paid to it."

W.H. Vanderburg comes to engineering students as one of them (his Ph. D. thesis was in fluid mechanics). He went to France for four and a half years to study the social sciences "to see what they knew that would be useful to me." He found a contradiction: that while science dominates and shapes our culture, our lives, it was not regarded as a serious phenomenon in the social sciences. As he pursued his studies he became convinced that there is a whole sociology of science, and he approaches students as a sociologist with a solid engineering background. This year he has been nominated for a teaching award and course evaluations from his students are high.

He tells his students that to be a good engineer means more than improving the responsiveness of a transistor or the strength of a bridge, that engineers must have a sense of the impact of what they do, that "many of these moral and ethical dilemmas become invisible when you subdivide a particular job or project down to its metallurgical aspect, or its chemical engineering aspect."

By dealing with cases involving transportation of technology to hypothetical but specific situations where the people and their institutions are not prepared for them, he forces students to deal with them "not in a naive way but by looking at the constraints the system has and asking what can be done within them, what the options may be.

"It's sort of applied social science," he says, "within an engineering context. The most common tools I use I borrow from sociology."

We are talking of acid rain and disposal of hazardous wastes, of toasters with faulty wiring and automobiles with defective gas tanks, of urban development and environmental protection, of computers and privacy. There is little in our lives that is unaffected by scientific and technological advances often accompanied by the threat or reality of disaster and disruption. What the students are being asked to consider is the extent to which they must assume responsibility for the mischief that may be inflicted on society when things go wrong.

The students are, many of them, single-minded and uninterested rather than reluctant to consider the moral and social implications of what they do.

Engineering students, says Jack Stevenson, a philosopher who has taken up the cause with almost missionary zeal, are self-selected for strength in maths and science, further culled by the University which demands a 90 per cent high school average for admission. It isn't surprising that they have little interest in the arts and humanities, that they have little skill in writing, in expressing themselves outside their fields.

Deans of engineering had seen the changes occurring in society and in the profession. U of T has included ethics and other non-technical electives in its curriculum for almost 20 years, but these courses have now become mandatory and engineering students will spend one-eighth of their time here in them. That's new. Also new is the revised Professional Engineers Act, which came into being on Sept. 1, 1984, and for the first time spells out clearly and unequivocally that the essential purpose of the profession is to serve the public, that safety and health are paramount.

Dean Gordon Slemon had already moved. In 1980 he established a task force headed by Morris Wayman, a professor in the Department of Chemical Engineering and Applied Chemistry, to look into "what we should be doing in courses that link engineering with society." Such courses were already being tried but, as Wayman noted in an article in the *Bulletin,* the campus fortnightly newspaper, there were problems. One professor of philosophy spent an entire term discussing the pros and cons of capital punishment. "He was," wrote Wayman, "trying to teach them how to approach moral problems. But the students have moral problems far more relevant to engineers than capital punishment."

In the same article Wayman wrote of the roots of engineering, which "did not arise from science but from the practical arts, from military engineering and from agricultural engineering, from construction and surveying and the building of cathedrals, pyramids or Stonehenge, or to go further back, from the making of bread and wine, from metallurgy and the many other non-scientific ways in which people feed, clothe, house, transport and protect themselves."

But there is little sense among engineering students today that arts and science professors have anything relevant to teach them. I caught something of this as I left Friedman's lecture and heard one student muttering to another: "Man, you can get a heavy if you think about this kind of thing too much." And another: "What does Plato matter anyway? I mean he's *dead*, isn't he?"

Early in 1981 Peter M. Wright, a professor of civil engineering who was a member of the Wayman committee and is now associate dean of engineering and acting dean of architecture, observed in another *Bulletin* article that "Marshall McLuhan, in *The Gutenberg Galaxy*, stated 'any technology tends to create a new human environment'." Was study of these changes not central to much of the humanities? "Engineers," observed Wright, "over the years have not been fully aware of the impact of their works and of the technology with which they are associated . . . The question for the rest of the University is, what role will it play in developing in engineers a better sense of perspective of their impact on the human environment. And conversely what place will engineering have in the university of the future."

There was much debate about importing philosophers, sociologists and historians. Not even all engineering faculty members were fully responsive, let alone the students. So much to be taught within the discipline, so much pressure on the students, was it reasonable to require them to spend a substantial part of their time studying such irrelevancies?

It certainly was and is, and the way had been prepared by, among others, Harold Innis and Marcus Long. "Innis," wrote Wayman, "was above all concerned from the beginning with the social impact of technology." Long, whom Slemon describes as "the famous raconteur of philosophy", was attracting interest which cut across disciplinary boundaries. "It's a long tradition," says Slemon. The result today is a cluster of courses designed to help engineering students understand professional ethics and comprehend the greater issues of social responsibility and moral awareness. They are also taught the complexities and confusions of whistle blowing and the heresy of the uncertainty principle.

Slemon is candid and pragmatic. Most engineers, he says, are employees. If their company is working on a design they know may be disadvantageous (not necessarily unsafe) to the public, what should they, as professionals, do about it? Blow the whistle? Talk to their supervisor? Call a press conference? He doesn't attempt to provide answers but feels strongly that nothing can be achieved without risk, and that the proper role of a professional engineer is to provide reliable information to both sides, especially in cases — the use of nuclear power for generating electricity is a good example — where neither side is right or wrong, simply polarized. "It is the most difficult position of all," says Slemon, "for the engineers will be castigated, they'll be thought of as traitors to both sides."

It is arrogance, says Slemon, for an engineer to say that something has been designed so that accidents cannot happen again. "There's hardly anything we can do without creating some difficulty, some danger for somebody else. And conversely if we don't do something, that will cause difficulty or danger to somebody else. The best we can do is to come to the best judgement of the best answer under existing circumstances, and that may not be the best answer next year. The only truth is many instances is that there is a part of it that we don't know."

Another thing that worries Slemon and Stevenson both is the misconception many engineering students seem to have about the work they'll be doing. Increasingly, says Slemon, "the engineer has to communicate, in a factory for example, with upper management, with the men on the floor, with union officials across a bargaining table, with the local city council or a protest group of concerned citizens — many different audiences. The same message has to go out in almost different languages and few engineers are prepared for that."

It was Jack Stevenson who developed the course in ethics and engineering. He studied the engineering code of ethics, and went on from there.

"One of the things I do," says Stevenson, "is put what I call a plate of spaghetti on the blackboard, a look at engineering as an activity under constraints of various kinds. It's not just the code of ethics, there are regulations under many acts, there's common law, civil actions, and by the time I put this up — all the various boxes, laws, regulations, moral obligations, rights — they get some sense that it's a very complex situation. Then I try to show the sources of all these restraints, a host of regulatory agencies they have to deal with. It's a concept they have to get hold of eventually. An engineer walking into a job situation can be very naive about this. I feel that my job is to inject a little realism into them."

It's one thing to say an engineer's duty to the public is paramount, but what does he do when his supervisor tells him to come in to the plant early Sunday morning and turn a valve that will release a 45-gallon barrel of dioxins into the lake? If he obeys he is ignoring the code and breaking the law. If he disobeys it's very likely that he'll be fired. "What's the welfare of the world?" asks Stevenson. "How do you measure it? You have to immerse the students in something close to reality and still be able to abstract from it to make it manageable. It's a process that involves finding some middle ground that's realistic on the one hand and yet simplified enough to see the issues and how to balance things off. You have to knock that simple-minded view out of their heads."

Stevenson does not teach philosophy by itself, out of context. "I'll discuss an ethical theory like utilitarianism but we only have 13 weeks so there's very little you can do and the students are very overworked. I have a kind intellectual ballast that I carry around with me that I can draw on. I don't pull Plato out of my back pocket, but he's in there, in what I'm saying."

He concentrates on cases drawn from reports or created hypothetically from his own knowledge and explores with the students their responsibilities, moral and legal obligations and options. Whistle blowing, for example. But again, he can't tell them how to react in a given situation. "That's cookbook science," he scoffs.

"There are methods that work a good deal of the time but they're not infallible. The students have to learn to recognize and deal with the relation between the known and the unknown; they have to understand the role of luck and serendipity, and that you can only improve your judgement with practice."

Is this ethics, philosophy or survival?

THE GRADUATE

EXPLORING THE ARTICLE

1. Familiarize yourself with this vocabulary: philosophy, moral, ethical, sociology, pragmatic, humanities, heresy, naive, dioxin, utilitarianism, serendipity, candid.

2. State the thesis of Aitkin's article and select three types of evidence used to prove it.

3. Arts and Humanities departments usually teach such subjects as languages, history, philosophy, visual arts, sociology, psychology, and anthropology. Given this information, what do you think is meant by the term "anti-arts credo?"

4. What indications are there that Friedman sometimes feels discouraged about educating students who hold an "anti-arts credo?"

5. (a) Why is the language used in this article suitable for its audience?
    (b) Why is it unlikely that this essay would appear in a city's mass circulation tabloid?

EXTENSIVE STUDY

1. The teaching of ethics and social issues to engineers is based on a specific value judgment. What is this premise or assumption?

2. (a) Does this article offer sufficient evidence to support the generalization that certain personality types are drawn to various professions?

   (b) What commonly held assumptions (stereotypes) exist about the personality traits of accountants, research scientists, artists, teachers, and media celebrities? How do these stereotypes develop? What is your reaction to this type of stereotyping?

3. Do you feel more comfortable working with information that is technical and quantitative or abstract and open-ended? Relate these preferences and feelings to the school subjects in which you do well. Consider how these reactions may affect your choice of a career.

4. Create a hypothetical situation that involves a young engineer or other professional in a conflict of values which forces a choice between personal and corporate values. List the conflicts involved, the value judgments that must be made, the options available, and the pros and cons of each choice.

5. (a) Find evidence to support, refute, or qualify this statement as the basis for a seminar:

   "A professional — engineer, doctor, lawyer, or teacher — should have a well-rounded education, which teaches the technical expertise of the field, but also instructs the whole human being about the pleasures and responsibilities of being a contributing member of society."

   (b) Debate one of these statements. Resolved that:

   The state is responsible for providing universal employment.

   It is better to be happily employed than waste your life working at a lucrative job that does not fulfill you.

6. Read the accompanying interview with David Suzuki, taking note of where it was originally published. Compare its purpose, language, and audience with Aitken's article.

7. Both these pieces of contemporary journalism raise questions about the individual's responsibility to society. Explore your views about how we can balance individual and collective needs.

8. What reactions have been provoked by Aitken's article, judging from the accompanying letters to the editor of *The Graduate*?

9. How does Suzuki's life illustrate the idea that life is what you make of it?

10. Suzuki claims that "As a tool within a framework of social values, science is valuable. But science can never provide answers to

important questions like what is right or wrong."

   (a) How does Wideman's interview with Suzuki underscore the idea behind teaching ethics to engineers?

   (b) Can art or artists help us understand moral issues?

   (c) If you have read any of the essays by Russell, Thoreau (see The Generic Essay, page 26), Hales (see The Scholarly Essay, page 47) or Gardner (see The Review, page 137), how might each author feel about Suzuki's comment?

THE WRITING FOLDER

1.   Assume the role of a professional in one of these fields: a classical or rock musician, a nurse, an athlete or sports figure, a psychiatrist, a lawyer, a writer or police officer. Write an after-dinner speech, using one of the topics listed below, for a specified audience using language appropriate for the occasion.

> The Mixed Blessings of My Work
> If I'd Known Then What I Know Now. . .
> Professional Secrets I'll Pass On to My Children
> If I Had It To Do Over Again

2.   Write an interview in which you ask Suzuki other questions that have arisen in response to issues he raised.

3.   Write a column on a topic of interest for a magazine that is currently popular with your peers.

INDEPENDENT STUDY

1.   "In order that people may be happy in their work, these three things are needed: they must be for it; they must not do too much of it; and they must have a sense of success in it."

          — John Ruskin, *Pre-Raphaelitism*

  Prepare a report based on published research and personal interviews that deals with job satisfaction in contemporary North American society.   +

2.   " 'A fair day's wages for a fair day's work': it is as just a demand as governed men ever made of governing. It is the everlasting right of man."

          — Thomas Carlyle, *Past and Present*

  Research and write a report on some aspect of the effects of Canada's traditionally high unemployment on the individuals involved. You might focus on the psychological and social effects of unemployment on the family, for example. Define a specific topic with the help of your teachers.   +

3.   Locate a copy of *The Professional Engineers Act* (September 1, 1984).

Prepare a seminar based on your study of the document. Consider such issues as the obligations and duties specified and the ethical responsibilities entailed. You might interview one or more engineers about these matters. Submit a written report or essay. (*Hint:* some mathematics and science teachers have engineering papers.) +

4. Examine one or more mass-circulation publications such as *Chatelaine, Arrowsmith,* or *Homemakers.* Compare how the editors use language, editorials, advertising and over-all image to make a successful package. +

5. Read two works such as Miller's *Death of a Salesman,* Ibsen's *The Master Builder,* or Ayn Rand's *The Fountainhead* that involve the protagonist in a conflict between personal values and professional demands. Compare the manner in which the protagonists resolve their conflict. ++

TIMED READING AND WRITING

1. Write an essay on one of these topics in the time specified by your teacher.

> Qualities Needed for Success in the Medical Profession (or substitute another field)
> Why I'd Like To Be an Engineer (or substitute another field)
> Society's Reverence of the Medical Profession Is Harmful to Our Health

2. Compare Suzuki's remarks about the impact of television on people with the ideas Reed raises in "T.V. As a Shaper" (see The Report, page 85).

3. Assume the role of L.F. Thomay and compose a response to J.D. Gardiner's letter.

LETTERS OF RESPONSE

THE GRADUATE

I WISH TO COMMEND THE EXCELLENT article "Ethics and Engineering" (Jan./Feb.). It ranged widely beyond ethics and touched on several deficiencies of engineering training as I see it — too narrow and academic. I am also impressed by Jack Stevenson's pragmatic approach to teaching the course in ethics — relevance is the key element.

I'm of the class of 4T0 Mechanical and now retired. After several years in the Navy I joined the work force in industrial manufacturing after the war. Obviously unprepared for management, business economics and communication, a number of us found ourselves taking extension courses to broaden our perspective. Many of these were irrelevant, too. Ethics did not arise until later in more responsible positions.

Over the past 30 years in an engineering capacity I have been amazed by the general lack of pragmatism of engineers providing consulting services. I was involved in high speed machinery using both flammable and toxic substances. It was a continuous struggle to keep the work place safe for people and the environment. Management was generally co-operative but I had to lean heavily on various regulatory and licensing authorities to counteract the ever-present cost/benefit pressure.

Now I am doing a little consulting work for a firm in B.C., working with a pair of Ontario-trained engineers. They are aware of the toxic, explosive and environmental hazards of several key products being processed and accept the need for certain general precautions.

However, I am astounded at their almost complete ignorance of the impact of regulatory authorities and absence of personal concern for the omissions in their design concepts. My ethical problem is that this aspect of the larger project is outside my terms of reference. I have warned them as to the costly extent of these fire and safety requirements in general but so far they have had soothing reassurances from the local building and fire underwriter consultants. Time will tell.

These real life work experiences account for my favourable response to the article and the awareness at U of T. It is encouraging to think that the current crop of engineers will receive a more rounded education to face today's hazards and responsibilities.

J.D. Gardiner
Rexdale

———————

Do you realize how deeply the article "Ethics and Engineering" offended all engineering students, past and present?

Not interested in ethics and morals, indeed! Just reflect a minute on why a young man would tinker with mechanical objects, why he would take up engineering in the first place. (I am a man and only know how men think, but probably all I am saying applies to women as well.) He does that in order to create something that is better, cheaper, simpler and, yes, safer, than what we had before. This is an absolutely basic idea behind engineering. And if we do create something better, cheaper and safer, then the entire community is well served; otherwise we wouldn't see any sense in doing it.

Ethics is, by definition, one of the major motivating factors for a young person taking up engineering. It is an integral part of his personality. Just as a medical student goes into medicine to learn to cure people and not to poison them, the young engineer wants to create something worthwhile, not to contribute to the destruction of the planet.

As to the "hypothetical situations" these courses deal with, in three decades as a telephone engineer I have never once encountered any situation where I would have been asked to falsify technical facts (or any other). When judging the merits of a project, the ultimate criterion was always: "is it service affecting?" and the project would have no chance if it was. Is this not an ethical attitude?

L.F. Thomay
Ottawa

"Nothing but trade schools," said a senior U of T official, as he described Ontario's community colleges a few years ago. "Do you know," he asked, "that they actually try to teach social science? And the humanities?" He went on to insist that if the liberal arts were to have a place in the colleges, then surely only university faculty ought to teach them.

As a then 12-year veteran of community college teaching, who also possesses a B.A. and three post-graduate degrees. I bristled a little but soon dismissed the matter largely as an unfortunate instance of post-doctoral snobbery. I cheerfully returned to my labours where I have been "trying to teach social sciences and the humanities" since 1969.

I was reminded of this incident by the article "Ethics and Engineering", wherein it became apparent that some university professors are facing problems and working on solutions that are not unfamiliar to those of us who have made careers teaching not only engineering technologists but also students in the dozens of vocational programs that colleges provide.

It is difficult to bridge the gap between the arts and the applied sciences, but is it too much to imagine that the equally large gap that separates college and university faculty might be narrowed with salutary benefits for all? A mutual recognition of shared problems and a genuinely reciprocal discussion of successful teaching methods might make for considerable progress. Too often arrogance on the one hand and defensiveness on the other have obscured the fact that college teaching and undergraduate university teaching are not all that dissimilar. At least as far as post-secondary instruction is concerned, we could learn much from each other.

Howard A. Doughty
Co-ordinator, Electives Program,
Seneca College of Applied Arts and Technology
King City

AN INTERVIEW WITH DAVID SUZUKI

RON WIDEMAN

DURING THE PAST three years David Suzuki has travelled the planet, gathering material for what he calls "the single most important project I have ever worked on." The result is A Planet for the Taking, *a controversial eight-part CBC special that challenges our most fundamental assumptions about the human species and our place in nature.*

Controversy is not new to this university professor, television host, and world renowned geneticist. He has never shied from being critical of his own scientific community. His overriding concern centres on the moral implications of research being undertaken for profit and power, without regard to social consequences.

Ron Wideman spoke with David Suzuki at a CBC press preview of A Planet for the Taking. *Suzuki explains what motivated his involvement and why this mini-series will provoke widespread public reaction.*

Forum: *You've been the host of numerous successful programs* — Suzuki on Science, Science Magazine, Quirks & Quarks, *and* The Nature of Things. *You're now launching* A Planet for the Taking. *What prompted the production of this new series?*

Suzuki: *A Planet for the Taking* is a one-shot deal and certainly isn't intended to be the first season of an ongoing TV series. Essentially, it's a summation of the thinking John Livingston and I have been doing. Livingston, an environmentalist at York University, is an important part of this production. He worked with *The Nature of Things* for a long time and was once the executive producer. We put together a radical look at some current issues and explored how these led to environmental problems.

After watching people fight developments like the Spadina Expressway and the Pickering Airport, we realized even when they win, the same issues keep recurring. Why do we spend so much energy yet never seem to get anywhere? What is the philosophical underpinning that generates these problems?

In our view it's a Western attitude, which regards humans as special and somehow separate from the rest of nature. This stems from the belief that we were created in God's image and placed on this planet to have dominion over everything. Our definition of progress is measured by the extent to which we can dominate nature — how well we can predict and control weather and earthquakes, find oil and extract it. That's progress!

With that attitude we don't really examine our biological roots. We don't consider ourselves part of the earth's ecosystem or recognize that our actions have enormous impact. If we continue this way, we will not only extinguish a large number of other species, which we've already been doing successfully, but we are going to create a planet that won't ever support us. This TV program says, "Look at what we are doing! Look at our assumptions. Do we have the right to make these assumptions?" If the answer is no, then the question is what can we do about it.

Forum: You don't see this dominating attitude as being a product of science so much as science being a product of that attitude.

Suzuki: Science is a result of the natural enquiring mind. We aren't very strong, we aren't very fast, our senses aren't as keen as those of other animals. But we have a large brain. We are able to examine and understand our world. We learned when plants would ripen, where and when animals would migrate, how animals would behave. That was our survival strategy. That has been our evolutionary history. But it has gone too far.

The Judeo-Christian tradition goes back over 2,000 years and at that time it saw humans as separate from nature and superior to it. When science came along in the 16th century, it was just an extension of that same drive to dominate and control.

Forum: A Planet for the Taking promises to be a provocative series. Who is going to like it?

Suzuki: Anyone who has felt frustrated about issues like the nuclear arms race, the degradation of the environment, the continual development of "natural resources" at the expense of values like the right of animals or plants to exist — these people will be pleased with it.

But anytime you are asked to take a hard look at your society, your lifestyle, it is going to be painful. There are going to be things you don't like. There are things that I find extremely painful. For example, the section on our use of animals for feed, I find extremely uncomfortable to watch. I am not a vegetarian and yet when I see what is being done to serve my food I find it quite horrendous.

Forum: *Where will the criticism come from?*

Suzuki: People who feel progress is absolutely necessary (progress being defined as continual growth in the GNP, as continual development of our "resources") and those who see nature as ours for the taking will not like the series. These people would be outraged if someone suggested that extracting oil in the high Arctic, which might provide southern areas with more oil and gas for five years, is not worth the risk of upsetting the northern ecosystem.

People who do not believe in evolution will hate it. The show runs on the assumption that evolution is fact.

Forum: *Is it possible to develop another kind of science — a science that is based on seeing humankind as part of the ecosystem?*

Suzuki: The problem is not with science. The series is more about putting science in its place. It exposes the myth that science is value free. We should understand that when we use science, we are using it with all kinds of social and cultural assumptions.

Science is a powerful but limited way of knowing. Scientists began by saying, "We can't explain everything that's happening in the universe. It's just too complex." Science is good at isolating part of nature, examining it under a microscope, and then assuming that that's an indication of what the whole thing is. Well, we know from the 20th century on that this doesn't apply in physics. You can't isolate an electron or a neutron and study it in isolation from the atom in which it belongs. And if you try to isolate it you change it. There is no way of knowing what nature is like in its native state, because in order to study it, you disturb it.

As a tool within the a framework of social values, science is valuable. But science can never provide answers to important questions like what is right or wrong.

Forum: *Someone said that we are technological giants and ethical pygmies. That suggests that we need to develop an ethical system.*

Suzuki: That's right. But what we must do is bring this juggernaut into proper perspective. We believe that somehow scientists can provide all the answers. Scientists, doctors, technologists, and engineers seem to promise a lot of goodies — "We'll solve cancer" . . . "We'll extend your life" . . . "We may conquer death."

We never ask, "Why should we try to beat death?" There is no one who has ever lived or who is alive today who will not die.

Medicine has postponed death, but it can never beat death. We see cancer, stroke, heart disease, and other terrible things and say science is going to conquer them.

Well, maybe it's a part of getting old. Because we now are approaching the theoretical limits of our lifespan, perhaps no amount of science is going to get us over the hump. The average life expectancy today is 74. The absolute limit for all people will be 84. The longest that anyone has ever lived is less than 120 years. We ought to ask science not to promise all those goodies but to put them in a framework in which we maximize the quality of our life but accept aging and death as a natural consequence of being biological creatures.

Forum: I suspect you believe it possible for humankind to change because so much of your work has been an attempt to inform the public. Is your belief in TV as a medium for education still strong?

Suzuki: I'm very pessimistic about TV. It is without a doubt the most powerful medium for transferring information today. But what's being transferred is not what we think.

I used to think that people examined the TV schedule, turned on the set, watched it for an hour, turned it off, had a heated discussion, and later read a book. They don't.

Canadians watch six to eight hours of television a day but they watch it in blocks of time. Regardless of how high the quality of the show, it's going to be sandwiched between *Quincy* and *Charlie's Angels* or *Dallas* and *Dynasty*. The "education" people are getting is very different from what we suppose.

Viewers remember programs in bits and pieces. They don't watch in a concentrated, intense way as they would intellectually. A child is crying, the dog's barking, the telephone rings — there are all kinds of interruptions. So people float in and out of the room while they watch. God knows what they really get out of TV.

The kind of change our new series is asking for is comparable to Paul or Saul of Tarsus being knocked off a horse. Examples of changing values in that profound a way are very, very rare. John DeLorean found God, but he had a pistol put to his head. Charles Colson, one of Nixon's lieutenants, had a similar conversion. He found God, but he was going to jail.

We've been conditioned with these values from the time we were born. But it doesn't matter what the end result is. What matters is that people believe something can be done. You have to be optimistic. It's the doing and trying to change that matters.

Forum: In schools we've found that to examine values students need an opportunity to challenge their beliefs and to reflect on issues in terms of their own experience.

Suzuki: In school situations TV can be extremely useful because you can focus on particular programs and then use them as your springboard to questions. That, to me, is the ideal use of TV.

In many ways I'm optimistic about VCRs. They have the potential to free us from the tyranny of the TV schedule. My children, for example, are *not* allowed to watch TV. I control what they watch through the VCR. There are no commercials. They are allowed to watch what I rent or tape for them, when I say they can watch. Television watching is mesmerizing. Once on, it is very difficult to turn off. Unless you have some structure like a VCR, kids tend to watch everything.

Forum: *Adolescents need skills for TV viewing, for information sorting, and for distinguishing between good and poor ideas.*

Suzuki: I've been in TV work over 20 years and I believe the most important lesson to get across is not the latest scandal or environmental issue. People have so much information that my show will be just another drop in the bucket. What's important is to show viewers how to assess information for themselves.

Forum: *There are implications in what you say regarding how science should be taught in schools.*

Suzuki: What discourages me is that educational institutions are built on a knowledge pyramid. Teachers are under pressure to cover a given amount of material so the students taking next year's course will have the facts under their belt and can progress. By Grade 12 or 13, those students graduating in science are expected to have a base to take first-year university physics or chemistry.

But at each level the school system shucks off large numbers of students who no longer feel the curriculum is relevant because they are not going to continue in science. By the time they graduate, it's as if science isn't part of their lives, because teachers had to fill them with information. Yet it's crazy because 90 percent of what is taught today is going to be totally irrelevant in five or six years. What's important is emphasizing that science is a way of learning about the world.

I know that teachers are under the gun because universities make these demands, but students don't need the latest DNA, RNA, and protein stuff. They are going to get that in university. Teachers ought to tell the universities to stuff it.

I remember going to Slave Lake, Alberta, to judge a science fair and being asked to address the high school students. The night before the address I was in a local pub. A biology teacher from the school introduced himself and mentioned that the kids were a tough audience. He said all they cared about was sex, drugs, and cars. When I went in the next day, half the student body were Natives and

I have not had much experience with Natives. I had no idea how the students would react and I was apprehensive.

I started by saying, "When you are in high school all you think about is sex. You are walking gonads. Your puberty has arrived. You've lost 50 IQ points. You're walking around with your knuckles dragging on the ground. What the hell have I got to tell you of interest? Obviously I've got to talk about sex."

I went on to talk about the biology of sex and got into X and Y chromosomes and what alcohol and drugs do to chromosomes. Well, you could have heard a pin drop. I talked for an hour and a half and for another hour they just kept me there asking questions. And I thought, if a high school biology teacher can't get those kids hooked, we are in bad shape.

Forum: Let's look at the broad educational picture. What does the citizen in the 1990s look like in your estimation?

Suzuki: I never dreamed television would be a daily part of our world when I was in grade school. There were no computers, birth control pills, plastics, tranquilizers, or organ transplants then. We didn't know how many chromosomes humans had or what DNA did. This has all happened in my lifetime. My youngest child is going to become an adult after the year 2000. I simply cannot imagine what her world will be like. But it will be totally different.

It's insane the way high schools are jumping on computers. Everyone seems panicked and wants their children to become computer literate. At five years of age they are sent off to computer schools and summer camps. The computer is going to be a daily part of the world our children grow up in — there is no doubt about it. But the computers that our children encounter as adults will be vastly different from those we have today. What's the point of teaching them on a Model A? All you have to do is encourage them to become aware of computers and not be afraid of them.

Forum: Planet for the Taking has to do with basic beliefs, values, and ethics. Should ethical issues be discussed as part of the science curriculum?

Suzuki: Only when you see the history of science do you realize the profound effect of the social context within which science is conducted. You realize, for example, that the race purification activity in Nazi Germany did not spring up in the mind of one madman. It was a consequence of the ideas of the leading biologists of the day, who were pushing the idea that humankind could be improved by selective breeding. It ended up in this grotesque thing we call the Holocaust.

I had a liberal arts education and yet what astounds me is in all of my background there was no history of science. Today, students coming through universities are specializing from the time they enter first year. They don't take a liberal arts degree. They take a bachelor of science degree and very small amounts of course work outside science. They get no grounding at all in history or philosophy.

Forum: *Opposition to your series will come from creationists who object to the evolutionary view of life. A lot of people want creation science taught as an alternative to evolution.*

Suzuki: There aren't a lot of people — there is a very vocal minority.

Forum: *Is creation science science?*

Suzuki: No. It appalls me to see the juxtaposition of creation and science. It is not science. I have no objection to people who, in discussions of religion, want to believe creation theories. But it is not science. The thing that astounds me is the number of people who cave in when a vocal minority puts on pressure. At what point do you as a teacher say, "This is not science. This is not education. And don't tell me what my profession is"? Creation science has no business being in a science curriculum — period.

Forum: *Why isn't creation science scientific?*

Suzuki: Science begins with a basic assumption and that is a basic faith in the experimental process within the scientific technique. There is no recourse to any absolute truth in science. You are constantly in the business of using the scientific method and proving your ideas wrong.

Scientific creationism begins with the assumption that what is in the Bible is true. That is fine for them, but it lies outside of science. In science, what has value is an idea, a theory that unifies a broad number of bits of data. It brings it together and it makes sense of it. And it suggests further experimentation. You can test it. In that way evolution has been incredibly useful. It has explained the enormous diversity of life around us. And it has provided us with ways of testing to prove whether or not this idea has validity.

From the standpoint of science, scientific creation is totally worthless because it gives you nothing testable. It tells you right from the start, this is the way it was. In scientific terms, that is of no value at all.

Forum: *You have a varied background — scientist, educator, media personality. How did this broad career orientation come about?*

Suzuki: It is grounded in the fact that I spent four years in a Canadian concentration camp. I say concentration camp in contrast to the death camps in Germany, which is what they were. The

Canadian concentration camps were established on the assumption that deceit and treachery are hereditary.

It didn't matter if you were born in Canada, were a Canadian citizen, spoke English as your first language. If you were a "Jap" it was assumed that you were potentially capable of disloyalty, that you had greater allegiance to another country. We had no rights of citizenship. We were incarcerated.

Now that was a very important event in my life. It shaped a great deal of my extracurricular activity in civil liberties. After graduating from university I began to look at the history of genetics. I realized that we were imprisoned because geneticists had propagated the notion that many human behaviours were hereditary, that you could characterize races as shiftless, as vagrant, as nomadic, as unreliable — all of these things.

As a scientist, I loved this area and yet it had implications in other areas that were equally important to me in civil rights. I realized you can not ignore science, you must take it seriously, and it has to be brought to the public in a broader context.

Since that time I have spent more and more time trying to demystify the process, trying to say to people, "For God's sake, think about the implications. Don't say, 'I don't understand it. It is beyond me. Let the experts judge.'" If the public doesn't take science seriously and insist on a role in determining how politicians should treat the issues, then we are going to get into trouble again.

Forum: *One last question. I expect* Planet for the Taking *will be used extensively by educators. Where do you see it being used?*

Suzuki: The most important impact will be felt through its reuse in science curricula in high schools. Just as Bronowski's series *The Ascent of Man* has been used extensively, I hope this one will also be bought by school boards across the country and used as a point of departure for discussion.

Forum Interview

E|SSAYS FOR THE CRAFT OF WRITING AND STUDIES IN LITERATURE

INTRODUCTION

The essays In Part B go beyond the material generally studied in core English courses; they have been selected especially for students taking courses in the craft of writing or the study of literature. They provide a stimulus for exploring the specialized skills required in these particular areas. Teachers and students may wish to use them for further application of skills developed in Part A or for enrichment. Each essay is introduced with a biographical sketch of the writer, two questions that focus on the work, and, usually, suggestions for related or further readings.

■ Famous Quotations: Food for Thought and Discussion opens this section of the text and offers relevant statements of opinion on writing and literature by writers, scholars, and critics.
■ The first seven essays — by Alderich, Cowley, Laurence, Boles, Wilder, Ibsen, and McGill — focus on specific aspects of the writing process.
■ The final five works — by Mannes, Pope, Ciardi, Atwood, and Frye — offer various insights about the study of literature.
■ An Overview: Questions for Discussion rounds out this section of the text.

Suggested Supplementary Resources

Students of the craft of writing will find it useful to have the periodicals and texts listed below in their school's Resource Centre. These sources provide detailed, practical assignments and/or advice which could be used independently. *Note:* Not all resources provide exercises at the same level of difficulty.

Eileen Goodman, *The Canadian Writer's Market,* 6th ed. (Toronto: McClelland and Stewart, 1981)

The Writer's Digest (205 West Center Street, Marion, Ohio 43305)

R. Davey, *The Writing Process* (Toronto: Prentice-Hall of Canada, 1984)

Peter Elbow, *Writing without teachers* (London: Oxford University Press, 1973)

L. Mueller and J.D. Reynolds, *Creative Writing* (Toronto: Doubleday Canada, 1982)

W.H. New and W.E. Messinger, eds., *The Active Stylist* (Toronto: Prentice-Hall of Canada, 1981)

J. Norton and F. Gretton, *Writing Incredibly Short Plays, Poems, Stories* (New York: Harcourt Brace Jovanovich, 1972)

J.F. Parker, *The Writer's Craft* and *The Process of Writing* (Toronto: Addison-Wesley Publishers, 1983)

F.W. Shaw, *30 Ways To Help You Write* (New York: Bantam, 1980)

Students of specialized literary studies courses might find some of the references listed below useful Resource Centre materials, depending on the nature and content of their course.

Margaret Atwood, *Survival: A Thematic Guide to Canadian Literature* (Toronto: House of Anansi Press, 1972)

A.C. Bradley, *Shakespearean Tragedy* (London: Macmillian, 1964)

E.M. Forster, *Aspects of the Novel* (Markham: Penguin Books Canada, 1963)

Northrop Frye, *The Educated Imagination* (Toronto: CBC Enterprises, 1963)

D.G. Jones, *Butterfly on Rock* (Toronto: University of Toronto Press, 1971)

D.H. Lawrence, *Studies in Classic American Literature* (London: Heinemann Group, 1924)

J.E. Miller, ed., *Myth and Method* (University of Nebraska, 1960)

FAMOUS QUOTATIONS: FOOD FOR THOUGHT AND DISCUSSION

■ What common threads run through these famous statements listed below by writers, scholars, and thinkers?

■ Are there any statements that provoke a strong response in you?

"People put down Canadian literature and ask us why there isn't a *Moby Dick.* The reason there isn't a *Moby Dick* is that if a Canadian did a *Moby Dick,* it would be done from the point of view of the whale. Nobody ever thought of that."

— Margaret Atwood, *Saturday Night* (Nov. 1972)

"He [the writer] must teach himself that the basest of all things is to be afraid; and, teaching himself that, forget it forever, leaving no room in his workshop for anything but the old verities and truths of the heart . . . [without which] any story is ephemeral and doomed — love and honour and pity and pride and sacrifice."
— William Faulkner, *Speech Upon Receiving the Nobel Prize* (Dec. 10, 1950)

"Against the disease of writing one must take special precautions, since it is a dangerous and contagious disease."
— Peter Abelard, "Letter 8, Abelard to Heloise"

"The next thing most like living one's life over again seems to be the recollection of that life, and to make that recollection as durable as possible by putting it down in writing."
— Benjamin Franklin, *Autobiography*

"The original writer is not one who imitates nobody, but one whom nobody can imitate."
— F.R. de Chateaubriand, *Le Genie du Christianisme*

"Every great and original writer, in proportion as he is great or original, must himself create the taste by which he is to be relished."
— William Wordsworth, "Letter to Lady Beaumont" (May 21, 1807)

"Omit needless words. Vigorous writing is concise. . . . This requires not that the writer make all his sentences short, or that he avoid all detail and treat his subjects only in outline, but that every word tell."
— William Strunk, Jr. and E.B. White, *The Elements of Style*

"No tears in the writer, no tears in the reader."
— Robert Frost, "The Figure a Poem Makes." Preface to *Collected Poems*

"A good many young writers make the mistake of enclosing a stamped, self-addressed envelope, big enough for the manuscript to come back in. This is too much of a temptation to the editor."
— Ring Lardner, *How To Write Short Stories*

"All good books are alike in that they are truer than if they had really happened and after you have finished reading one you will feel that all that happened to you and afterwards it all belongs to you. . . . If you can . . . give that to people then you are a writer."
— Ernest Hemingway, "Old Newsman Writes," from *Esquire*

"Writing, when properly managed (as you may be sure I think mine is), is but a different name for conversation."
— Laurence Sterne, *Sermons,* I

"Reading maketh a full man, conference a ready man and writing an exact man."
— Francis Bacon, "Of Studies," *Apothegms*

"True ease in writing comes from art, not chance,
As those move easiest who have learned to dance.
'Tis not enough no harshness gives offence;
The sound must seem an echo to the sense."
> — Alexander Pope, *An Essay on Criticism*

"The only reason for the existence of the novel is that it does attempt to represent life."
> — Henry James, *The Art of Fiction*

"The power to guess the unseen from the seen, to trace the implications of things, to judge the whole piece by the pattern, the condition of feeling life so completely that you are well on your way to knowing any particular corner of it — this cluster of gifts may be said to constitute experience. . . . If experience consists of impressions, it may be said that impressions *are* experience. . . . Therefore, if I should say to a novice [writer], 'Write from experience and experience only,' I should feel that this was a rather tantalizing monition if I were not careful immediately to add, 'Try to be one of the people on whom nothing is lost.'"
> — Henry James, (*The Art of Fiction*)

"Lyric poets generally come from homes run by women."
> — Milan Kundera, *Life Is Elsewhere*

"One must not always think that feeling is everything. Art is nothing without form."
> — Gustave Flaubert, "Letter to Madame Louise Colet"

"Never pursue literature as a trade."
> — Samuel Coleridge, *Biographia Literaria*

HOW TO READ LIKE A WRITER
— Robert S. Aldrich

Aldrich has written many stories for western and mystery magazines such as *Ellery Queen's Mystery Magazine* and *Alfred Hitchcock's Mystery Magazine.*

■ What is the difference between reading for entertainment and reading with the critical eye of a professional writer?
■ What can you learn about effective story-telling techniques by adopting this critical reading approach?

Aldrich contends that reading like a writer helps you learn the secrets and techniques of successful authors. You may want to try some of his suggestions the next time you read.

You've seen those entertaining picture-puzzles, where some object is lost or disguised until, by tilting the picture, or suddenly looking at it in a different way, you perceive the object standing out vividly from all that surrounds it. Something very much like that is involved when we study the work of other writers.

Most writers are great readers to begin with. But it's one thing to absorb what is laid before you — to read as the ordinary reader reads — for interest, amusement, entertainment. It's something else to read in order to understand how the writer has worked, what he or she had to do to create the particular effects produced in you, the reader.

To read that way, to grasp an author's technique instead of simply following after his content and material or his characters, you must examine a short story, a novel, or nonfiction in such a way that the author's *methods* can be clearly seen. For it is the published writer's methods that one seeks to study and at times to borrow.

Yes, borrow. Nothing is shameful in adopting the universal *methods* used by successful writers. Using practiced techniques is not plagiarism; stealing another writer's *words, ideas,* or *characters* is plagiarism. Writers have always learned their craft from the writers who have gone before them.

Why, then, can't anybody with a mild interest in writing pick out a writer's "secrets" like raisins from a pudding and put them to use? Because you need, also, that *method of reading,* a way of tilting the puzzle, that allows these technical devices to come clear, stand out, rather than being lost or obscured amid your fascination with the characters and what is happening in the story.

It wasn't until I enrolled in the courses taught by the University of Oklahoma's Professional Writing School that I encountered a workable way to analyze stories. A professor there, Walter S. Campbell, taught a reading method close to the one I'm about to describe.

The Last Shall Be First

The stories and novels you choose to study need not be (though of course they may be) classics of their kinds. You may simply want some representative sample of the type of work you want to do. In college, I was encouraged to admire Keats and Coleridge, but when I sought to sell to the pulps, I studied *Dime Western, Bluebook* and the like as if they were sacred writ. Well, almost.

For the moment, let's assume your model is a short story. With an unborrowed copy, you can scribble in the margins. You might find a couple of crayons handy; say, green to underscore devices of interest, red for plausibility, other colors for additional fictional elements you want to identify.

Begin to read from the start as you would ordinarily. But read slowly. You're not reading for entertainment, but to note what is happening to the reader.

When you have read far enough to get some notion of what the story is going to be about, *stop.* (There is no set wordage for any of this; you can be quite arbitrary about it.)

Now, turn to read the end of the story. (Again, exactly how much you call the end doesn't much matter. Often an editor will conveniently mark off both beginning and end sections of a story with white spaces.)

You have, now, some idea of the conclusion, the destination toward which the whole story is aimed. ("Plot is destination, said British novelist Elizabeth Bowen.)

Next, take your pencil and mark the story into parts. Five or six parts might do for an average-length short story. In time, you may want to work with 10 or 12 smaller parts.

Next, read the section just *before* the last — e.g., part 5 of 6 parts. Then read the part before that one — e.g., part 4 of 6. And then the part before *that.* And so on, back to the beginning, rereading the first part last.

Finally, begin at the beginning again and *read the whole story* from start to finish.

Studying a book-length story for technique is basically similar. However, reading a whole book "backward" chapter by chapter can be tedious. So it is perhaps more sensible, and enlightening, to read by parts or sections. Some novels and nonfiction books are divided into Part One, Part Two, etc., some not. If not, divide the book yourself.

For instance, study a 24-chapter novel like this: First, read the opening four chapters, then turn to the last four chapters. Then read the four chapters just before the final four — and so on back to the beginning. Then, later on, pick up the book again and go through it start to finish. There is, by the way, no time requirement involved in this reading method. You can pick the book up when it's convenient. But, after finishing your "backward" study, wait awhile before reading straight through. You may gain more from the reading by giving yourself time to digest what you've learned.

I must emphasize that reading for technique necessarily involves the reading of a whole work, not just a part. You remember, in school, being assigned to read brief excerpts, "selected passages," from an author's story. These cuttings can be interesting, but they differ in effect from the whole story. To understand techniques, you must try to see the underlying pattern of a story, and this can only be done by reading the whole.

When you read this way, you always know *what follows.* So, for example, when you read the part that comes just before the ending, you know what is coming. You can see exactly how the author prepares his reader for the ending before it actually arrives. When you have worked your way back to study the beginning once more, you know all that comes after, what the characters did, and so you can notice precisely *why* the author chose his devices to use at the start.

You have, in short, a position from which you can observe the author at work, seeing why he did what he did. To quote Professor Campbell: "Before you realize it, you are attending to the technique of writing, instead of following the story like a donkey after a bundle of hay."

When at last you return to the beginning and read the story straight through, you will observe any number of things about the author's technique you would *not* have noticed in an ordinary first reading. For by this time you will be aware of the writer's scheming; you will see not only what design he used to attract you and hold you spellbound, but also how he used his devices and to what purposes.

Dissecting the Devices

When you study a story for technique, look primarily for devices for fueling *interest*, and devices for maintaining *plausibility*. The two go hand in hand. If a story doesn't interest readers, what difference does believability make? And if readers can't believe in the characters, how long can the story hold their interest? Therefore, when you study a story, look for the methods by which interest in aroused and deepened, but also for whatever enables readers to believe in the characters and occurrences.

Interest may initially be aroused by our identification with human nature or through curiosity; but to maintain interest, to keep readers involved, there must be a *complication* of some sort. A complication plunges your chief character into worse trouble. At the same time, by making things as bad as possible for him, new opportunities for solution arise. This is the real "secret" of plotting. When you can't bring your story to a conclusion, it is because you haven't made things *bad enough* for your character. Reading for technique shows you this much more vividly than can any explanation.

The chief devices for *plausibility* are *planting* and *pointing*. *Planting* is informing the reader *in advance* of any facts, objects, conditions or circumstances that will figure later, at the climax. Revealing at a high point of the story that a condition exists, that a tool or weapon is available for the hero's use, or whatever, is simply too late. For example, if the hero is going to solve his problem by blowing up the villain's works with dynamite, readers must know early in the tale that dynamite is available, and you must at least hint that the hero can get his hands on it.

Such hints, shadowings or forewarnings of something to come, are called *pointers.* In the beginning of your story there should be at least a faint pointer indicating the ultimate means of solution or the outcome of the problem. Of course such hints mustn't give the whole show away too soon, but they more or less subtly "point" to what is actually coming. When you read for technique, pointers lift right off the page, making themselves very apparent — something that *doesn't* happen on an ordinary run-through reading.

Tea Time

Let's watch how this reading technique works by applying it to a search for pointers in one of my own stories, "A Cup of Herbal Tea," which I sold to *Alfred Hitchcock's Mystery Magazine.* Reading the story's opening, you learn that my viewpoint character, Jenkins, is a shady lawyer who has bilked Bowen, an old chemist, out of his soft-drink company — whereupon Bowen has apparently killed himself.

Now, skipping to the end, you find Jenkins having tea with Bowen's widow. Jenkins thinks he's dying and confesses to Bowen's murder — and the police, concealed behind a door, hear the confession. The story's cap is that the self-taught chemist was illiterate, so couldn't have written the suicide note Jenkins left with the corpse.

Next, when reading the section just before the end, you learn that Jenkins is having tea with Bowen's widow. The widow talks so pointedly about the moles in her garden, and the arsenic her gardener has been using, that Jenkins becomes convinced she has poisoned him. That's why Jenkins later confesses. Reading on, section by section, toward the beginning of the story, you find this pointer early in the tale:

> Jenkins remembered with pleasure the moment when, with tears brimming his rheumy eyes, Bowen had at last reached for a pen and scrawled his signature on the closing agreement, his fingers pushing the pen falteringly, as if it were a great effort to sign away the business into which he had poured his life and hopes. That childlike scrawl fulfilled the dream of months for the scheming attorney.

Scrawled, falteringly, great effort, childlike — these are little hints of the revelation-to-come, that the only thing Bowen *can* write is his signature, that his wife has covered for him all these years. But readers don't (I assume) think, "Aha, Bowen can't read or write!" Rather, they take the description as indicating Bowen's grief. Reading for technique, on the other hand, makes this marvelously clear, as you study a well-constructed story. Knowing the outcome, you can see just how readers are led to it, step by convincing step.

More Pieces of the Puzzle

Reading for technique also reveals other devices — as well as solutions to your writing problems. You may, for example, have difficulty bringing on a character new to the reader. How shall he or she be made to arrive? Closely studying published fiction will demonstrate a variety of ways, most commonly a character doing or speaking something on his very first appearance — demonstrating a characteristic trait through action or speech. But, also, first appearances are often forewarned; that is, a character is mentioned or somehow referred to before he or she appears in the flesh, thus turning the reader's attention to that character even before he shows up. For instance, a heroine sees a man's name on a mailbox before she meets him.

Other devices, strategies, techniques and solutions include:

General Questions

1. For what sort of reader is this story intended? Estimate the probable age group, type of employment, income range, education. If the story is in a magazine, survey the publication's advertisements. With a book, the tone, style, vocabulary, subject matter, the jacket blurb, all suggest a "typical" reader.

2. What is the story's principal subject matter? It's about love, sex, crime, espionage, religion — something. Answer concisely.

3. In whose point of view is the story presented? a) Author's own; b) first-person narrator; c) third-person protagonist; d) multiple viewpoint (switches from one character to another); e) other.

4. Apart from subject matter as such, what *treatment* — theme, idea, impression — does the story convey? In other words, what attitude does the author take to his subject? Approving? Scornful? Sentimental? Cynical? Humorous?

5. What emotions, or emotional values, are in conflict? This may seem hard to say at first. Read the whole story before answering. (Examples: love and pride, ambition-honor, greed-jealousy.)

6. Who are the principal characters? List them by name and at least one identifying "tag." A tag is something that helps the reader see and identify a character. For example:

"Hey, man. . ." (Speech tag.)
She was *short, blonde,* with a *dimpled* chin. (Appearance.)
He *waddled* to the door. (Action, movement.)
Tim *hated* all rich people. (Social attitude.)

7. How is dialogue handled? How long is the longest sentence in quotes? The longest unbroken passage of speech? Does speech sound natural? How does it differ from real-life talk? How does the author let you know who's speaking? Is *he said, she said* used? Note little gestures accompanying speech. Are wild lines (lines with

speaker unnamed) used; how long do they run before the speaker is again identified?

8. What is the plot? Summarize it, including the outcome, as *briefly* as possible.

9. How are narrative, descriptive matter, dialogue, action and exposition balanced? (It is not always easy to determine if a passage is, say, description or exposition; make your best guess.)

10. At the end of the story, has the protagonist been advanced (rewarded) or retarded (punished)? Is this apparently the result of his own efforts and decisions or of Fate? Do readers feel the outcome is appropriate? Satisfying? Does the character deserve what happens to him or her?

Devices of the Beginning

1. After you've read the story and have returned to the Beginning, ask yourself why the author chose to begin this way? You should be able to tell why the author began with: information (exposition), narrative action (with or without dialogue), description (of place, person, condition, atmosphere), dialogue, narrative recollection, other (specify).

2. What question is implied in the first few lines or paragraphs to catch readers' interest and curiosity, making them *want* to read on? (Be precise.)

3. Now that you know the Outcome, can you find a hint or indication of what eventually is going to occur, particularly in regard to some crucial Decision the protagonist will make later on? Is there more than one such *pointer*? How expressed? How does perception of these pointers differ between that of a first-time reader and that of one who already knows the Outcome?

4. If there is a Complication, how early is it first introduced? (A Complication stems from the initial problem, but is not just the same thing.) How does Complication worsen the hero's problem?

5. Is there a major flashback? A series of small flashbacks? Is the story kept consistently in the fictional "present," rather than flashing either back or forward in time? (As a rule of thumb, a flashback is useful only if it adds fuel and power to the struggle of the present.)

6. How rapidly are all principal characters introduced, at least by name? (Everybody important in the cast should either be onstage or mentioned in the first quarter of a story.)

7. What was the chief problem of *plausibility* the author had to overcome? (Don't say none; there's always at least one.) List three ways the writer overcame this problem.

Devices of the Middle

1. Does the Middle merely repeat the fact that a Problem exits for the protagonist, or does the story advance? Is the protagonist

compelled to act, *do* something, as a result of his now-complicated situation?

2. Knowing the whole story, can you describe exactly how Problem and Complication lead to Crisis (Decision Point)?

Devices of the Ending

1. What vital choice (Decision) must the protagonist make at the high point or Crisis? Is this decision expressed in action? Does he make the "right," solving, choice, or take the wrong road? Is he immediately rewarded, or is there a Black Moment of uncertainty?

2. Is the protagonist's reward tangible or intangible?

3. If the story ends unhappily for the protagonist, does he deserve what happens? Are readers satisfied? Why?

4. What important tool, weapon, acquired knowledge or information is involved in the climax? Where and how is it first planted in the story?

The Puzzle Solved

This is not at all a restricting method of reading, nor are the "rules" binding. You can develop your own system. The main purpose is to get a different perspective on the work, to become more aware of patterns and effects, to tilt the picture a little . . . to solve a portion of the fiction-writing puzzle.

HOW WRITERS WRITE

– Malcolm Cowley

An American critic and poet of international reputation, Cowley was one of the colony of American writers and artists such as Hemingway and Fitzgerald who lived in France during the 1920s. His books include two volumes of verse, *Blue Juanita* and *The Dry Season,* a study of William Faulkner in *The Viking Portable Faulkner,* and *The Literary Situation,* which analyzes the place of the writer in American society.

■ What are the four stages in the composition of a story?
■ What observations about their craft have been made by such famous writers as Henry James, Frank O'Connor, Dorothy Parker, Katherine Anne Porter, James Thurber, Guy de Maupassant and Truman Capote?

You might like to read further; consult the interviews of individual artists in Cowley's text, *Writers at Work.*

There would seem to be four stages in the composition of a story. First comes the germ of the story, then a period of more or less conscious meditation, then the first draft, and finally the revision, which may be simply "pencil work," as John O'Hara calls it — that is, minor changes in wording — or may lead to writing several drafts and what amounts to a new work.

The germ of a story is something seen or heard, or heard about, or suddenly remembered; it may be a remark casually dropped at the dinner table (as in the case of Henry James's story, *The Spoils of Poynton*), or again it may be the look on a stranger's face. Almost always it is a new and simple element introduced into an existing situation or mood; something that expresses the mood in one sharp detail; something that serves as a focal point for a hitherto disorganized mass of remembered material in the author's mind. James describes it as "the precious particle . . . the stray suggestion, the wandering word, the vague echo, at a touch of which the novelist's imagination winces as at the prick of some sharp point," and he adds that "its virtue is all in its needle-like quality, the power to penetrate as finely as possible."

In the case of one story by the late Joyce Cary, the "precious particle" was the wrinkles on a young woman's forehead. He had seen her on the little boat that goes around Manhattan Island, "a girl of about thirty," he says, "wearing a shabby skirt. She was enjoying herself. A nice expression, with a wrinkled forehead, a good many wrinkles. I said to my friend, 'I could write about that girl . . .' " but then he forgot her. Three weeks later, in San Francisco, Cary woke up at four in the morning with a story in his head — a purely English story with an English heroine. When he came to revise the story he kept wondering, "Why all these wrinkles? That's the third time they come in. And I suddenly realized," he says, "that my English heroine was the girl on the Manhattan boat. Somehow she had gone down into my subconscious, and came up again with a full-sized story."

The woman with the wrinkled forehead could hardly have served as the germ of anything by Frank O'Connor, for his imagination is auditive, not visual. "If you're the sort of person," he says, "that meets a girl in the street and instantly notices the color of her eyes and of her hair and the sort of dress she's wearing, then you're not in the least like me. . . . I have terribly sensitive hearing and I'm terribly aware of voices." Often his stories develop from a remark he has overheard. That may also be the case with Dorothy Parker, who says, "I haven't got a visual mind. I hear things." Faulkner does have a visual mind, and he says that *The Sound and the Fury* "began with a mental picture. I didn't realize at the time it was symbolical. The picture was of the muddy seat of a little girl's drawers in a pear tree, where she could see through a window where her grandmother's funeral was taking place and report what was happening to her brothers on the ground below. By the time I explained who they were and what they were doing and how her pants got muddy, I realized it would be impossible to get all of it into a short story and it would have to be a book.'' At other times the precious particle is something the author has read — preferably a book of memoirs or history or travel, one that lies outside his own field of writing. Robert Penn Warren says, "I always remember the date, the place, the room, the road, when I first was struck. For instance, *World Enough and Time.* Katherine Anne Porter and I were both in the Library of Congress as fellows. We were in the same pew, had offices next to each other. She came in one day with an old pamphlet, the trial of Beauchamp for killing Colonel Sharp. She said, 'Well, Red, you better read this.' There it was. I read it in five minutes. But I was six years making the book. Any book I write starts with a flash, but takes a long time to shape up.''

The book or story shapes up — assumes its own specific form, that is — during a process of meditation that is the second stage in composition. Angus Wilson calls it "the gestatory period" and says that it is "very important to me. That's when I'm persuading myself of the truth of what I want to say, and I don't think I could persuade my readers unless I'd persuaded myself first." The period may last for years, as with Warren's novels (and most of Henry James's), or it may last exactly two days, as in the extraordinary case of Georges Simenon. "As soon as I have the beginning," Simenon explains, "I can't bear it very long. . . . And two days later I begin writing." The meditation may be, or seem to be, wholly conscious. The writer asks himself questions — "What should the characters do at this point? How can I build to a climax?" — and answers them in various fashions before choosing the final answers. Or most of the process, including all the early steps, may be carried on without the writer's volition. He wakes before daybreak with the whole story in his head, as Joyce Cary did in San Francisco, and hastily writes it down. Or again — and I think most frequently — the meditation is a mixture of conscious and unconscious elements, as if a cry from the depths of sleep were being heard and revised by the waking mind.

Often the meditation continues while the writer is engaged in other occupations: gardening, driving his wife to town (as Walter Mitty did), or going out to dinner. "I never quite know when I'm not writing," says James Thurber. "Sometimes my wife comes up to me at a dinner party and says, 'Dammit, Thurber, stop writing.' She usually catches me in the middle of a paragraph. Or my daughter will look up from the dinner table and ask, 'Is he sick?' 'No,' my wife says, 'he's writing.' I have to do it that way on account of my eyes.'' When Thurber had better vision he used to do his meditating at the typewriter, as many other writers do. Nelson Algren, for example, finds his plots simply by writing page after page, night after night. "I always figured," he says, "the only way I could finish a book and get a plot was just to keep making it longer and longer until something happens.''

The first draft of a story is often written at top speed; probably that is the best way to write it. Dorothy Canfield Fisher, who is not among the authors interviewed, once compared the writing of a first draft with skiing down a steep slope that she wasn't sure she was clever enough to manage. "Sitting at my desk one morning, she says, "I 'pushed off' and with a tingle of not altogether pleasurable excitement and alarm, felt myself 'going.' I 'went' almost as precipitately as skis go down a long white slope, scribbling as rapidly as my pencil could go, indicating whole words with a dash and a jiggle, filling page after page with scrawls." Frank O'Connor explains the need for haste in his own case. "Get black on white," he says, "used to be Maupassant's advice — that's what I always do. I don't give a hoot what the writing's like, I write any sort of rubbish which will cover the main outlines of the story, then I can begin to see it." There are other writers, however, who work ahead laboriously, revising as they go. William Styron says, "I seem to have some neurotic need to perfect each paragraph — each sentence, even — as I go along." Dorothy Parker reports that it takes her six months to do a story: "I think it out and then write it sentence by sentence — no first draft. I can't write five words but that I change seven."

O'Connor doesn't start changing words until the first draft is finished, but then he rewrites, so he says, "endlessly, endlessly, endlessly." There is no stage of composition at which these authors differ more from one another than in this final stage of preparing a manuscript for the printer. Even that isn't a final stage for O'Connor. "I keep on rewriting," he says, "and after it's published, and then after it's published in book form, I usually rewrite it again. I've rewritten versions of most of my early stories, and one of these days, God help, I'll publish these as well." Françoise Sagan, on the other hand, spends "very little" time in revision. Simenon spends exactly three days in revising each of his short novels. Most of that time is devoted to tracking down and crossing out the literary touches — "adjectives, adverbs, and every word which is there just to make an effect. Every sentence which is there just for the sentence. You know, you have a beautiful sentence — cut it." Joyce Cary was another deletionist. Many of the passages he crossed out of his first drafts were those dealing explicitly with ideas. "I work over the whole book," he says, "and cut out anything that does not belong to the emotional development, the texture of feeling." Thurber revises his stories by rewriting them from the beginning, time and again. "A story I've been working on," he says, ". . . was rewritten fifteen complete times. There must have been close to two hundred and forty thousand words in all the manuscripts put together, and I must have spent two thousand hours working at it. Yet the finished story can't be more than twenty thousand words." That would make it about the longest piece of fiction he has written. Men like

Thurber and O'Connor, who rewrite "endlessly, endlessly," find it hard to face the interminable prospect of writing a full-length novel.

For short-story writers the four stages of composition are usually distinct, and there may even be a fifth, or rather a first, stage. Before seizing upon the germ of a story, the writer may find himself in a state of "generally intensified emotional sensitivity . . . when events that usually pass unnoticed suddenly move you deeply, when a sunset lifts you to exaltation, when a squeaking door throws you into a fit of exasperation, when a clear look of trust in a child's eyes moves you to tears." I am quoting again from Dorothy Canfield Fisher, who "cannot conceive," she says, "of any creative fiction written from any other beginning." There is not much doubt, in any case, that the germ is precious largely because it serves to crystallize a prior state of feeling. Then comes the brooding or meditation, then the rapidly written first draft, then the slow revision; for the story writer everything is likely to happen in more or less its proper order. For the novelist, however, the stages are often confused. The meditation may have to be repeated for each new episode. The revision of one chapter may precede or follow the first draft of the next.

That is not the only difference between writing a short story and writing a novel. Reading the interviews together, I was confirmed in an old belief that the two forms are separate and that mere length is not their distinguishing feature. A long short story — say of forty thousand words — is not the same as a novel of forty thousand words, nor is it likely to be written by the same person. Among the authors interviewed, the division that goes deepest is not between older and younger writers, or men and women writers, or French and English writers; it is the division between those who think in terms of the short story and those who are essentially novelists.

Truman Capote might stand for those who think in terms of the short story, since he tells us that his "more unswerving ambitions still revolve around this form." A moment later he says, "I invariably have the illusion that the whole play of a story, its start and middle and finish, occur in my mind simultaneously — that I'm seeing it in one flash." He likes to know the end of a story before writing the first word of it. Indeed, he doesn't start writing until he has brooded over the story long enough to exhaust his emotional response to the material. "I seem to remember reading," he says, "that Dickens, as he wrote, choked with laughter over his own humor and dripped tears all over the page when one of his characters died. My own theory is that the writer should have considered his wit and dried his tears long, long before setting out to evoke similar reactions in a reader." The reactions of the reader, not of the writer, are Capote's principal concern.

For contrast take the interview with Simenon, who is a true novelist even if his separate works, written and revised in about two weeks, are not much longer than some short stories. Each of them starts in the same fashion. "It is almost a geometrical problem," he says. "I have such a man, such a woman, in such surroundings. What can happen to them to oblige them to go to their limit? That's the question. It will be sometimes a very simple incident, anything which will change their lives. Then I write my novel chapter by chapter." Before setting to work Simenon has scrawled a few notes on a big manila envelope. The interviewer asks whether these are an outline of the action. "No, no," Simenon answers. ". . . On the envelope I put only the names of the characters, their ages, their families. I know nothing whatever about the events which will occur later. Otherwise" — and I can't help putting the statement in italics — "*it would not be interesting to me.*"

Unlike Capote, who says that he is physically incapable of writing anything he doesn't think will be paid for (though I take it that payment is, for him, merely a necessary token of public admiration), Simenon would "certainly," he says, continue writing novels if they were never published. But he wouldn't bother to write them if he knew what the end of each novel would be, for then *it would not be interesting.* He discovers his fable not in one flash, but chapter by chapter, as if he were telling a continued story to himself. "On the eve of the first day," he says, "I know what will happen in the first chapter. Then day after day, chapter after chapter, I find what comes later. After I have started a novel I write a chapter each day, without ever missing a day. Because it is a strain, I have to keep pace with the novel. If, for example, I am ill for forty-eight hours I have to throw away the previous chapters. And I never return to that novel." Like Dickens he lets himself be moved, even shattered, by what he is writing. "All the day," he says, "I am one of my characters" — always the one who is driven to his limit. "I feel what he feels. . . . And it's almost unbearable after five or six days. That is one of the reasons why my novels are so short; after eleven days I can't — it's impossible. I have to — It's physical. I am too tired."

Nobody else writes in quite the same fashion as Simenon. He carries a certain attitude toward fiction to the furthest point that it can be carried by anyone who writes books to be published and read. But the attitude in itself is not unusual, and in fact it is shared to some extent by all the true novelists who explain their methods in this book. Not one of them starts by making a scene-by-scene outline, as Henry James did before writing each of his later novels. James had discovered what he called the "divine principle of the Scenario" after writing several unsuccessful plays, and in essence the principle, or method, seems to be dramatistic rather than novelistic. The dramatist, like the short-story writer, has to know where he is going and how he will get there, scene by scene, whereas all the novelists interviewed by *The Paris Review* are accustomed to making voyages of exploration with only the roughest of maps. Mauriac says, "There is a point of departure, and there are some characters. It often happens that the first characters don't go any further and, on the other hand, vaguer, more inconsistent characters show new possibilities as the story goes on and assume a place we hadn't foreseen." Françoise Sagan says that she has to start writing to have ideas. In the beginning she has "a character, or a few characters, and perhaps an idea for a few of the scenes up to the middle of the book, but it all changes in the writing. For me writing is a question of finding a certain rhythm." (One thinks of Simenon and his feeling that he has to keep pace with the novel.) "My work," says Moravia, ". . . is not prepared beforehand in any way. I might add, too, that when I'm not working I don't think of my work at all." Forster does lay plans for his work, but they are subject to change. "The novelist," he says, "should, I think, always settle when he starts what is going to happen, what his major event is to be. He may alter this event as he approaches it, indeed he probably will, indeed he probably had better, or the novel becomes tied up and tight. But the sense of a solid mass ahead, a mountain round or over which or through which the story must go, is most valuable and, for the novels I've tried to write, essential. . . . When I began *A Passage to India* I knew that something important happened in the Malabar Caves, and that it would have a central place in the novel — but I didn't know what it would be."

Most novelists, one might generalize on this evidence, are like the chiefs of exploring expeditions. They know who their companions are (and keep learning more about them); they know what sort of territory they will have to traverse on the following day or week; they know the general object of the expedition, the mountain they are trying to reach, the river of which they are trying to discover the source. But they don't know exactly what their route will be, or what adventures they will meet along the way, or how their companions will act when pushed to the limit. They don't even know whether the continent they are trying to map exists in space or only within themselves. "I think that if a man has the urge to be an artist," Simenon muses, "it is because he needs to find himself. Every writer tries to find himself through his characters, through all his writing." He is speaking for the novelist in particular. Short-story writers come back from their briefer explorations to brood over the meaning of their discoveries; then they perfect the stories for an audience. The short story is an *exposition*; the novel is often and perhaps at its best an *inquisition* into the unknown depths of the novelist's mind.

TIME AND THE NARRATIVE VOICE

— Margaret Laurence

One of Canada's most famous writers, Laurence has written short stories for children and adults, commentaries, reviews, and criticism. She is probably best known, however, for her novels such as *The Stone Angel, The Diviners,* and *Jest of God.*

■ What problems do writers encounter in conveying within a work a sense of time?

■ How does the writer's selection of narrative voice or point of view influence the manner in which a sense of time may be conveyed?

Laurence contends that "the past and future are both always present." You might find it useful to relate ideas in this essay to Hales's analysis of Laurence's fiction in "Spiritual Longing in Laurence's Manawaka Women" in Part A, page 48.

The treatment of time and the handling of the narrative voice — these two things are of paramount importance to me in the writing of fiction. Oddly enough, although they might seem to be two quite separate aspects of technique, in fact they are inextricably bound together. When I say "time," I don't mean clock-time, in this context, nor do I mean any kind of absolute time — which I don't believe to exist, in any event. I mean historical time, variable and fluctuating.

In any work of fiction, the span of time present in the story is not only as long as the time-span of every character's life and memory; it also represents everything acquired and passed on in a kind of memory-heritage from one generation to another. The time which is present in any story, therefore, must — by implication at least — include not only the totality of the characters' lives but also the inherited time of perhaps two or even three past generations, in terms of parents' and grandparents' recollections, and the much much longer past which has become legend, the past of a collective cultural memory. Obviously, not all of this can be conveyed in a single piece of prose. Some of it can only be hinted at; some of it may not be touched on at all. Nevertheless, it is *there* because it exists in the minds of the characters. How can one even begin to convey this sense of time? What parts of the time-span should be conveyed? These are questions which I always find enormously troubling, and before beginning any piece of writing, I tend to brood for quite a long time (clockwise) on these things. Not that the brooding does very much good, usually, or perhaps it bears fruit at some unrecognized subconscious level, because when the writing begins, a process of selection takes place in a way not consciously chosen, and this is where the long-time-span implicit in every story or novel is directly and intimately related to the narrative voice.

Most of the fiction I have written in recent years has been written in the first person, with the main character assuming the narrative voice. Even when I have written in the third person, as I did in part of my novel *The Fire-Dwellers,* it is really a first-person narrative which happens to be written in the third person, for the narrative voice even here is essentially that of the main character, and the writer does not enter in as commentator. Some people hold the erroneous belief that this kind of fiction is an evasion — the writer is hiding behind a mask, namely one of the characters. Untrue. The writer is every bit as vulnerable here as in directly autobiographical fiction. The character is not a mask but an individual, separate from the writer. At the same time, the character is one of the writer's voices and selves, and fiction writers tend to have a mental trunk full of these — in writers, this quality is known as richness of imagination; in certain inmates of mental hospitals it has other names, the only significant difference being that writers are creating their private worlds with the ultimate hope of throwing open the doors to other humans. This means of writing fiction, oriented almost totally towards an individual character, is obviously not the only way, but it appears to be the only way I can write.

Once the narrative voice is truly established — that is, once the writer has listened, really listened, to the speech and idiom and outlook of the character — it is then not the writer but the character who, by some process of transferal, bears the responsibility for the treatment of time within the work. It is the character who chooses which parts of the personal past, the family past and the ancestral past have to be revealed in order for the present to be realized and the future to happen. This is not a morbid dwelling on the past on the part of the writer or the character. It is, rather, an expression of the feeling which I strongly hold about time — that the past and the future are both always present, *present* in both senses of the word, always now and always here with us. It is only through the individual presence of the characters that the writer can hope to convey even a fragment of this sense of time, and this is one reason, among others, why it is so desperately important to discover the true narrative voice — which really means knowing the characters so well that one can take on their past, their thoughts, their responses, can in effect for awhile *become* them. It has sometimes occurred to me that I must be a kind of Method writer, in the same way that some actors become the characters they play for the moments when they are portraying these characters. I didn't plan it this way, and possibly it sounds like gibberish, but this is how it appears to take place.

Theorizing, by itself, is meaningless in connection with fiction, just as any concept of form is meaningless in isolation from the flesh and blood of content and personality, just as a skeleton is only dry bone by itself but when it exists inside a living being it provides the support for the whole creature. I'll try to show something of what I mean about time and voice by reference to the two stories of mine which appear in this book.

These stories are part of a collection called *A Bird in the House*, eight in all, published separately before they were collected in a single volume, but conceived from the beginning as a related group. Each story is self-contained in the sense that it is definitely a short story and not a chapter from a novel, but the net effect is not unlike that of a novel. Structurally, however, these stories as a group are totally unlike a novel. I think the outlines of a novel (mine, anyway) and those of a group of stories such as these interrelated ones may be approximately represented in visual terms. In a novel, one might perhaps imagine the various themes and experiences and the inter-action of characters with one another and with themselves as a series of wavy lines, converging, separating, touching, drawing apart, but moving in a *horizontal* direction. The short stories have flow-lines which are different. They move very close together but parallel and in a *vertical* direction. Each story takes the girl Vanessa along some specific course of her life and each follows that particular thread closely, but the threads are presented separately and not simultaneously. To this extent, the structure of these stories is a good deal simpler than that of a novel. Nevertheless, the relationship of time and the narrative voice can be seen just as plainly in the stories as in a novel.

''To Set Our House in Order'' takes place when Vanessa is ten years old. Her age remains constant throughout the story. The actual time-span of the story itself is short, a few days in her life, immediately before, during and after the birth of her brother. The things which happen on the surface are simple, but the things that happen inside Vanessa's head are more complex.

The narrative voice is, of course, that of Vanessa herself, but an older Vanessa, herself grown up, remembering how it was when she was ten. When I was trying to write this story, I felt as I did with all the stories in *A Bird in the House*, that this particular narrative device was a tricky one, and I cannot even now personally judge how well it succeeds. What I tried to do was definitely *not* to tell the story as though it were being narrated by a child. This would have been impossible for me and also would have meant denying the story one of its dimensions, a time-dimension, the viewing from a distance of events which had happened in childhood. The narrative voice had to be that of an older Vanessa, but at the same time the narration had to be done in such a way that the ten-year-old would be conveyed. The narrative voice, therefore, had to speak as though from two points in time, simultaneously.

Given this double sense of time-present, Vanessa herself had to recollect those things which were most meaningful to her, and in doing so, she reveals (at least I hope she does to the reader as she does to me) what the story is really about. It is actually a story about the generations, about the pain and bewilderment of one's knowledge of other people, about the reality of other people which is one way of realizing one's own reality, about the fluctuating and accidental quality of life (God really doesn't love Order), and perhaps more than anything, about the strangeness and mystery of the very concepts of *past, present* and *future*. Who is Vanessa's father? The doctor who is struggling to support his family during the depression and who seems a pillar of strength to the little girl? Or the man who has collected dozens of travel books because once he passionately wanted to go far beyond Manawaka and now knows he won't? Or the boy who long ago half-blinded his brother accidentally with an air-rifle? Or the nineteen-year-old soldier who watched his brother die in the First World War? Ewen is all of these, and many many more, and in the story Vanessa has the sudden painful knowledge of his reality and his intricacy as a person, bearing with him the mental baggage of a lifetime, as all people do, and as she will have to do. The events of the story will become (and have become, to the older Vanessa) part of her mental baggage, part of her own spiritual fabric. Similarly, her father passes on to her some actual sense of her grandparents, his parents — the adamant Grandmother MacLeod, whose need it has been to appear a lady in her own image of herself; the dead Grandfather MacLeod, who momentarily lives for his granddaughter when she sees for the first time the loneliness of a man who could read the Greek tragedies in their original language and who never knew anyone in the small prairie town with whom he could communicate.

In "The Loons," the narrative voice is also that of the older Vanessa, but in her portrayal of herself in past years, she ranges in age from eleven to eighteen. This meant, of course, that the tone of the narration had to change as Vanessa recalled herself at different ages, and this meant, for me, trying to feel my way into her mind at each age. Here again, the narrative voice chooses what will be recalled, and here again, the element of time is of great importance in the story. The eleven-year-old Vanessa sees the Métis girl, Piquette Tonnerre, in terms of romanticized notions of Indians, and is hurt when Piquette does not respond in the expected way. That summer lies submerged in Vanessa's mind until she encounters Piquette at a later time, but even then her reaction is one mainly of embarrassment and pity, not any real touching, and Piquette's long experience of hurt precludes anything except self-protectiveness on her part. It is only when Vanessa hears of Piquette's death that she realizes that she, too, like the entire town, is in part responsible. But the harm and alienation started a long way back, longer even than the semi-mythical figure of Piquette's grandfather, Jules Tonnerre, who fought with Riel at Batoche. The loons, recurring in the story both in their presence and in their absence, are connected to an ancestral past which belongs to Piquette, and the older Vanessa can see the irony of the only way in which Piquette's people are recognized by the community, in the changing of the name Diamond Lake to the more tourist-appealing Lake Wapakata.

What I said earlier may perhaps be more clearly seen now to show a little of the relationship between the narrative voice and the treatment of time — it is the character who chooses which parts of the personal past, the family past and the ancestral past have to be revealed in order for the present to be realized and the future to happen.

MASTERING THE SHORT STORY

— Paul Darcy Boles

Boles's short stories have appeared in the old *Saturday Evening Post* as well as contemporary publications. This essay is an excerpt from *Storycrafting,* which appeared shortly before his death in 1984.

- What elements make a short story especially readable?
- If you want to sell your short stories, what qualities may increase their appeal in today's market?

Boles addresses these and other questions asked by budding writers. After you have read his suggestions, you might apply them to your next short story project.

The short story has as many definitions as the blind men had for their fabulous elephant.

Its bright and buoyant virtue is that it's traditionally short.

Somerset Maugham said that it must have a beginning, a middle, and an end.

But some beautiful stories are as long as young novels.

And some excellent stories have no more beginning, middle, and end than a plate of lasagna.

Its forward motion may be like the catapult, sudden and fierce and moving from *here* to *there* in a parabola of impact that hits the reader straight between the eyes.

Or it may be artfully slow, rising around the reader in a tide of sensation and revelation.

The best all-around description of the short story was given by Stephen Vincent Benét: "Something that can be read in an hour and remembered for a lifetime."

Writing the marketable story can't be taught.

It can be guided.

If you have talent, your talent can be sharpened toward the making of stories which will have a fighting chance with a magazine editor. Your special fund of emotion and skill can be channeled into the story that gets the editor's attention and starts you on a published career. There is no mystery about this. There are no tricks to it.

There is a lot of work, coupled with the joy of mastering an art almost as old as time — one which many believe to be the most rewarding of any.

Your story will stand a far better chance in today's market if it can be told in 3,000 words or less. This is ten pages, double-spaced. If this restriction bothers your sense of story-values, cheer yourself by reflecting that the Gettysburg Address is very brief, and that the Song of Solomon takes up only modest space in the Bible.

The days of voluminous magazine-room for short fiction are over. Thinking in story-space will encourage you to trim your story as you plan it — to leave out the fat, eliminate side trips, and hold back your self-indulgence for other pursuits.

It will cut down on characters, help you aim in the manner of a rifle rather than a scattergun, and bring in focus what was fuzzy.

It will eliminate all the dreary padding by means of which so many former long-winded tale-tellers gave the effect of importance by loading their work with detail.

Your detail will improve simply by being vital to the story and not dragged in by the heels.

If you throw up your hands in alarm and say that these artificial boundaries stifle you, that you need room to let the story breathe, and that Reader's Digest condensation is a curse meant to squeeze decent prose into palatable capsules, perhaps you were a novelist all the time and shouldn't come near the story except to sneer.

But if you rise to the challenge of capturing on paper a story strong enough to compete with television, movies and radio for the attention of the much-assaulted general reader, you will teach yourself economy.

By doing so, you will improve your writing in all other forms.

Thinking Story

The novel has an up-and-down motion. It goes in a series of wave crests and troughs. It moves with undulance. Even in the pared-down, almost bald novels of the late James M. Cain, which are restricted to action and dialogue whittled to their simplest elements, the movement is Alpine, roller-coaster, rising, falling and rising.

The story is a straight line. The marketable story is nearly always held in tight reins of time. The time elapsed in most stories is at most a season, usually a few days or hours. Chekhov's marvelous observation, "The art of writing is the art of abbreviation," applies to the commercial story of today more than it ever did.

Abbreviation is not private code. It is the clarification of the complex. In the story, large ideas are briskly implied. What is between the lines looms as large as what appears on the page. But there can be no cryptic semaphoring, no messages held so close to the chest they're unreadable. The modern story is like the modern poem in that it relies on the reader's informed imagination much more than did the stories of Sir Walter Scott or Thomas Hardy or Robert Louis Stevenson. Today's reader simply doesn't need excessive explanation — he can see clearly when he is given a few clear-cut hints. But the modern story is not dense and it doesn't require footnotes or translators. Its words may be simple in the extreme, as in the stories of Hemingway. (His story vocabulary has been estimated at about 800 words — that of an average high school sophomore.) A story's words may glitter with light and allusion, as in tales by John Cheever and J.D. Salinger. They may be serviceable earthenware with flashes of gold, as are Scott Fitzgerald's. They may be as full of fireworks as Faulkner's. But their common ground is that they are intensely readable.

The more you train yourself to think in terms of the story, the more readable your stories will be.

You can save yourself extra hours of editing grief by building a few dams in your mind at the start. This doesn't mean that you'll "write short" for the sake of shortness alone, or leave out anything vital that you'll have to insert later with a shoehorn.

It means you'll write in a controlled state of mind, conscious with part of yourself that the market won't stand for self-indulgent excess, and caring enough about your story to make it occupy a tidy space at full strength.

Kipling said he never "wrote short" — that he'd tried it, and found the story weakened by too much vigilance. His way with a story — and it was quite a way — was to drift until it was ready, then to let it come out, then to set it aside — sometimes for months, in a few cases for years — and, at intervals, have at it with black India ink and a brush, until he'd cut out everything extraneous and the story spun like a top in righteous balance.

Saying enough is as necessary as not saying too much.

Skimping during the composition of a story is slow death. Stopping after every sentence for arduous stock-taking, asking yourself

"Did I need that?" instead of "What comes next?" is a strong indication that you haven't spent enough time testing the story before you began it, that you're not yet involved enough to know, emotionally, where you're going, and that you're making a formidable mountain out of the process of creation when you should be skipping along the hills.

Knowing emotionally where you're going is different from knowing mentally where you're going.

Fitzgerald — who should be quoted, daily, by every working story writer as a matter of habit — said that *all good writing is swimming under water and holding your breath.*

Pronouncing Sentence

A story is *not* putting one sentence after another.

It's a series of aimed sentences.

The opening of James Joyce's "Two Gallants" is a series of nearly protoplasmic impressions, floating like light above tepid water, breaking most of the "rules" and leaving the reader puzzled as though he had been dipped in a murky bath, yet intrigued and even entranced.

> The grey warm evening of August had descended upon the city and a mild warm air, a memory of summer, circulated in the streets. The streets, shuttered for the repose of Sunday, swarmed with a gaily coloured crowd. Like illumined pearls the lamps shone from the summits of their tall poles upon the living texture below which, changing shape and hue unceasingly, sent up into the warm grey evening air an unchanging, unceasing murmur.

Reading that, even casually, you'll be struck by an apparent laziness, a repetition of such words as *grey, warm,* an inner chiming and murmuration that sounds a bit like an elderly lady talking in her sleep. It is one long metaphor of sleepwalking, and it sets the scene as nothing else could.

There is no repetition, no incantation, only a direct series of extremely vivid pictures, all in flowing motion, in the opening paragraph of E.M. Forster's "The Story of the Siren":

> Few things have been more beautiful than my notebook on the Deist Controversy as it fell downward through the waters of the Mediterranean. It dived, like a piece of black slate, but opened soon, disclosing leaves of pale green, which quivered into blue. Now it had vanished, now it was a piece of magical India rubber stretching out to infinity, now it was a book again, but bigger than the book of all knowledge. It grew more fantastic as it reached the bottom, where a puff of sand welcomed it and obscured it from view. But it reappeared, quite sane though a little tremulous, lying decently open on its back, while unseen fingers fidgeted among its leaves.

The sentences in both of those stories are aimed at what the story wants. For all its seeming amorphousness, the Joyce story exerts a powerful mood like a rising fog in which specific people will presently be encountered. The Forster story has a sliding, plunging underwater motion which follows that lost notebook like the eye of a whimsical god and gives it specific personality — "quite sane though a little tremulous" — as it rests in sight but drowning.

Your sentences are servants of your story mood, each pulling its proper weight as it enters and makes way for the next, and each related to the other by more than the mere fact that the same person is writing them. Get and read Flannery O'Connor's "A Good Man Is Hard to Find" and notice that in its commentary on good and evil — and the fatuous helplessness of mankind when faced by pure evil — it's as succinctly told as though a lucid stream of icy air had been turned on and then off. Look up Eudora Welty's "Powerhouse" and see how the sentences jump into the skin of a black musician — Fats Waller — seeing him from the inside as a bolt of lightning might be felt. Take any Damon Runyon story and hear in it the stylized voice of a professional Broadway "character" speaking nasally and from a guarded mouth-corner.

Good sentences pace in step with their story.

If you're writing a light story about a mother's struggle with her eight-year-old daughter who wants to enter a dubious neighbourhood theater beauty contest, and is asking for the ten-dollar entry fee, your sentences won't be heavy and overdramatic. They'll be humorous, straightforward, concerned. A story about a husband and wife on the verge of breaking up because he's a slipshod driver will have its contemporary pulse in every sentence, using brief description and dialogue to bring out what they're really fighting about — which may not be his driving at all. If your story is told by a young woman and concerns a radio announcer in love with his own chest tones, its sentences will be crisp, sardonic, pungent.

In ten years of reading stories by beginners, I have come across too many in which the sentence is regarded as a slack noose, aimlessly thrown in the hope of surrounding a story.

If you stiffen up and go cold in your center when you think about aiming a sentence, look on it as malleable, fluid, subject to your will. The poor thing needs your direction. It wants to say as much as it can for the story you have in mind. It's waiting to be modeled into kindness, curtness, flexible grace, gleaming steel. It asks to be fitted into your story — to be part of the ambience. Give it a nudge here and there until it's part of the crowd, feels at home. If it opens your story on too high a note, tone it down. If it's flabby, make it work until its muscles show. If it's just a wrong sentence and belongs in some other story you may write later, set it aside with a good word.

All good sentences are organic, belonging in their stories as cherries grown in the same orchard have the same family taste.

In most stories, you'll want to keep the sentences short. The attention span of the reader of marketable short stories varies from the flick of an eyelash to the dart of a lizard. Most readers aren't familiar with the long, looping and wonderfully prolix sentences of Proust, and Faulkner even at his most intense and grand makes them itchy. They're conditioned to television, in which images flitting by keep the eye in a steady state of daze and semi-stupor. By asking them to read a story, you're taxing them with the job of cooperating with you. Brief sentences insult nobody's intelligence. Nor do they have to be in baby talk to be immediately comprehended. Maupassant's stories, even in so-so translations, clip along with the eagerness of horses heading for a stable. He was the short story writer most in demand in his time. He's not in favour with critics today, but critics don't read popular magazines.

The Fat and the Lean

The story itself, like the sentences that comprise it, must also be aimed. Keep it lean and uncluttered.

First stories can, like Christmas geese, be packed with too much stuffing. There is sometimes a pressing need to get everything in, to make a story overflow its space by holding more than it comfortably can. The old and pleasantly ribald anecdote about the *Reader's Digest* editor who wanted a tale which would be All Things to All Men, and came up with the man who assaulted a bear in an iron lung for the FBI and found God, is a good case in point. So is the apocryphal story sometimes called "Lincoln's Doctor's Wife's Dog," which was wonderfully calculated to please everybody, but which would be too much for mortal readers to accept.

So look around your story for too much obvious meaning. Meaning in a story is not injected with a hypodermic needle, but issues from it after it has been written. It's highly doubtful that Aesop ever said to himself. "Now I shall produce a profound fable upon the subject of Envy, and I think I'll call this one 'The Fox and the Grapes.'" Meaning lurks inside a story, between the lines; it is not always completely clear to the writer while the story is being written, or for that matter afterward. He or she leaves meaning to perceptive readers to interpret for themselves.

Similarly, stroll around your story plot. Study it with narrow eyes and critical objectivity. If it has a rococo touch — if there appears, already, to be too much detail in it, too many possible side shows — clear them away. If it still seems amorphous, merely a fuzzy far-in-the distance suggestion of two or three characters thrown together, start focusing on just one of the people, and ask what is making this person tick.

When you think you know, begin plumbing the depths of your

other protagonists. You may well find that you have imagined a straw doll for your more real people to react to.

The first draft of my short story "Sweet Chariot" was not lean and uncluttered; it was 24 pages long. It was all there, complete, making its point without shouting at the reader; but it was also too leisurely in rhythm, and self-indulgent when it came to halting the forward motion and giving the reader a guided tour of scenic wonders and outside appearances of people. At one juncture, its main character was described as if he weren't inhabiting a *short* story at all, but happened to be in a roomy Sir Walter Scott sort of novel:

> Journey was a looming, rangy man with the high cheek-bones of middle Appalachia, descended from hunters, ballad-singers, keepers of their own secret counsels. His eyes, the color of very good, sun-faded denim, sometimes held hints of wildness — of wanting to rush away, like a deer startled from dreaming.

That is passable character-drawing; but it stands by itself without any kinship to the quick, demanding music of character-in-action called for in a short story. It's a trifle show-offy, like a set piece meant for recitation rather than reading in silence. In the process of cutting the first draft from 24 pages to 10, it was thrown out without a qualm. All that remained in the final draft was:

> His eyes held hints of wildness and rushing away.

That line does the job, summarizing everything in the original windy passage and allowing the story to move on without hanging fire.

Let's assume, for a moment, that part of your story is about the reaction of a woman to a snake. (Excellent stories along this line have been done — in the King James version of the Old Testament, for instance; and in more recent times by John Steinbeck.) Your task, to be performed in a minimum of words and space, is to make your reader know the essence of snakedom, the elixir of the woman. You may have read half a hundred volumes about herpetology; you may have spent an instructive summer working in the snake-house at your local zoo. But in your story what you're after is the valid center of the experience — the point, for instance, that dormant snakes smell like new-cut cucumbers; that they inspire atavistic fear, even though they're amazingly sentient, easy to handle and over-maligned. And without doing an essay on it, you will need to quickly interpret the woman's reaction to the encounter; to tell how she takes it, what she does, which will give immediate insight into the middle of her character. This is a section from a short story of mine, which was later, with slight changes, incorporated into a novel, *Glory Day*. Among other things, I wanted to show the impeccable calm of the woman, Phyllis, in a moment of natural crisis. The writing comes in on a slant, by indirection, embedded in the action so that inside and outside factors are working in harness. The reader sees what is going on, and feels it at the same time:

> She took hold of another weed; this one deep, calling for a side twist to bring the root webs out. When she had tossed it back and was reaching for another, she saw the intruder. It was uncoiled, a flake of sun touching the triangular, turned-away head. The serrate, arid scales looked as though, if touched, they would whisper like autumn leaves. The body of the copperhead was a thick single muscle, relaxing. She sat back, hand hanging in air, then withdrew it gradually, from shade to sun.

Woman and snake are somehow together; the confrontation in mysterious and double. Here, the word *description* is misleading as a cover-word for what is actually happening. The eye sees, the ear listens, the skin feels; the hand of the woman becomes the hand of the reader as it is drawn back from the shadow into the sunlight. The inwardness of snake and woman are respected and let alone to be themselves. There are just sufficient words to allow the reader to participate wholly in the experience.

And here, for full contrast, is a sample from Elizabeth Bowen's short story, "Maria." The story is one of the funniest ever written, and the intricately horrible character of young Maria comes through without one extraneous label offered by the author:

> "I can't tell you what I think of this place you're sending me to," said Maria. "I bounced on the bed in the attic they're giving me and it's like iron. I suppose you realize that rectories are always full of diseases? Of course, I shall make the best of it, Aunt Ena. I shouldn't like you to feel I'd complained. But of course you don't realize a bit, do you, what I may be exposed to? So often carelessness about a girl my age just ruins her life."
>
> Aunt Ena said nothing; she settled herself a little further down in the rugs and lowered her eyelids as though a strong wind were blowing.

A thousand labored "signpost" sentences couldn't tell you more about Maria, or more about Aunt Ena's stoic endurance. Their inwardness has been expertly and beautifully externalized.

What I am calling inwardness here — a certain center of within-ness in all people, and in animals and birds, and in sunlight and rain — is nearly always seen and simultaneously felt in what we name, too lightly, "good story description."

This withinness, insideness, is there in so-called inanimate objects as well as in the obviously living and breathing. An awareness of it informs the story (even a fantasy) with reality, and it can make the *unsaid* more potent than what is put on paper, and richer than if it were stridently spelled out. When you admire understatement in a story, this is what you are admiring. You are

praising considerably more than good taste, which, like fastidi-
ousness, is not a particular virtue when it stands alone; you are
impressed by the author's constant consciousness of the entire
world of people and things, as well as that author's ability to suggest
these in microcosm without turning up the volume.

So for a minute now, consider:

The In-ness of Things

Going into a raw, newly constructed house which nobody has
lived in, touching the fresh wood, sniffing the plaster, you feel
neither alien nor at home. You are in the no man's land of the
untenanted.

But after a few years, when the house has been occupied and
rubbed by humanity, it gains a special aura, even when its occu-
pants are not at home. A quality more important than furniture or
familiar belongings or food and light is there. People have brought to
things a felt impact of themselves.

The lived-in story is very like this. Each corner of it reflects,
refracts and responds to the tone of whoever lives there . . . whoever
wrote it with innate understanding of its inmost character.

There are stories which have never been lived in. They may be
built of the most durable material; their authors may have applied
every rule laid down by generations of good, indifferent and long-
retired or defunct teachers, and still have produced handsome and
hollow shells.

Stories such as this are sometimes published — but when they
lack the heat that lies outside technique, readers forget them. They
suffer in silence from a need for the character of people *and* things.

The things of a lived-in story don't have to be "described" —
sometimes they don't even require mentioning. Yet during the writing they were known by the writer as familiarly as his or her hands
and feet and heart and bloodstream; they were *felt all through.*

In the paragraph about the discovery of the snake by the
woman, while she was weeding an onion patch, I left out the intense
fury of the late-afternoon, Fourth of July heat above the simmering
Ohio River, the arcade of sun-stunned, leaf-drooping oaks in the
near distance, the musky smell of the riverbank, the friable, powd-
ery touch of the baking earth. But they are there. They're in the
silence around the snake, around the woman.

And the in-ness of Things is present to a touchable degree in
"Maria," whose voice needs no description because we know it is
pinched, haughty and insufferable, from hearing it on the page in
her words, which characterize her completely — as do Aunt Ena's
eyes, barely visible above the rugs as she lowers her eyelids "as
though a strong wind were blowing."

Your story's foreground, and the people in it, should be lighted
by your feeling for background — the shape and presence of Things.

Now, this so-called background is no stage flat, put there to give an audience the easily destroyed illusion that it is looking at a drawing room or a doctor's office. Its windows are real. Its walls have substance. It is never merely imagined. It is made of your ability to bring out the whole solidity of place. It reminds the reader of *something she or he has known*; and it influences the depth of a story as well as its topsoil. In many commercial stories of the kind published up through the '20s and into the '30s, such background was a bulky as a horsehair sofa, dominating the induction of a story while its characters, and its readers, waited for the action to start. Dress styles were lingered upon, furnishings were depicted at paragraph-length, fabrics were named and sometimes priced. This opulent sandbag approach to a story is no longer necessary or at all desirable — but without *some* fragrance of background reaching the reader, the story will hang in the air, a depthless and curious mobile.

Place is the Greek *Locus* — creator of the atmosphere where drama happens.

Bringing it closer, it's your own hand gripping the rocks of a gulley down which your chief character is perilously moving; your observation that these rocks are stippled with tiny deposits of quartz, which glitter in late sun beside the shadow of the mountains; your nostrils expanding to smell time-worn stone; your eye catching the light on a circling hawk's wing; your ear listening to the shuffle of pebbles as they slide below you with the sound of snare-drum brushes; the taste of danger drying the roots of your tongue. Even a story delivered entirely in dialogue — an experiment not to be encouraged — should have this thereness, withness, the felt knowledge of background beating behind the words.

But background is double-edged. When it begins to take over, it can slowly swallow up and cover what began as a story with a clean line of action and event. A story drenched in background is always on the verge of becoming an essay. Every writer has, inside, a pendulum that swings toward background and foreground — and if you allow this to linger in the direction of mood and scene, you'll discover that your main character has turned into an observer and *only* an observer; that his or her vitality has become muffled.

Keeping the character alive to the least hair in her or his eyebrows, neither dominating the background nor subservient to it, but *in* it, is one of your primary concerns. At this point, if I believed in illustrative charts — which I do not — I would draw one, splitting the page in halves, and at the top of one half I would inscribe BACKGROUND, while at the top of the other I would write CHARACTER. I'd much rather you would imagine this; as a writer, it's considerably more healthy for you to think in words than in geometric designs. But consider the chart as limned in your head. The moment you feel yourself spending too much time, too many sentences, on one side or the other, go back to using your personal pendulum in steady balance; back to the rhythm of Background Place and Foreground Character.

But we are not clocks, we are people, and to point out this necessity for balance between human character and the character of place, a story of mine, "The Thief," is useful. This one depends more than most of my work on a careful division of character and a full realization of background, for the background becomes a "character" in its own right, yet it cannot be allowed to obliterate or even slightly to dim the reader's understanding of the boy, Raoul.

"The Thief" begins with Raoul awkwardly shoving open the screen door of the summer cabin he shares with his father on the Altamaha River in lower Georgia. He carries a rod, a reel, a creel. It is a blue-hot morning. His father, a judgmatic sportsman-broker on vacation, nods over his first gin and tonic of the day and wishes him luck. The saturating heat and quiet mystery of the morning take over; Raoul is a noticer, a see-er of the small and the large; he appreciates the minuscular flowers that go to make up a bed of moss; the enormity and silence of the river. As he comes to the river, the reader enters its aura of mysticism — and is reminded, in a few lines, that once, before General Oglethorpe's men drove them away, elk roared along its banks, and that until naturalist and explorer William Bartram discovered it, it was known only to Indians and wild animals. The river is, in essence, a god.

As he casts and waits for a strike, Raoul breathes into himself its agelessness, its biding self against his puny humanity. Yet his humanity is important; he is more alert than ever before in his brief years to the presence of the Things — to being watched, perhaps judged. Seeing an egret on the far bank of the sun-mirroring water, he recalls that egrets are called cowbirds by farmers — considered pests and casually shot as such. He has started on this morning to become someone else — someone who was waiting within him to appear . . . older, more alive and aware. And what he wants, tangibly and terribly, is to catch just one decent fish, to carry it back to his father and remark offhandedly that it isn't such a bad catch.

And then he has his strike — a respectable trout of about two pounds. It fights with fury, and for the first time in his life he remembers to apply the controlled skill his father has tried to teach him, to play it as an old hand would; almost miraculously, he lands it, swinging it over his shoulder and back in a shining arc to the firm sand beach. But before he can touch it, a red-tailed hawk is upon it and has snapped the line and sailed to the mesa-like top of a sandstone-and-shell cliff. The cliff is sheer, 30 feet almost straight up, appearing to be unscalable. But in his stricken, ice-hard rage, Raoul climbs without real consciousness of anything but raw injustice. He finds barely enough handholds to keep moving, but never pauses to look down. Attaining the tabletop ledge where the hawk's nest is built, he dives at the hawk, finds his hands around its thin throat, its life under his fingers. The hawk's wings, its crazed and courageous saffron eyes, with their own rage like a lion's, and its searching beak, are all demonic. And in one blinding second, impossible to sustain but only to recall later and to keep with him perhaps to his own death, Raoul understands that the hawk's need is infinitely greater than his own. He drops it. He looks at the already torn, diminished trout, its live river-self faded and gone, its colors paling semblances of what they were. With strong caution, going slowly and nursing his bloody scratches, he makes his way down the side of the cliff. He gathers his snarled gear, and starts back; the revelation he has experienced stays with him, invisible, but as hoary and intense as the river and the heat; he knows an exaltation he will never be able to speak completely.

At the cabin, he merely mentions to his father that the line got tangled in brush, and that he was scratched getting it out. But he has changed completely, and we feel he will forever be.

Keeping Raoul in balance, never allowing him to be subsumed under descriptions of Nature, or the story — which was only seven pages long — to turn into a "nature study" piece of charm, were the only recognizable problems at the time of writing. The rest was swimming under water — perhaps the water of the Altamaha. So far as I know, "The Thief" has no easily explicable theme. It would be simple to say "A ten-year-old child becomes a discerning man," but it wouldn't be true. The internal wrestling in Raoul is strong, and it is brought to an end by his recognition of the purer and more violent wrestling in the hawk, yet there are overtones there which I can only hear, not define.

All of which tells us that mystery is at the heart of many stories, and that unraveling the mystery as far as words can is one of the challenges that keep writers of stories young in their nimble minds.

Of Beginnings and Endings

Crafting two important elements of your short stories

I. Beginnings

Make your openings as memorable as you can. Get the reader's attention, but get it in a way that leads naturally to the next fact or picture you want the reader to see. An opening is a compressed emotional promise of things to come. It may be terse or leisurely, but it contains the seed of everything that will grow from it. It sets the rhythm of the story. It is not merely a dramatic hook. It is as unself-conscious as possible, sliding into the reader's mind like a voice at the shoulder.

Bad openings are those that stretch the longbow of reader cred-ulity and can't be followed up. (" 'Hell,' said the duchess as she fell off the leaning tower of Pisa" is a striking opening, but hard to follow.) Weak openings are those that stroll in vaguely like actors who have forgotten their lines. "I wandered lonely as a cloud on that grand April morning, or possibly it was May because I've really forgotten the month, but then I'd been watching so many soap operas I might have had amnesia." What bad openings signal to the reader is blatant false confidence; what weak openings signal is confusion.

Readers don't have time to sort out what you mean. They'll believe what you say if you say it well from the start.

Write your openings over as many times as it takes to make them shapely and packed with promise.

Then begin to think about going on.

II. *Endings*

Somewhere in the untapped reaches of your convoluted story-making mind you might cherish the notion that your story ought to end happily for the sake of pleasing an editor. If this is the sole reason you have for making such a decision, it's a very bad one. The story itself will tell you where to go. There are stories which, to be true to themselves, must end on a note of resolution that may well be optimistic. Others resist the intrusion of cheerfulness for all they are worth — they may not be unrelentingly grim, but their subject matter is such that to twist them, however slightly, in order to bring about an ending which is out of key with the rest will ruin them as believable experiences for both editor and reader. Cling to the story's own innards, which are a sacrosanct part of your own *persona* — if you envision any editor or eventual reader as an arbitrary Pollyanna, you are creating a false image that, like a will-o'-the-wisp, can lead you into swamps of fatuity. No outside force, teacher, guide, mentor or imagined editorial reaction should be allowed to interfere with your essential writing self once the story is in progress.

A useful guideline for knowing *when* to end a short story is this: As soon as wrestling (which is a better term for what most writers call "conflict") has evolved into revelation, your story is over. This doesn't simply mean that you've kept a variant of the O. Henry trick ending in reserve until the last. It means that the reader has been given a clear look at a change that the wrestling has brought about, and that it's time to stop. You, the author, have wrestled within *yourself* to understand your people, and to make the reader understand them as they grappled with themselves or with others, and now that the lightning of change, or sometimes even the flicker of possible change, has been shown, the story must stand on its own. A meeting has been achieved. Nothing may have been permanently solved — but something has been apprehended.

In first stories especially, the temptation is to run on past the story's natural stop — to embroider slightly, to give one last parting sentence or so as a goodbye, a rounding off and farewell. This is an orator's impulse. Good storytellers learn early to suppress it. The best stories stop when their wrestling stops and a little light has been shed on the reasons for it. They don't stop with a big bang or a trailing whimper; they stop for the excellent reason that they are finished.

SOME THOUGHTS ON PLAYWRITING

— Thornton Wilder

A critically acclaimed American playwright and novelist, Wilder has won three Pulitzer Prizes for *The Bridge of San Luis Rey, Our Town,* and *The Skin of Our Teeth.* He also taught writing at the University of Chicago. Wilder is known for his intriguing experimentation with theatrical technique and the ironic and witty tone which characterizes his work.

■ What are the differences in how information is conveyed in drama and fiction?
■ Does one genre offer more imaginative scope to the artist than the other?

Wilder's observations may help you to decide which genre you want to begin writing.

Novels are written in the past tense. The characters in them, it is true, are represented as living moment by moment their present time, but the constant running commentary of the novelist ("Tess slowly descended into the valley"; "Anna Karenina laughed") inevitably conveys to the reader the fact that these events are long since past and over.

The novel is a past reported in the present. On the stage it is always now. This confers upon the action an increased vitality which the novelist longs in vain to incorporate into his work.

This condition in the theatre brings with it another important element:

In the theatre we are not aware of the intervening storyteller. The speeches arise from the characters in an apparently pure spontaneity.

A play is what takes place.

A novel is what one person tells us took place.

A play visibly represents pure existing. A novel is what one mind, claiming to omniscience, asserts to have existed.

Many dramatists have regretted this absence of the narrator from the stage, with his point of view, his powers of analyzing the behaviour of the characters, his ability to interfere and supply further facts about the past, about simultaneous actions not visible on the stage, and above *all* his function of pointing the moral and emphasizing the significance of the action. In some periods of the theatre he has been present as chorus, or prologue and epilogue or as *raisonneur*. But surely this absence constitutes an additional force to the form, as well as an additional tax upon the writer's skill. It is the task of the dramatist so to co-ordinate his play, through the selection of episodes and speeches, that, though he is himself not visible, his point of view and his governing intention will impose themselves on the spectator's attention, not as dogmatic assertion or motto, but as self-evident truth and inevitable deduction.

Imaginative narration — the invention of souls and destinies — is to a philosopher an all but indefensible activity.

Its justification lies in the fact that the communication of ideas from one mind to another inevitably reaches the point where exposition passes into illustration, into parable, metaphor, allegory, and myth.

It is no accident that when Plato arrived at the height of his argument and attempted to convey a theory of knowledge and a theory of the structure of man's nature he passed over into story telling, into the myths of the Cave and the Charioteer; and that the great religious teachers have constantly had recourse to the parable as a means of imparting their deepest intuitions.

The theatre offers to imaginative narration its highest possibilities. It has many pitfalls and its very vitality betrays it into service as mere diversion and the enhancement of insignificant matter; but it is well to remember that it was the theatre that rose to the highest place during those epochs that aftertime has chosen to call "great ages" and that the Athens of Pericles and the reigns of Elizabeth, Philip II, and Louis XIV were also the ages that gave to the world the greatest dramas it has known.

THE TASK OF THE POET

— Henrik Ibsen

Although his parents intended him to be a druggist, Ibsen became a world-renowned playwright. The father of modern drama, Ibsen invented the realistic play built around psychological conflict, rather than following in the tradition of plot emphasis.

- What are the implications of being a "poet"?
- What moves or inspires the writer?

Ibsen believes that the "poet" must see in a special way and convey the precise perception to the audience. Compare this focus with Ciardi's observations about poetry in "Robert Frost: The Way to the Poem" (see Part B, page 283) and Davies's contentions about the artist in "The Conscience of the Writer" in Part A, page 173.

. . .AND WHAT does it mean, then, to be a poet? It was a long time before I realized that to be a poet means essentially to see, but mark well, to see in such a way that whatever is seen is perceived by the audience just as the poet saw it. But only what has been lived through can be seen in that way and accepted in that way. And the secret of modern literature lies precisely in this matter of experiences that are lived through. All that I have written these last ten years, I have lived through spiritually. But no poet lives through anything in isolation. What he lives through all of his countrymen live through with him. If that were not so, what would bridge the gap between the producing and the receiving minds?

And what is it, then, that I have lived through and that has inspired me? The range has been large. In part I have been inspired by something which only rarely and only in my best moments has stirred vividly within me as something great and beautiful. I have been inspired by that which, so to speak, has stood higher than my everyday self, and I have been inspired by this because I wanted to confront it and make it part of myself.

But I have also been inspired by the opposite, by what appears on introspection as the dregs and sediment of one's own nature. Writing has in this case been to me like a bath from which I have risen feeling cleaner, healthier and freer. Yes, gentlemen, nobody can picture poetically anything for which he himself has not to a certain degree and at least at times served as a model. And who is the man among us who has not now and then felt and recognized within himself a contradiction between word and deed, between will and duty, between life and theory in general? Or who is there among us who has not, at least at times, been egoistically sufficient unto himself, and self unconsciously, half in good faith, sought to extenuate his conduct both to others and to himself?

I believe that in saying all this to you, to the students, my remarks have found exactly the right audience. You will understand them as they are meant to be understood. For a student has essentially the same task as the poet: to make clear to himself, and thereby to others, the temperal and eternal questions which are astir in the age and in the community to which he belongs.

In this respect I dare to say of myself that I have endeavored to be a good student during my stay abroad. A poet is by nature farsighted. Never have I seen my homeland and the true life of my homeland so fully, so clearly, and at such close range, as I did in my absence when I was far away from it.

And now, my dear countrymen, in conclusion a few words which are also related to something I have lived through. When Emperor Julian stands at the end of his career, and everything collapses around him, there is nothing which makes him so despondent as the thought that all he has gained was this: to be remembered by cool and clear heads with respectful appreciation, while his opponents live on, rich in the love of warm, living hearts. This thought was the result of much that I had lived through; it had its origin in a question that I had sometimes asked myself, down there in my solitude. Now the young people of Norway have come to me here tonight and given me my answer in word and song, have given me my answer more warmly and clearly than I had ever expected to hear it. I shall take this answer with me as the richest reward of my visit with my countrymen at home, and it is my hope and my belief that what I experience tonight will be an experience to "live through" which will sometime be reflected in a work of mine. And if this happens, if sometimes I shall send such a book home, then I ask that the students receive it as a handshake and a thanks for this meeting. I ask you to receive it as the ones who had a share in the making of it.

Henrik Ibsen: "Speech to the Norwegian Students, September 10, 1874," *Speeches and New Letters,* translated by Arne Kildal (Boston. Richard G. Badger, 1910), pp. 49-52. After an absence of ten years, Ibsen spent a couple of months in Norway during the summer of 1874. On September 10, Norwegian students marched in procession to Ibsen's home. This speech is Ibsen's reply to their greeting.

GIVE YOUR HOW-TO ARTICLES THE VOICE OF AUTHORITY

— Leonard McGill

Leonard McGill has written several popular books, including *Stylewise: A Man's Guide to Looking Good for Less.*

■ Are writers able to write convincingly about subjects on which they are not experts?

■ What techniques convince readers they are learning something from "how-to" articles?

McGill contends you should adopt the "voice" of an expert to convince your readers of the legitimacy of your advice. The next time you read a "how-to" article, check to see if its writer has employed any of McGill's strategies to achieve a persuasive tone.

Too many writers believe they must be experts on an activity to write about it. After all, if you're not a mechanic, you couldn't possibly tell someone how to buy a used car, right?

Not necessarily. Other than getting the right facts, you only have to *sound* like an expert.

You don't have to practice scales to develop an effective how-to "voice," but following some simple guidelines will help impart this special, *salable* ring to your words. It's almost as easy as do re mi.

Two traits are essential: Curiosity. And a willingness to use your inquisitive pick and shovel to unearth information that makes you sound authoritative. I've recently sold articles on how to order clothing from Hong Kong, how to combine various sports in an exercise program, and how to cut the cost of shaving. Before researching these subjects, I knew as much about them as I do about building submarines. Nothing. But in each case I acquired the type of knowledge that made me sound like I'd been ordering outfits from the Orient, swimming to develop aerobic capacity, and shaving for pennies all my life. As Susan Crandell, editor of *Direct Newsletter*, puts it, "The best how-to writers can assume a mantle of authority on a subject by becoming quick experts."

Always look for four categories of information when researching: specific descriptions, "subject-bound" terminology, concrete examples, and "expert facts."

When experts talk shop, they don't generalize. A good wine steward doesn't recommend "red" or "white," but "Bordeaux" or "Chablis" or whatever. He's specific. In assuming the mantle of authority, you must be specific, too. This is a good credo in all nonfiction writing, but in doing how-tos, specifics are the fodder you'll turn into acceptance checks. If you're writing about how to cut children's hair, don't suggest using "barber's shears" if the best barber's shears are five inches long and made of stainless steel. Such facts add resonance to your writing voice.

So does "subject-bound" terminology. Almost every profession or activity has its own vocabulary. For example, sailors speak of "tacks," "tillers" and "running bowsprits" when talking to each other. So, when writing "How to Survive Your First Day of Sailing," use such words (and explain what they mean). They'll make you sound like an old sea salt, even if you've spent only a day under the mast yourself.

Just as you're more likely to believe I know what I'm saying in this article if I back it up with specific examples, so your own how-to pieces will sound more authoritative if you back up the kind of statements authorities make. My book *Style Wise* (a guide to saving money on men's clothing and grooming), contained a small section on how to give yourself a home haircut. Obviously, most men wouldn't usually consider trying this. To convince them it was possible to save money and have good-looking hair, too, I told how I halved the cost of keeping my hair neat by alternating visits to the barber with home trimmings, and how my wife actually said my hair looked *better* with this routine.

Also, watch for "expert facts" that add depth and credibility to your writing. For example, in writing a piece on creating home-made jewelry, I read several books on gemstones. This wasn't "must" research, because several jewelers already had explained what materials (gemstones included) to use and how to use them. In writing the article, however, my reading allowed me to mention several authoritative "gems," such as the fact that agates, a type of stone frequently used in home jewelry, are formed by volcanic action. This made the article a bit more interesting, and, just as important, made me sound more like an expert.

When conducting research, consult as many sources as possible, for two reasons:

First, you want to be certain you are presenting facts, and not opinion. Charles Hix, the bestselling author of *Looking Good* (a how-to book on men's grooming) and *Working Out* (on exercise), researches until he accumulates a "base of facts": "I tend to gravitate toward the type of fact that's basic to a subject. In *Looking Good*, all the grooming tips were based on medical information on how the human body functions. In researching, I always try to get to a base where I'll know if the authorities I talk to are working out of self-interest. For example, I certainly wasn't an expert when I started my exercise book, but I read books and articles on the basic functioning of muscle, the bloodstream and digestion, and how these were affected by exercise, instead of just interviewing someone with a string of health clubs."

Second, you want to present facts and instruction as being yours, not someone else's. In writing a *Gentlemen's Quarterly* article on how to buy a pen, I interviewed the owner of the largest pen shop in Manhattan. She told me pens had to be "tried on" like clothing. Had I not done further research, I would have been forced to quote the owner if I used her opinion that pens should be tried on. After talking with other pen shop owners, I discovered that each thought the correct way to buy a pen was to handle several to see which fit your hand the best. Thus, I could state in the article, without quoting anyone, that pens should in fact be "tried on," again using research information to make myself sound more like an authority.

On the first day of class in high school or college, instructors invariably give an introductory talk to establish the teacher's role, and break the ice between instructor and student. Similarly, in how-to writing, your voice will resound without authority if you establish your role as an educator from the start.

In general terms, this means letting readers know you will teach them something valuable. If the topic is aimed at improving their lifestyle, simply state the benefits of following your advice. My *Gentlemen's Quarterly* article on selecting alligator fashion accessories began: "Domestically illegal for over a decade, alligator shoes and accessories are once again being hungrily snapped up by fashion-conscious men. . . . Here's a guide to the skins and styles on today's market and, since they're likely to take a sizable bite out of your wardrobe dollars, the best way to care for them."

If your article solves a problem, state the problem and tell readers you're going to explain how solving it is possible. My article on organizing a cluttered closet began: "Has your dressing routine become an act of frustration? Do you dig into your wardrobe, wrenching wrinkled clothes from a packed and jumbled closet? What if opening your clothes vault showcased a wardrobe arranged as neatly as eggs in cartons? It can. And rather easily. Your closet reorganization can range from streamlining to customizing. Ahead; how to put your wardrobe's house in order."

The sentences "It can. And rather easily." illustrate another way to assume the mantle of authority at the very beginning of your article. Instead of moving into the body of the article after establishing your role as teacher, give your readers a dose of inspiration. They'll think you must know *something* if you're so confident that they can accomplish what you propose. I call such inspirational sentences "confidence builders." Used at the beginning of an article, and sprinkled through longer pieces, they grab readers and draw them through how-to information.

See how author Duane Newcomb, after establishing himself as a teacher in his book's introduction, immediately draws readers into *A Complete Guide to Marketing Magazine Articles* by inspiring confidence in the first sentence of chapter one: "There's money to be made out there in the writing field, and you, if you can write a letter other people can understand, can cash in on it."

In school, we learn the ABCs before we learn to spell, because experts present information in a logical order. In most how-tos, a simple chronological order works best. Move readers along through a sequence of instructions, ordered as they will perform them. If the project or activity involves more than one task, start with the simplest and move toward the most complex.

After establishing myself as a teacher and injecting a confidence builder, I started the body of my closet cleanup piece at the logical beginning: "A good first step toward quelling closet turmoil is to set aside an afternoon and proceed as if moving, taking everything out of your closet."

After telling how to prune unwanted wardrobe items, I gave some simple ideas on what to do with the closet before reinstating the newly groomed wardrobe. Then I told how to restructure the closet: moving rods and shelves, or adding a vertical partition. Next came other modifications, each increasing in complexity, until, finally, I told how to hire a professional to build a custom closet.

While proper research and the right structure add to the substance and range of your how-to voice, several writing conventions round it out and keep it on key. For example, when you read how-tos — and you should read a lot of them in training your how-to voice — you'll notice a "ring" to the writing, a style as straightforward as a bulldozer, using short sentences. I call it the "cookbook cadence," because it sounds like the writing used in recipes. (Preheat oven to 375 degrees. Place chicken in shallow baking pan, skin side up. Sprinkle with onion, garlic, salt and . . . .)

Readers expect to receive how-to information in such a cadence. Recipes, instruction manuals, and directions on food containers and other products are all written in this form. When you use it in your how-to writing, readers recognize the ring, and your writing voice takes on authority. Obviously, you can't maintain a cookbook cadence throughout an article or book, but it's the best way for giving a series of short directions. Newcomb uses such a cadence in his book when discussing how to find salable article ideas: "Article ideas are everywhere. You can stand on any street corner and find hundreds. In the beginning, you won't be able to see them — but as you begin to think of what readers are particularly interested in, it will start to clear up. Start asking yourself, Why? What's behind this? What are the reasons for this, and finally, who would be interested in reading about it?"

Note the command form used in recipes and instructions; it's direct, confident and authoritative. Use this form whenever possible, and don't dilute the impact of "commands" with quibbling phrases like "I think," "I suggest" and "You should." Such throat-clearing muffles your authoritative how-to voice.

Also, address the reader as "you." You want readers to feel as though you're beside them, a reassuring voice guiding their every move. As Charles Hix puts it, "I use 'you' in my writing much more now; it seems like the most direct connection."

However, many editors complain of the too-frequent use of "you" in how-to articles. "The easiest mistake a writer can make is trying to draw readers into an article by relying solely on addressing them directly as 'you,'" says Susan Crandell of *Direct.* "It works very well if used in a limited way, but it gets overdone. Since we deal in how-to articles quite often, I must be careful that the entire magazine isn't couched in the second person."

A last writing convention — again borrowed from the teaching profession — is to use analogies to strengthen your expert stance. When teaching readers how to shop for a pen, I wrote that selecting the proper model "is easier if you assess these tools as you would any fashion accessory — considering both your needs and personal taste." The reader is comforted by the fact that choosing a pen won't be foreign — it's like shopping for something he already knows about. Making the unfamiliar familiar shows you know your stuff. If you can work analogies into how-to articles, readers and editors are more likely to view you as an expert.

Especially if you use a trained writing voice; research for "expert" facts, include specific descriptions, "subject-bound" terminology and concrete examples; establish yourself as a teacher; add "confidence builders"; follow a chronological or simple-to-complex order; and speak in "cookbook cadence."

Such authoritative writing will have editors exercising their voices, singing *your* praises.

HOW DO YOU KNOW IT'S GOOD?

— Mayra Mannes

Mayra Mannes is a social critic whose commentaries have appeared in American publications.

- Are there absolute standards by which a work of art can be validly judged?
- Is it valid to say a creative piece of work is "good" or "bad"?

Mannes contends that the individual's judgment is the key to appreciating art.

Suppose there were no critics to tell us how to react to a picture, a play, or a new composition of music. Suppose we wandered innocent as the dawn into an art exhibition of unsigned paintings. By what standards, by what values would we decide whether they were good or bad, talented or untalented, successes or failures? How can we ever know that what we think is right?

For the last fifteen or twenty years the fashion in criticism or appreciation of the arts has been to deny the existence of any valid criteria and to make the words "good" or "bad" irrelevant, immaterial, and inapplicable. There is no such thing, we are told, as a set of standards, first acquired through experience and knowledge and later imposed on the subject under discussion. This has been a popular approach, for it relieves the critic of the responsibility of judgment and the public of the necessity of knowledge. It pleases those resentful of disciplines, it flatters the empty-minded by calling them open-minded, it comforts the confused. Under the banner of democracy and the kind of equality which our forefathers did *not* mean, it says, in effect, "Who are you to tell us what is good or bad?" This is the same cry used so long and so effectively by the producers of mass media who insist that it is the public, not they, who decides what it wants to hear and see, and that for a critic to say that *this* program is bad and this program is good is purely a reflection of personal taste. Nobody recently has expressed this philosophy more succinctly than Dr. Frank Stanton, the highly intelligent president of CBS television. At a hearing before the Federal Communications Commission, this phrase escaped him under questioning: "One man's mediocrity is another man's good program."

There is no better way of saying, "No values are absolute." There is another important aspect to this philosophy of *laissez-faire:* It is the fear, in all observers of all forms of art, of guessing wrong. This fear is well come by, for who has not heard of the contemporary outcries against artists who later were called great? Every age has its arbiters who do not grow with their times, who cannot tell evolution from revolution or the difference between frivolous faddism, amateurish experimentation, and profound and necessary change. Who wants to be caught *flagrante delicto* with an error of judgment as serious as this? It is far safer, and certainly easier, to look at a picture or a play or a poem and to say, "This is hard to understand, but it may be good," or simply to welcome it as a new form. The word "new" — in our country especially — has magical connotations. What is new must be good; what is old is probably bad. And if a critic can describe the new in language that nobody can understand, he's safer still. If he has mastered the art of saying nothing with exquisite complexity, nobody can quote him later as saying anything.

But all these, I maintain, are forms of abdication from the

responsibility of judgment. In creating, the artist commits himself; in appreciating, you have a commitment of your own. For after all, it is the audience which makes the arts. A climate of appreciation is essential to its flowering, and the higher the expectations of the public, the better the performance of the artist. Conversely, only a public ill-served by its critics could have accepted as art and as literature so much in these last years that has been neither. If anything goes, everything goes; and at the bottom of the junkpile lie the discarded standards too.

But what are these standards? How do you get them? How do you know they're the right ones? How can you make a clear pattern out of so many intangibles, including that greatest one, the very private I?

Well for one thing, it's fairly obvious that the more you read and see and hear, the more equipped you'll be to practice that art of association which is at the basis of all understanding and judgment. The more you live and the more you look, the more aware you are of a consistent pattern — as universal as the stars, as the tides, as breathing, as night and day — underlying everything. I would call this pattern and this rhythm an order. Not order — *an* order. Within it exists an incredible diversity of forms. Without it lies chaos. I would further call this order — this incredible diversity held within one pattern — health. And I would call chaos — the wild cells of destruction — sickness. It is in the end up to you to distinguish between the diversity that is health and the chaos that is sickness, and you can't do this without a process of association that can link a bar of Mozart with the corner of a Vermeer painting, or a Stravinsky score with a Picasso abstraction; or that can relate an aggressive act with a Franz Kline painting and a fit of coughing with a John Cage composition.

There is no accident in the fact that certain expressions of art live for all time and that others die with the moment, and although you may not always define the reasons, you can ask the questions. What does an artist say that is timeless; how does he say it? How much is fashion, how much is merely reflection? Why is Sir Walter Scott so hard to read now, and Jane Austen not? Why is baroque right for one age and too effulgent for another?

Can a standard of craftsmanship apply to art of all ages, or does each have its own, and different, definitions? You may have been aware, inadvertently, that craftsmanship has become a dirty word these years because, again, it implies standards — something done well or done badly. The result of this convenient avoidance is a plenitude of actors who can't project their voices, singers who can't phrase their songs, poets who can't communicate emotion, and writers who have no vocabulary — not to speak of painters who can't draw. The dogma now is that craftsmanship gets in the way of expression. You can do better if you don't know *how* you do it, let alone *what* you're doing.

I think it is time you helped reverse this trend by trying to rediscover craft: the command of the chosen instrument, whether it is a brush, a word, or a voice. When you begin to detect the difference between freedom and sloppiness, between serious experimentation and egotherapy, between skill and slickness, between strength and violence, you are on your way to separating the sheep from the goats, a form of segregation denied us for quite a while. All you need to restore it is a small bundle of standards and a Geiger counter that detects fraud, and we might begin our tour of the arts in an area where both are urgently needed: contemporary painting.

I don't know what's worse: to have to look at acres of bad art to find the little good, or to read what the critics say about it all. In no other field of expression has so much double-talk flourished, so much confusion prevailed, and so much nonsense been circulated: further evidence of the close interdependence between the arts and the critical climate they inhabit. It will be my pleasure to share with you some of this double-talk so typical of our times.

Item one: preface for a catalogue of an abstract painter:

"Time-bound meditation experiencing a life; sincere with plastic piety at the threshold of hallowed arcana; a striving for pure ideation giving shape to inner drive; formalized patterns where neural balances reach a fiction." End of quote. Know what this artist paints like now?

Item two: a review in the *Art News:*

". . . a weird and disparate assortment of material, but the monstrosity which bloomed into his most recent cancer of aggregations is present in some form everywhere. . . ." Then, later, "A gluttony of things and processes terminated by a glorious constipation."

Item three, same magazine, review of an artist who welds automobile fragments into abstract shapes:

"Each fragment . . . is made an extreme of human exasperation, torn at and fought all the way, and has its rightness of form as if by accident. *Any technique that requires order or discipline would just be the human ego.* No, these must be egoless, uncontrolled, undesigned and different enough to give you a bang — fifty miles an hour around a telephone pole. . . ."

"Any technique that requires order of discipline would just be the human ego." What does he mean — "just be"? What are they really talking about? Is this journalism? Is it criticism? Or is it that other convenient abdication from standards of performance and judgment practiced by so many artists and critics that they, like certain writers who deal only in sickness and depravity, "reflect the chaos about them"? Again, whose chaos? Whose depravity?

I had always thought that the prime function of art was to create order *out* of chaos — again, not the order of neatness or rigidity or convention or artifice, but the order of clarity by which one will and one vision could draw the essential truth out of apparent confusion. I still do. It is not enough to use parts of a car to convey the brutality of the machine. This is as lavishly representative, and just as easy, as arranging dried flowers under glass to convey nature.

Speaking of which, i.e., the use of real materials (burlap, old gloves, bottletops) in lieu of pigment, this is what one critic had to say about an exhibition of Assemblage at the Museum of Modern Art last year:

> Spotted throughout the show are indisputable works of art, accounting for a quarter or even a half of the total display. But the remainder are works of non-art, anti-art, and art substitutes that are the aesthetic counterparts of the social deficiencies that land people in the clink on charges of vagrancy. These aesthetic bankrupts . . . have no legitimate ideological roof over their heads and not the price of a square intellectual meal, much less a spiritual sandwich, in their pockets.

I quote these words of John Canaday of *The New York Times* as an example of the kind of criticism which puts responsibility to an intelligent public above popularity with an intellectual coterie. Canaday has the courage to say what he thinks and the capacity to say it clearly: two qualities notably absent from his profession.

Next to art, I would say that appreciation and evaluation in the field of music is the most difficult. For it is rarely possible to judge a new composition at one hearing only. What seems confusing or fragmented at first might well become clear and organic a third time. Or it might not. The only salvation here for the listener is, again, an instinct born of experience and association which allows him to separate intent from accident, design from experimentation, and pretense from conviction. Much of contemporary music is, like its sister art, merely a reflection of the composer's own fragmentation: an absorption in self and symbols at the expense of communication with others. The artist, in short, says to the public: If you don't understand this, it's because you're dumb. I maintain that you are not. You may have to go part way or even halfway to meet the artist, but if you must go the whole way, it's his fault, not yours. Hold fast to that. And remember it too when you read new poetry, that estranged sister of music.

> A multitude of causes, unknown to former times, are now acting with a combined force to blunt the discriminating powers of the mind, and, unfitting it for all voluntary exertion, to reduce it to a state of almost savage torpor. The most effective of these causes are the great national events which are daily taking place and the increasing accumulation of men in cities, where the

uniformity of their occupations produces a craving for extraordinary incident, which the rapid communication of intelligence hourly gratifies. To this tendency of life and manners, the literature and theatrical exhibitions of the country have conformed themselves.

This startlingly applicable comment was written in the year 1800 by William Wordsworth in the preface to his *Lyrical Ballads*; and it has been cited by Edwin Muir in his recently published book, *The Estate of Poetry*. Muir states that poetry's effective range and influence have diminished alarmingly in the modern world. He believes in the inherent and indestructible qualities of the human mind and the great and permanent objects that act upon it, and suggests that the audience will increase when "poetry loses what obscurity is left in it by attempting greater themes, for great themes have to be stated clearly." If you keep that firmly in mind and resist, in Muir's words, "the vast dissemination of secondary objects that isolate us from the natural world," you have gone a long way toward equipping yourself for the examination of any work of art.

When you come to theatre, in this extremely hasty tour of the arts, you can approach it on two different levels. You can bring to it anticipation and innocence, giving yourself up, as it were, to the life on the stage and reacting to it emotionally, if the play is good, or listlessly, if the play is boring; a part of the audience organism that expresses its favor by silence or laughter and its disfavor by coughing and rustling. Or you can bring to it certain critical faculties that may heighten, rather than diminish, your enjoyment.

You can ask yourselves whether the actors are truly in their parts or merely projecting themselves; whether the scenery helps or hurts the mood; whether the playright is honest with himself, his characters, and you. Somewhere along the line you can learn to distinguish between the true creative act and the false arbitrary gesture; between fresh observation and stale cliché; between the avant-garde play that is pretentious drivel and the avant-garde play that finds new ways to say old truths.

Purpose and craftsmanship — end and means — these are the keys to your judgment in all the arts. What is this painter trying to say when he slashes a broad band of black across a white canvas and lets the edges dribble down? Is it a statement of violence? Is it a self-portrait? If it is *one* of these, has he made you believe it? Or is this a gesture of the ego or a form of therapy? If it shocks you, what does it shock you into?

And what of this tight little painting of bright flowers in a vase? Is the painter saying anything new about flowers? Is it different from a million other canvases of flowers? Has it any life, any meaning, beyond its statement? Is there any pleasure in its forms or texture? The question is not whether a thing is abstract or representational, whether it is "modern" or conventional. The question, inexorably, is whether it is good. And this is a decision which only you, on the basis of instinct, experience, and association, can make for yourself. It takes independence and courage. It involves, moreover, the risk of wrong decision and the humility, after the passage of time, of recognizing it as such. As we grow and change and learn, our attitudes can change too, and what we once thought obscure or "difficult" can later emerge as coherent and illuminating. Entrenched prejudices, obdurate opinions are as sterile as no opinions at all.

Yet standards there are, timeless as the universe itself. And when you have committed yourself to them, you have acquired a passport to that elusive but immutable realm of truth. Keep it with you in the forests of bewilderment. And never be afraid to speak up.

EXCERPT FROM "AN ESSAY ON CRITICISM"

— Alexander Pope

This essay, written in rhyming couplets, made Pope famous at the age of 23. He became England's literary dictator during his lifetime (1688-1744), a period when other classic writers such as Swift and Dryden worked. Best known for his technical polish and satirical abilities, Pope's other famous publications include *Rape of the Lock* and *Epistle from Eloise to Abelard*.

■ What fundamental error do people often make when forming judgments?
■ In what spirit should a work of art be read?

One of the most famous poets in the English language suggests approaches to literature which you might like to compare to Mannes's "How Do You Know It's Good?" in Part B, page 275.

PART II

Of all the causes which conspire to blind
Man's erring judgment, and misguide the mind,
What the weak head with strongest bias rules,
Is pride, the never-failing vice of fools.
Whatever Nature has in worth deni'd,
She gives in large recruits of needful pride;
For as in bodies, thus in souls, we find
What wants in blood and spirits, swell'd with wind:
Pride, where wit fails, steps in to our defence,
And fills up all the mighty void of sense:
If once right reason drives that cloud away,

Truth breaks upon us with resistless day.
Trust not yourself; but, your defects to know,
Make use of ev'ry friend — and ev'ry foe.
    A little learning is a dang'rous thing;
Drink deep, or taste not the Pierian spring:
There shallow draughts intoxicate the brain,
And drinking largely sobers us again.
Fir'd at first sight with what the Muse imparts,
In fearless youth we tempt the heights of arts,
While from the bounded level of our mind,
Short views we take, nor see the lengths behind;
But more advanc'd, behold with strange surprise,
New distant scenes of endless science rise!
So pleas'd at first the tow'ring Alps we try,
Mount o'er the vales, and seem to tread the sky,
Th' eternal snows appear already past,
And the first clouds and mountains seem the last:
But those attain'd, we tremble to survey
The growing labours of the lengthen'd way;
Th' increasing prospect tires our wand'ring eyes,
Hills peep o'er hills, and Alps on Alps arise!
    A perfect judge will read each work of wit
With the same spirit that its author writ;
Survey the whole, nor seek slight faults to find
Where Nature moves, and rapture warms the mind;
Nor lose for that malignant dull delight,
The gen'rous pleasure to be charm'd with wit.
But in such lays as neither ebb nor flow,
Correctly cold, and regularly low,
That, shunning faults, one quiet tenour keep,
We cannot blame indeed — but we may sleep.
In wit, as Nature, what affects our hearts
Is not th' exactness of peculiar parts;
'Tis not a lip, or eye, we beauty call,
But the joint force and full result of all.
Thus when we view some well-proportion'd dome,
(The world's just wonder, and ev'n thine, O Rome!)
No single parts unequally surprise,
All comes united to th' admiring eyes;
No monstrous height, or breadth, or length, appear;
The whole at once is bold, and regular.
    Whoever thinks a faultless piece to see,
Thinks what ne'er was, nor is, nor e'er shall be.
In ev'ry work regard the writer's end,
Since none can compass more than they intend;
And if the means be just, the conduct true,

Applause, in spite of trivial faults, is due.
As men of breeding, sometimes men of wit,
T' avoid great errors, must the less commit;
Neglect the rules each verbal critic lays,
For not to know some trifles is a praise.
Most critics, fond of some subservient art,
Still make the whole depend upon a part:
They talk of principles, but notions prize,
And all to one lov'd folly sacrifice.
Good nature and good sense must ever join;
To err is human, to forgive, divine.

ROBERT FROST: THE WAY TO THE POEM

— John Ciardi

An American teacher, critic and poet, Ciardi offers common-sense advice in his commentaries about appreciating poetry. His publications include numerous volumes of poetry, collections of critical writings, and a translation of Dante's *Inferno* into idiomatic English.

■ What is the difference between what a poem means and how it means?
■ Is there one best way to approach the study of poetry?

Ciardi offers a no-nonsense perspective which may help you more fully enjoy poetry. You may find it instructive to read this essay in conjunction with Ibsen's "Task of the Poet" in Part B (page 269), and Orwell's "Politics and the English Language" (see The Core Essays in Part A, page 4).

Stopping by Woods on a Snowy Evening
by Robert Frost

Whose woods these are I think I know.
His house is in the village though;
He will not see me stopping here
To watch his woods fill up with snow.

My little horse must think it queer
To stop without a farmhouse near
Between the wood and frozen lake
The darkest evening of the year.

He gives his harness bells a shake
To ask if there is some mistake.
The only other sound's the sweep
Of easy wind and downy flake.

The woods are lovely, dark and deep.
But I have promises to keep,
And miles to go before I sleep,
And miles to go before I sleep.

The School System has much to say these days of the virtue of reading widely, and not enough about the virtues of reading less but in depth. There are any number of reading lists for poetry, but there is not enough talk about individual poems. Poetry, finally, is one poem at a time. To read any one poem carefully is the ideal preparation for reading another. Only a poem can illustrate how poetry works.

Above, therefore, is a poem — one of the master lyrics of the English language, and almost certainly the best-known poem by an American poet. What happens in it? — which is to say, not *what* does it mean, but *how* does it mean? How does it go about being a human reenactment of a human experience? The author — perhaps the thousandth reader would need to be told — is Robert Frost.

Even the TV audience can see that this poem begins as a seemingly simple narration of a seemingly simple incident but ends by suggesting meanings far beyond anything specifically referred to in the narrative. And even readers with only the most casual interest in poetry might be made to note the additional fact that, though the poem suggests those larger meanings, it is very careful never to abandon its pretense to being simple narration. There is duplicity at work. The poet pretends to be talking about one thing, and all the while he is talking about many others.

Many readers are forever unable to accept the poet's essential duplicity. It is almost safe to say that a poem is never about what it seems to be about. As much could be said of the proverb. The bird in the hand, the rolling stone, the stitch in time never (except by an artful double-deception) intend any sort of statement about birds, stones, or sewing. The incident of this poem, one must conclude, is at root a metaphor.

Duplicity aside, this poem's movement from the specific to the general illustrates one of the basic formulas of all poetry. Such a grand poem as Arnold's "Dover Beach" and such lesser, though unfortunately better-known, poems as Longfellow's "The Village Blacksmith" and Holmes's "The Chambered Nautilus" are built on the same progression. In these three poems, however, the generalization is markedly set apart from the specific narration, and even seems additional to the telling rather than intrinsic to it. It is this sense of division one has in mind in speaking of "a tacked-on moral."

There is nothing wrong-in-itself with a tacked-on moral. Frost, in fact, makes excellent use of the device at times. In this poem, however, Frost is careful to let the whatever-the-moral-is grow out of the poem itself. When the action ends the poem ends. There is no epilogue and no explanation. Everything pretends to be about the narrated incident. And that pretense sets the basic tone of the poem's performance of itself.

The dramatic force of that performance is best observable, I believe, as a progression in three scenes.

In scene one, which coincides with stanza one, a man — a New Englander — is driving his sleigh somewhere at night. It is snowing, and as the man passes a dark patch of woods he stops to watch the snow descend into the darkness. We know, moreover, that the man is familiar with those parts (he knows who owns the woods and where the owner lives), and we know that no one has seen him stop. As scene one forms itself in the theatre of the mind's eye, therefore, it serves to establish some as yet unspecified relation between the man and the woods.

It is necessary, however, to stop here for a long parenthesis: Even so simple an opening statement raises any number of questions. It is impossible to address all the questions that rise from the poem stanza by stanza, but two that arise from stanza one illustrate the sort of thing one might well ask of the poem detail by detail.

Why, for example, does the man not say what errand he is on? What is the force of leaving the errand generalized? He might just as well have told us that he was going to the general store, or returning from it with a jug of molasses he had promised to bring Aunt Harriet and two suits of long underwear he had promised to bring the hired man. Frost, moreover, can handle homely detail to great effect. He preferred to leave his motive generalized. Why?

And why, on the other hand, does he say so much about knowing the absent owner of the woods and where he lives? Is it simply that one set of details happened-in whereas another did not? To speak of things "happening-in" is to assault the integrity of a poem. Poetry cannot be discussed meaningfully unless one can assume that everything in the poem — every last comma and variant spelling — is in it by the poet's specific act of choice. Only bad poets allow into their poems what is haphazard or cheaply chosen.

The errand, I will venture a bit brashly for lack of space, is left generalized in order the more aptly to suggest *any* errand in life and, therefore, life itself. The owner is there because he is one of the forces of the poem. Let it do to say that the force he represents is the village of mankind (that village at the edge of winter) from which the poet finds himself separated (has separated himself?) in his moment by the woods (and to which, he recalls finally, he has promised to keep). The owner is he-who-lives-in-his-village-house, thereby locked away from the poet's awareness of the-time-the-snow-tells as it engulfs and obliterates the world the village man allows himself to believe he "owns." Thus, the owner is a representative of an order of reality from which the poet has divided himself for the moment, though to a certain extent he ends by reuniting with it. Scene one, therefore, establishes not only a relation between the man and the woods, but the fact that the man's relation begins with his separation (though momentarily) from mankind.

End parenthesis one, begin parenthesis two.

Still considering the first scene as a kind of dramatic performance of forces, one must note that the poet has meticulously matched the simplicity of his language to the pretended simplicity of the narrative. Clearly, the man stopped because the beauty of the scene moved him, but he neither tells us that the scene is beautiful nor that he is moved. A bad writer, always ready to overdo, might have written: "The vastness gripped me, filling my spirit with the slow steady sinking of the snow's crystalline perfection into the glimmerless profundities of the hushed primeval wood." Frost's avoidance of such a spate illustrates two principles of good writing. The first, he has stated himself in "The Mowing": "Anything *more* than the truth would have seemed too weak" (italics mine). Understatement is one of the basic sources of power in English poetry. The second principle is to let the action speak for itself. A good novelist does not tell us that a given character is good or bad (at least not since the passing of the Dickens tradition): he shows us the character in action and then, watching him, we know. Poetry, too, has fictional obligations: even when the characters are ideas and metaphors rather than people, they must be *characterized in action*. A poem does not *talk about* ideas; it *enacts* them. The force of the poem's performance, in fact, is precisely to act out (and thereby to make us act out emphatically — that is, to *feel out*, that is, to *identify with*) the speaker and why he stopped. The man is the principal actor in this little "drama of why" and in scene one he is the only character, though as noted, he is somehow related to the absent owner.

End second parenthesis.

In scene two (stanzas two and three) a *foil* is introduced. In fiction and drama, a foil is a character who "plays against" a more important character. By presenting a different point of view or an opposed set of motives, the foil moves the more important character to react in ways that might not have found expression without such opposition. The more important character is thus more fully revealed — to the reader and to himself. The foil is the horse.

The horse forces the question, Why did the man stop? Until it occurs to him that his "little horse must think it queer" he had not asked himself for reasons. He had simply stopped. But the man finds himself faced with the question he imagines the horse to be asking: What *is* there to stop for out there in the cold, away from bin and stall (house and village and mankind?) and all that any self-respecting beast could value on such a night? In sensing that other view, the man is forced to examine his own more deeply.

In stanza two the question arises only as a feeling within the man. In stanza three, however (still scene two), the horse acts. He gives his harness bells a shake. "What's wrong?" he seems to say. "What are we waiting for?"

By now, obviously, the horse — without losing its identity as horse — has also become a symbol. (A symbol is something that stands for something else.) Whatever that something else may be, it certainly begins at that order of life that does not understand why a man stops in the wintry middle of nowhere to watch the snow come down. (Can one fail to sense by now that the dark and the snow-fall symbolize a death-wish, however momentary, i.e., that hunger for final rest and oblivion that a man may feel, but not a beast?)

So by the end of scene two the performance has given dramatic force to three elements that work upon the man. There is his relation to the world of the owner. There is his relation to the brute world of the horse. And there is that third presence of the unownable world, the movement of the all-engulfing snow across all the orders of life, the man's, the owner's, and the horse's — with the difference that the man knows of that second dark-within-the-dark of which the horse cannot, and the owner will not, know.

The man ends scene two with all these forces working upon him simultaneously. He feels himself moved to a decision. And he feels a last call from the darkness: "the sweep/ Of easy wind and downy flake." It would be so easy and so downy to go into the woods and let himself be covered over.

But scene three (stanza four) produces a fourth force. This fourth force can be given many names. It is certainly better, in fact, to give it many names than to attempt to limit it to one. It is social obligation, or personal commitment, or duty, or just the realization that a man cannot indulge a mood forever. All of these and more. But finally he has a simple decision to make. He may go into the woods and let the darkness and the snow swallow him from the world of beast and man. Or he must move on. And unless he is going to stop here forever, it is time to remember that he has a long way to go and that he had best be getting there. (So there is something to be said for the horse, too.)

There and only then, his question driven more and more deeply into himself by these cross-forces, does the man venture a comment on what attracted him: "The woods are lovely, dark and deep." His mood lingers over the thought of that lovely dark-and-deep (as do the very syllables in which he phrases the thought), but the final decision is to put off the mood and move on. He has his man's way to go and his man's obligations to tend to before he can yield. He has miles to go before his sleep. He repeats that thought and the performance ends.

But why the repetition? The first time Frost says, "And miles to go before I sleep," there can be little doubt that the primary meaning is: "I have a long way to go before I get to bed tonight." The second time he says it, however, "miles to go" and "sleep" are suddenly transformed into symbols. What are those "something-elses" the symbols stand for? Hundreds of people have tried to ask Mr. Frost that question and he has always turned it away. He has turned it away *because he cannot answer it.* He could answer some part of it. But some part is not enough.

For a symbol is like a rock dropped into a pool: it sends out ripples in all directions, and the ripples are in motion. Who can say where the last ripple disappears? One may have a sense that he knows the approximate center point of the ripples, the point at which the stone struck the water. Yet even then he has trouble marking it surely. How does one make a mark on water? Oh very well — the center point of that second "miles to go" is probably approximately in the neighborhood of being close to meaning, perhaps, "the road of life"; and the second "before I sleep" is maybe that close to meaning "before I take my final rest," the rest in darkness that seemed so temptingly dark-and-deep for the moment of the mood. But the ripples continue to move and the light to change on the water, and the longer one watches the more changes he sees. Such shifting-and-being-at-the-same-instant is of the very sparkle and life of poetry. One experiences it as one experiences life, for everytime he looks at an experience he sees something new, and he sees it change as he watches it. And that sense of continuity in fluidity is one of the primary kinds of knowledge, and one that only the arts can teach, poetry foremost among them.

Frost himself certainly did not ask what that repeated last line meant. It came to him and he received it. He "felt right" about it. And what he "felt right" about was in no sense a "meaning" that, say, an essay could apprehend, but an act of experience that could be fully presented only by the dramatic enactment of forces which is the performance of the poem.

Now look at the poem in another way. Did Frost know what he was going to do when he began? Considering the poem simply as an act of skill, as a piece of juggling, one cannot fail to respond to the magnificent turn at the end where, with one flip, seven of the simplest words in the language suddenly dazzle full of never-ending waves of thought and feeling. Or, more precisely, of felt-thought. Certainly an equivalent stunt by a juggler — could there be an equivalent — would bring the house down. Was it to cap his performance with that grand stunt that Frost wrote the poem?

Far from it. The obvious fact is that *Frost could not have known he was going to write those lines until he wrote them.* Then a second fact must be registered: *he wrote them because, for the fun of it, he had got himself into trouble.*

Frost, like every good poet, began by playing a game with himself. The most usual way of writing a four-line stanza with four feet to the line is to rhyme the third line with the first, and the fourth with the second. Even that much rhyme is so difficult in English that many poets and almost all of the anonymous ballad makers do not bother to rhyme the first and third lines at all, settling for two rhymes in four lines as good enough. For English is a rhyme-poor language. In Italian and in French, for example, so many words end with the same sounds that rhyming is relatively easy—so easy that many modern French and Italian poets do not bother to rhyme at all. English, being a more agglomerate language, has far more final sounds, hence fewer of them rhyme. When an Italian poet writes a line ending with "vita" (life) he has literally hundreds of rhyme choices available. When an English poet writes "life" at the end of a line he can summon "strife, wife, knife, fife, rife," and then he is in trouble. No "life-strife" and "life-rife" and "life-wife" seem to offer a combination of possible ideas that can be related by more than just the rhyme. Inevitably, therefore, the poets have had to work and rework these combinations until the sparkle has gone out of them. The reader is normally tired of such rhyme-led associations. When he encounters "life-strife" he is certainly entitled to suspect that the poet did not really want to say "strife" — that had there been in English such a word as, say, "hife," meaning "infinite peace and harmony," the poet would as gladly have used that word instead of "strife." Thus, the reader feels that the writing is haphazard, that the rhyme is making the poet say things he does not really feel, and which, therefore, the reader does not feel except as boredom. One likes to see the rhymes fall into place, but he must end with the belief that it is the poet who is deciding what is said and not the rhyme scheme that is forcing the saying.

So rhyme is a kind of game, and an especially difficult one in English. As in every game, the fun of the rhyme is to set one's difficulties high and then to meet them skilfully. As Frost himself once defined freedom, it consists of "moving easy in harness."

In "Stopping by Woods on a Snowy Evening" Frost took a long chance. He decided to rhyme not two lines in each stanza, but three. Not even Frost could have sustained that much rhyme in a long poem (as Dante, for example, with the advantage of writing in

Italian, sustained triple rhyme for thousands of lines in *The Divine Comedy*). Frost would have known instantly, therefore, when he took the original chance, that he was going to write a short poem. He would have had that much foretaste of it.

So the first stanza emerged rhymed *a-a-b-a*. And with the sure sense that this was to be a short poem, Frost decided to take an additional chance and to redouble: in English three rhymes in four lines is more than enough; there is no need to rhyme the fourth line. For the fun of it, however, Frost set himself to pick up that loose rhyme and to weave it into the pattern, thereby accepting the all but impossible burden of quadruple rhyme.

The miracle is that it worked. Despite the enormous freight of rhyme, the poem not only came out as a neat pattern, but managed to do so with no sense of strain. Every word and every rhyme falls into place as naturally and as inevitably as if there were no rhyme restricting the poet's choices.

That ease-in-difficulty is certainly inseparable from the success of the poem's performance. One watches the skillman juggle three balls, then four, then five, and every addition makes the trick more wonderful. But unless he makes the hard trick seem as easy as an easy trick, then all is lost.

The real point, however, is not only that Frost took on a hard rhyme-trick and made it seem easy. It is rather as if the juggler, carried away, had tossed up one more ball than he could really handle, and then amazed himself by actually handling it. So with the real triumph of this poem. Frost could not have known what a stunning effect his repetition of the last line was going to produce. He could not even know he was going to repeat the line. He simply found himself up against a difficulty he almost certainly had not foreseen and he had to improvise to meet it. For in picking up the rhyme from the third line of stanza one and carrying it over into stanza two, he had created an endless chain-link form within which each stanza left a hook sticking out for the next stanza to hang on. So by stanza four, feeling the poem rounding to its end, Frost had to do something about that extra rhyme.

He might have tucked it back into a third line rhyming with the *know-though-snow* of stanza one. He could thus have rounded the poem out to the mathematical symmetry of using each rhyme four times. But though such a device might be defensible in theory, a rhyme repeated after eleven lines is so far from its original rhyme sound that its feeling as rhyme must certainly be lost. And what good is theory if the reader is not moved by the writing?

It must have been in some such quandary that the final repetition suggested itself — a suggestion born of the very difficulties the poet had let himself in for. So there is that point beyond mere ease in handling a hard thing, the point at which the very difficulty offers the poet the opportunity to do better than he knew he could. What, aside from having that happen to oneself, could be more self-delighting than to participate in its happening by one's reader-identification with the poem?

And by now a further point will have suggested itself: that the human-insight of the poem and the technicalities of its poetic artifice are inseparable. Each feeds the other. That interplay is the poem's meaning, a matter not of WHAT DOES IT MEAN, for no one can ever say entirely what a good poem means, but of HOW DOES IT MEAN, a process one can come much closer to discussing.

There is a necessary epilogue. Mr. Frost has often discussed this poem on the platform, or more usually in the course of a long-evening-after a talk. Time and again I have heard him say that he just wrote it off, that it just came to him, and that he set it down as it came.

Once at Bread Loaf, however, I heard him add one very essential piece to the discussion of how it "just came." One night, he said, he had sat down after supper to work at a long piece of blank verse. The piece never worked out, but Mr. Frost found himself so absorbed in it that, when next he looked up, dawn was at his window. He rose, crossed to the window, stood looking out for a few minutes, and then it was that "Stopping by Woods" suddenly "just came," so that all he had to do was cross the room and write it down.

Robert Frost is the sort of artist who hides his traces. I know of no Frost worksheets anywhere. If someone has raided his wastebasket in secret, it is possible that such worksheets exist somewhere, but Frost would not willingly allow anything but the finished product to leave him. Almost certainly, therefore, no one will ever know what was in that piece of unsuccessful blank verse he had been working at with such concentration, but I for one would stake my life that could that worksheet be uncovered, it would be found to contain the germinal stuff of "Stopping by Woods"; that what was a-simmer in him all night without finding its proper form, suddenly, when he let his still-occupied mind look away, came at him from a different direction, offered itself in a different form, and that finding that form exactly right the impulse proceeded to marry itself to the new shape in one of the most miraculous performances of English lyricism.

And that, too — whether or not one can accept so hypothetical a discussion — is part of HOW the poem means. It means that marriage to the perfect form, the poem's shapen declaration of itself, its moment's monument fixed beyond all possibility of change. And thus, finally, in every truly good poem, "How does it mean?" must always be answered "Triumphantly." Whatever the poem "is about," *how* it means is always how Genesis means: the word become a form, and the form become a thing, and — when the becoming is true — the thing become a part of the knowledge and experience of the race forever.

EXCERPT FROM SURVIVAL

— Margaret Atwood

A Canadian writer and critic of great talent, Atwood has written volumes of verse, novels, and criticism including *The Circle Game,* which won the Governor General's Award in 1960. Other works include *The Journals of Susanna Moodie, Surfacing,* and *The Edible Woman.*

■ Does every country have a unique symbol that unifies it and is reflected in its literature?
■ What national factors contribute to the form this symbol assumes?

Atwood contends that Canada's informing symbol is Survival, *la Survivance.* You may wish to compare the ideas Atwood raises with Shadbolt's comments about Carr's artistry in "Foreword to *Klee Wyck*" in Part A, page 197, and Hales's analysis in "Spiritual Longing in Laurence's Manawaka Women" in Part A, page 48 or Smart's "Our Two Cultures," in Part A, page 59.

I'd like to begin with a sweeping generalization and argue that every country or culture has a single unifying and informing symbol at its core. (Please don't take any of my oversimplifications as articles of dogma which allow of no exceptions; they are proposed simply to create vantage points from which the literature may be viewed.) The symbol, then — be it word, phrase, idea, image, or all of these — functions like a system of beliefs (it *is* a system of beliefs, though not always a formal one) which holds the country together and helps the people in it to co-operate for common ends. Possibly the symbol for America is The Frontier, a flexible idea that contains many elements dear to the American heart: it suggests a place that is *new,* where the old order can be discarded (as it was when America was instituted by a crop of disaffected Protestants, and later at the time of the Revolution); a line that is always expanding, taking in or "conquering" everfresh virgin territory (be it The West, the rest of the world, outer space, Poverty or The Regions of the Mind); it holds out a hope, never fulfilled but always promised, of Utopia, the perfect human society. Most twentieth century American literature is about the gap between the promise and the actuality, between the imagined ideal Golden West or City Upon a Hill, the model for all the world postulated by the Puritans, and the actual squalid materialism, dotty small town, nasty city, or redneck-filled outback. Some Americans have even confused the actuality with the promise: in that case Heaven is a Hilton hotel with a coke machine in it.

The corresponding symbol for England is perhaps The Island,

convenient for obvious reasons. In the seventeenth century a poet called Phineas Fletcher wrote a long poem called *The Purple Island,* which is based on an extended body-as-island metaphor, and, dreadful though the poem is, that's the kind of island I mean: island-as-body, self-contained, a Body Politic, evolving organically, with a hierarchical structure in which the King is the Head, the statesmen the hands, the peasants or farmers or workers the feet, and so on. The Englishman's home as his castle is the popular form of this symbol, the feudal castle being not only an insular structure but a self-contained microcosm of the entire Body Politic.

The central symbol for Canada — and this is based on numerous instances of its occurrence in both English and French Canadian literature — is undoubtedly Survival, *la Survivance.* Like the Frontier and The Island, it is a multi-faceted and adaptable idea. For early explorers and settlers, it meant bare survival in the face of "hostile" elements and/or natives: carving out a place and a way of keeping alive. But the word can also suggest survival of a crisis or disaster, like a hurricane or a wreck, and many Canadian poems have this kind of survival as a theme; what you might call 'grim' survival as opposed to 'bare' survival. For French Canada after the English took over it became cultural survival, hanging on as a people, retaining a religion and a language under an alien government. And in English Canada now while the Americans are taking over it is acquiring a similar meaning. There is another use of the word as well: a survival can be a vestige of a vanished order which has managed to persist after its time is past, like a primitive reptile. This version crops up in Canadian thinking too, usually among those who believe that Canada is obsolete.

But the main idea is the first one: hanging on, staying alive. Canadians are forever taking the national pulse like doctors at a sickbed: the aim is not to see whether the patient will live well but simply whether he will live at all. Our central idea is one which generates, not the excitement and sense of adventure or danger which The Frontier holds out, not the smugness and/or sense of security, of everything in its place, which The Island can offer, but an almost intolerable anxiety. Our stories are likely to be tales not of those who made it but of those who made it back, from the awful experience — the North, the snowstorm, the sinking ship — that killed everyone else. The survivor has no triumph or victory but the fact of his survival; he has little after his ordeal that he did not have before, except gratitude for having escaped with his life.

A preoccupation with one's survival is necessarily also a preoccupation with the obstacles to that survival. In earlier writers these obstacles are external — the land, the climate, and so forth. In later writers the obstacles tend to become both harder to identify and more internal; they are no longer obstacles to physical survival but obstacles to what we may call spiritual survival, to life as anything more than a minimally human being. Sometimes fear of these obstacles becomes itself the obstacle, and a character is paralyzed by terror (either of what he thinks is threatening him from the outside, or of elements in his own nature that threaten him from within). It may even be life itself that he fears; and when life becomes a threat to life, you have a moderately vicious circle. If a man feels he can survive only by amputating himself, turning himself into a cripple or a eunuch, what price survival?

Just to give you a quick sample of what I'm talking about, here are a few capsule Canadian plots. Some contain attempts to survive which fail. Some contain bare survivals. Some contain crippled successes (the character does more than survive, but is mutilated in the process).

Pratt:	*The Titanic:* Ship crashes into iceberg. Most passengers drown.
Pratt:	*Brébeuf and His Brethren:* After crushing ordeals, priests survive briefly and are massacred by Indians.
Laurence:	*The Stone Angel:* Old woman hangs on grimly to life and dies at the end.
Carrier:	*Is It The Sun, Philibert?* Hero escapes incredible rural poverty and horrid urban conditions, almost makes it financially, dies when he wrecks his car.
Marlyn:	*Under The Ribs of Death:* Hero amputates himself spiritually in order to make it financially, fails anyway.
Ross:	*As For Me and My House:* Prairie minister who hates his job and has crippled himself artistically by sticking with it is offered a dubious chance of escape at the end.
Buckler:	*The Mountain and the Valley:* Writer who has been unable to write has vision of possibility at the end but dies before he can implement it.
Gibson:	*Communion:* Man who can no longer make human contact tries to save sick dog, fails, and is burned up at the end.

And just to round things out, we might add that the two English Canadian feature films (apart from Allan King's documentaries) to have had much success so far, *Goin' Down the Road* and *The Rowdyman,* are both dramatizations of failure. The heroes survive, but just barely; they are born losers, and their failure to do anything but keep alive has nothing to do with the Maritime Provinces or 'regionalism.' It's pure Canadian, from sea to sea.

My sample plots are taken from both prose and poetry, and from regions all across Canada; they span four decades, from the thirties to the early seventies. And they hint at another facet of Survivalism: at some point the failure to survive, or the failure to achieve anything beyond survival, becomes not a necessity imposed by a hostile outside world but a choice made from within. Pushed far enough, the obsession with surviving can become the will *not* to survive.

Certainly Canadian authors spend a disproportionate amount of time making sure that their heroes die or fail. Much Canadian writing suggests that failure is required because it is felt — consciously or unconsciously — to be the only 'right' ending, the only thing that will support the characters' (or their authors') view of the universe. When such endings are well-handled and consistent with the whole book, one can't quarrel with them on aesthetic grounds. But when Canadian writers are writing clumsy or manipulated endings, they are much less likely to manipulate in a positive than they are in a negative direction: that is, the author is less likely to produce a sudden inheritance from a rich old uncle or the surprising news that his hero is really the son of a Count than he is to conjure up an unexpected natural disaster or an out-of-control car, tree or minor character so that the protagonist may achieve a satisfactory *failure*. Why should this be so? Could it be that Canadians have a will to lose which is as strong and pervasive as the Americans' will to win?

It might be argued that, since most Canlit has been written in the twentieth century and since the twentieth century has produced a generally pessimistic or "ironic" literature, Canada has simply been reflecting a trend. Also, though it's possible to write a short lyric poem about joy and glee, no novel of any length can exclude all but these elements. A novel about unalloyed happiness would have to be either very short or very boring: "Once upon a time John and Mary lived happily ever after, The End." Both of these arguments have some validity, but surely the Canadian gloom is more unrelieved than most and the death and failure toll out of proportion. Given a choice of the negative or positive aspects of any symbol — sea as life-giving Mother, sea as what your ship goes down in; tree as symbol of growth, tree as what falls on your head — Canadians show a marked preference for the negative.

ARCHETYPES OF LITERATURE

— Northrop Frye

Perhaps Canada's most well-known literary scholar, Frye is also an ordained United Church minister, a professor at University of Toronto, and the recipient of over 20 honorary degrees. *Anatomy of Criticism,* which explores the subject of this essay, helped establish his international reputation. Other famous books include *The Educated Imagination* and *The Bush Garden.*

■ What differentiates criticism from art?
■ Is it possible to "learn literature"?

Frye contends there are four phases of myth which form archetypal patterns in art — dawn, zenith, sunset, and darkness. These archetypes may provide you with a fresh approach to your study of literature.

I

Every organized body of knowledge can be learned progressively; and experience shows that there is also something progressive about the learning of literature. Our opening sentence has already got us into a semantic difficulty. Physics is an organized body of knowledge about nature, and a student of it says the he is learning physics, not that he is learning nature. Art, like nature, is the subject of a systematic study, and has to be distinguished from the study itself, which is criticism. It is therefore impossible to "learn literature": one learns about it in a certain way, but what one learns, transitively, is the criticism of literature. Similarly, the difficulty often felt in "teaching literature" arises from the fact that it cannot be done: the criticism of literature is all that can be directly taught. So while no one expects literature itself to behave like a science, there is surely no reason why criticism, as a systematic and organized study, should not be, at least partly, a science. Not a "pure" or "exact" science, perhaps, but these phrases form part of a 19th Century cosmology which is no longer with us. Criticism deals with the arts and may well be something of an art itself, but it does not follow that it must be unsystematic. If it is to be related to the sciences too, it does not follow that it must be deprived of the graces of culture.

Certainly criticism as we find it in learned journals and scholarly monography has every characteristic of a science. Evidence is examined scientifically; previous authorities are used scientifically; fields are investigated scientifically; texts are edited scientifically. Prosody is scientific in structure; so is phonetics; so is philology. And yet in studying this kind of critical science the student becomes aware of a centrifugal movement carrying him away from literature. He finds that literature is the central division of the "humanities," flanked on one side by history and on the other by philosophy. Criticism so far ranks only as a subdivision of literature; and hence, for the systematic mental organization of the subject, the student has to turn to the conceptual framework of the historian for events, and to that of the philosopher for ideas. Even the more centrally placed critical sciences, such as textual editing, seem to be part of a "background" that recedes into history or some other non-literary field. The thought suggests itself that the ancillary critical disciplines may be related to a central expanding pattern of systematic comprehension which has not yet been established, but which, if it were established, would prevent them from being centrifugal. If such a pattern exists, then criticism would be to art what philosophy is to wisdom and history to action.

Most of the central area of criticism is at present, and doubtless always will be, the area of commentary. But the commentators have little sense, unlike the researchers, of being contained within some sort of scientific discipline: they are chiefly engaged, in the words of the gospel hymn, in brightening the corner where they are. If we attempt to get a more comprehensive idea of what criticism is about, we find ourselves wandering over quaking bogs of generalities, judicious pronouncements of value, reflective comments, perorations to works of research, and other consequences of taking the large view. But this part of the critical field is so full of pseudo-propositions, sonorous nonsense that constrains no truth and no falsehood, that it obviously exists only because criticism, like nature, prefers a waste space to an empty one.

The term "pseudo-proposition" may imply some sort of logical positivist attitude on my own part. But I would not confuse the significant proposition with the factual one; nor should I consider it advisable to muddle the study of literature with a schizophrenic dichotomy between subjective-emotional and objective-descriptive aspects of meaning, considering that in order to produce any literary meaning at all one has to ignore this dichotomy. I say only that the principles by which one can distinguish a significant from a meaningless statement in criticism are not clearly defined. Our first step, therefore, is to recognize and get rid of meaningless criticism: that is, talking about literature in a way that cannot help to build up a systematic structure of knowledge. Casual value-judgments belong not to criticism but to the history of taste, and reflect, at best, only the social and psychological compulsions which prompted their utterance. All judgments in which the values are not based on literary experience but are sentimental or derived from religious or political prejudice may be regarded as casual. Sentimental judgments are usually based either on nonexistent categories or antitheses ("Shakespeare studied life, Milton books") or on a visceral reaction to the writer's personality. The literary chit-chat which makes the reputations of poets boom and crash in an imaginary stock exchange is pseudo-criticism. That wealthy investor Mr. Eliot, after dumping Milton on the market, is now buying him again; Donne has probably reached his peak and will begin to taper off; Tennyson may be in for a slight flutter but the Shelley stocks are still bearish. This sort of thing cannot be part of any systematic study, for a systematic study can only progress: whatever dithers or vacillates or reacts is merely leisure-class conversation.

We next meet a more serious group of critics who say: the

foreground of criticism is the impact of literature on the reader. Let us, then, keep the study of literature centripetal, and base the learning process on a structural analysis of the literary work itself. The texture of any great work of art is complex and ambiguous, and in unravelling the complexities we may take in as much history and philosophy as we please, if the subject of our study remains at the center. If it does not, we may find that in our anxiety to write about literature we have forgotten how to read it.

The only weakness in this approach is that it is conceived primarily as the antithesis of centrifugal or "background" criticism, and so lands us in a somewhat unreal dilemma, like the conflict of internal and external relations in philosophy. Antitheses are usually resolved, not by picking one side and refuting the other, or by making eclectic choices between them, but by trying to get past the antithetical way of stating the problem. It is right that the first effort of critical apprehension should take the form of a rhetorical or structural analysis of a work of art. But a purely structural approach has the same limitation in criticism that it has in biology. In itself it is simply a discrete series of analyses based on the mere existence of the literary structure, without developing any explanation of how the structure came to be what it was and what its nearest relatives are. Structural analysis brings rhetoric back to criticism, but we need a new poetics as well, and the attempt to construct a new poetics out of rhetoric alone can hardly avoid a mere complication of rhetorical terms into a sterile jargon. I suggest that what is at present missing from literary criticism is a coordinating principle, a central hypothesis which, like the theory of evolution in biology, will see the phenomena it deals with as parts of a whole. Such a principle, though it would retain the centripetal perspective of structural analysis, would try to give the same perspective to other kinds of criticism too.

The first postulate of this hypothesis is the same as that of any science: the assumption of total coherence. The assumption refers to the science, not to what it deals with. A belief in an order of nature is an inference from the intelligibility of the natural sciences; and if the natural sciences ever completely demonstrated the order of nature they would presumably exhaust their subject. Criticism, as a science, is totally intelligible; literature, as the subject of a science, is, so far as we know, an inexhaustible source of new critical discoveries, and would be even if new works of literature ceased to be written. If so, then the search for a limiting principle in literature in order to discourage the development of criticism is mistaken. The assertion that the critic should not look for more in a poem than the poet may safely be assumed to have been conscious of putting there is a common form of what may be called the fallacy of premature teleology. It corresponds to the assertion that a natural phenomenon is as it is because Providence in its inscrutable wisdom made it so.

Simple as the assumption appears, it takes a long time for a science to discover that it is in fact a totally intelligible body of knowledge. Until it makes this discovery it has not been born as an individual science, but remains an embryo within the body of some other subject. The birth of physics from "natural philosophy" and of sociology from "moral philosophy" will illustrate the process. It is also very approximately true that the modern sciences have developed in the order of their closeness to mathematics. Thus physics and astronomy assumed their modern form in the Renaissance, chemistry in the 18th Century, biology in the 19th, and the social sciences in the 20th. If systematic criticism, then, is developing only in our day, the fact is at least not an anachronism.

We are now looking for classifying principles lying in an area between two points that we have fixed. The first of these is the preliminary effort of criticism, the structural analysis of the work of art. The second is the assumption that there is such a subject as criticism, and that it makes, or could make, complete sense. We may next proceed inductively from structural analysis, associating the data we collect and trying to see larger patterns in them. Or we may proceed deductively, with the consequences that follow from postulating the unity of criticism. It is clear, of course, that neither procedure will work indefinitely without correction from the other. Pure induction will get us lost in haphazard guessing; pure deduction will lead to inflexible and over-simplified pigeon-holing. Let us now attempt a few tentative steps in each direction, beginning with the inductive one.

II

The unity of a work of art, the basis of structural analysis, has not been produced solely by the unconditioned will of the artist, for the artist is only its efficient cause: it has form, and consequently a formal cause. The fact that revision is possible, that the poet makes changes not because he likes them better but because they are better, means that poems, like poets, are born and not made. The poet's task is to deliver the poem in as uninjured a state as possible, and if the poem is alive, it is equally anxious to be rid of him, and screams to be cut loose from his private memories and associations, his desire for self-expression, and all other navel-strings and feeding tubes of his ego. The critic takes over where the poet leaves off, and criticism can hardly do without a kind of literary psychology connecting the poet with the poem. Part of this may be a psychological study of the poet, though this is useful chiefly in analysing the failures in his expression, the things in him which are still attached to his work. More important is the fact that every poet has his private mythology, his own spectroscopic band or peculiar formation of symbols, of much of which he is quite unconscious. In works with characters of their own, such as dramas and novels, the same psychological analysis may be extended to the interplay of characters, though of course literary psychology would analyse the behavior of such characters only in relation to literary convention.

There is still before us the problem of the formal cause of the poem, a problem deeply involved with the question of genres. We cannot say much about genres, for criticism does not know much about them. A good many critical efforts to grapple with such words as "novel" or "epic" are chiefly interesting as examples of the psychology of rumor. Two conceptions of the genre, however, are obviously fallacious, and as they are opposite extremes, the truth must lie somewhere between them. One is the pseudo-Platonic conception of genres as existing prior to and independently of creation, which confuses them with mere conventions of form like the sonnet. The other is that pseudo-biological conception of them as evolving species which turns up in so many surveys of the "development" of this or that form.

We next inquire for the origin of the genre, and turn first of all to the social conditions and cultural demands which produced it — in other words to the material cause of the work of art. This leads us into literary history, which differs from ordinary history in that its containing categories, "Gothic," "Baroque," "Romantic," and the like are cultural categories, of little use to the ordinary historian. Most literary history does not get as far as these categories, but even so we know more about it than about most kinds of critical scholarship. The historian treats literature and philosophy historically; the philosopher treats history and literature philosophically; and the so-called "history of ideas" approach marks the beginning of an attempt to treat history and philosophy from the point of view of an autonomous criticism.

But still we feel that there is 'something missing. We say that every poet has his own peculiar formation of images. But when so many poets use so many of the same images, surely there are much bigger critical problems involved than biographical ones. As Mr. Auden's brilliant essay *The Enchaféd Flood* shows, an important symbol like the sea cannot remain within the poetry of Shelley or Keats or Coleridge: it is bound to expand over many poets into an archetypal symbol of literature. And if the genre has a historical origin, why does the genre of drama emerge from medieval religion in a way so strikingly similar to the way it emerged from Greek religion centuries before? This is a problem of structure rather than origin, and suggests that there may be archetypes of genres as well as of images.

It is clear that criticism cannot be systematic unless there is a quality in literature which enables it to be so, an order of words corresponding to the order of nature in the natural sciences. An archetype should be not only a unifying category of criticism, but itself a part of a total form, and it leads us at once to the question of what sort of total form criticism can see in literature. Our survey of critical techniques has taken us as far as literary history. Total literary history moves from the primitive to the sophisticated, and here we glimpse the possibility of seeing literature as a complication of a relatively restricted and simple group of formulas that can be studied in primitive culture.

If so, then the search for archetypes is a kind of literary anthropology, concerned with the way that literature is informed by preliterary categories such as ritual, myth and folk tale. We next realize that the relation between these categories and literature is by no means purely one of descent, as we find them reappearing in the greatest classics — in fact there seems to be a general tendency on the part of great classics to revert to them. This coincides with a feeling that we have all had: that the study of mediocre works of art, however energetic, obstinately remains a random and peripheral form of critical experience, whereas the profound masterpiece seems to draw us to a point at which we can see an enormous number of converging patterns of significance. Here we begin to wonder if we cannot see literature, not only as complicating itself in time, but as spread out in conceptual space from some unseen center.

This inductive movement towards the archetype is a process of backing up, as it were, from structural analysis, as we back up from a painting if we want to see composition instead of brushwork. In the foreground of the grave-digger scene in *Hamlet*, for instance, is an intricate verbal texture, ranging from the puns of the first clown to the *danse macabre* of the Yorick soliloquy, which we study in the printed text. One step back, and we are in the Wilson Knight and Spurgeon group of critics, listening to the steady rain of images of corruption and decay. Here too, as the sense of the place of this scene in the whole play begins to dawn on us, we are in the network of psychological relationships which were the main interest of Bradley. But after all, we say, we are forgetting the genre: *Hamlet* is a play, and an Elizabethan play. So we take another step back into the Stoll and Shaw group and see the scene conventionally as part of its dramatic context. One step more, and we can begin to glimpse the archetype of the scene, as the hero's *Liebestod* and first unequivocal declaration of his love, his struggle with Laertes and the sealing of his own fate, and the sudden sobering of his mood that marks the transition to the final scene, all take shape around a leap into and return from the grave that has so weirdly yawned open on the stage.

At each stage of understanding this scene we are dependent on a certain kind of scholarly organization. We need first an editor to clean up the text for us, then the rhetorician and philologist, then the literary psychologist. We cannot study the genre without the help of the literary social historian, the literary philosopher and the student of the "history of ideas," and for the archetype we need a literary anthropologist. But now that we have got our central pattern of criticism established, all these interests are seen as converging on literary criticism instead of receding from it into psychology and history and the rest. In particular, the literary anthropologist who chases the source of the Hamlet legend from the pre-Shakespeare play to Saxo, and from Saxo to nature-myths, is not running away from Shakespeare: he is drawing closer to the archetypal form which Shakespeare recreated. A minor result of our new perspective is that contradictions among critics, and assertions that this and not that critical approach is the right one, show a remarkable tendency to dissolve into unreality. Let us now see what we can get from the deductive end.

III

Some arts move in time, like music; others are presented in space, like painting. In both cases the organizing principle is recurrence, which is called rhythm when it is temporal and pattern when it is spatial. Thus we speak of the rhythm of music and the pattern of painting; but later, to show off our sophistication, we may begin to speak of the rhythm of painting and the pattern of music. In other words, all arts may be conceived both temporarily and spatially. The score of a musical composition may be studied all at once; a picture may be seen as the track of an intricate dance of the eye. Literature seems to be intermediate between music and painting: its words form rhythms which approach a musical sequence of sounds at one of its boundaries, and form patterns which approach the hieroglyphic or pictorial image at the other. The attempts to get as near to these boundaries as possible form the main body of what is called experimental writing. We may call the rhythm of literature the narrative, and the pattern, the simultaneous mental grasp of the verbal structure, the meaning or significance. We hear or listen to a narrative, but when we grasp a writer's total pattern we "see" what he means.

The criticism of literature is much more hampered by the representational fallacy than even the criticism of painting. That is why we are apt to think of narrative as a sequential representation of events in an outside "life," and of meaning as a reflection of some external "idea." Properly used as critical terms, an author's narrative is his linear movement; his meaning is the integrity of his completed form. Similarily an image is not merely a verbal replica of an external object, but any unit of a verbal structure seen as part of a total pattern or rhythm. Even the letters an author spells his words with form part of his imagery, though only in special cases (such as alliteration) would they call for critical notice. Narrative and meaning thus become respectively, to borrow musical terms, the melodic and harmonic contexts of the imagery.

Rhythm, or recurrent movement, is deeply founded on the natural cycle, and everything in nature that we think of as having some analogy with works of art, like the flower or the bird's song, grows out of a profound synchronization between an organism and the rhythms of its environment, especially that of the solar year. With animals some expressions of synchronization, like the mating dances of birds, could almost be called rituals. But in human life a ritual seems to be something of a voluntary effort (hence the magical element in it) to recapture a lost rapport with the natural cycle. A farmer must harvest his crop at a certain time of year, but because this is involuntary, harvesting itself is not precisely a ritual. It is the deliberate expression of a will to synchronize human and natural energies at that time which produces the harvest songs, harvest sacrifices and harvest folk customs that we call rituals. In ritual, then, we may find the origin of narrative, a ritual being a temporal sequence of acts in which the conscious meaning or significance is latent: it can be seen by an observer, but is largely concealed from the participators themselves. The pull of ritual is toward pure narrative, which, if there could be such a thing, would be automatic and unconscious repetition. We should notice too the regular tendency of ritual to become encyclopedic. All the important recurrences in nature, the day, the phases of the moon, the seasons and solstices of the year, the crises of existence from birth to death, get rituals attached to them, and most of the higher religions are equipped with a definitive total body of rituals suggestive, if we may put it so, of the entire range of potentially significant actions in human life.

Patterns of imagery, on the other hand, or fragments of significance, are oracular in origin, and derive from the epiphanic moment, the flash of instantaneous comprehension with no direct reference to time, the importance of which is indicated by Cassirer in *Myth and Language*. By the time we get them, in the form of proverbs, riddles, commandments and etiological folk tales, there is already a considerable element of narrative in them. They too are encyclopedic in tendency, building up a total structure of significance, or doctrine, from random and empiric fragments. And just as pure narrative would be unconscious act, so pure significance would be an incommunicable state of consciousness, for communication begins by constructing narrative.

The myth is the central informing power that gives archetypal significance to the ritual and archetypal narrative to the oracle. Hence the myth *is* the archetype, though it might be convenient to say myth only when referring to narrative, and archetype when speaking of significance. In the solar cycle of the day, the seasonal cycle of the year, and the organic cycle of human life, there is a single pattern of significance, out of which myth constructs a central narrative around a figure who is partly the sun, partly vegetative fertility and partly a god or archetypal human being. The crucial importance of this myth has been forced on literary critics by Jung and Frazer in particular, but the several books now available on it are not always systematic in their approach, for which reason I supply the following table of its phases:

1. The dawn, spring and birth phase. Myths of the birth of the hero, of revival and resurrection, of creation and (because the four phases are a cycle) of the defeat of the powers of darkness, winter and death. Subordinate characters: the father and the mother. The archetype of romance and of most dithyrambic and rhapsodic poetry.

2. The zenith, summer, and marriage or triumph phase. Myths of apotheosis, of the sacred marriage, and of entering into Paradise. Subordinate characters: the companion and the bride. The archetype of comedy, pastoral and idyll.

3. The sunset, autumn and death phase. Myths of fall, of the dying god, of violent death and sacrifice and of the isolation of the hero. Subordinate characters: the traitor and the siren. The archetype of tragedy and elegy.

4. The darkness, winter and dissolution phase. Myths of the triumph of these powers; myths of floods and the return of chaos, of the defeat of the hero, and Götterdämmerung myths. Subordinate characters: the ogre and the witch. The archetype of satire (see, for instance, the conclusion of *The Dunciad*).

The quest of the hero also tends to assimilate the oracular and random verbal structures, as we can see when we watch the chaos of local legends that results from prophetic epiphanies consolidating into a narrative mythology of departmental gods. In most of the higher religions this in turn has become the same central quest-myth that emerges from ritual, as the Messiah myth became the narrative structure of the oracles of Judaism. A local flood may beget a folk tale by accident, but a comparison of flood stories will show how quickly such tales became examples of the myth of dissolution. Finally, the tendency of both ritual and epiphany to become encyclopedic is realized in the definitive body of myth which constitutes the sacred scriptures of religions. These sacred scriptures are consequently the first documents that the literary critic has to study to gain a comprehensive view of his subject. After he has understood their structure, then he can descend from archetypes to genres, and see how the drama emerges from the ritual side of myth and lyric from the epiphanic or fragmented side, while the epic carries on the central encyclopedic structure.

Some words of caution and encouragement are necessary before literary criticism has clearly staked out its boundaries in these fields. It is part of the critic's business to show how all literary genres are derived from the quest-myth, but the derivation is a logical one within the science of criticism: the quest-myth will constitute the first chapter of whatever future handbooks of criticism may be written that will be based on enough organized critical knowledge to call themselves "introductions" or "outlines" and still be able to live up to their titles. It is only when we try to expound the derivation chronologically that we find ourselves writing pseudo-prehistorical fictions and theories of mythological contract. Again, because psychology and anthropology are more highly developed sciences, the critic who deals with this kind of material is bound to appear, for some time, a dilettante of those subjects. These two phases of criticism are largely undeveloped in comparison with literary history and rhetoric, the reason being the later development of the sciences they are related to. But the fascination which *The Golden Bough* and Jung's book on libido symbols have for literary critics is not based on dilettantism, but on the fact that these books are primarily studies in literary criticism, and very important ones.

In any case the critic who is studying the principles of literary form has a quite different interest from the psychologist's concern with states of mind or the anthropologist's with social institutions. For instance: the mental response to narrative is mainly passive; to significance mainly active. From this fact Ruth Benedict's *Patterns of Culture* develops a distinction between "Apollonian" cultures based on obedience to ritual and "Dionysiac" ones based on a tense exposure of the prophetic mind to epiphany. The critic would tend rather to note how popular literature which appeals to the inertia of the untrained mind puts a heavy emphasis on narrative values, whereas a sophisticated attempt to disrupt the connection between the poet and his environment produces the Rimbaud type of *illumination*, Joyce's solitary epiphanies, and Baudelaire's conception of nature as a source of oracles. Also how literature, as it develops from the primitive to the self-conscious, shows a gradual shift of the poet's attention from narrative to significant values, this shift of attention being the basis of Schiller's distinction between naive and sentimental poetry.

The relation of criticism to religion, when they deal with the same documents, is more complicated. In criticism, as in history, the divine is always treated as a human artifact. God for the critic, whether he finds him in *Paradise Lost* or the Bible, is a character in a human story; and for the critic all epiphanies are explained, not in terms of the riddle of a possessing god or devil, but as mental phenomena closely associated in their origin with dreams. This once established, it is then necessary to say that nothing in criticism or art compels the critic to take the attitude of ordinary waking consciousness towards the dream or the god. Art deals not with the real but with the conceivable; and criticism, though it will eventually have to have some theory of conceivability, can never be justified in trying to develop, much less assume, any theory of actuality. It is necessary to understand this before our next and final point can be made.

We have identified the central myth of literature, in its narrative aspect, with the quest-myth. Now if we wish to see this central myth as a pattern of meaning also, we have to start with the workings of the subconscious where the epiphany originates, in other words in the dream. The human cycle of waking and dreaming corresponds closely to the natural cycle of light and darkness, and it is perhaps in this correspondence that all imaginative life begins. The correspondence is largely an antithesis: it is in daylight that man is really in the power of darkness, a prey to frustration and weakness; it is in the darkness of nature that the "libido" or conquering heroic self awakes. Hence art, which Plato called a dream for awakened minds, seems to have as its final cause the resolution of the antithesis, the mingling of the sun and the hero, the realizing of a world in which the inner desire and the outward circumstance coincide. This is the same goal, of course, that the attempt to combine human and natural power in ritual has. The social function of the arts, therefore, seems to be closely connected with visualizing the goal of work in human life. So in terms of significance, the central myth of art must be the vision of the end of social effort, the innocent world of fulfilled desires, the free human society. Once this is understood, the integral place of criticism among the other social sciences, in interpreting and systematizing the vision of the artist, will be easier to see. It is at this point that we can see how religious conceptions of the final cause of human effort are as relevant as any others to criticism.

The importance of the god or hero in the myth lies in the fact that such characters, who are conceived in human likeness and yet have more power over nature, gradually build up the vision of an omnipotent personal community beyond an indifferent nature. It is this community which the hero regularly enters in his apotheosis. The world of this apotheosis thus begins to pull away from the rotary cycle of the quest in which all triumph is temporary. Hence if we look at the quest-myth as a pattern of imagery, we see the hero's quest first of all in terms of its fulfillment. This gives us our central pattern of archetypal images, the vision of innocence which sees the world in terms of total human intelligibility. It corresponds to, and is usually found in the form of, the vision of the unfallen world or heaven in religion. We may call it the comic vision of life, in contrast to the tragic vision, which sees the quest only in the form of its ordained cycle.

We conclude with a second table of contents, in which we shall attempt to set forth the central pattern of the comic and tragic visions. One essential principle of archetypal criticism is that the individual and the universal forms of an image are identical, the reasons being too complicated for us just now. We proceed according to the general plan of the game of Twenty Questions, or, if we prefer, of the Great Chain of Being:

1. In the comic vision the *human* world is a community, or a hero who represents the wish-fulfillment of the reader. The archetype of images of symposium, communion, order, friendship and love. In the tragic vision the human world is a tyranny or anarchy, or an individual or isolated man, the leader with his back to his followers, the bullying giant of romance, the deserted or betrayed hero. Marriage or some equivalent consummation belongs to the comic vision; the harlot, witch and other varieties of Jung's "terrible mother" belong to the tragic one. All divine, heroic, angelic or other superhuman communities follow the human pattern.

2. In the comic vision the *animal* world is a community of domesticated animals, usually a flock of sheep, or a lamb, or one of the gentler birds, usually a dove. The archetype of pastoral images. In the tragic vision the animal world is seen in terms of beasts and birds of prey, wolves, vultures, serpents, dragons and the like.

3. In the comic vision the *vegetable* world is a garden, grove or park, or a tree of life, or a rose or lotus. The archetype of Arcadian images, such as that of Marvell's green world or of Shakespeare's forest comedies. In the tragic vision it is a sinister forest like the one in *Comus* or at the opening of the *Inferno*, or a heath or wilderness, or a tree of death.

4. In the comic vision the *mineral* world is a city, or one building or temple, or one stone, normally a glowing precious stone — in fact the whole comic series, especially the tree, can be conceived as luminous or fiery. The archetype of geometrical images: the "starlit dome" belongs here. In the tragic vision the mineral world is seen in terms of deserts, rocks and ruins, or of sinister geometrical images like the cross.

5. In the comic vision the *unformed* world is a river, traditionally fourfold, which influenced the Renaissance image of the temperate body with its four humors. In the tragic vision this world usually becomes the sea, as the narrative myth of dissolution is so often a flood myth. The combination of the sea and beast images gives us the leviathan and similar water-monsters.

Obvious as this table looks, a great variety of poetic images and forms will be found to fit it. Yeats's "Sailing to Byzantium," to take a famous example of the comic vision at random, has the city, the tree, the bird, the community of sages, the geometrical gyre and the detachment from the cyclic world. It is, of course, only the general comic or tragic context that determines the interpretation of any symbol: this is obvious with relatively neutral archetypes like the island, which may be Prospero's island or Circe's.

Our tables are, of course, not only elementary but grossly over-simplified, just as our inductive approach to the archetype was a mere hunch. The important point is not the deficiencies of either procedure, taken by itself, but the fact that, somewhere and some-how, the two are clearly going to meet in the middle. And if they do meet, the ground plan of a systematic and comprehensive develop-ment of criticism has been established.

An Overview: Questions for Discussion

1. What common problems and rewards face writers?

2. Judging from the essays in Part B and your own experience, do you think creative writing can be taught? You might wish to read Hatcher's "Whole Brain Learning," Part A, page 74.

3. Of the essays in this section, which ones offered you the most insight into the craft of writing and/or approaches to the study of literature? Give reasons.

4. Is there valid evidence to suggest that writing in one genre is more difficult than in another? Give reasons.

5. Show that the language advice given in this section echoes Orwell's "rules" in "Politics and the English Language," page 4.

6. Are there common guidelines that help writers of both fiction and nonfiction? Explain your position.

7. If you have read Davies's "Conscience of the Writer" (see "The University Lecture," page 173), compare his remarks about different types of writers with the depiction of writers in one or more of the essays in this section.

8. (a) Show that Ciardi in "Robert Frost: The Way to the Poem" and Mayra Mannes in "How Do You Know It's Good?" judge literary works by similar standards.

    (b) Show that Frye and Atwood use similar approaches to their criticism.

    (c) In your view what, if anything, might the student of literature learn from literary criticism?

9. Account for the antipathy between writers and critics, even though some critics are authors in their own right.

10. What is the role of the literary arts in society?

T IPS
FOR STUDENTS

INTRODUCTION

The tips in this section provide strategies to help you improve your scholastic performance and save time. Not only will they help you complete the assignments in this text, they also will help prepare you for post-secondary endeavours.

We suggest you skim through the tips and use them as the need arises.

The model essays in this text serve as examples of how to write in a particular format such as a review, report, or scholarly essay. The preliminary comments which precede each format also contain useful information about purpose, tone, evidence, and audience.

Suggested Supplementary Resources

For in-depth help with assignments, consult one or more of the texts listed under Suggested Supplementary Resources in the Preface and in the Introduction in Parts A and B. Especially useful sources for independent use are:

Diane Brown, *Notemaking* (Toronto: Gage Publishing, 1977)

Q. Gehle and D. Rollo, *The Writing Process* (Nelson Canada, 1981)

Margot Northey, *Making Sense: A Student's Guide to Writing Style* (Toronto: Oxford University Press, 1983)

John Parker, The Process of Writing (Toronto: Addison-Wesley, 1983)

K. Stewart and M. Freeman, *Essay Writing for Canadian Students* (Scarborough: Prentice-Hall Canada, 1981)

TIPS ON COMPOSING ESSAYS

Composing good critical essays requires an ability to form an opinion (to generalize) and to argue and defend that opinion (to analyze); in other words, you are required to argue deductively and inductively. Evidence of logical errors or personal and/or emotional biases can seriously undermine a critical essay.

Thinking and language are inseparable; thinking is refined and clarified through writing and speaking, just as writing and speaking are refined and clarified through thinking. Some people, who compose with ease, have developed their own system of working through the writing process. However, if, like many writers, you feel you don't know how to approach your assignments with confidence or you are dissatisfied with the results of your efforts, the following suggestions will save time and effort and ensure that you become adept at thinking through the essay.

1. *Acquire a thorough knowledge:*

■ Know your material, whether it is a single work of literature or a variety of information on a general subject.
■ Know your intended audience.
■ Know the format and particular form of essay you will be writing (e.g., follow the conventions of the scholarly essay, report, or review).

This step is crucial. Thought without learning is perilous. There is no substitute for knowledge as a basis for critical thinking. Most weaknesses in argument result from an attempt to generalize and analyze from insufficient information.

2. *Engage in exploratory thinking and preliminary investigation:*

■ Examine your material from various viewpoints; make educated guesses, play hunches, and look for biases in your material and approach to it.
■ Talk through your ideas with someone else who can help you clarify your thoughts.

This step takes time, but ultimately saves effort. It helps you to avoid zeroing in on a thesis too quickly and then having to abandon it because of its weaknesses.

3. *Arrive at a tentative thesis:*

■ Formulate a working thesis, a generalization which states the main idea you wish to prove.
■ Check your generalization for biases — particularly narrow egocentric bias (as "I think it, therefore it's right" approach) and cultural biases (for example, racial and sexist biases).
■ Test your thesis for validity by listing evidence and tentative steps of logical development.
■ Identify exceptions to your argument and other possible interpretations so that you can develop a well-rounded defence of your position.

This step helps you avoid a thesis that is overly simplified, one-sided, or too broad in scope.

4. *Make an outline:*

- State your thesis.
- Use the rough notes you took in step 3 to organize and group the various stages and approaches that develop your argument. (Check for logical connections.)
- If necessary, rearrange the stages in their most effective order. (Some authorities say that, generally, you should begin with your second strongest point and end with your most convincing piece of evidence.)
- Give your conclusion — not merely a restatement of your thesis, but a comment on its significance. (Never add new material in your conclusion; instead rework your argument, if necessary.)

This organizational step prevents wasting working time later and gives you an overview of the logical progression of your argument — a crucial element in the writing of successful essays.

(Steps 5 through 8 have been set out in sequence to clarify the various tasks involved in moving from the original draft to the final copy. In reality, revising, editing, and polishing are interactive and concurrent.)

5. *Write the draft:*

- Using your outline, begin with the thesis paragraph; include an attention-getting lead if this suits the type of essay and audience, and an elaboration of the basic point of your essay. (Some people call this a sentence of enumeration).
- Without stopping to rearrange or polish, "chunk down" the major sections of your argument in numbered paragraphs according to your outline; leave plenty of space for additions and changes.
- Check the whole draft for clarity, deleting, adding, and rearranging "chunks" as necessary (word processors make this a relatively easy task).

Set your work aside; in a day or two, you'll be able to come back to it with a fresh mind.

6. *Revise the draft:*

- A day or two later, reread your draft with more objectivity; check for possible biases, overlapping information, irrelevant material, and illogical order
- If possible, have a classmate check your draft to make sure your thesis is clear and your argument is carefully developed.
- Delete or alter material; don't be afraid to discard any material that does not directly prove your thesis. (Again, a word processor facilitates this work.)
- Ensure that your changes have retained the required elements of the particular format (e.g., report, review, scholarly essay).
- When the order of your argument is established, add any necessary

transitions that contribute to the logical flow of your argument (e.g., however, in addition, on the other hand).

Note that this revision stage often requires crucial alterations. Without them your argument may fail.

7. *Edit and polish the revised draft:*

■ Look for any remaining mechanical and language convention errors (spelling, grammar, standard language usage). Ask someone to proofread your material; often a fresh pair of eyes is better able to "see" things you've overlooked. Or read it aloud, as this process often helps you find your own errors.

■ Check for proper format in your documentation (e.g., quotations, footnotes, bibliography).

■ Make sure that you have not unconsciously used diction and/or imagery that may undermine your argument and offend your audience (e.g., unflattering references).

■ Strive for freshness and originality, keeping in mind Orwell's six rules, particularly the one stating thought must control language and not vice versa (see The Core Essays, page 3); this is your opportunity to imprint the essay with your personal stamp.

Attention to these details often makes the difference of a grade or two in your essay.

8. *Self-Evaluation:*

■ Apply the tips on how to evaluate an essay to your finished work.
■ Further polishing will enhance the final product.

TIPS ON PREPARING FOR THE EXAMINATION

Working under time limitations strains people's critical abilities. But time constraints are a fact of life. Therefore, a major objective of the senior English examination is to determine your ability to think, read, and write effectively under pressure. The following suggestions should improve your performance.

1. *Practise working under time limitations:*

■ The suggested timed reading and writing assignments in this text offer practice that develops your response to working under pressure.

2. *Anticipate the questions:*

There are three general types of questions to prepare for:

■ Questions on reading which usually involve thesis identification, methods of development, evaluating effective use of rhetorical devices, summarizing and assessing ideas and opinions expressed.

■ General topic questions which may call upon you to offer and support your views about social and political issues in an essay; you should rely upon well-known methods of orderly argument such as cause and effect, pro and con and analogy.

■ Literature-based questions which require an essay response. Such questions demand that you decide upon your thesis and set up your plan as quickly as possible, again by relying upon the well-known patterns of orderly development mentioned in the above point. Study for literature questions by forming possible hypotheses that synthesize the key ideas in each work and then try to formulate generalizations that link the ideas in various works. Finally, look for evidence to support these generalizations and consider how you would organize your proof in a written answer. (Many people find that annotating their notebooks and textbooks helps them to identify the key ideas which run through the material.)

3. *Decoding an examination question:*

As you read an examination question, note that most have three key parts: a key verb, an object, and a limiting factor.

■ Consider this example:

"Writers create unique hero/heroines who depict the inner reality of humanity. They search out not only the sources of nobility and dignity, but also the elements of darkness and violence which form an integral part of humanity."

Evaluate the validity of this generalization with reference to (name of character) in (name of work) and the protagonists of two other works studied.

key verb — the word "evaluate" tells you what to do

object — the phrase "the validity of this generalization" tells you the object on which you are to perform the task

limiting factor — the phrase "reference to the main characters in three works" suggests how you are to go about your task

Caution: Some questions have only a key verb after a quotation. Be prepared for such a question by clarifying with your teacher what is expected when such words as the following are used: state, explain, evaluate, analyze, compare, assess, comment on, debate, justify, paraphrase, describe or discuss (discuss is an especially vague word which needs careful definition to elicit the desired response).

TIPS ON NOTE-TAKING

The ability to take effective notes is a vital skill, regardless of your future plans. Whether the situation is class discussion, a seminar or lecture, or reading a text, note-taking helps you to analyze the material presented. Learning to listen and to think critically are, therefore, an integral part of this process. The suggestions listed below should help you to develop successful strategies for note-taking.

1. General tips:

- Develop a form of personal shorthand. You might consider one or a combination of the following approaches:

    — leave out all or most of the vowels: therefore, the above statement reads, lv out al or mst of th vwls
    — develop symbols or codes for commonly used words: the = x, for example = e.g., therefore or thus = .·., percent = %, number = #, and = &, that is = ie, express surprise = !, references to money = $, more or plus = +, with = w, very = v, not = ~
    — omit words such as the, an, a, for, unless they are essential to the meaning
    — use only the first few and final letters in a long word: definition = defn, complication = compn, satisfaction = satn
    — generally, the context should provide the meaning of each word when you reread your work

- Write out a proper name in full the first time it is mentioned
- Take notes under headings and subheadings:

    — begin with a title (if one is not provided, compose one)
    — underline and number headings and subheadings, using symbols to indicate their relative importance for the argument.

2. Working with written material:

- Record pertinent information about the source:

    — author(s), title, and date and place of publication, editor(s), and pages consulted

- Record information for accurate footnotes:

    — for any phrases or sentences transcribed word-for-word
    — when you summarize a writer's concept or use an idea or approach

3. Working with oral material:

- Record main ideas using headings and subheadings.
- Fill in appropriate supporting detail.

4. An example:

- Ira Dilworth's ''Foreword to *Klee Wyck*,'' page 197, provides a convenient example:

Dilworth's Tribute to Friend, Emily Carr

A. Erlst Mmrs EC
   1. Vctria, BC   — erly 1900s
                          — unnkwn + rdcld
                          — strng dly trps w. crrge + anmls
                          — reptn eccntrc eg dg knnls

B. EC x grt pntr
    1. Childhd tlnt   — apprd erly — drwng
                             — oils, lftme exprmtatn
                             — mny dffclts bt v crgous
    2. stdies   — San Fran, Engl set gls fr styl
    3. styl   — cncrn devlp styl to trnslte visl imprssns +
                              flngs
                           — spcl intrst Wst Cst Indns + Pcfc Cst forst
                           — alwys flt inadqt
                           — Lawren Harris disagrd — sys EC 1st sw
                            uniqnss of Can Ind + B.C.

What is the next heading required?

TIPS ON PREPARING A SEMINAR

A seminar is an oral presentation. Its purpose is similar to the essay, but the format is somewhat different:

- The audience participates in the learning experience through discussion encouraged by the seminar leader.
- The leader learns from the audience.

Seminar assignments help participants to develop and refine skills useful in post-secondary institutions and professional life. The skills developed will be in great demand in your post-secondary career:

- to organize and articulate with clarity and confidence
- to listen with discrimination to the reactions of others
- to revise your thoughts, taking into account what you have learned.

These steps should help create a successful experience.

1. Gather your material:

- Since preparing for a seminar is a form of independent study, follow the steps outlined in the tips on independent study.
- Refine the process according to the nature of your project.

2. Organize to deliver your seminar:

- Transfer your main points to a series of index cards; write one main idea in coloured ink across the top of each card.
- For emphasis, underline the main idea or use block capitals.
- In point form, list the subheadings and details (proof).

Hint: If your presentation includes quotations from texts, don't write them out; attach small pieces of paper with paperclips to the relevant pages.

- If your seminar involves audiovisual aids (always a good idea), prepare them carefully (slides, charts, photographs, films). Always check machinery to ensure it is in working order.

■ Provide students with a written overview of your seminar, giving only the thesis, main headings, and page references.

■ Using one ditto, you might leave spaces under each heading for participants to make notes or use one transparency.

■ You might want to go through the motions before presentation day when the classroom is empty, or invite a sympathetic friend or use a tape recorder to act as your audience; it is important to appear poised and confident.

■ Prepare your audience with some preliminary information before the seminar date (e.g., assign specific reading or thinking exercises).

3. *Deliver your seminar:*

■ Be on time.

■ Indicate when questions should be posed.

■ Speak slowly and clearly, using your index cards for guidelines; do not read your notes, as that puts people to sleep.

■ Keep an eye open for reactions: puzzled looks, questions, and signs of boredom.

■ Make sure you leave enough time for discussion; if necessary, help break the ice by asking specific people questions you have prepared in advance.

■ Listen carefully and respond in a reasoned manner to questions, comments, and criticisms.

4. *The final steps:*

■ Revise your material to incorporate valid points raised in discussion.

■ Write and submit the final draft of your essay or report.

TIPS ON EVALUATING AN ESSAY

Essays vary a great deal in form, purpose, and presentation, as you have seen from the models used in this text. However, whether you are evaluating a work written by yourself or someone else, certain elements are constant. Consider these factors:

1. *Purpose*

Is the author's purpose clear?
Has the writer successfully addressed the intended audience?

2. *Structure*

Introduction: is the introduction appropriate for the format or approach?
Body: is the body coherently organized in a manner suitable for the author's purpose, format, and audience? Appropriate types of evidence (again consider purpose, format, and audience) may include:

■ a survey or statistics (is the source reliable?)
■ quotations from an authority on the subject

- anecdotes
- first-hand observation
- contrast or comparison
- dialogue
- rhetorical questions
- humour, exaggeration, irony
- illustrations, diagrams, charts
- analogy
- appeals to logic (check for generalizations based on a false premise)
- appeals to emotion

Conclusion: does it pull together the significance of the argument?

3. *Style*

Diction:

- Is the vocabulary appropriate for the audience?
- Are words freshly and cleverly used to achieve an effective tone?
- Are rhetorical devices repeated for emphasis or effect?
- Is effective ornamentation employed when appropriate?
Sentence structure:
- Is sentence structure appropriate for the audience, subject, and format?

4. *Appreciation*

- In what ways did you find this essay effective?
- If it fell short of your expectations, what audience might be more receptive?

TIPS ON INDEPENDENT STUDY

Independent study refers to any self-directed learning project completed in co-operation with the teacher. Regardless of the particular focus or approach, the project will most likely be evaluated for both process and product. You will learn to take charge of your own learning experiences, just as you will be expected to do in your post-secondary career. Every project has three common stages, as set out below.

1. *The preliminary investigation and organization stage:*

- If your project involves writing an essay, read tips on "Composing Essays," page 309; pay particular attention to the suggestions in 1 through 3 at this point.
- Meet with your teacher to establish a clear working topic and approach; keep up-to-date logs which record due dates and other expectations (index cards are handy).
- If you are planning to write an essay, you might consult one or more of the suggested resources in the Introduction to Part C; consult your teacher-librarian about other in- and out-of-school library resources.

■ If your project entails creative writing, the first two suggestions in "Composing Essays," on page 309, are relevant; one or more of the books listed as resources in the Introduction to Part B and some of the "how-to" essays in Part B may provide helpful hints.

■ If your project has an out-of-school component, consider what community resources are available; set up appropriate interviews, discussions, and meetings (your school's teacher-librarian or Student Services Department may be able to provide names of relevant agencies or personnel).

2. The composing stage:

■ Reread "Composing Essays," page 309, and apply its suggestions to your project; even if you are doing a piece of creative writing, parts of 4 through 7 are relevant. All writers could benefit from following Orwell's six rules of language usage (see page 4).

■ If you are writing an essay, refer to the model essays in Part A which apply to the format you are employing (e.g., report, scholarly essay, review); the introductory notes to each format also offer helpful information.

■ Meet with your teacher as often as you both feel necessary to work smoothly through the various stages of the composing process.

■ Consider asking the advice of a classmate, as well; reliable peers may offer just the advice you need to solve a particular problem.

■ If your project involves a seminar, read the tips on "Preparing a Seminar," page 315.

3. The evaluation stage:

■ If appropriate to the nature of your project, apply the criteria from the tips on how to evaluate an essay; a number of the points also apply to creative writing (you might discuss this with the teacher or develop a checklist for evaluation with a classmate working on a similar type of project.

■ Your teacher will most likely evaluate both process and product in your work in considering such questions as:

1. Did you arrive punctually at interviews, prepared with appropriate notes and materials for discussion?

2. Did you demonstrate an understanding of the project, and a willingness to ask questions and discuss problems during interviews?

3. Did you demonstrate initiative, curiosity, self-motivation, the ability to organize and set goals, and thoughtfulness when dealing with others?

4. Does the finished project demonstrate your defined goals have been achieved, sufficient effort has been expended, and a high-quality product (written and oral) has resulted?

GUIDE TO THEMES AND SPECIAL SKILLS EXERCISES

Thematic Study

Although this text is not organized thematically, teachers may wish to pursue certain threads that are developed in more than one essay or unit. This list outlines some of these interconnecting ideas (with corresponding page numbers shown at right).

1. *The role of art and the artist:*

2. *The critic in society:*

3. *The role of language in communication:*

4. *The craft of writing:*

5. *The Canadian identity:*